TWAYNE'S WORLD AUTHORS SERIES
A Survey of the World's Literature

FRANCE

Maxwell Smith
Guerry Professor of French, Emeritus
The University of Chatanooga
Former Visiting Professor in Modern Languages
The Florida State University

EDITOR

Roland Barthes

TWAS 614

ROLAND BARTHES

By GEORGE R. WASSERMAN

Russell Sage College

TWAYNE PUBLISHERS
A DIVISION OF G.K. HALL & CO., BOSTON

Library of Congress Cataloging in Publication Data

Wasserman, George R. (George Russell), 1927–
Roland Barthes.

(Twayne's world authors series ; TWAS 614. France)
Bibliography: pp. 130–32
Includes index.
1. Barthes, Roland. 2. Criticism. 3. Semiotics. 4. Discourse
analysis.
I. Title. II. Series: Twayne's world authors series ; TWAS 614.
III. Series: Twayne's world authors series. France.
P85.B33W3   808'.00141   81–4118
ISBN 0–8057-6456-9   AACR2

For Kyle
a la recherche du temps perdu

Contents

About the Author

George Wasserman is professor of English, specializing in Restoration and Augustan literature, at Russell Sage College, Troy, New York. He received his B.A. and M.A. degrees from the University of Pittsburgh, and his Ph.D. in 1958, from the University of Michigan. He has published numerous articles in scholarly journals and is the author of the Twayne English Authors Series volumes *John Dryden* and *Samuel "Hudibras" Butler.*

Preface

The chief difficulty in writing a book about Roland Barthes is that the closer one tries to get to the man and his writing as critical objects, the more interested one becomes in oneself as a critical subject. Although this admission may serve as the author's credentials for writing such a book (since it testifies to his involvement in the Barthesian problematics of criticism), it must be accompanied by two apologies. Apology must be made to Barthes himself for the inevitable tendency of critical commentary to reduce him to an image, his books and essays to a set of intentions, his whole production to an *oeuvre*, when every text he has written is, before anything else, an act of resistance to such closures. The second apology is offered to the reader for whom these transgressions have been committed (the reader, after all, wants to "get hold" of Barthes), but who nevertheless may feel that the explanation is inadequate or wants explaining itself. The first apology defines an ethical problem that is handled rhetorically in the first and last chapters of the present study ("Barthes in Spite of Himself" and "Barthes as Text"); the second covers the practical problems of omissions (both of Barthes's writings and of the broad philosophical ramifications of his thought) and the treatment of the contents of the book. Practically speaking, the thought of surveying Barthes in totality is unfeasible in a book of this size: his writings are too numerous and too difficult to admit of a general overview. I have therefore taken a somewhat Barthesian view of this second problem, allowing my own interest and pleasure in Barthes to be the chief determinant of the contents and their treatment, requiring only that the selected topics of interest be also representative of the range of Barthes's critical interests.

For the most part, these "sites" of my attention to Barthes may be identified with one or more of his major texts. I begin, therefore, after a general survey of Barthes's career, with the important concept of *écriture*, the focus of Barthes's early ideological criticism in *Writing Degree Zero;* included in this initial discussion, as a conceptual tool, is the scheme of semiological analysis that first appeared as an explanation of Barthes's essays on popular "mythologies" and then was formalized in his more technical *Elements of Semiology*. Chapter 3 deals with his theory of criticism as that was set forth in several early essays and consolidated, in *Critique et vérité*, as a reply to Raymond Picard's attack on the *nouvelle critique*. Chapters 4 and 5 look at Barthes's allegiance to and defection from Structuralism—his "euphoric dream," in the "Introduction to the Structural Analysis of Narrative," of a single structure in which all the world's stories would be seen, and, in *Système de la mode*, of a definitive "language" of fashion writing; and his subsequent reactive attraction, in *S/Z*, to "structuration," "difference," and "plurality." Barthes's current posture as a critical hedonist and his redefinition of the Text, exemplified by *L'Empire des signes*, *The Pleasure of the Text*, and *Roland Barthes*, are taken up in the last two chapters. On the other hand, I have said little about Barthes's commentary in his early volume of selections from Michelet, the early essays on the theater (Brechtian, for the most part), his studies of Racine, Sade, Fourier, and Loyola, or his most recent works, *A Lover's Discourse* and the as yet untranslated *Sollers écrivain;* reluctantly, I have also had to ignore the bulk of his shorter essays.

As the preceding summary of inclusions and exclusions suggests, Barthes's criticism is of interest to me largely for its own sake, quite apart from what it has to say *about* another writer or work (Racine or "Sarrasine," for example), or *about* a particular cultural scene (France in *Mythologies*, Japan in *L'Empire des signes*); or even, when the meaning of one of his texts appears to "name" or cancel the meaning of another of them, what it says *about* Barthes and his "intellectual development." Barthes's writing has done much to weaken the tyranny of this concept of "the author," to celebrate literature not by immortalizing its origin or past, but by giving its *writing* a future. (For this reason, too, I feel obliged merely to note here that since the completion of my manuscript a Frenchman named Roland Barthes died in a Paris hospital.) This study is therefore offered as an introduction to the writing of one who, I believe, will be read and studied with the kind of attention usually given only to "creative writers," and for whom we therefore need to redefine our categories of literary classification. As a critic, Barthes is interested in writers who make or remake their language in the act of writing it; and it is our view that he is engaged in a similar production as he thinks and writes about these writers. In other words, we are suggesting that the Barthesian text is like a literary text: it is less a communication or metalanguage than a poetry, and that is to say it is above all a language to be enjoyed. Unfortunately, the present study must remain a language *about* the Barthesian language, and such a metalanguage cannot be a "site" of pleasure. For that, the reader must turn to the Barthesian Text itself.

Chronology

1915 Barthes born November 12 in Cherbourg.

1916 Death of Louis Barthes, the critic's father, in a naval battle on the North Sea.

1924 Move, with his mother, to Paris.

1934 Onset of tuberculosis. Treatment in the Pyrénées, at Bedous until 1935.

1935 Until 1939, at the Sorbonne, where he founded the Groupe de Théâtre Antique.

1937 Exempted from military service.

1938 Trip to Greece with the Groupe de Théâtre Antique.

1939 Professor of fourth and third forms at the new lycée of Biarritz.

1940 Tutor and professor at the Lycées Voltaire and Carnot, in Paris.

1941 Relapse of tuberculosis.

1942 Treatment in the Sanatorium des Étudiants, at Saint-Hilaire-du-Touvet, in the French Alps. In July, his first publication "*Note sur André Gide et son Journal,*" appeared in *Existences,* the review of the sanitorium.

1943 Convalescence at the Post-Cure, in Paris. In June, another relapse in the right lung. Underwent treatment until 1945 in the Sanatorium des Étudiants, where for several months he engaged in pre-medical studies.

1946 Convalescence in Paris until 1947, when his first article, called "*Le Degré zéro de l'écriture,*" appeared in *Combat.*

1948 In Bucharest until 1949, as librarian and then professor at the Institut Français, and as reader in the university of this city.

1949 Reader at the University of Alexandria (Egypt) until 1950.

1950 Attaché at the Direction génerale des Relations culturelles until 1952.

1952 Until 1954, Officer of Instruction (in lexicology) at the Centre National de Recherche Scientifique. First of the *Mythologies* essays, "The World of Wrestling," published in *Esprit.*

1953 *Writing Degree Zero,* Barthes's first book.

1954 *Michelet par lui-même.*

1955 Research in sociology at the C.N.R.S., until 1959.

1957 *Mythologies.* Work begun on *Systeme de la mode.*

1960 Chairman of Section VI (the social and ecomonic sciences) at the École Pratique des Hautes Études until 1962. "Racinian Man" published as preface to the Club Français du Livre edition of Racine's plays.

1962 Appointed Director of Studies at the École Pratique des Hautes Études.

1963 *Sur Racine* and "L'Activité structuraliste."

1964 *Critical Essays* and *Elements of Semiology.*

1966 *Critique et Vérité,* Barthes's reply to Raymond Picard's *Nouvelle critique ou novelle imposture?* which appeared the previous year. "Introduction to the Structural Analysis of Narrative" published. Visits to Japan and America; at the International Symposium on "The Languages of Criticism and the Sciences of Man," held at Johns Hopkins University, he delivered his paper "To Write: an Intransitive Verb?"

1967 *Système de la mode.*

1970 *S/Z* and *L'Empire des signes.*

1971 *Sade/Fourier/Loyola.*

1973 *The Pleasure of the Text.*

1975 *Roland Barthes.*

1977 Elected to the faculty of the Collège de France, to fill the chair in Semiologie Littéraire.

1977 *A Lover's Discourse.*

1979 *Sollers écrivain.*

1980 Barthes dies in Paris, March 25.

CHAPTER 1

Barthes in Spite of Himself

READERS familiar only with the fact that Roland Barthes is a contemporary French literary critic may regard the present volume, in a series dedicated to creative artists, as somewhat gratuitous; for literary critics (even one who, on unimpeachable authority, has been called "the most interesting, fertile, and ambitious critic now writing")[1] are, after all, writers of a second order—not artists themselves, but merely writers about artists and their works. Let us understand at the outset, however, that Barthes himself would disapprove of this book—not for the reason just mentioned, but because traditional literary history-biography-criticism, as he understands it, is produced by denying the life of its subject, and he would no sooner condone the embalming of himself than of Rabelais or Balzac. Nevertheless, from Barthes's point of view, that is what we are about to do here. Traditional literary study operates on the assumption that there "naturally" exists a one–and–only subject behind every work of literature, a Barthesian "essence" in this case, that can be collected from his writings, and that (just as "naturally," it assumes) this essence exists to be "understood." For Barthes, however, these assumptions are not natural; they are historical, ideological, a product of our culture. He would further object that such an assumed essence, along with our efforts to possess it as knowledge, sets limits to the subject of our study; when we will have finished, the subject (which will now have become an object) will occupy not its own space, but the space we have created for it. Neither the end of our endeavor nor the means by which we attain it has its own integrity; each justifies and valorizes the other. Barthes, in short, repudiates all essences. Any "Barthes" we may succeed in isolating he will disown—not because it fails to conform to his sense of himself (fails here to do him credit, goes too far there), nor because we cannot avoid lapsing into subjectivity (for Barthes, objectivity is not synonymous with reality or truth), but simply because he believes there is no essential Barthes. The subject

who says "I," he insists, is not the same as the subject referred to by
the pronoun. In Barthes's eyes, then, we are about to commit an act of
"bad faith" (existentially speaking)—we are about to contribute to *a
mythology of Barthes*. Perhaps in thus acknowledging this bad faith,
we may somehow redeem our enterprise.

Barthes, then, does not at all fit our stereotype of the literary critic.
He is neither a historian nor, in the usual sense, an explicator; and,
although he began as a teacher of French literature and has held
several university appointments, he is not what we would call an
"academic" or—to use his word—a "university" critic; moreover,
although recently honored by election to the prestigious faculty of the
Collège de France, he has throughout his career practiced a sort of
academic apostasy in his writings that has not endeared him to his
colleagues outside the untraditional École Pratique des Hautes
Études. Moreover, Barthes's criticism and theoretical writing tend to
blur the conventional distinction between literature and writing that
purports to discuss literature. Criticism, he encourages us to believe,
is actually another form of literature; the critic reads a writing, and
writes his reading. Since few of Barthes's notions are more discon-
certing than this one—at least to students of Anglo-American or
French academic criticism—it may be useful to begin this study of
Barthes by trying to become more familiar with it; in doing so we shall
also be acquainting ourselves with one of the major concerns of
literary modernism, the critical acceptance of which Barthes, as the
recognized leader of the *nouvelle critique* of the 1950s and '60s, did
much to further.

I   *Criticism and Literature*

It should first be understood that Barthes himself is not responsible
for this unification of literature and criticism: its origin is to be found
in the poetics of Paul Valéry and Stéphan Mallarmé. Its impetus, in
other words, has come not from criticism, but from literature itself.
If, as Barthes believes, the critic's purpose is no longer to discover the
meaning of a literary work, but rather "to *cover*" the work as completely as possible with his own language,[2] the reason is that the
modern author no longer conceives of his work as the container of a
meaning. To say that a work "contains a meaning" implies that the
meaning existed before the work existed—in the world or in the
author's mind—and that the work imitates or expresses this meaning.

But modern writers have become increasingly skeptical that there are objective meanings in the world, and literature has accordingly become less representational and expressive. That meaning, once said to lie deep inside things—their "nature," as it was called—was, they began to suspect, of their own invention—a product, that is, of history, not nature.

According to Barthes, this change in the conception of the relation of literature to "the world" occured for French writers around the middle of the nineteenth century. At that time, he tells us in *Writing Degree Zero*, "literature" (and he frequently reminds us that the word *littérature* had come into being only shortly before this time) began to become truly conscious of itself, no longer trying to make its form and linguistic surface as unnoticeable as possible in the interest of a "reality" it was written to reveal, but instead calling attention to that surface, its *writing*, as its entire being. For Barthes, this change implies a new relation between the critic and the literary text. It is no longer appropriate, he has said, to think of a text as "a species of fruit with a kernel (an apricot, for example), the flesh being the form and the pit being the content"; "it would be better to see it as an onion, a construction of layers (or levels, or systems) whose body contains, finally, no heart, no kernel, no secret, no irreducible principle, nothing except the infinity of its own envelopes—which envelop nothing except the infinity of its own surfaces."[3]

As Barthes explains it, what happened around 1850 was nothing less than an alteration of human consciousness, a new awareness of the mind's creative role in the perception of the world it inhabited. For centuries, men had believed in their own innocence before an objective world, and in the innocence of language as the means of communicating information about that world. The world, they assumed, existed independently of both language and themselves, prior to both; it was eternal "nature" itself, not a product of human history. Language, it was understood, was the means of gaining access to objective experience of such a world. According to Barthes, the nineteenth century brought an end to this innocence. Men now recognized not only that nature takes the shape of their own minds, but also that language is the means by which they shape and perceive nature. As Dorothy Lee explains, "a member of a given society— who, of course, codifies experienced reality through the use of the specific languages and other patterned behavior characteristic of his culture—can actually grasp reality only as it is presented to him in

this code."[4] In other words, men recognized that their experience
of the world is determined largely by their language, and that their
ability to express themselves is determined by the culture in which
they find their language. Seen in this light, language can no longer be
taken for granted; it becomes, in Barthes's word, "problematic"—
i.e., it reveals its own complicity in history; it is significative in itself,
quite apart from any content with which a writer may wish to fill it.
For Barthes, the most important consequence of these views is that
the modern writer has come to feel an urgent need to justify himself
as a writer—to doubt the very possibility of expression without
somehow trying to make language innocent again.

It is this effort to remake language in the act of writing it that
accounts for the characteristic absence of traditional content in much
modern literature. The writer as "subject," Barthes says, no longer
thinks of himself as an "individual plenitude," a *fullness* that may be
evacuated in language, but instead as an "emptiness" (*vide*) around
which he "weaves a discourse that is infinitely transformed . . . in
such a way that all writing *which does not lie* designates not the
internal attributes of the subject, but the absence of subject. Language is not the predicate of a subject . . . it is the subject."[5] Modern
literature, as Gerald Bruns therefore characterizes it, no longer
expresses itself through language; "it is rather language which now
expresses itself through literature."[6]

Since 1850, then, serious literature (and we shall henceforth use
the word "modern" in quotes to distinguish this feature) has been
written not merely to communicate a specific meaning or subject; it
has been written as well to present a language. This no doubt sounds
tautological, since most people would say that literature is made out
of language—though they would probably add that this language
seems to disappear as soon as it calls to our minds the world it refers
to. Barthes would say that such people are pretending that language
never lost its original innocence, or that they are genuinely innocent
of the fact that such language only repeats the image of its own
encoding of the world. The "modern" writer attempts to avoid such
self-deception by trying to reduce language to pure form, to a truly
innocent or neutral state which Barthes calls its "zero-degree of
signification." As we shall see, however, this pure form of language is
unrealizable, for emptiness and absence are themselves significant.

Barthes's point is that "modern" literature aims to be a potentiality,
the empty form of a meaning *to be filled*—but filled by the critic or
reader. That is what he is getting at when he says that the critic covers

the text with his own language. Thus, there is a "problematics" of language for the critic as well as for the writer; according to Barthes, "the writer and the critic meet in the same difficult situation, facing the same object: language" (*CV*, p. 47). The critic's task is to determine not whether the author's language conforms to reality, but whether the new system of signs the author has made of that language is coherent—not whether the work contains *a* meaning, but whether it contains the conditions of meaning. The critic assimilates his author's language, and then turns it back on the work, so that critical discourse "is never anything but tautological" (*CE*, p. 259).

Barthes's view of criticism as a "second writing" of an original is given a novel application in one of his more recent works, a biography or autobiography (one simply can't be sure which to call it) ambiguously entitled either *Roland Barthes* or *Roland Barthes by Roland Barthes*, published in 1975. (Apparently, if a book has no determinate subject, even its title becomes problematical—or else the purest of conventions.) Barthes's title parodies that of a well-known French series of introductions to celebrated authors, in which a critic pieces together selected passages of an author in order to present a portrait of him. The critic, in this case, would normally be invisible, subordinated to his "subject"; he selected the passages, but it is the author's words that we read. Hence the formula for the title of the series: *X by Himself*; for example, *Rabelais par lui-meme*, or (to cite a contribution to the series by Barthes himself) *Michelet par lui-meme*. But in *Roland Barthes par Roland Barthes*, it is impossible to distinguish between the creative "subject" and the assembling critic. In this instance, the former appears not as a series of quotations intended to stand for the man, but as a collection of random thoughts presented for the first time—and presented by the critic. One of these Barthes is conceived of as a "text," a formal object to be "read"; the other quite literally "writes" that object, "covers" it with a discourse of his own. Barthes presenting Barthes is a literal illustration of the tautological function of all criticism.

The chapters on Barthes that follow here are tautological in a more familiar way. Rather than attempt to *rewrite* Barthes's language, they aim to state what we *presume* is its intended meaning. Of the critical dilemma we face here, Barthes has counselled us not to despair: "there is no reason to complain," he has said; "there is reason only to ask for the candor of the [critical] system."[7] In the interest of an "understanding," let us say then, we propose to make singular, at as many places as possible in his writing, a Barthes who is by temperament and conviction plural, and to limit, by rendering in a language already filled with meaning, the freedom of Barthes's language.

II *Barthes's Career*

Barthes was born in Cherbourg in 1915 of an eminently bourgeois family. We are told in *Roland Barthes* that he was raised a Protestant—"in no way a severe situation," he writes there in retrospect, "but one which somewhat marks the whole of social existence," and may—along with certain other social "deficiences"—be the origin of his lifelong devaluation of what he calls "the natural"; "who," he observes, "does not feel how *natural* it is, in France, to be Catholic, married, and properly accredited with the right degrees?"[8] At the age of nine, Barthes moved with his mother (his father was killed in a naval battle in 1916) to Paris, where he received most of his education. Between 1935 and 1939 he was at the Sorbonne, receiving in the latter year a license in classical letters. Here too he founded the Groupe de Théâtre Antique. Exempted from military service (at nineteen, he had suffered an attack of tuberculosis), he was tutor and professor at the Lycées Voltaire and Carnot in Paris when the Nazis occupied the city. His academic career was interrupted, however, by a second attack of tuberculosis in 1941 and a six-year absence from active work, during which he received a license in grammar and philology, published his first article (on the journal of André Gide), and, for a time, engaged in pre-medical study with the intention of pursuing a career in psychiatric medicine. It was not until 1948 that he returned to academic work, first at the Institute Français in Bucharest, and, in 1949 and 1950, at the University of Alexandria in Egypt. The latter appointment we must regard as highly consequential, since it was here, according to Jonathan Culler, that Barthes had his "linguistic 'initiation' . . . through the good offices of A. J. Grimas."[9]

Toward the end of this decade—in 1947 and 1950, to be exact— Barthes contributed a number of articles on literary criticism to the Paris paper *Combat*, edited by the leftist critic Maurice Nadeau. These articles were the germ of Barthes's first book, a volume of eighty pages entitled *Writing Degree Zero*, which appeared in 1953. In her preface to the English translation of this book (1967), the American critic Susan Sontag (whose call for "an erotics of art" in an essay called "Against Interpretation" [1964], sounds now like a messianic prophecy of Barthes) introduced this new work by quite rightly placing it in a context of modernist critical theory and political debate; Barthes himself has said that he was a "Sartrian and Marxist" at the time the *Combat* pieces appeared.[10] We should observe here that by 1956, French Marxism and Existentialism had ceased to be the competing ideologies they were at the end of World War II, and had begun to coalesce into a "New Left," or what has been called "existential Marxism." Mark Poster has described this coalition as a "non-Leninist Marxism . . . that picks up from existentialism the effort to capture human beings in the moment of their active creation of their world, in their subjectivity; and . . . rejects the attempt to have a closed theory complete within itself."[11] It is interesting that the clearing house for the diverse doctrines of this position was a journal called *Arguments* which was initiated in 1956 by Barthes and Edgar Morin.

Political allegiance is not usually so easy to assign to Barthes. Though indiscriminately critical of all political ideologies, his views seem generally to be those of a Marxist intellectual, but which Marxism? "What provenance, what brand?" he later asks in *Roland Barthes:* "Lenin, Trotsky, Luxemburg, Bakunin, Mao, Bordiga, etc.?" (*RB*, p. 156) *Writing Degree Zero*, however, leaves little doubt about the ideological roots of his thought: neither do his early essays on Brecht—celebrating a "theater of solidarity" capable of bringing about change by intervening in history (*CE*, pp. 35-38)—published in 1955 and 1956 in the review *Théâtre Populaire*, which Barthes also had helped to found.

In 1952 Barthes joined the Centre National de Recherche Scientifique, where, until 1959, he was engaged in research, first in lexicology, and then in sociology. The earliest apparent product of these studies was the sequence of entertaining analyses or "demystifications" of contemporary "myths," the languages of mass culture (e.g., wrestling, soap-powders, Garbo's face, Einstein's brain, wine and milk, steak and chips) which he initially contributed each month, from 1954 to 1956, to *Les Lettres Nouvelles*, and at last gathered and published as *Mythologies* in 1957. At the same time, there were "repercussions" (to use Barthes's word) and influences from other quarters. The years 1954 and 1955 are the dates of Barthes's two early essays on Alain Robbe-Grillet's experimental fiction ("Objective Literature" and "Literal Literature") which helped establish the critical category of what shortly became known as the *nouveau roman*. In the former year, too, he produced *Michelet par lui-meme*, a selection of representative passages by the historian together with commentary by the selector. This rather inflexible format, tailored to the specifications of the series for which the volume was written (*Écrivains de Toujours*), Barthes did not find uncongenial, however; simply as a matter of practical expedience, it brought about that separation of biography and criticism that he would go on to practice and profess for more theoretical reasons.

In *Michelet,* biography consists of nothing more than several lists of plain facts; on the other hand, the criticism in the book aims to present a coherence, "the structure of an existence (I do not say of a life), a thematic . . . or better still, an organized network of obsessions"[12] which is identified with the structure of the world in Michelet's works. It is important that we do not identify (as Barthes's critical adversary, Raymond Picard, has) this statement of purpose with that of conventional psychological criticism. Barthes is not interested in tracing the roots of Michelet's themes to events in his childhood; his rationale is less Freudian than Bachelardian, a "psycho-analysis of substance" which postulates the four elements (fire, air, earth, and water) out of which ancient cosmology constructed its worlds as the elements of all imaginative experience. These elements become physical humors in Barthes's *Michelet,* the constituents of a language of the body out of which this historian conceived his objects. Thus, whereas the traditional or "classical" historian "accumulates adjectives—an infinite number of them"—in portraying the personages of history, in Michelet the "adjective is unique; it renders . . . an ideal palpation which has found the elementary substance of the body under study and makes the man inconceivable under any other qualification."[13] Thus, although this language has as its source the historical Michelet, the only subject for Barthes's analysis is the historian as he reveals himself in his works.

In 1960 Barthes joined the faculty of the École Pratique des Hautes Études as Chairman of the Section of Social and Economic Sciences. This may seem an unusual appointment for a literary critic, but, as Barthes wrote at that time, "the forms of education follow the ideology of their times," and today "the form explodes," as is demonstrated by "the adjunction of Sciences Humaines to Lettres in the name of the new Faculté" and in "the teaching at the École . . ." (*R,* p. 159). The human sciences that Barthes spoke of here are a reformation of traditional humanism along lines of several modern intellectual movements—especially those in linguistics, which was now employed as a tool for analyzing any social practice as a language. As a result, the imprecise concept of "the human" could be demystified and studied scientifically. But it is one thing to demonstrate these progressive ideas in a series of popular analyses of modern "mythologies," and quite another to direct them at the vested interests of literary scholarship and the French university establishment, which in fact is what Barthes began to do. In particular, two of his essays, published the year of his academic appointment, had ultimately a polarizing effect on French literary criticism at the time. One of these, "History or Literature," can be read as an outright polemic against traditional "university" criticism, arguing that its claims to both historicism and objectivity are mythical expressions of an academic ideology; the other, "Racinian Man," is a reconstruction of "a kind of Racinian anthropology, both structural and psychoanalytic," and thus an example of the *nouvelle critique* directed at one of the sacred objects of French literature. Both essays were republished (with a third, "Racine Spoken") as *On Racine* in 1963. By this time, Barthes's principal critical opponent had emerged, the Sorbonne Racine specialist, Raymond Picard, whose *Nouvelle Critique ou Nouvelle Imposture* appeared two years later. In 1966 Barthes consolidated his position in *Critique et Vérité*, and so ended what the French press of the time had called a second "battle of ancients and moderns."

Picard's criticism of the *nouvelle critique* was for the most part a reaction against what he considered a misuse of psychoanalytic techniques in literary criticism; for Barthes, however, the term *nouvelle critique* covered the use of any modern "language" (or conceptual framework) which a critic might choose as a metalanguage with which to speak about a literary work: Marxism, Existentialism, Phenomenology, Structuralism, as well as psychoanalysis. Barthes's familiarity with all these "languages" is demonstrated in his *Critical Essays* (1964), a selection of thirty-four articles, prefaces, and interviews published between 1953 and 1963. The essays also give us an indication of the range of his critical interests during this first decade of his professional career. Here are the important critical introductions to new writing (works by Michel Foucault, Alain Robbe-Grillet, Yves Velan, Michel Butor, and Georges Bataille), along with fresh views of established figures (Raymond Queneau, Kafka, Voltaire, Tacitus, Michelet, and La Bruyère), and a surprising resurrection (the seventeenth-century Dutch painter, Saenredam). There is an emphasis on the theater in the earlier pieces (nine essays, most of them on Brecht); from 1959 on, polemics and theory predominate. Among the latter is Barthes's most widely anthologized essay, "The Structuralist Activity," first published in 1963.

It is difficult to mark with precision the beginning and end of
Barthes's Structuralist phase. Intellectual histories normally associate the rise of Structuralism as a modern movement with the
publication of Claude Lévi-Strauss's *Tristes tropiques* in 1955;
Barthes, who uses the label more sparingly than most, associates it
always with Saussure's linguistics, which he appears not to have
studied until just before composing the earliest *Mythologies*
essays—perhaps as early as 1952, then. But there is always an air of
prematurity about Barthes's references to Structuralism—at least as a
literary movement; Structuralist criticism seems always an un-
realized promise, something more valued *in the process* of realizing
itself than in any realized product. The titles of Barthes's two most
explicitly Structuralist studies suggest this: "The Structuralist *Activity*" and "An *Introduction* to the Structural Analysis of Narrative,"
the latter published in 1966 in the journal *Communications*, of which
Barthes was a founding editor. The same precocity is apparent in
Barthes's *Elements of Semiology* (1964) which, because of its Saussurean genealogy, may also be regarded as a Structuralist study. It is
worth noticing in this connection that when the Structuralist activity
does eventuate in an object, Barthes is likely to be unhappy with it;
this is the case with his analysis of fashion writing, *Système de la
mode*, which he labored over from 1957 to 1963, deciding not until
three years later to publish it, and then merely as a document in the
history of semiology. His self-criticism here is typical of the French
Structuralist movement generally; by 1968 it had all but extinguished
itself in the pages of *Tel Quel* [Such As It Is], the journal it had
established in 1960 to promote itself.

The rise and fall of Structuralism is an extremely complex phenomenon; in this study we can deal with it on only the most superficial
level. Here we shall merely note that Structuralism tended to separate its product (a model structure or system or "language") from the
process of its production—a shortcoming that Barthes (at least on the
level of theory) attempted to overcome by explaining Structuralism
as an "activity"—and if the product is separated from the production,
it is also separated from the producer, the "subject." Since Structuralism aims to construct a "language," and since—according to
Saussure—it is the language-making faculty that distinguishes men
from animals, then all men are, in a manner of speaking, Structuralists. But the language we "make" as we speak or write is produced in an endless "process of difference"; it is not *fixed* as is the

static system produced in structural analysis. In short, Structuralism was seen to bear little relation to the everyday world, a fact that was dramatized by the silence of its adherents in the riots of students and workers in May 1968.[14] As Lévi-Strauss explained, those who ("wrongly") had embraced Structuralism as "the philosophy of modern times turned abruptly away from it with even a kind of spite at having bet on the wrong horse."[15]

Outside France, this reaction against Structuralism went largely unnoticed; indeed the rest of the world at this time was only beginning to hear about something called Structuralism and about one of its proponents named Roland Barthes. Until 1967 only one of Barthes's books had been translated into English *(On Racine)*, but in that year translations of *Writing Degree Zero* and *Elements of Semiology* appeared, and Barthes's reputation (no doubt as a Structuralist) spread widely. This identification was helped by his visits in 1966 to Japan and the United States; at Johns Hopkins University he delivered a paper at the International Symposium on "The Languages of Criticism and the Sciences of Man." Nevertheless, by 1968, in his seminar at the École Pratique, he was already engaged in the analysis of Balzac's "Sarrasine," which appeared as *S/Z* and marked what, for want of a better term, has been called his "post-Structuralist" phase.

Barthes himself has described this phase as a concern with "textuality," a word that is to be understood in the technically expanded sense it has been given in the magazine *Tel Quel* by Philippe Sollers and Julia Kristeva, and in the criticism of Jacques Derrida and the psychoanalytic theory of Jacques Lacan. The "textual" in this sense is not to be identified with the state of a physical text; the *texts* these writers deal with are held only *in* language, not in the hand. Barthes's next three books each supply an example. In *S/Z*, published in 1970, the text is not Balzac's "Sarrasine," but Barthes's *reading* of that story as a language; in *L'Empire des signes* [The Empire of Signs], published the same year, the text is "Japan," a country which Barthes manages to "read"; and in *Sade/Fourier/Loyola*, published the following year, we are given three texts, three languages, founded by these "logothetes": sadism, utopian "passion," and "indifference." We may see that, in distinction to the earlier structural analyses, these textual studies emphasize the *process* of the text, not a structure, but a "structuration" of a text by the subject-reader.

Though there is a certain logical consistency in this movement from ideological criticism, through Structuralism, to "Textualism,"

Barthes would regard as irrelevant any unifying conclusion we might draw from it. As far as he is concerned each of these critical moves has been nothing more than a source of personal pleasure, the transformation of himself as a text. That, at any rate is how he most recently viewed his critical progress, a view that might in turn be regarded as still one more transformation of the Barthesian subject. In two of his most recent books, *The Pleasure of the Text* (1973) and *Roland Barthes* (1975, he has given the name "morality" to this latest phase of his work, "morality" being the thinking of the body in a state of language."

"Writing" and the "Myth" of Literature

ACCORDING to Susan Sontag, *Writing Degree Zero* was Barthes's reply to Jean Paul Sartre's *What Is Literature?*[1] an important statement of the Existentialist critical position, which appeared while Barthes was composing his early *Combat* essays. This does not mean that there are not many similarities between Barthes's thought and Existentialist philosophy. Barthes's insistence upon the radical freedom of the writer, for instance, his concern with authenticity (with writing "which does not lie"), his criticism of bourgeois ideology, and skepticism of essences and *a priori* meanings will sound familiar to any reader of Sartre's earlier *Being and Nothingness* (1943). It is only when Sartre looks specifically at literature from his philosophical position—the ends of which are primarily social and political—that Barthes's independence becomes apparent. According to Sartre, the freedom of literature must serve these ends: literature must be socially "committed," the writer politically "engaged." "The end of language," Sartre wrote, "is to communicate," to impart to others the results one has obtained; "by speaking, I reveal the situation . . . I reveal it to others *in order* to change it."[2] For Sartre, "engagement" presupposes prose (words used as signs of objects); poetry (words used as objects in themselves) is necessarily disengaged, he believes; to speak is to act, and it is only prose that speaks. "The man who talks is beyond words and near the object," he writes, "whereas the poet is on this side of them."[3] Even prose will become mute when it uses language self-consciously—when, for example, its style becomes noticeable. Hence Sartre's criticism of Modernist literature which does not speak to a reader *about* anything, solicit him to share its author's situation.

For Barthes, however, the distinction to be made is not that between the unadorned prose that communicates and a self-conscious style or poetry that does not, but that between literal speech (which is always produced in a situation or in the midst of contingencies) and writing (which is always removed from contingencies, "closed," "self-contained"). Since, according to Barthes, it is contingency (or context) that makes the meaning of language clear—makes it *speak* or communicate—writing (whether prose or verse) is necessarily ambiguous, "an anti-communication" (*W*, p. 20). A writer cannot, then, make a reader share his situation, as Sartre believes is possible; that is an illusion based upon the illusion that writing *speaks*. Sartre's demand for a literature of commitment has no place, then, in Barthes's criticism—not for political reasons, but for purely technical ones. Barthes's conception of literature starts "farther back" than Sartre's, placing "the need for a free language at the sources of this language [at each moment of its being written] and not [where Sartre places it] in its eventual consumption" (*W*, p. 16). As we shall see, Barthes does not so much reject the idea of commitment as redefine it as a critical concept: what matters for the writer, he believes, is his awareness of "the commitment of his form."

The purpose of *Writing Degree Zero* is not only polemical or ideological, then; it is also formal or technical. Barthes ascribed a similar twofold purpose to another of his works, *Mythologies*, published in 1957. This book, he wrote in the preface to the 1970 edition, was both "an ideological critique bearing on the language of so-called mass-culture," and "a first attempt to analyze semiologically [i.e., as a system of signs] the mechanics of this language."[4] The purpose of *Writing Degree Zero* may be stated in similar terms: an ideological critique of "the language of literature" (one that would also defend Modernist literature against Sartre's ideological attack), and an attempt to explain the mechanics of this "language." "What we hope to do here," Barthes wrote in the introduction to the earlier book, is "affirm the existence of a formal reality independent of language and style" (*W*, p. 5). The ideological concerns of the book grow logically out of the consideration of this "third-dimension of Form," which Barthes calls *écriture* or "writing." Nevertheless, *Writing Degree Zero* is a one-sided book, and it is the technical side that is slighted. Barthes tells us in "Myth Today," the concluding essay in *Mythologies*, that he "began to discuss this problem [i.e., the idea that literature is a "mythical system"] in *Writing Degree Zero*" (*M*, p. 134). But what he lacked in the earlier book was a theoretical model of language and a technical vocabulary to articulate it. As the later *Mythologies* amply illustrates, he found these only after he had read the work of the Swiss linguist Ferdinand de Saussure, sometime in the 1950s. For this reason, our discussion of Barthes's first book will draw extensively upon the more fully developed scheme of technical analysis offered in *Mythologies*.

I *"Writing"*

Besides its usual meanings, the noun "writing" is used by Barthes in two technical senses that are probably unfamiliar to many readers; we are now concerned with only one of these, and shall henceforth use the English word in quotation marks to refer to it; the second sense, distinguished by the use of its French equivalent, *écriture*, will be taken up later in this chapter. Here, then, "a writing" for Barthes is something like a *style*, though, because the latter word designates for him the most personal and individual quality of a writer, we must hasten to say that a "writing" is a very general style, a public style, in fact. We shall think of it as the literary manner of a particular society, the conventions governing the writing of a language that identify its intention to be literature. Barthes puts this in somewhat more technical terms: "writing" is a *function* of language; it is also the formal sign of literature. As we have already noticed, language for Barthes "is never innocent," never pure; "words have a second-order memory which mysteriously persists" (*W*, p. 16). Because written language is separated from its author—nothing more than fixed marks on a page—"it must," he argues, "signify something other than [i.e., something besides] its content and its individual form, something which defines its limits and imposes it as Literature" (*W*, pp. 1-2). Without its formal memory, then, written language could not express its intention to a reader.

Jonathan Culler, in his valuable *Structuralist Poetics*, gives us the following illustration of this self-signifying function of written language. When, in the eighteenth century, Madame de Lafayette wrote that the Comte de Tende learned that his wife was pregnant by another man, it was unnecessary for her to tell her reader what he thought; her language needed only to gesture formally toward the world where such thoughts and accidents occur. The Comte, she had only to write, "thought everything that it was natural to think in such circumstances."[5] The emptiness and transparency of this language (its "decorum," a contemporary critic would have said), compelling the reader to fill it himself with his own or society's knowledge of the world, is a sign of an accepted conception of literature, i.e., of literature "institutionalized"; it is, in Barthes's early sense of the word, a particular "writing."

But there is more than this to Barthes's elucidation of the significance of "writing." A writer wishes to express himself freely; but a "writing" expresses the social and political intentions of the language's former uses. What written language says, then, is only in part what its writer intends to say: what it says is also what the language, simply as an enduring (i.e., a written) form says. Madame de Lafayette, in our previous example, does not freely record what *she* believes the Comte de Tende thought; rather, she uses a public style of *not saying* something in order to let the language express a cultural preconception of "the natural." The content of her language tells the reader that the Comte "thought everything that it was natural to think in such circumstances"; but the conventional form of that language (its "writing") tells him more: "Literature," it says in effect, "represents the 'universal,' i.e., *nature*, and *natural* things 'go-without-saying': so I am a work of literature." Clearly, such a public style is a great convenience. Here, for instance, it does away with the difficult job (for Mme de Lafayette) of articulating and (for the reader) of imagining what the Comte thought—and above all it manages this *naturally*, i.e., without seeming to be a style at all. Barthes's point is that this "writing" (and the conception of literature it signifies) only seems "natural"; it was in fact historically determined by social and political forces—by ideology.

Madame de Lafayette, of course, was not in the least conscious of any of this. She simply wrote her sentence with an intuitive assurance that her reader would not wonder about what the Comte thought, an assurance that was rooted in perhaps the most general assumption of her culture and her time: that the truth was *in the world* for anyone to see—the truth was obvious. Literature, then, which aimed to express truth, could do no better than merely gesture at the world. Thus her sentence justifies itself in justifying the assumption on which it rests. It is only when the ideological forces that produce such a public style (and that the style in turn helps to perpetuate) weaken that the style reveals itself as a style, and the writer becomes aware that merely the "writing," simply the *written form,* is what speaks.

As we have already noted, Barthes dated this fall from literary innocence at around 1850. From the moment the writer recognized "the morality" of the form of his language, he became aware, in a new way, of his own responsibility as a writer. His question was no longer "*Why* write?" but "*How* to write?" for he had now a conscious choice to make: either to adopt the "writing" of his past along with all that it stood for, or to reject it and, attempting to return language to its original innocence, devise new modes of free expression. For Barthes, then, there is a history of "writing" (distinct from that history of themes and individual styles known as "literary history"): the history of those "modern" attempts to purge language of its

historical meaning—to write without a preconception of Literature. *Writing Degree Zero* is an introduction to such a history.

But "writing" is a generic as well as a period concept; literature is conceived in terms not only of the period in which it is produced, but also of the various genres (poetry, the novel, journalism, etc.) which constitute it. Though Barthes makes the distinction between these two conceptions of "writing" the primary principle of organization in *Writing Degree Zero* (Part I of the book discussing the generic significance of the term, and Part II tracing the sequence of its historical modes from the seventeenth century to the present), it is important to recognize that in fact these functions exist simultaneously. The "writing" of poetry, for example, alerts a reader to a different set of intentions than does the "writing" of narrative; but the significance of the "writing" of an eighteenth-century poem will be of little help in deciphering one written in the twentieth century. The former consists of those highly conspicuous forms (rhyme, meter, imagery) that signify the "technique of projecting out an inner thought" (*W*, p. 42), traditional poetry, for Barthes, being nothing more than the language of prose augmented by ornament. One thinks of Alexander Pope transcribing the thought of an essay on man in prose, and then translating it into the couplets of *An Essay on Man.* Pope's thought, we know, consisted of the great truths of the world ("what oft was thought"); his rhyme and meter make us think of it as his thought. The "writing" of eighteenth-century literature demands that we look for meaning in the world to which its language refers, and interpret as poetic what does not make literal sense there. But "modern" poetry, Barthes says, "carries its own nature within itself, and does not need to signal its identity outwardly" (*W*, p. 34).

On the other hand, formal features like the preterite tense and the third person are operative in the "writing" of the novel. The function of the preterite (in French, the *passé simple*), for instance, "is no longer that of tense," according to Barthes, but a sign of "the presence of Art." The preterite presupposes the existence of an order, an already constructed world whose beginning is conceivable because its end is already known. Thus, it brings the past within reach, makes it clearer and more intelligible—but also slighter and less rich. So when we read "The duc de Guise died on December 23rd, 1588," we feel reassured that the world to be presented has been "purged of the uncertainty of existence," that it is not set "sprawling before us," but has been reduced to "a slim and pure logos" (*W*, pp. 30-31). We know, that is, that we are reading a story and a history.

II *"Myth" and Ideology*

Early in *Writing Degree Zero* Barthes defines "writing" as "a set of signs unrelated to the ideas, the language or the style, and setting out to give definition, within the body of every possible mode of expression, to the utter separateness of a ritual language. This hieratic quality of written Signs," he says, "establishes Literature as an institution" (*W*, pp. 1-2). What Barthes is saying here is that "writing" makes literature itself a sort of language, separate from the language that generates it (French or English)—but separate also as a ritual language. The last phrase is especially obscure in the context of *Writing Degree Zero;* it suggests that Barthes had already, in his earliest criticism, begun to think of literature as a "mythical system." As this is an idea that is best understood in terms of his semiological analysis, we must now review the main points of his semiology as these were soon to appear in his book *Mythologies*.

The so-called "myths" with which Barthes is concerned in *Mythologies* are not, we should first of all understand, the primitive stories studied by anthropologists, but the "collective representations" (sociologist Émil Durkheim's phrase) of mass culture such as magazine illustrations, films, advertisements, newspaper articles. Specifically, Barthes wishes to account for a certain duplicity in such artifacts: the signification of a *naturalness* that somehow "dresses up" the representation of a reality that is "undoubtedly determined by history" or society—not, in other words, a fact of nature at all. The end-product of his study is the conception of a structure of double-function in sign systems, the ability of one signification to generate a second. As an example, Barthes asks us to think of a cover of the French magazine *Paris-Match* on which a young black, dressed in French military uniform is saluting, eyes raised as if to the tri-colored flag. This, Barthes explains, is "the meaning" of the picture. But grafted on to this primary message is a second signification: "that France is a great Empire, that all her sons, without any colour discrimination, faithfully serve under her flag, and that there is no better answer to the detractors of an alleged colonialism than the zeal shown by this Negro in serving his so-called oppressors" (*M*, p. 116). What particularly interests Barthes here (irritates him, actually) is that this new signification seems "natural," "obvious," "what-goes-without-saying," when in fact it is historically determined—in this case, by a threatened colonialism. This transformation of history into "nature," he concludes, is "the very principle of myth" (*M*, p. 129).

"The notion of myth," Barthes wrote in the preface to *Mythologies*, "seemed to me to explain these examples of the falsely obvious. . . . I was already certain of a fact from which I later tried to draw all the consequences: myth is a language. So that while concerning myself with phenomena apparently most unlike literature . . . I did not feel I was leaving the field of this general semiology of our bourgeois world, the literary aspect of which I had begun to study in earlier essays" (*M*, p.11). As we have already suggested, the earliest of those essays to which Barthes refers is *Writing Degree Zero*, which he describes at the end of *Mythologies* as "nothing but a mythology of literary language" (*M*, p. 134). In other words, he was trying to say in his first book that literature is a system of signs, a *semiology*, and that "writing" is part of a second-order signification by which the historical memory of language is *institutionalized* or transformed into a conventional image of what is literarily "natural." Literature as "myth," then, is "literature as an institution."

But these ideas are only faintly adumbrated in *Writing Degree Zero;* in 1953 Barthes had probably not even heard of the word "semiology," coined by the Swiss linguist Ferdinand de Saussure. Barthes's preface to the second French edition of *Mythologies* (1970), then, is both a restrospective judgment of his first major critical effort and an announcement of a new one: he "had just read Saussure," he writes there, and had become convinced "that by treating 'collective representations' as sign-systems, one might hope to go further than the pious show of unmasking" these systems (apparently that was how he then regarded his achievement in *Writing Degree Zero*); in *Mythologies*, he hoped to "account *in detail* for the mystification which transforms . . . culture into a universal nature" (*M*, p. 9).

The proto-semiological character of *Writing Degree Zero* becomes clear when we consider several features of the analytical method of *Mythologies*. Our starting point, like Barthes's will be Saussure's analysis of the form of a sign, which Barthes found in Saussure's *Course in General Linguistics* (1915). Saussure regarded the linguistic sign (a word, for instance) as a three-part unity: a sound-image (or *signifier*). a concept (or *signified*), and the associational totality of these two halves (the *sign*).[6] The important feature of Saussure's analysis is that it works not with two, but three terms. In everyday experience we make no distinction between a signifier and a sign. Under analysis, however, they are different: the sign has meaning; the signifier is merely a sound-image.

This difference is what interested Barthes. "Take a bunch of roses," he wrote in *Mythologies;* "I use it to *signify* my passion. Do we have

here, then, only a signifier and a signified, the roses and my passion?"
Not, he answers, when we analyze this sign. "We do have three
terms; for these roses weighted with passion perfectly and correctly
allow themselves to be decomposed into roses and passion: the
former and the latter existed before uniting and forming this third
object, which is the sign. . . . On the plane of analysis I cannot
confuse the roses as signifier and the roses as sign: the signifier is
empty, the sign is full, it is a meaning" (M, p. 113).

Language, then, is a sign system that uses "sound-images" for its
signifiers, combining these with concepts in order to produce linguistic signs. Barthes thinks of it as a *first-order semiological system*. We
can diagram it as a box divided into three compartments:

1. Signifier	2. Signified
3. Sign	

Now the word *myth*, in the technical sense in which Barthes uses it,
designates a message that is made out of a preexisting sign system; it is
a *second-order semiological system*. Like language, it makes its signs
by combining signifiers and signifieds; its uniqueness is that its
signifier is an already existing sign, which now becomes only a part of
a greater system. Our three-compartment language-box, then, will
become the first compartment of a three-compartment myth-box:

Language {	1. Signifier	2. Signified	
	3. Sign		
MYTH {	I. SIGNIFIER		II. SIGNIFIED
	III. SIGN		

(M, p. 155)

Barthes illustrates this conception of "mythical speech" with the
following example:

I am a pupil in the second form in a French *lycée*. I open my Latin grammar,
and I read a sentence from Aesop or Phaedrus: *quia ego nominor leo*. I stop
and think. There is something ambiguous about this statement: on the one
hand, the words in it do have a simple meaning: *because my name is lion*. And
on the other hand, the sentence is evidently there in order to signify something else to me. Inasmuch as it is addressed to me, a pupil in the second
form, it tells me clearly: I am a grammatical example meant to illustrate the
rule about the agreement of the predicate. (M, p. 115–16)

The student in this example pays little attention to the "meaning" of the first-order linguistic system (*because my name is lion*). Instead, a second-order system "imposes" itself on his attention: there is a signifier (the whole first-order system, now to be called a "form"); there is a signified (now to be called a "concept": *I am a grammatical example*); and the relation of this "form" and "concept" is a new, larger sign or "signification." The sentence, then, is both a meaning and a label of itself.

The preceding example demonstrates the principle of double-functionality in sign systems; it sheds little light, however, on Barthes's critical purpose in *Mythologies*. What, after all, is reprehensible about a sentence in a grammar that says both *my name is lion and I am a grammatical example*? To grasp the deceptiveness of cultural "myths"—that characteristic of them that provoked Barthes's analysis—we shall have to look at another of Barthes's examples. But let us first notice two additional features of the signifier (form) and the signified (concept) of second-order sign-systems. The signifier of a myth is curiously ambiguous, owing to the fact that it is both a first-order sign full of meaning *and* an empty form, a mere sound-image. If we were to take our Latin sentence out of the second-order system of the grammar book and replace it in the fable from which it was taken, we would see that it originally had a life and history of its own. Barthes attempts to summarize it: "I am an animal, a lion, I live in a certain country, I have just been hunting, they would have me share my prey with a heifer, a cow and a goat; but being the stronger, I award myself all the shares for . . . *my name is lion*" (*M*, p. 118). When this final clause enters the second-order system, it leaves behind much of this story (it would be an unsatisfactory grammatical example if it did not)—much, but not all of it; enough of it remains in the new signifier to make the grammatical example "lively." Barthes puts it this way: "the [original] meaning loses its value, but keeps its life, from which the form of the myth will draw its nourishment. . . . the form must constantly be able to be rooted again in the meaning and to get there what nature it needs for its nutriment" (*M*, p. 118). On the other hand, the *signified* of a myth is always the intention that calls the myth into existence (e.g., the wish to justify colonialism, or to make a grammatical example); the "concept" is "filled with a situation," and thereby implants a "a whole new history" in the myth. Can we perhaps now begin to see the point of Barthes's argument that myth transforms history into nature? But let us get to that example that will explain his displeasure with myth.

Walking in the Basque country of Spain, Barthes says, I may well notice a common style in the houses of the area which causes me to acknowledge this sort of house as "a definite ethnic product." This architectural unity "does not provoke me into naming it," however; it does not impose itself on me. I recognize that "it was here before me, without me. It is a complex product which has its determinations at the level of a very wide history: it does not call out to me." But, Barthes continues, if I happen to see such a house in Paris, "I feel as if I were personally receiving an imperious injunction to name this object a Basque chalet: or better, to see it as the very essence of *basquity*" (*M*, p. 124–25). In the Basque country, in other words, the architectural style is a first-order sign. In Paris, it is a second-order signification or myth; its signifier is the first-order sign (i.e., the architectural style, deprived, however, of much of its reason-for-being, its history); its signified is the concept of *basquity;* the two together make up the myth.

Now the *signified* or concept of myth, we have said, is both intentional and historical; the builder of the house "comes and seeks me out," Barthes says, "in order to oblige me to acknowledge the body of intentions which have motivated it and arranged it there as the sequel of an individual history, as a confidence and a complicity" (*M*, p. 125). The myth, that is, "appropriates me" as its reader; it has "an imperative, buttonholing character." But at the same time it seems to do just the opposite of this. Because its signifier is not only a form (certain architectural specifications), but also a meaning (the association of these specifications with houses in the Basque country), this myth seems to exist quite independently of me, seems just *to be there*, innocently, *naturally*. For Barthes, a thing is "naturalized" when it is made to seem eternal, i.e., not due to history—and this is precisely what happens in myth, thanks to the ubiquity of its signifier which is a sort of constantly moving turnstile, presenting now an absent, but full meaning, now a present, but empty form (*M*, pp. 123–24). As a kind of utterance, myth is defined by its intention (to label itself *basquity,* or French colonialism, or a grammatical example) rather than by its literal sense (the architectural specifications of houses in the Basque country, a black soldier saluting, *my name is lion);* nevertheless, its intention is always neutralized, made "absent" by this literal sense. Myth is best characterized, Barthes says, as a "perpetual alibi," in that it always has "an 'elsewhere' at its disposal" (*M*, p. 123).

Here at last we have come to the main point of Barthes's criticism of modern cultural "myth" and, let us also bear in mind, of traditional literature. This criticism is the consequence of a new way of viewing language, the model (since Saussure's linguistics) for investigating any sign system. The old view of language (which, nevertheless, is probably still the popular view) assumes that words possess meanings in themselves, that when we make an utterance, we start with a meaning and then look for words that will translate it. But Saussure has taught us that the signifier and signified of a linguistic sign are arbitrarily related; words do not derive their meanings from their sounds; nor do the sounds of words, in and of themselves, connote their meanings. Rather, meaning is said to come about through the relations of words to one another, as a function of the differences between words in the language system. It is produced not in the reference of words to discrete objects, but in the very process of discourse. As Maurice Merleau-Ponty says, the choice of a sign requires that we "evoke some of the other expressions which might have taken its place and were rejected, and we must feel the way in which they might have touched and shaken the chain of language in another manner and the extent to which this particular expression was really the only possible one if that signification was to come into the world."[7] There is surely something admirable in this integrity of language; Barthes speaks of it as the "health of language" (*M*, p. 126).

But in myth the relation between the signifier (form) and the signified (concept) is not arbitrary, but "motivated"; the form is not empty, but filled with a first-order meaning, and it is the analogy of this meaning to the concept that "motivates" the myth to choose its signifier. Myth lacks the integrity of language. The meaning that should be generated within the system is taken at the start from outside the system. History supplies it. But the innocent reader or consumer of myth is unaware of this. Because he senses an excess of meaning (the loaded signifier), the intentionality of the concept goes unnoticed—the intention, Barthes says, "can remain manifest without however appearing to have an interest in the matter . . . everything happens as if the picture *naturally* conjured up the concept, as if the signifier *gave a foundation* to the signified" (*M*, pp. 129–30). As a result, the reader "lives the myth as a story at once true and unreal" (*M*, p. 128).

But in what way is this criticism of myth, in the language of Barthes's preface, "ideological"? As we have seen, Barthes's interest in semiology centered, at least in the beginning, on society's representation of reality, and his analysis has so far shown us that the goal of myth is to give "an historical intention a natural justification," to make "contingency appear eternal"; in myth, that is, things forget that they once were made. Barthes's criticism of myth starts from a personal disgust with the fact that society accepts its own made-up images of nature as nature itself. This criticism becomes ideological when we recognize that the loss in myth of historical reality is a loss of *political reality*—using this term to describe "the whole of human relations in their real, social structure, in their power of making the world" (*M*, p. 143). Thus, what is left out of the Basque chalet when it is mythicized in Paris is the environment of work of which the original chalet is a "political expression." In the Basque country the chalet works as a primary language or "language-object"—it *"speaks things," enacts* them; in Paris, it works as a "metalanguage" that *"speaks of* [or about] *things"* (*M*, p. 144). Myth, therefore, is "depoliticized speech"; in passing from history to nature, "it abolishes the complexity of human acts . . . it does away with all dialectics, with any going back beyond what is immediately visible" (*M*, p. 143). Now according to Barthes, political ideologies are themselves mythic in character, and none more so than that of the bourgeoisie, which he defines as *"the social class which does not want to be named"* (*M*, p. 138). Bourgeois ideology does not wish to be recognized as an ideology at all, but as an order of nature, eternal and universal; it is itself, in other words, a second-order signification. By putting aside its name, the first-order sign of its historical origin, "the bourgeoisie transforms the reality of the world into an image of the world, History into Nature" (*M*, p. 141). For this reason, Barthes regards myth as the appropriate instrument of bourgeois ideology; and because ours is still a bourgeois society, we live in a world that is "a privileged field of mythical significations."

III   *"Classical" Literature as Myth*

We should now be in a position to understand better Barthes's statement that *Writing Degree Zero* was an attempt to deal with literature as an aspect of the "general semiology of our bourgeois world" (*M*, p. 11). Literature—traditional literature, that is—is a mythical or second-order system. There is, Barthes explains, *a meaning*, "that of the discourse" (what the words of a text actually mean); there is a *signifier* (the same discourse considered as form); there is a *signified*, "the concept of literature"; and there is *a signification*, "the literary discourse" (i.e., the alternating relations of the *concept* with both the *form* and the *meaning*). What Barthes calls "writing" is the signifier of the literary myth, a form already filled with meaning which receives from the concept of literature a new signification (*M*, p. 134). Thus, in addition to communicating its own determinate content, a literary work (just like Barthes's illustrative Latin sentence) also labels itself "literature," thereby involving us in the particular historical activity of "consuming literature." It is difficult to slow down the process of signification to the point that we may demonstrate this process in a specific literary work; but we can observe one or two of the anomalous features of literature that result from it. Here, for example, are the opening sentences of Balzac's story called "Sarrasine" (1830), a text which Barthes is later to study in exhaustive detail:

I was deep in one of those daydreams which overtake even the shallowest of men, in the midst of the most tumultuous parties. Midnight had just sounded from the clock of the Elysée-Bourbon. Seated in a window recess and hidden behind the sinuous folds of a silk curtain, I could contemplate at my leisure the garden of the mansion where I was spending the evening.[8]

We should first of all notice that, since a man "speaks" to us here of his presence at a party, we have therefore to deal with both an "instance of discourse"—a narrative situation—and an "instance of reality"—a situation narrated. The "I" of this discourse belongs logically to the former, for "I," as a linguistic form, is defined as "the one who says 'I' in the present instance of discourse."[9] Nevertheless, although the instance of discourse exists to express the instance of reality, the former is curiously indeterminate until it is combined with the latter—and it is this combination that produces the anomalies of the text. Consider, for example, the fact that a narrator *deep in a daydream* would be unlikely to say he was *deep in a daydream*. The past tense of the verb does not explain this difficulty, for we are next told that midnight "had just" sounded—sounded, of course, at the party, in the fashionable district of the Elysée-Bourbon; but "had just" also tends to draw itself into the time-frame of "the present instance of discourse." There is, then, in the mind of any reader of this passage, a sort of rapid alternation between the instance of discourse and the instance of reality, as if the reality must exist prior to the discourse in order for the discourse to make the reality seem to exist. In other words, the signifier of this second-order system is a form (the instance of discourse) already filled with a meaning (the instance of reality); and as the character of the mythical signifier is always *to be somewhere else* (a "perpetual alibi," in Barthes's words) we are unable to confine it to one or the other of these instances. But although the form all but disappears in the interests of the meaning, enough of it remains to receive a new signification from the concept "literature."

Of course, the ambiguities of "Sarrasine" are apparent only because we have adopted the perspectives of Barthes's "modern" critical consciousness. Generations of readers have encountered not the slightest perplexity in the opening sentences of the story—have probably identified it as the most *natural* sort of literature. But that is just the point, Barthes would say: myth always passes itself off as "nature"; because of its excess of meaning, "things appear to mean something by themselves" (*M*, p. 143). That too is the way we must characterize the literarily "natural": its meaning (the instance of reality in "Sarrasine") appears not to have been caused. To the extent that the form of the signifier "hides" in its meaning, Balzac's language disposes of itself as it is read—much as spoken language does in the speaking. The language is transparent, permitting the reader to look *through* it to a meaning which seems independent of the language that conveys it, but which was in fact part of the language system to begin with, and so awaits the reader at the end of the disposable utterance. In more familiar terms, we say that Balzac's work is mimetic or realistic.

For Barthes, however, this function of language to dispose of itself (and thereby to signify its literary nature) is an identifiable *écriture* or "writing"—a "spectacular commitment of language" (*W*, p. 25), though in this case it is a spectacle that tries to make itself as unnoticeable as possible. Barthes distinguishes this particular "writing" as the "classical," a writing that "universalized" itself as the only "writing" of the period 1650 to 1850, and in the process universalized a conception of literature as an image of reality, a "literature of the referent." Not until history altered human consciousness was this literature in fact recognized as an "institutionalized" entity—i.e., as a "myth" with "writing" as its signifier. At that moment, according to Barthes, "the whole of literature . . . became the problematics of language" (*W*, p.3)—"modern" literature was born.

But let us return to Barthes's criticism of traditional (i.e., "classical") literature as bourgeois myth. We have noticed that, in *Mythologies*, myth is defined as "depoliticized speech," an image of the world that "passes off" the structure of actual human relations that underlies it. Now to innocently "read" such myth, to receive its ambiguous signification unquestioningly (as Barthes believes most of us in a bourgeois society do much of the time) is one thing; but to recognize a myth for what it is, to "decipher" it or understand it as a distortion is another. One may say that the polemical purpose of *Mythologies* is to make us "mythographers" of the second sort, make us aware, that is, of the hidden commitment of the language forms of contemporary bourgeois society; the purpose of *Writing Degree Zero* is to describe the historical moment at which French writers became aware of the commitment of the form of "classical" language, and to define the consequences of that awareness for literature. Barthes has said that "bad faith" adheres to "any language which is ignorant of itself"[10]—not just myth (the Basque chalet in Paris, for instance), but any primary language (present-day French, let us say) that has become "established on a national scale," become, that is, a body of prescriptions of what is permissible or forbidden in the language, but without any longer concerning itself about the "political" or historical "origins or the justification for such a taboo" (*W*, p. 56).

The phrase "bad faith" is used in an Existentialist sense here: it is Sartre's name for the belief in a delusory freedom or authenticity. In *Being and Nothingness* he illustrated the concept with an amusing description of a woman who, when her escort speaks to her ambiguously—using words that at face value are merely admiring, yet not without obvious amorous suggestion—prolongs the excitement of the moment without risk to herself by pretending that only his admiration is real. She emphasizes the "facticity" of the situation, the absoluteness of the present. But as the man takes her hand, and she pretends not to notice it—seeming to etherealize the situation with lofty talk about life—she frees herself completely from the present. There is "at once a facticity and a transcendence," Sartre says, and this is an instance of bad faith because the woman attempts to constitute herself as being what she is not.[11] Barthes discovers a parallel between this sort of ethical equivocation and the ubiquity of the mythical signifiers in "classical" literature. Thus, Balzac's use of the first-person pronoun produces a "proprietary consciousness which retains the mastery of what it states without participating in it"[12]—much like the sexually uncommitted woman of Sartre's illustration. "Modern" literature's consciousness of language, Barthes says, is "a weapon against the general 'bad faith' of discourse which would make a literary form simply the expression of an interiority constituted previous to and outside of language."[13]

But "classical" literature was defenseless against this "bad faith." By the middle of the seventeenth century the French language had achieved a normative status. Systematizing usage according to an

"intemporal" rational principle, the Port Royal grammarians so
purified and "naturalized" the language that its regularized forms
were taken as "universal," without a thought of their historical origin.
The troublesome substance of language (variations in usage, for instance) was refined away, leaving only an abstract system that a writer
could complacently ignore in the interests of what he wished to say *by
means of* the language—i.e., in the interests of the referents of its
words. For two hundred years this transparent language became
itself the sole "mode of writing" available to French authors.
Barthes's name for it—"classical"—reveals its implicit bad faith by
ironically punning on its origin: "classical writing," he says, merely
"wears a universal look"; it is in fact "a class writing," a "bourgeois
writing," produced "in the group which was closest to the people in
power, shaped by force of dogmatic decisions, [and] promptly ridding
itself of all grammatical turns of speech forged by the spontaneous
subjectivity of ordinary people . . ." (W, p. 57). Bourgeois ideology
not only "gave the measure of the universal," i.e., of reality; it also
fulfilled it unchallenged. As a result, the "classical" or bourgeois
writer enjoyed the unique privilege of being the "sole judge of other
peoples' woes without anyone else to gaze on him" (W, p. 60); he
wrote in innocence of any tension between his vocation as a writer
and his social condition.

But all this changed, according to Barthes, with the revolution of
1848, the failure of which brought about the disintegration of French
society into "three mutually hostile classes" (the aristocracy, the
bourgeoisie, and the proletariate) and with it "the definitive ruin of
liberal illusions" (W, p. 60). The consequence was a change in consciousness. The unified consciousness of the "classical" age was fragmented, and the bourgeois writer found himself in a new historical
situation; his "reality" was no longer *the* reality. As Barthes put it, the
universal escaped his ideology, which now became only one among
many possible ideologies. Similarly, his language, which until now
could be taken for granted—a "common property," supposedly neutral, and hence universal—betrayed its class origin in history. Language began, in other words, to lose its transparency, to draw attention to itself; it became a visible object, not the vehicle of a meaning,
but something with a meaning of its own, an intentionality that could
not be ignored. History now confronted the writer with "a necessary
option between several moral attitudes connected with language,"
forced him "to choose the commitment of his form, either by adopting
or rejecting" the "classical" as "a mode of writing" (W, pp. 2-3).

IV   *"Modern" Literature*

Barthes, then, sees the development of what he calls "modern" literature as the effort of writers to reject the false "nature" of "classical writing," to achieve "an object wholly delivered of History, and find again the freshness of a pristine state of language" (*W*, p. 74). This "modern" reaction against "classical writing" was not, of course, cataclysmic; most writers today must, by Barthes's norms, still be called "classical." Moreover, since a "writing" presupposes a particular consciousness, any deliberate attempt to substitute a new "writing" for an old one is necessarily an individual act. There is, therefore, no single "modern writing," but a variety of "modes" of the "modern." It will be useful here to have a specimen of one—and perhaps the more "modern" the better. For this reason we shall glance at the work of Alain Robbe-Grillet, even though it appeared too late to influence Barthes's thinking in *Writing Degree Zero.* Here is the opening paragraph of his 1959 novel, *In the Labyrinth:*

I am alone here now, under cover. Outside it is raining, outside you walk through the rain with your head down, shielding your eyes with one hand while you stare ahead nevertheless, a few yards ahead, at a few yards of wet asphalt; outside it is cold, the wind blows between the bare black branches; the wind blows through the leaves, rocking whole boughs, rocking them, rocking, their shadows swaying across the white roughcast walls. Outside the sun is shining, there is no tree, no bush to cast a shadow, and you walk under the sun shielding your eyes with one hand while you stare ahead, only a few yards in front of you, at a few yards of dusty asphalt where the wind makes patterns of parallel lines, forks, and spirals.[14]

We have seen that the "naturalness" of the "classical" text is proof of its mythical order; what we might call the "unnaturalness" of *In the Labyrinth* is proof of its primarily linguistic order. Balzac reads "naturally" because he began with a meaning, a reference to the world—the subjective experience of a party-goer, the late night sounds of Paris, the tumult of a bright ballroom; the assumption is that the meaning existed prior to the text. The task of the writer, then, was one of finding the right language to "translate" this meaning—and for Balzac, the right language was that which attracted the least attention to itself, the most transparent language. Robbe-Grillet's novel seems "unnatural" because it does not begin with a meaning, to be deferred for the reader to the end of the passage; hence we cannot identify the world to which it refers. Is it sunny there, or raining, or snowing? hot or cold? Is there a tree growing there or not? Robbe-Grillet's language demands that we look *at* it rather than *through* it, that we regard it primarily as form. Its meaning develops internally, just as the meaning of every linguistic statement, according to modern linguistics, develops inside the language system.

Conceptually, Barthes locates the "classical" writer "outside" his language; he is the *user* of a "relational" instrument, a language whose "words are abstracted as much as possible in the interest of relationships . . . of conveying a connection" (*W*, p. 44). To this instrumentality of the language is due the sequential flow of "classical" discourse, the transparency of its "writing." Its "connections lead the word on," Barthes says, "and at once carry it towards a meaning . . ." (*W*, p. 47). "Classical" literature, we have observed, is received as an instance of reality, of the referent. But Robbe-Grillet's language interrupts the flow of sequential discourse; it seems unable even to get started, let alone to make connections: "Outside it is raining, outside you walk through the rain . . . outside it is cold . . . Outside the sun is shining . . ." Having no meaning to start with, it has none to refer to us. Rather, its meaning inheres in our consciousness of the play of these simple linguistic forms or signifiers. The passage from *In the Labyrinth* is *about* nothing but the process of its own coming into existence—its *writing*—and the range of possibility in that process: beginning in one direction, then in another, and so on. As Barthes has more recently remarked, "Language is literature's Being, its very world; the whole of literature is contained in the act of writing, and no longer in those of 'thinking,' 'portraying,' 'telling' or 'feeling'."[15]

The point of this distinction becomes clear when we compare the use, by Robbe-Grillet and Balzac, of the first-person pronoun. We noted that, linguistically, "I" signifies "the one who says 'I' in the present instance of discourse"[16]; and clearly that is all the pronoun does in the carefully composed first sentence of Robbe-Grillet's text: "I *am alone here now*" (italics added)—not "I," a recording self together with "I," a recorded self, but "I" who (at a particular place (on the paper) and at a particular moment) *writes* the word "I." In Balzac, "I" is a mythical signifier, i.e., both a form signifying "the one who says 'I'" and a meaning, a previously made-up person who is written about; there is a "confusion," Barthes says, "between the subject of the discourse and the subject of the reported action, as if—and this is a common belief—he who is speaking today were the same as he who acted yesterday."[17] Barthes believes that "modern" writers have become more and more aware of this ambiguity of the mythical signifier of "classical" literature, and that accordingly "the *I* of discourse can no longer be a place where a previously stored-up person is innocently restored."[18] Thus the "field" of the "modern" writer has become the process of writing itself. As the "agent" of the act of writing, it is the only "place" where he can locate himself. And because, as we have already suggested, the task of the reader of "modern" literature parallels the writer's, constituting a sort of "second-writing" of the work, the reader too is internalized. Barthes's conception of literature as "an institution" implies that every work of literature is socially situated. As Fredric Jameson says, "there is an obligatory distance that obtains at any given period between the reader and the literary product and between the writer and the product as well."[19] Compared, then, to the social situation of Balzac's language—in which the writer and reader stand outside the language, at either end of it—the distance of writer and reader from Robbe-Grillet's language has diminished radically. By substituting the "instance of discourse for the instance of reality," the "modern" work includes them.

Barthes's recognition of the "bad faith" of "classical writing" leads him not only to defend "modern" literature against Sartre's charge of bourgeois irresponsibility, but also to use Sartre's own term of disapprobation to characterize a "writing" that, in Sartre's sense, is "engaged." Sartre's "engaged" literature is revolutionary literature; it assumes a universal or classless audience. But it reaches this audience through its content, not its form: "there is nothing to be said about form in advance, and we have said nothing," Sartre wrote in defense of his position.[20] For Barthes, however, there is everything to be said about form "in advance" (i.e., before we presume to fill it with a content); the forms of language are filled with meaning when we take them up, and it is by means of these "loaded" forms—the "writing," not its content—that a work selects its public.

From Barthes's point of view, Sartre's insistence upon a literature of commitment to social revolution is a form of linguistic innocence. Sartre's "engaged" writer, by rebelling against established literary conventions, is assumed to have restored language to a "clean" or neutral state, the only medium in which free expression is supposed to be possible to the writer and available to all readers. To Barthes, however, this freedom is an illusion; the very stylelessness of "committed" language becomes another closed "mode of writing," another style—in this case, "the sufficient sign of [a] commitment," functioning "as an economy signal whereby the scriptor [or writer] constantly

imposes his conversion without ever revealing how it came about"—
if indeed it ever did (W, p. 26-27). "Commitment," then, is only a
myth; it is only the convention of commitment.

But, granted that every revolt against literary convention eventually becomes a convention, a "mode of writing," is it not possible to
believe that at least the first writer who rebelled against the established convention wrote freely? Barthes's answer is that this writer's
freedom is literally only momentary, a freedom of "the gesture of
choice," but not a freedom "within duration" (W, pp. 16-17). If, as
Barthes maintains, the forms of language retain "the recollection of
[their] previous usage," and become thereby meaning-filled signifiers of a second-order system, then to write freely, the "modern"
writer must destroy language's "memory," try to make language
"innocent" again. But since "language is never innocent" (W, p. 16),
this writer too becomes a prisoner of his own words, those he has just
written in a previous paragraph. As Barthes puts it, "a stubborn
after-image, which comes from all the previous modes of writing and
even from the past of my own, drowns the sound of my present
words. . . . mere duration gradually reveals in suspension a whole
past of increasing density, like a cryptogram" (W, p. 17). It is "duration," "the ineffable binding force running through existence," that
"reconquers the writer . . . for it is impossible to develop a negative
within time, without elaborating a positive art, an order which must
be destroyed anew" (W, pp. 38-39). From Barthes's point of view, no
writing can ever be truly revolutionary.

We have mentioned the fact that no single mode of "modern
writing" has achieved the triumphant status of "classical writing" in
its time, but that "modern writing" must exist as a plurality of modes,
the sequence of which constitutes the history to which *Writing
Degree Zero* purports to be an introduction; Part II of the book
devotes an essay to each of three "typical stages" in this "modern"
movement. In the first of these stages, what Barthes calls the
"usage-value" of "classical writing"—i.e., its value as an instrument,
a conveyer of thought—was replaced by a "work-value." "Classical
writing," we have said, was a sort of window that gave access to a
"reality" outside itself, the "reality" sanctioned by bourgeois ideology; as long as bourgeois consciousness remained unified, "writing"
could justify itself solely in terms of *what it existed for:* "thought alone
bore the weight of being different," Barthes says (W, p. 62). But with
the fragmentation of bourgeois consciousness, the ideological guarantee of thought expired, and "classical writing" called attention to itself

as an anachronistic language. Aware now of a "disjunction" between the inherited convention of "writing" and their historical condition, writers felt an urgent need to justify themselves, and did so by placing a premium upon the form of their work. If the end for which "classical writing" existed was no longer valued, then writing itself must be made more valuable—be made to "cost more" in the expenditure of labor upon its own form. So grew up, Barthes says, the image of the writer as "a craftsman who shuts himself away in some legendary place, like a workman operating at home, and who . . . sets his form exactly as a jeweller extracts art from his material, devoting to his work regular hours of solitary effort" (W, p. 63). The evidence of this labor, as found in the work of writers like Théophile Gautier, Paul Valéry, André Gide, and especially Flaubert, becomes a new sign of literature, a new "writing."

But craftsmanlike "writing" was not, according to Barthes, a complete break with "classical writing"; it did not disturb the bourgeois order: it was essentially representational. In fact, the "Flaubertization of writing," as Barthes calls it, ultimately produced an important "sub-writing" that was just as strictly governed by rules, just as "mythical," as the "classical"—i.e., "realist writing," as that was adapted to the aims of Naturalism by Maupassant, Zola, and Alphonse Daudet. Historically considered, the words *realism* and *naturalism* imply the following criticism of earlier "writing": that now, for the first time, language would present not literature, but reality or nature. "Classical" language had rendered only a "verbal nature"; Flaubert's language made literary form a conspicuous commodity; but the "modern realists" would be "authors without a style," handlers of the naked objects of the world, and recorders of "incongruous snippets of popular speech, strong language or dialect words" (W, p. 68,67). What happened, though, is that these unobtrusive details became themselves "the most spectacular signs of fabrication," a mode of "writing" that is "the image *par excellence* of a Literature which has all the striking and intelligible signs of its identity" (W, p. 70): everyone, that is, recognizes realist writing as "Realism." In semiological terms, the language of the realists is "a form which is already filled with a meaning and which receives from the concept of Literature a new signification" (M, p. 134).

For Barthes, let us not forget, the aim of the "modern" writer has been the creation of forms that are not mythical (in his special sense of that word), forms that try to escape their own formal past, transcend history to exist purely as writing, without receiving the signification

"Literature." This is what Barthes means by the "zero-degree" of writing: language emptied of is historical associations and "values," and thus made innocent again. Barthes likens this notion of the "writer without Literature" (the writer *before the existence of Literature*) to the problem of Orpheus who could bring Eurydice back from death only by not looking at her. The "modern" writer too feels he can save literature only by renouncing it, yet "cannot resist glancing round a little: it is Literature brought to the gates of the Promised Land," Barthes says: "a world without Literature, but one to which writers would nevertheless have to bear witness" (*W*, p. 76). Just as Orpheus resurrected Eurydice only to kill her with his glance, so the "modern" writer can create literature only by destroying it, i.e., by making it cease to communicate—dislocating the language, disordering its syntax, and finally silencing it completely, "murdering" it (or arranging its self-destruction). For Barthes, the exemplar of such linguistic homicide was the poet Mallarmé (a critical hypothesis he acknowledges taking from Maurice Blanchot [*W*, p. 76]). In a poem like *Un Coup de dés*, Mallarmé causes language to work spatially rather than temporally, using typography and the positioning of words on the page in place of their normal syntactical relations. The word, suspended in the silent white space surrounding it, is thereby "liberated from its guilty social overtones"; "freed from responsibility in relation to all possible context . . . [it] declares its solitude, and therefore its innocence" (*W*, p. 75).

The "zero-degree of writing" (and here we shall use the French equivalent for distinction, since a zero-degree *écriture* aims *not to be a "writing"*) is a "neutral," "colourless writing"; in *Writing Degree Zero*, it is Albert Camus, in *The Outsider* (more frequently translated *The Stranger*), who is credited with "almost" having achieved it. Barthes took the idea of "zero-degree" from linguistics, where it is used to designate a third term that stands between the two terms of a polarity; "thus between the subjunctive and the imperative moods, the indicative is . . . an amodal form" (*W*, p. 76). This, of course, is only an analogy: we are to understand that there is a polarity of "writings" with a medial zero-degree *écriture* which parallels these grammatical moods. The point, as Barthes was later to clarify it in *Mythologies*, is that the imperative and subjunctive moods are mythically disposed forms: each is "the form of a particular signified, different from the meaning": the signified of the imperative is "my will," that of the subjunctive "my request" (*M*, pp. 131-32). The corresponding "writings" are similarly compromised: to adopt the "classical" "writing" is, we have seen, to assent to notions of "intemporal" reason and "universal nature," the props of bourgeois ideology; to write in it is to signify "literature" as a bourgeois institution. But a zero-degree *écriture*, like the indicative mood, would mean something without manifesting "the intention which led to its being used"; it would eradicate the sign of literature, resist myth. If "writing" is a public style that carries with it some sort of commitment, then its zero-degree will be a "style of absence which is almost an ideal absence of style," and therefore ideologically neutral. It will take its place, Barthes says, "in the midst of all those ejaculations and judgments, without becoming involved in any of them" (*W*, pp. 77). Thus, in *The Outsider*, Barthes says, Camus tried to reduce "writing" to a "sort of negative mood" which would abolish the mythical character of language in favor of "a neutral and inert state of form"; "thought," then, would be "wholly responsible," uncompromised by any "secondary commitment of form to a History not its own" (*W*, p. 77). But "neutral writing" (i.e. *écriture*) is subject to the fate of every other form: it can be neutral, or colorless, or transparent only at the outset; language produces its own "automatisms, constants, themes, in which there is no innocence, since they indicate the return of myth, that is, of literature."[21]

Does Barthes, then, see no way out of this dilemma? In 1953, the year *Writing Degree Zero* appeared, he apparently did not. The book ends, therefore, somewhat dispiritedly: "writing is a blind alley"; "a modern masterpiece is impossible," it concludes (*W*, pp. 86-87). The quest for the zero-degree of "writing" is the "philosopher's stone of present day writers," a futile quest, possible only "by a kind of ideal anticipation of some new Adamic world where language would no longer be alienated." In such a view, "literature becomes the Utopia of language" (*W*, p. 88).

But in 1954 and 1955 Barthes published two articles—"Objective Literature" and "Literal Literature"—that sound a more enthusiastic note. These publications signaled the appearance of Alain Robbe-Grillet's first two novels, *The Erasers* (1953) and *The Voyeur* (1955), and announced a new approach to the problematic of *écriture*. The problem, as we have seen, is that language, being a human product, humanizes everything it touches; it pretends to find an objective meaning in whatever it records, which is, however, the meaning history has encoded in it. From Barthes's point of view, the healthful austerity of Robbe-Grillet's work is that it does not attempt to disguise or escape this fact, but accepts it as a primary condition, using language not to speak for something beyond itself, but to illuminate its own workings. The result, Barthes admitted, cannot be separated from "what is today [1955] the constitutively reactionary status of literature"; it is, however, "preparing, without yet achieving, a de-conditioning of the reader in relation to the essentialist art of the bourgeois novel" (*CE*, p. 58).

CHAPTER 3

Ancients and Moderns

B Y THE END of 1965 Barthes had become involved in a literary quarrel which attached to his name a notoriety in excess of any celebrity generated by the six books he had to that date published. Commentators have likened this quarrel to the seventeenth-century confrontation of traditional and modern views known in literary history as the Quarrel between the Ancients and Moderns, the word *Ancient* designating now a half-century-old prescription for critical objectivity and methodological rigor which had achieved a privileged status in the French university establishment, and *Modern,* the adoption of any contemporary ideological viewpoint from which a literary work may be systematically read for a deliberately ideological interpretation. Barthes, of course, has been the spokesman for the latter position, generally referred to as the *nouvelle critique,* though, as he has explained, its presence is no newer than the end of World War II, and reflects little other reason for distinction than the complete absorption of its constituents in "a certain ideological present" and their reluctance "to acknowledge any participation" in the older critical tradition.

In an essay published in 1963 ("What Is Criticism?") Barthes gives us a convenient, but simplified directory to the movement, reducing the major ideological "languages" of modern French criticism to four "philosophies," and supplying the name of a representative critic in each: Existentialism (Sartre); Marxism (not at its "avowed center," but at its "frontier," as in the work of Lucien Goldmann); psychoanalysis (here on the Bachelardian "margins" of Freud); and Structuralism, an exponent of which Barthes does not name because in 1963 its critical products were yet, he says, "in preparation." Since Barthes is conversant in all these critical languages—"in a certain sense I subscribe to each of them at the same time" (*CE,* p. 257)—it is understandable that he should have emerged as the chief polemicist and champion of the *nouvelle critique,* as well as the most visible target of its opponents.

Barthes's principal opponent in this brief but widely publicized quarrel was Raymond Picard, a professor at the Sorbonne and a respected Racine scholar. Barthes had first of all come to Picard's attention with his own very unorthodox book *On Racine* (1963), which included, as a sort of apology for itself, Barthes's earliest statement of his views on academic criticism, an essay called "History or Literature," first published in *Annales,* one of the most influential journals in historical studies today. Picard's initial shot, "M. Barthes et la 'Critique Universitaire'"—published in *Le Monde* in March 1964—was aimed not at this essay, however. It addressed itself to two others, collected in Barthes's *Critical Essays* (1964), but originally published outside of France, "The Two Criticisms," published (in French) in 1964 in the American scholarly journal *Modern Language Notes,* and "What Is Criticism?" which appeared the year before in a special "modern criticism issue" of the (London) *Times Literary Supplement* (there, under the title "Criticism as Language"). Since this issue also included an essay by Picard, it was as an embarrassed French academician, indicting Barthes for irresponsibly defaming French "university criticism" before a foreign audience, that Picard entered the fray. Picard's more widely known *Nouvelle Critique ou Nouvelle Imposture?* [*New Criticism or New Fraud?*], taking Barthes's *On Racine* as the point of departure for a more extensive attack on the *nouvelle critique,* appeared the following year. Ironically, this inflammatory book only gave a wider fame to the name of its adversary, and prompted Barthes in 1966 to present a more systematic statement of his critical position, a book called *Critique et Vérité.*

The ambiguously coordinated words, *criticism* and *truth,* in Barthes's title set in high relief the basic question on which the academic and new critic disagree: What is the relation of criticism to truth? To the academic critic, as Barthes understands his position, the truth of a literary work consists in its relation to something other than itself, an "elsewhere": its "source" (an earlier work) or the circumstances in which it was written (the historical "background" or biographical "context"); accordingly, Barthes maintains, academic criticism is true to the extent that it *objectively* establishes this relation, points out the analogies between the work and its model. For Barthes and the new critics, however, "criticism is more than discourse in the name of 'true' principles"; its proof is not of "an 'alethic' order"—it does not, that is, come from anything *other* than itself (*CE,* pp. 257,259).

Picard, on the other hand, takes almost the opposite view of the way these two criticisms regard the truth of criticism. Academic criticism is not, he insists, a stereotyped "Lansonism," i.e., a "biographical criticism which . . . finds resemblances between life and literature"[1]; on the contrary, he argues, the charge that the new critics have made against academic criticism should be levelled at the new criticism itself: for in saying that a literary work is only "a collection of signs," are they not saying that its meaning is elsewhere?—

in a psychoanalytic *elsewhere* (placed, for example, in the writer's childhood), or in the pseudo-Marxist *elsewhere* of an economic-political structure, or in the *elsewhere* of whatever metaphysical universe the author's may be, etc. And of course this *elsewhere* is to be found at the very center of the work, since it is its reason for being. Thus, penetrated, peopled, obsessed by worlds that it seems to be unaware of, and on the other hand prolonged, explicated, justified beyond itself, the work is no longer in the work. External to itself, it consists in relations which go beyond it. Existing as a multiplicity of signs the sense of which must be sought in a truth which is not of a literary order, it is secondary in relation to the psychological, sociological, or philosophical reality that conditions and clarifies it.[2]

What Picard implicitly objects to here is the subjectivity of interpretive criticism (its pursuit of its own obsessions); but for Barthes, this alleged "elsewhere" of *a* meaning is an "immanence" of meaning*s*: "how could we believe," he asks, "that the work is an object exterior to the psyche and history of the man who interrogates it" (*CE*, p. 257)? Criticism, for Barthes, is "the dialogue of two histories and two subjectivities, the author's and the critic's. But this dialogue is egoistically shifted toward the present"; it "is not an 'homage' to the truth of the past or to the truth of 'others'—it is a construction of the intelligibility of our own time" (*CE*, p. 260).

Thus far, the quarrel between Picard and Barthes sounds like a quarrel between a historian and an "anti-historian," i.e., between a view which attaches importance to the historical circumstances in which a work is produced and one which attaches importance to the circumstances in which it is read. But as *Writing Degree Zero* amply demonstrates, Barthes's views are anything but anti-historical. Indeed, the trouble with academic criticism, as he finds it, is that it is untrue to its avowedly historical program—it is not historical enough. Why did Racine write? Barthes considers this a proper question for the academic critic, a historical question equivalent to asking "what literature could be for a man of his [Racine's] period" (*CE*, p. 251). But in limiting himself to the "facts" of a work, the academic critic ignores this *general* question, the answer to which would enable him to explain his "facts." In failing to question "the Being of literature," then, the academic critic rejects history, for not to ask this question is also to answer it: i.e., by tacitly accrediting "the notion that this Being is eternal or 'natural'—in short, that literature is *a matter of course*" (*CE*, p. 250).

But history, according to Barthes, teaches just the reverse: that the word *literature*, which is of quite recent origin, designates "a process of very different forms, functions, institutions, reasons, and projects" (*CE*, p. 251). Seen in this light, academic criticism, transforming the historical into the natural or eternal, repeats the function of myth. For all its vaunted objectivity and scientific rigor, university criticism is only another ideology—specifically, positivism—implying certain general convictions about man, history, and literature. How else can we regard its insistence upon a "timeless essence" of literature which guarantees the validity of present-day interpretations of older works, and its insistence upon the mimetic character of all writing? Barthes's point is not that university criticism is to be blamed for its ideological commitments (though he does make the passing remark that positivist psychology is outdated), but for the fact that it conceals these prejudices, "masks them under the moral alibi of rigor and objectivity" (*CE*, p. 257).

No such alibi functions in the *nouvelle critique* which might, Barthes, says, call itself "*ideological*, in opposition to the first kind [university criticism] which rejects every ideology and claims to derive only from an objective method" (*CE*, p. 249). Such candor is indeed admirable. But what is the justification of this translation of a literary work into another language of the critic's choice—psychoanalysis or Structuralism, for example? Barthes dismisses this question since, for him, such translation (or interpretation) is itself the justification of criticism. "There is nothing astonishing in a nation's taking up the works of its past and describing them anew in order to know *what can be done with them*: this," he wrote in the opening of *Critique et Vérité*, "ought to be the regular procedure of evaluation" (*CV*, p. 9). True, the object of criticism is "the discourse of someone else." But for this very reason, criticism is a "discourse upon a discourse"—hence "a second language or *metalanguage* . . . which operates on a first language (or language object)" (*CE*, p. 258);

and since, for Barthes, no language is innocent or ideologically neutral, the critic's choice of one, like the writer's choice of a mode of "writing," is a responsibility. It is morally wrong, as well as impracticable, he would argue, to subject Robbe-Grillet's *In the Labyrinth*—which deliberately violates the conventions of mimetic literature—to the methods of academic criticism, the assumptions of which (he would further assert) have upheld the ethical and political status quo that makes mimesis still possible. For criticism is concerned not only with the relation between an author's language and the world he records in it, but also with the relation between that language and the language of the critic who studies it. It is precisely "the 'friction' of these two languages [the author's and the critic's] which defines criticism" (*CE*, p. 258).

We must return for a moment to the description of criticism as metalanguage, a term that is likely to be troublesome for the reader of Barthes (indeed, it has been a source of trouble for Barthes, too). Originally, this word designated the "artificial language" devised by logicians and linguists to speak about the logical relations that constitute sentences in a "real language" or "language object." Barthes therefore used the word in *Mythologies* to define the analogous function of myth, "a second language, *in which* one speaks about the first" (*M*, p. 115). Literature is also metalanguage, then, for it, too, is myth. The details of realistic literature, for example, do not constitute a primary or "natural" language that "speaks" reality, but a secondary language that speaks *about* reality. This was the reason, as we observed earlier, that Barthes was skeptical of the Existentialist faith in a "committed" literature to bring about social action. Only a "transitive" language that "spoke" its object could bring this about—and that, he believed as early as *Writing Degree Zero*—was a "utopian" notion. Even the most conscientious effort to make literature "unliterary," its content more assertive, more "natural" (the "styleless" or "blank writing" of Camus, for instance), becomes in time as elitist as any literature, a style of stylelessness.

Confusion arises, however, when we find Barthes using this now negatively charged term to define not only the literature of "bad faith," but also the critical and literary programs he obviously wishes to promote. In an essay entitled "Literature and Metalanguage," published in 1959, for example, he characterized "modern" literature as that which had begun "to regard itself as double: at once object and scrutiny of that object, utterance and utterance of that utterance, literature object and metaliterature" (*CE*, p. 97). The fact of the matter is that Barthes's description of criticism as metalanguage in "What Is Criticism?" (1963) constitutes a new understanding of the workings of metalanguage which would be explicitly defined the following year in his *Elements of Semiology*. Moreover, it became necessary, in view of this new understanding, for him to differentiate between the two secondary languages, criticism and literature, and to designate the latter by a new term, "connotation."

The clarifying agent here was the Danish linguist Louis Hjelmslev, whose *Prolegomena to a Theory of Language* (1943) was for Barthes an important development of the semiological implications of Saussure's ideas. In particular, Barthes adopted Hjelmslev's distinction between "connotative semiotics" and "metalanguage." Now, in each of these phenomena, there is a relation between two distinct signification systems; their difference depends solely on "the point of insertion of the first system into the second."[3] In "connotation" a complete sign system becomes the signifier of the second system, or as Barthes now expresses it, using Hjelmslev's more efficient formula, a first system consisting of the relation (R) between a "plane of expression" (E) and a "plane of content" (C) becomes the "plane of expression" of a second system. Thus:

System 2	E	R	C
System 1	ERC		

This is precisely the scheme that Barthes had earlier labelled "myth," and he observes in the *Elements* that literature is an instance of connotation (*ES*, p. 90). In metalanguage, however, a first system (ERC) becomes the *signified* or "plane of content" (C) of the second:

System 2	E	R	C
System 1			ERC

A metalanguage, Barthes says, is "a semiotics which treats of a semiotics" (*ES*, p. 90).

Interpretive or ideological criticism is metalinguistic, then, since it takes a primary language (a play of Racine's, let us say) as its signified and signifies or *expresses* it with a "form" of its own choice (a system of psychoanalytic principles, for instance). Its aim is to test the validity or coherence of the Racinian language. Academic criticism, on the

other hand, remains mythological in that it proceeds *as if* the Racinian play—the signifier, in this case—calls forth its own critical
commentary, which is therefore supposed to be objective, but, in
Barthes's view, is silently ideological and intentional. It appears "to
work" for the same reason that "classical" language appears to express
the world; both have forgotten that the worlds "to be expressed"—
real or literary—have already been encoded in the language used to
express them. Little wonder, then, that academic criticism is compla-
cent about the "truth" of the analogies it discovers between a literary
work and the world: no "friction" can exist between the critical
language and that of the literature it studies.

This "friction" or, as Barthes later put it, "distance" between the
literary and the critical languages, between, say, Michelet's historical
writing and Barthes's Bachelardian psychoanalysis of it (the feature of
the *nouvelle critique* which academic criticism finds least to its liking:
a license to the critic to say anything he pleases about the work), is
unremittingly argued for by Barthes. His purpose, however, is not
critical libertinism, as Picard suggests. Though the choice of a language is an "absolute freedom" of the critic's, once made, it becomes
his responsibility: "we do not choose a language because it seems
necessary to us"; rather, Barthes says, "we make necessary the
language we choose" (*CE*, p. 273). It is, in fact, only in the "resistance" of the work to the critical language that the work may be said to
be "discovered." What, Barthes asks, would be the value of subject-
ing Michelet to ideological criticism when Michelet's ideology is
perfectly clear to begin with? But a psychoanalysis of substance
"recuperates" or takes back from the work not only the historian's
"experience of things," but his ideology as well (*CE*, p. 273). On the
other hand, the distance a critical language must traverse to join its
object is not infinite, and the critic must recognize the point at which
the work's resistance to the language becomes too powerful. When
this occurs, he is obliged to change his critical language—not because
his first choice is now seen as a bad one, but because it has revealed "a
new problem," requiring another language for its solution. The "classical" or Freudian psychoanalytic "form" of *On Racine*, Barthes has
explained, came about in just this manner. He originally conceived of
the book as another psychoanalysis of substance, but found that
Racine's tragic image system offered too many resistances to such an
analysis. What these resistances revealed, however, was that the
Racinian image system was not the personal language of an individual, as was the case in Michelet's writing, but a dialect of a "general

code" or the "rhetorical language of a whole society." Barthes consequently "veered toward a psychoanalysis both more classical . . . and more structural" (*CE*, p. 274).

From Barthes's point of view criticism is ethical only when it realizes its freedom. We may perhaps gain more respect for such an ethic if we set beside it the ethic of "truth" by which academic criticism governs itself. When confronted by resistances in its object, the latter applies a "brake" to itself, believing that it thereby "guarantees a greater objectivity," as if "by remaining on the surface of the facts, one respects them more, the timidity or banality of the hypothesis being a pledge of its validity" (*R*, p. 166). It is as though, at some point in an analysis, the critic suffers a failure of confidence in his critical method: his interpretation seems farfetched ("Racine cannot have meant *that!*"), causing him to take a more plausible line—i.e., a less "subjective" line. Barthes's point (sarcasm aside) is that such prudence is itself a contamination of objectivity, for it has already taken a systematic view of things. Barthes has stated that we ascertain a signifier inductively, that is, only after "*first* positing the signified, *before* the signifier" (*R*, p. 164). In stopping short of some deeper level of signification, in locating its signifieds in the world outside the work, academic criticism has already taken "a stand on the world"—albeit one that is difficult to defend. For "things do not signify more or less, they signify or they do not signify. . . . And all significations being acknowledged to be presumptive, how can we help preferring those that resolutely locate themselves at the deepest level of the person . . . or of the world . . . where one has some chance of achieving a genuine unity" (*R*, p. 166)?

Thus, the critic, according to Barthes, avoids "bad faith" in the same way as the author—by confronting the problematics of language. For if literature wishes only to signify the world, it succeeds in signifying only itself, and for that reason becomes a second language that can only connote or double reality. This problem exists, as we have seen, because language, the "substance" of literature, is already a signifying system when literature takes it up. What we consume when we read are the words and sentences of a primary system; but the "reality" of what we read is literature, not the world. How, then, can the task of criticism be the designation of some meaning or signified of the world? How can its "moral goal" be anything but the reconstruction of a system of signification?

From this conclusion Barthes derives both a critical standard of literary value and the justification of critical freedom. When an author understands that literature is nothing more than a parasitic language, able only to connote or double reality, he ceases to look for meaning in the world, but writes "as if the world signified though without saying *what*," using language "to constitute a world which is emphatically signifying but never finally signified" (*CE*, pp. 267, 268). Not until literature becomes such an "unfulfilled technique of meaning"—i.e., a technique for multiplying significations "without filling or closing them"—do "second meanings" appear and call for interpretation. In its struggle to advance and, at the same time, withhold meaning (for Barthes, this is the Orphean task of leading reality out of the unnamed, toward the light of meaning, while abstaining from looking at it, i.e., naming it), in its ability to leave meaning "open," unfulfilled, literature poses an indirect question that "jeopardizes" meaning in the world, challenges criticism to provide answers to it, and to endow (with its own substance the meaning it proposes. It is in the variety of those answers, the work's "accessibility" to various critical languages, that we find the measure of the work. Thus Racine is for Barthes "the greatest French author" not because he has transformed the world (literature, being a "second language," cannot do that), but because of his accessibility to the intelligence of any historical subject who reads him—the very reason for which Picard feels obliged to defend him against Barthes.

The curious fact about the quarrel between Barthes and Picard is that neither contestant ever actually engages the other. For Picard, the logocentrist, it is waged at the level of the word of the *nouvelle critique;* it is a police action against critical interference in literary self-determination. "No, you cannot say just anything," he insists; "Racine's words have a literal meaning which was obligatory for the spectators and readers of the seventeenth century, and which cannot be ignored without a game of chance being made of the language."[4] The assumption here is that Racine's play is an object, a monument to reality, to which it is related *naturally*. The critic, then, is a sort of scientist: "There is a Racinian truth, concerning which everyone can manage to agree. Relying especially on the certainties of language . . . the modest and patient scholar manages to spot pieces of evidence which in some measure determine zones of objectivity . . ."[5] But Barthes is arguing at another place altogether. Concerning his critical language, once its subjective historicity is admitted, there is nothing to say; it is beyond defense. Barthes argues at the ontological level of literature, the level of Picard's tacit assumptions. The mode of being of a literary work, its relation to reality, is *institutional*, not

natural. A play by Racine is not simply an object made of language,
that speaks according to the lexicon of seventeenth-century French;
it *is* a langue itself, the lexicon of which is the historical subject that
deciphers it. Of course, Racine's seventeenth-century French speaks
to us, but that is not "the reality of the work"; the reality is the second
language which *is* the work—and this language is silent until criticism
speaks it.

Institutionalized, literature is a process—much like respiration, as
Barthes describes it: as we give it life, "it permits us to breathe" (*CE*,
p. 267); "silence of the work even as it speaks, and speech of the man
who listens—that is the infinite respiration of literature in the world
and in history" (*R*, p. ix). "*To tell the truth*" about literature, therefore, is to acknowledge its paradoxical status: an "ensemble of objects
and rules, techniques and works, whose function in the general
economy of our society is precisely to *institutionalize* subjectivity"
(*R*, pp. 171-72).

Notwithstanding the rigor of Barthes's critical method—its need to
establish the coherence of the work as language before that language
can be "spoken"—it should be apparent that criticism, as Barthes
both writes it and of it, is not a science. For criticism always moves
toward a single meaning, and meaning presumes the existence of a
subject. It does not, in other words, articulate a meaning that was *in*
the work before the critic came along; a subject "produces" that
meaning, as it were, "for the first time." Criticism, for Barthes, is
radically subjective: it suspends the subject in order to make him
reappear. And yet, Barthes maintains in *Critique et Vérité*, "a *certain*
science of literature is possible," the goal of which would be not a
more objective way of producing the meaning of any work, but the
establishment of a logic of signs that would authorize all meaning in
written discourse. It would be a science "not of content" or meaning,
but of "the conditions of content"; its object would be not the "full" or
actualized meaning of a work, but the "empty" form that supports
that fullness, its potentiality (*CV*, p. 57). Now, since the potentiality
of any language for actualizing different possible sentences is far
greater (infinite, in fact) than that of a literary work to "accept"
possible meanings, the science of linguistics would logically suggest
itself as the model for Barthes's science of literature. "Confronted
with the impossibility of mastering all the sentences possible in a
language," Barthes says, "the linguist agrees to establish a *hypotheti-
cal model of description* by which he can explain how an infinite
number of sentences in the language are engendered"; and since

literary works are like "immense 'sentences' derived from the general language of symbols," there is "no reason not to try to apply such a method" to them (*CV*, p. 57).

It is interesting that although Barthes characterized the relation between literary science and "criticism" by an analogy to the relation between Ferdinand de Saussure's concepts of *langue* and *parole*, he did not find the model for his science in *langue*. Saussure used the first of these terms to designate the abstract system of forms deposited in the mind of every language user in a particular linguistic community; *parole*, on the other hand, designates the selection and combination of the elements of this system in their concrete manifestation as sound and meaning.[6] But as Noam Chomsky remarked, Saussure's *langue* was largely a system of forms, or "word-like elements" and phrases; it did not contain the rules needed to explain the formation of sentences, which was consequently regarded as a matter of "free and voluntary creation rather than systematic rule"—i.e., as a matter of *parole*.[7] Since Barthes wished to establish a finite set of "transformational rules" which would explain the derivation of "immense sentences," or literary works, from the "general language of symbols," Saussure's concept of *langue* is clearly inadequate; what Barthes wanted, as Jonathan Culler has said of Saussure, was "a notion of rule-governed creativity: individual creativity made possible by a system of rules."[8] According to Culler, Barthes found this notion in Noam Chomsky's concept of "competence," the system of rules, established by analyzing language into its elements and their rules of combination, which is present in everyone who has learned a language and which enables him to make and understand sentences.[9] *Literary* competence, then, would be the mastery of the forms of literary validity, the forms by which all written discourse signifies for its readers. Accordingly, Barthes's literary science would have for its object "not why a particular meaning ought to be accepted . . . but why it is *acceptable* [i.e., why it is *able to be* accepted] according to the workings of the linguistic laws of the symbol" (*CV*, p. 58).

CHAPTER 4

A Science of Literature

I The Structuralist Activity

THOUGH definitions of French Structuralism are often difficult to reconcile with one another, there seems to be at least popular agreement about attaching the term *Structuralist* to four particular Frenchmen: the anthropologist Claude Lévi-Strauss (everyone's "first choice"), the philosopher Michel Foucault (who angrily rejects the label), the psychologist Jacques Lacan (who is no more pleased with the identification than Foucault), and Roland Barthes (who accepts the term at least as a historical label for the work produced in the late 1950's and 60s). In "What Is Criticism?" (1963) Barthes admitted "subscribing" to Structuralist "ideological principles," and, as we shall see, his essay "The Structuralist Activity" takes a distinctively "inside" view of its object, defining it in terms not of the Structuralist's ideas, but of his imagination.

But Barthes very quickly makes our labels for him obsolete: "Who is still a structuralist?" he asked rhetorically in 1975 (*RB*, p. 117); and if it is not simply the momentum of his thought that allows him to keep ahead of his explainers, it is a complex reaction to being labeled or "fashioned" that provokes his intellectual energy: "By fashion," he writes, "I return in my text as farce, as caricature. A kind of collective 'id' replaces the image I thought I had of myself, and that 'id' is me" (*RB*, p. 146). Moreover, we should not forget that, even in 1963, Barthes's subscription to Structuralist principles was not an act of exclusion; "in a certain sense," he had said, "I subscribe to each of them [Existentialism, Marxism, psychoanalysis, and Structuralism] at the same time" (*CE*, pp. 254-57).

We shall certainly not go wrong to begin by stating that Structuralism is a concern with structures, and by structures here we mean the systems of relations human beings construct, consciously or unconsciously, in order to endow things with meaning. Speaking of the structures of phonemes in language, the anthropologist Claude

Lévi-Strauss observed that "meaning is always the result of a combination of elements which are not themselves significant . . . meaning is never the primary phenomenon . . . behind all meaning there is a non-meaning."[1] It is this substratum of "non-meaning" that is called "structure." Structuralism, then, can be regarded as the effort "to know how meaning is possible, at what cost and by what means" (*CE*, p. 218). Thus, in 1961, Barthes explained that, ever since his writing of "Myth Today" in 1956, he had been preoccupied with "a series of structural analyses, all of which aim at defining a certain number of extra-linguistic 'languages,'" i.e., with a number of "cultural objects" not significant in themselves—food, clothing, film, fashion, literature—but "which society has endowed with a signifying power"—turned, that is, into "extra-linguistic 'languages'" (*CE*, pp. 151-52). If cultural objects "speak" to us, then, they must be signs, and insofar as they are significant, they must derive their meaning not from themselves, but from structures or systems. Barthes's analyses attempted to reconstitute these structures.

Why did Barthes locate his Structuralist beginnings no earlier than the writing of "Myth Today"? It would seem that a case could be made for his always having been, in these terms, a Structuralist (albeit an eclectic one). Was not his quarrel with Raymond Picard both an attack upon the academic assumption that literary meaning is *in the work*— "primary," in Lévi-Strauss's sense—and a defense of the Structuralist view that meaning is the by-product of a critical act of "combination," such as he had made in his earlier studies of Michelet and Racine? The same issue underlies the distinction in *Writing Degree Zero* between "classical" art and "modern" art, just as his attacks there upon realism and bourgeois "myth" rest upon a rejection of *a priori*, essentialist, "primary" meaning.

Nevertheless, Barthes's use of the term *structuralist* is stricter than that we have just suggested. The Structuralist, he tells us, is identified by his language—especially by his "serious recourse to the nomenclature of signification" (*CE*, p. 214). His point, of course, is not that Structuralism is simply the use of a technical vocabulary (as its detractors often suggest); he is the first to admit that critics may use terms like *form, sign,* and *signification* in order to "camouflage" a completely traditional sort of criticism. Barthes is speaking of the distinctive use of certain specific "pairings" of terms first given prominence in the linguistics of Ferdinand de Saussure; "watch," he writes, "who uses *signifier* and *signified, synchrony* and *diachrony,* and you will know whether the structuralist vision is constituted"

(*CE*, p. 214). His point is that Structuralism is the offspring of Saussurean linguistics ("the true science of structure") and has inherited
from it that particular technique of analysis that such "pairs" of terms
articulate. As we are reminded by the first of the pairs cited by
Barthes, Saussure may also be considered the father of semiology,
and since Barthes links his own reading of Saussure with his "first
attempt" at semiological analysis, the *Mythologies* essays, since his
own use of the Saussurean pairs first becomes evident in its concluding essay, "Myth Today," we should properly date his Structuralist
phase from that point.

Barthes, of course, did not mean to limit the Saussurean influence
on Structuralism to the two pairs of terms cited above. Indeed, if we
are to appreciate the full extent of this influence, we must begin with
the more fundamental distinction mentioned in the previous chapter,
that between *parole*, the execution of language, and *langue*, the
system of a language. Pre-Saussurean linguistics was primarily a
study of the former, the tracing of the evolution of linguistic forms in
use. To understand why we speak or write English as we do today, it
assumed the necessity of knowing how it was spoken or written at an
earlier time. It was, in other words, a strictly historical or *diachronic*
study. Saussure, however, proposed a new focus of language study:
the system of forms and rules that makes the performance of language
possible. To understand the performance of a game of chess, he
argued, one can begin to deduce the rules which govern various
moves at any point in the progress of the game; one need not start
with the opening. In just this way, language is complete at any point
in its history; there may be, in other words, a *synchronic* study of the
static state of language.

For Structuralism, what is important here is the dialectical relationship beteen *langue* and *parole*, the fact that, in Barthes's words,
"there is no *langue* without *parole*, and no *parole* outside *langue*"
(*ES*, p. 15). *Langue* is what makes various acts of "speech" (*parole*)
possible; but *langue* is also the social product of *parole*, for its laws
may be abstracted at any moment (synchronically) from the evidence
of individual utterances. Thus, although my speech proves that I
know the system of a language, I am not conscious of that knowledge
when I speak the language: the *langue* is both in the mind and
"outside the will" of the subject or language user. But it also
follows—even though, according to Saussure, *langue* and not *parole*
is the field of linguistic study—that the structural linguist cannot, like

his linguist predecessors, ignore the subject in his field of study. "Saussure puts the subject right at the center of his analytic project," says Jonathan Culler; "in all cases where we are dealing with what Saussure calls . . . the social significance of objects and actions, the subject takes on a crucial role, in that the facts one is seeking to explain come from his intuitions and judgments."[2]

But what are the "intuitions and judgments" of the subject, and how does the linguist go about explaining the "facts" that come from them? To answer these questions, we must first understand that for Saussure language is only a system of differences "without positive terms"; it has "neither ideas nor sounds that existed before the linguistic system, but only conceptual and phonic differences that have issued from the system."[3] Neither element of a sign, then (i.e., neither the "sound-image" or *signifier* nor the "concept" or *signified*), preexists the other or has any meaning outside its relation in a system of differences. The combination of sounds we hear in the French word *poisson* is not a sign until it is opposed to a combination of similar but not identical sounds—those in *poison*, for example, where the voiceless phoneme /s/ is replaced by the voiced phoneme /z/. It is only this relational difference among similarities that creates the possibility of a signification. It is as though the subject, in thinking "*poisson*, not *poison*," cuts out or *articulates* a space which then becomes the signified or meaning "fish," not "poison," much as a missing piece of a jigsaw puzzle is defined by its relations to similar but different "in-place" pieces. Of course, the subject does not consciously perform this calculation: it is less a case of his speaking through language than of the language speaking through him. Our explanation means to suggest the subject's *implicit* knowledge of the system; it is the linguist's job to make it explicit. Nevertheless, the subject is the linguist's only source for the system. "Once the subject is firmly established at the center of the analytical domain," says Culler, the task of linguistics is one of "deconstructing the subject, of explaining meanings in terms of systems of convention which escape the subject's conscious grasp."[4]

Whether he is conscious of it or not, then, man is the signifying animal; what distinguishes him, Saussure wrote, "is not oral speech but the faculty of constructing a language."[5] To exercise, consciously, this faculty—as subject or analyst of language, creative artist or critic—is, properly speaking, to be a Structuralist. "*Homo significans:* such," writes Barthes, "would be the new man of structural inquiry" (*CE*, p. 218). But there is a danger here that the early Structuralists ran afoul of—that of thinking that the result of structural inquiry is a usable product, a "language" that can be returned to. Such a view would contradict the fundamental principle that *langue* has no concrete existence except in the performance of individual *paroles*. As Rosalind Coward and John Ellis observe, Saussure's initial distinction reveals language as "a system whose only reality is its realisations. This is the preliminary definition of a structure."[6] Significance or meaning is not a *product* of the fusion of signifier and signified; signification *is* that fusion, the carving-out or articulation of meaning. Structuralism, then, deals with meaning as function, not product, and Barthes, accordingly, prefers to think of structural analysis as an "activity" rather than a "work." True, this activity results in something Barthes calls an "object," but it is an object only insofar as it has been made: "the present being [of such objects, he says] *is* their past act: they are *having-been-mades*" (*CE*, p. 219). Structure is an object only in the sense that *langue* is an "object."

It will be helpful, as we follow Barthes's remarks here to have in mind an example of this "activity," and for this there is nothing better than his superb essay on the Eiffel Tower, itself both a non-technical account of how we "make Structuralism" in everyday experience, and a demystification of the Tower as a mythic image. Written as a preface to a collection of photographs in 1964 (the year *Elements of Semiology* was published), *The Eiffel Tower* has recently been republished in America in a second collection of "mythologies" essays omitted from the American edition of *Mythologies*. The Eiffel Tower exerts a double function for Barthes: it is both the point seen everywhere in Paris and the point from which all Paris may be seen (having, then, he says "both sexes of sight": *being seen* and *seeing*), a verb of both passive and active voice—or, considered another way, both an adventure of sight (when we look either at it or from it) and an adventure of intelligence (when we enter and explore its interior): it is, in other words, both myth and structure.

As a mythical image, the Tower—owing to its perfect uselessness, its absolute emptiness as a signifier—is a signification of all "the human meaning which it has assumed throughout the world," but especially of an "essence of Paris," a city converted to "a new nature": the Tower as "an immediate consumption of a humanity made natural by that glance [that function of seeing that is itself unseen] which transforms it into space."[7] But the view from the Tower also corresponds to "a new sensibility of vision"; at the top, one is able to transcend mere sensation, to see, *intellectually,* "things *in their structure,*" "a corpus of intelligent forms," "a concrete abstraction" (*ET,* p. 8). At the top of the Tower our minds become active; we are given the city "to *read,*" an object "exposed to the intelligence." With the city before us, we spontaneously separate and link certain known points, creating as we do a "functional space"; the city becomes for us a *panorama,* which Barthes defines as "an image we attempt to decipher":

> . . . here you make out the hill sloping down from Chaillot, there the Bois de Boulogne; but where is the Arc de Triomphe? You don't see it, and this absence compels you to inspect the panorama once again, to look for this point which is missing in your structure; your knowledge . . . struggles with your perception, and in a sense, that is what intelligence is: to *reconstitute,* to make memory and sensation cooperate so as to produce in your mind a simulacrum of Paris, of which the elements are in front of you . . . but nonetheless disoriented by the total space in which they are given to you, for this space was unknown to you. (*ET,* p. 10).

"Structuralism," Barthes writes in "The Structuralist Activity," "takes the real, decomposes it, then recomposes it" in order to make the functions of the real intelligible (*CE,* p. 215). The "object" resulting from these procedures is an image or "simulacrum" of the real object. Structuralism, then, is "essentially an activity of imitation"; but what is important in this imitation (as always with Barthes) is the technique, not the model or its copy. Its importance, Barthes says, consists in what happens "between" the two objects or "tenses" (the diachronic real and its synchronic image) of the activity, and what happens is an occurrence of "the generally intelligible: the simulacrum is intellect added to object . . . man himself . . ." (*CE,* p. 215). Indeed, Structuralist "imitation" does not seek to reproduce a model at all, but to *remake* one "in such a way as to manifest thereby the rules of [its] functioning," its intelligibility. Its mimesis is not constituted by an analogy of "substances" (as in traditional analysis, where the content of an interpretation is assumed to be analogous, if not equal, to the content of the work), but by an analogy of functions, in which the analysis establishes a relation between elements in the work, a fact which Barthes demonstrates in "The Eiffel Tower" by going on to articulate a historical structure in which "duration itself becomes panoramic" (*ET,* p. 11). Lévi-Strauss's analysis of the Oedipus myth, for a similar reason, does not give us "the meaning" of the narrative materials; it gives us a *location* in which meaning may be generated, the intersection of two pairs of functionally opposed elements. "We recompose the object," Barthes writes, "in order to make certain functions appear, and it is, so to speak, the way that makes the work" (*CE*, p. 216).

The "way" of Structuralism (and we should emphasize that this way is the same for both analysis and creation, i.e., for imitating an object already assembled and one that is "dispersed") consists of two operations: "dissection" and "articulation." It may help at this point to introduce another pair of Saussurean linguistic concepts. Saussure pointed out that the "value" of a sign is determined by two sorts of relations: those which it manifests with certain other signs in actual, present sequences or *syntagms,* and those which it bears to a virtual group or *paradigm* of similar, but not identical signs from which it was chosen for inclusion in a syntagm. In Terence Hawkes's serviceable example—"the boy kicked the girl"—meaning "unfolds" as each succeeding word is related to its predecessor, completing itself only when the last word joins these relationships. But this meaning also derives from the relation of each word to a group of associated words from which it was chosen (synonyms, antonyms, words of the same grammatical function or of similar sound), words which help to define the meaning of the chosen word by *not* having been chosen themselves. As Hawkes explains, "part of the meaning of 'kicked' derives from the fact that it turns out *not* to be 'kissed' or 'killed' as the full relationships of the words in the sentence are unrolled."[8]

Barthes's word *dissection* designates, first, a tentative isolating of certain fragments of the object operated upon, and, second, the ascertaining of their possible significance in a differential relation to other fragments in a paradigm: "dissection" is the means of deriving the significant units in the object. As Barthes explains: "the fragment has no meaning in itself, but it is nonetheless such that the slightest variation wrought in its configuration produces a change in the whole" (*CE*, p. 216). "Articulation," on the other hand, is the effort to determine the rules or forms which govern the combination of dissected fragments in a syntagm—not in order to resurrect the object as it was before dissection, but "to manifest thereby the rules of functioning (the 'functions') of this object" (*CE*, p. 214): "articulation" aims to establish a syntax of the object. Barthes conceives of this operation as "a kind of battle against chance," a seizing upon the recurrence of the units and their associations as "constraints" to which the units submit—evidence, then, of their not having been accidentally associated.

It is important that we do not think of these two operations as completely separate from one another. There is a tendency to regard dissection, the consciousness of a system, as a technique of analysis, and articulation, the "consciousness of the relations which unite signs on the level of discourse" (*CE*, p. 208), as a creative technique. To be sure, the real object given to the analyst (a work of art, say) is already composed; his first job, then, is one of dissection. The artist, on the other hand, begins with an "object" that is "dispersed"; for him, initially, there must be at least the tentative sense of a "composition." Nevertheless, the dispersed units of an object become signs only when they are placed in paradigms; and, of course, signification does not occur only *in* the paradigm—we signify again when we combine signs in discourse. Barthes's essay on Michel Butor's *Mobile*— "Literature and Discontinuity" (1962)—illustrates this point more fully than do any of the suggestive allusions in "The Structuralist Activity." Barthes is speaking of the special sense of the term "construction" which applies to Butor's "novels":

. . . it implies that the work reproduces an interior model assembled by the meticulous arrangement of parts: this model is, specifically, a *maquette* [i.e., a rough sketch]: the author works from a *maquette*, and we immediately see the structural signification of this art: the *maquette* is not, strictly speaking, a ready-made structure which the work must transform into an event; rather it is a structure to be realized starting from pieces of events, pieces which the author tries to bring together, to separate, to arrange, without altering their material figuration; this is why the *maquette* participates in that art of assemblage which Lévi-Strauss has just given its structural dignity. . . . the writer (the poet, novelist, chronicler [and critic, we shall add]) *sees* the meaning of the inert units in front of him only by *relating* them. . . . (*CE*, pp. 182–83)

There is still some ambiguity here. But one point is clear: Structuralism is a game played by rules that cannot be broken; but it is the player who makes up the rules as he plays the game.

In view of Barthes's reputation as a literary Structuralist and of his genuine enthusiasm about the value of structural linguistics as a methodological model for the analysis of literary works, it comes as a surprise to discover that he has given us no purely structural analysis of a literary work himself. (The closest thing to such an analysis is his essay called "The Structure of the *Fait-Divers*" (1962), which analyzes the "structure" of the unclassifiable items used as "filler" in newspapers.) The essay on Butor, to which we have just referred, is above all an apology for original literary creation—the sort of thing Barthes had earlier done for Robbe-Grillet's works—a definition of Butor's technique as an instance of Structuralist activity, but not itself an instance of that activity, i.e., the making of a simulacrum of *Mobile*. The same sort of exception must be made even of a work like "An Introduction to the Structural Analysis of Narrative," which has become one of the canonical texts of the Structuralist enterprise. "An Introduction . . ." is a practical textbook for Structuralists, spelling out in greater detail than "The Structuralist Activity" the use of linguistics as a model in analyzing narrative, but standing in the same relation to a structural analysis of narrative as *The Elements of Semiology* stands in relation to the analysis of fashion writing in *Système de la mode*.

On the other hand, such clearly analytical works as Barthes's study of Edgar Allan Poe's "The Facts in the Case of M. Valdemar" and the exhaustive examination of Balzac's "Sarrasine" called *S/Z* are carefully differentiated as "textual" rather than "structural" analyses. In another textual analysis of the biblical story of "Jacob's struggle with the angel," Barthes remarks that although he plans to show how the story lends itself to an "extremely classic and almost canonical structural analysis," he would in fact be presenting an analysis with which he is "more at home, textual analysis."[9] As far as literature is concerned, then, it appears that Barthes has never been a "practicing" literary Structuralist, that is, a practitioner of what Robert Scholes has called "low Structuralism," the purpose of which is "to be immediately useful," but "to be ultimately superseded."[10]

And yet, this view of Barthes's work makes a distinction between structural and semiological analysis that Barthes himself did not observe. The goal of structural linguistics is the reconstituting of the *langue* of verbal language, that of the structural analysis of literary texts, the establishing of a general model or *poetics* of those texts, and that of semiological analysis the establishing of the *langue* of "extralinguistic languages," one of which is literature institutionalized. Barthes speaks of his efforts in the last area as "structural analysis"; he has classified the "structural analysis of narrative" as a "part of the newly developing semiology," and included in a roster of "semiologists concerned with narrative" such recognized structural analysts as A. J. Greimas, Vladimir Propp, Claude Bremond, and

Lévi-Strauss (*IMT*, pp. 126, 137). It is, then, to his work in semiology that we shall now turn for illustrations of Barthes's own Structuralist activity.

II   *The "Languages" of Food and Fashion Writing*

Let us take as the simplest example of the identity of Structuralist and semiological means and ends Barthes's conception of the *langue* and *parole* of "the food system" or "alimentary language," as that is sketched out in the *Elements of Semiology*. Here, *langue* is a menu comprising a structure, *parole* the "filling" of this structure, i.e., a selecting and combining of various food items and modes of culinary preparation by an individual. The filling of the structure, the making of choices which will constitute a meal, is an utterance or "speech" in the language, and the structure or menu affords the freedom for a wide variety of speeches. But what allows Barthes to conceive of an alimentary language or system is not only the fact that the structure makes a sort of speech possible, but also that it makes certain other speeches impossible. A possible or, as the linguist would say, a "well-formed" meal, in other words, is due both to the "complete-ness" of the menu and to the existence in it of certain implicit rules or constraints that constitute the *forms* of our selections and combina-tions. Where has the menu come from, then? From the same source as the *langue* of a verbal language, i.e., from the collective "speech" of the language, the variety of individual meals that have been realized in a particular society; "a sort of sedimentation of many people's speech," Barthes says, "makes up the alimentary language" (*ES*, p. 28).

As we have summarized it here, the food language is a denotative system—not, that is, a "mythology," but a first-order "object-language" of the sort Barthes, in his book *Mythologies*, postulated as a starting-point for his analysis. It is important to emphasize the tentative character of this postulate. Barthes was well aware in his earliest essay of semiological analysis that first-order systems never manage to resist the usurpation of a second system. "Nothing," he wrote in "Myth Today," "can be safe from myth, myth can develop its second-order schema from any meaning and . . . from the very lack of meaning" (*M*, p. 131). "Steak and chips" (or "french-fries") denotes, because of a rule of the alimentary *langue*, a specific association of foods; but as Barthes showed in *Mythologies*, this sign-function also connotes the Gaulist myth—it is "the alimentary sign of Frenchness" (*M*, p. 64). Moreover, in the *Elements of Semiology* it is evident that object-languages are not absolutely independent of verbal language: "It is true that objects, images and patterns of behavior can signify, and do so on a large scale, but never autonomously; every semiological system has its linguistic admixture," either as a result of the linguistic model of the semiological analysis or because of some primary translation of the object-signs into linguistic equivalents or "relays" (*ES*, p. 10). In his long (over 300 pages) and detailed study of women's fashion, *Système de la mode*, this relation of verbal language to a system of clothes-objects is revealed with striking clarity.

Though Barthes's original intention in the *Système de la mode* was the reconstruction of a system of "real fashion as found in clothes actually worn, it quickly became apparent," he wrote in the preface to the book, "that a choice had to be made between the analysis of a real system and that of a written system."[11] Notwithstanding the sociological importance of a vestimentary language completely independent of verbal language, Barthes chose to analyze the written system of fashion, the verbal captions accompanying photographed models in the French fashion magazines *Elle* and *Jardin des modes*. In working with fashion writing rather than with the system of clothes-objects, Barthes felt he was "already in literature," another secondary, but more "formidable" system (*CE*, 152). Nevertheless, the analysis of written fashion also respected "a certain complexity and a certain order of the semiological project" (*SM*, p. 8); it provided, therefore, a necessary "apprenticeship" for the analysis of literature. But there is an important difference between the systems of literature and of fashion writing; whereas the former is a connotative system that takes over a verbal discourse as its signifier, the latter is first of all a metalanguage in which a verbal system "operates" upon an already-made object-system of garments which is its signified. "The fashion magazine 'speaks' the significations of garments, just as one speaks a language" (*ES*, p. 42). Moreover, fashion writing is complicated by the fact that magazines do not merely describe fashion denotatively: they also glamorize and "sell" it. The fashion statement, Barthes says, is "a complex ensemble" in that its language is both metalanguage, a nomenclatural or *terminological* system, and connotation or a *rhetorical* system.

To summarize the technique of Barthes's fashion analysis would require a lengthier examination than can be managed here; we shall instead merely try to suggest the complexity of this analysis in terms with which we have already become familiar from the semiological analysis of "Myth Today" and *The Elements of Semiology*. Take as an example of a fashion statement the following specimen: "Hats are back for work and play." At the root of this statement is a language of clothes-signs—i.e., signifiers (e.g., a cloth or felt object with a crown and brim) and signifieds (e.g., a covering for the head). This system now becomes the signified of a verbal metalanguage to which it supplies the name *hat* as a second-order signifier. Finally, this metalinguistic name-sign is taken over as the signifier of a connotative system, integrated into a system of rhetoric: "Hats are back for work and play." The signification of a connotation, we have already seen, is ambiguous; it is at once a meaning and a label, both historically determined and "natural," something that "goes-without-saying." Our fashion statement produces a similar ambiguity. It means not only what the English sentence says: that hats are being worn again by working women both at and away from their places of business; as Barthes would say, the statement has also become "a new sign whose signifier is the complete fashion utterance and whose signified is the image of the world ["Nature": or "naturally a hat"] and of fashion ["History": or "hats are 'in'"] that the journal wants to convey" (*SM*, p. 47). If this makes the fashion statement sound self-contradictory (the hat as both something to be taken for granted and the object of an attention), that is precisely Barthes's point: "The system of fashion thus offers the splendid paradox of a semantic system whose only goal is to undermine the meaning which it so luxuriantly elaborates" (*SM*, p. 287).

But this is only the beginning of Barthes's analysis; if written fashion is itself a language, one should be able to construct its system. What, in other words, are the units that combine to form the fashion syntagm or "sentence," and to what paradigmatic elements are these units opposed? Barthes describes the pattern of the syntagm as a three-term relationship: an "object" (0) that receives the significa-tion, a "variant" (V) of that object, and a "support" (S) of that variant. In the statement "A sweater with collar closed for dress," "sweater" is the object receiving the signification *dressiness*; "closed" is the variant (since the sweater-collar might also be worn *open*), and "col-lar" is the variant's support (*SM*, p. 73). Barthes also postulates certain *"systematic* modifications" of this basic scheme which can account, then, for any fashion statement. As for the paradigmatic system—i.e., the sets of associated items from which "sweater," "closed," and "collar" have been selected—Barthes's analysis recognizes that many terms ("species," he calls them) can fill both the *object* and the *support* positions of his model; for example, "collar," a *support* in the preceding example, is an *object* in the statement: "the collar asserted by a simple pin."

But a language system must be so arranged that the choice between items in the same paradigm (a dress and a ski outfit, for instance) will prevent their occurrence in the same syntagm. Barthes arrives at this constraint by distributing the *species* into groups or "kinds" *(genres)* on the basis of their syntagmatic incompatibility. Thus, he explains, "a dress and a ski outfit, although formally very different, belong to the same"kind" because one must 'choose' between them" (*SM*, p. 103). The paradims of the *variants* are established by the same principle of syntagmatic incompatibility. A collar cannot be at once both open and closed, but it can be both open and soft; "open" and "closed" are therefore units of the same "kind" *(genre)*, whereas "open" and "soft" are of different "kinds."

We can only begin to suggest here the complexity of Barthes's analysis of "the vestimentary code"; for we have still to notice his analysis of the connotative or rhetorical system of written fashion, that level of the fashion statement that most clearly reveals its affinities with literature. Fashion, as we know it, probably would not exist if it were not at last taken over by connotation, for the vestimentary code we have just looked at issues from "a fashion group" which decides what fashion will be in any particular year, and thus purposefully elaborates and revises the code in the light of this decision. In order for it to work, then, fashion manifests an ambiguity of being both "new" (novel) and "the-way-it-should-be"; its historical motivation must, in other words, be "naturalized." No fashion magazine declares a sign of fashion thus: "short skirts are a sign of fashion this year"; instead, it makes this point rhetorically: "this year, skirts are shorter." The determination to shorten skirts is concealed here by what appears to be already an observable phenomenon.

A more interesting rhetorical strategy (at least from the point of view of literature) naturalizes the function of a garment. As an example, Barthes gives us the following caption (accompanying, no doubt, a photograph of a modeled dress): "a young woman who lives twenty miles from the city, takes the train every day, and often lunches with friends." Barthes says that the very precision with which the mundane is expressed here makes the function of the dress so described "unreal"; but the more contingent that function becomes, the more "natural" it becomes. This is the technique of all realist art, according to which, says Barthes, "an accumulation of small and particular details sanctions the truth of the thing described" (*SM*, p. 268).

Realism, Barthes had shown in *Writing Degree Zero*, plays a curious game with itself: "it delineates an area of plausibility which reveals the possible in the very act of unmasking it as false" (*W*, p. 32). Fashion, we see in *Système de la mode*, does the same thing; Barthes calls it an "exemplary form of the act of signification" (*SM*, p. 287). First of all, it makes signs of objects, and the more it can compound objects by making distinctions, the more its signs abound (think of the potential signification riches in the variable hemline, lapel-width, or heel-height!). Having established these signs, fashion next goes about the task of masking or naturalizing them. Finally, the mask itself becomes a sign—the very effort of naturalizing betrays itself. Fashion, then—and in this, too, it is like literature—exists merely to maintain itself as an "equilibrium of operations": masking-unmasking-masking-unmasking, etc. It is a "homeostatic system." What do we, as consumers, "read" in the sign of fashion? Not a meaning, nothing but "the *signifying* of things"; its "being is in signification, not in what is signified" (*CE*, p. 152).

III The "Language" of Narrative

It is still a long step, however, from the analysis of fashion writing to the analysis of literature, and the reader who turns to Barthes's "Introduction to the Structural Analysis of Narrative" in hopes of finding a narrative *langue* as fully articulated as that of fashion is sure to be disappointed. Barthes made no such claim for the "Introduction," however. Written as an editorial preface to an issue of the journal *Communications* (vol. 8, 1966) devoted to the structural analysis of narrative, Barthes's contribution fully acknowledges its own provisional status. It is, however, an introduction in a broader sense than this, for whereas his fellow contributors concern themselves with the particular problems of individual analyses, Barthes—the "high structuralist"—sketches for us a "theory" of narrative structure based upon the model of linguistics. "A narrative," Barthes begins, "is a large sentence, just as any declarative sentence is . . . the outline of a little narrative."[12] We may therefore speak of narrative "subjects" and narrative "verbs," the latter bearing the narrative equivalents of tense, mode, and person. In short "from the point of view of linguistics, there is nothing in discourse [the "language" of which narrative is only one "idiom"] that is not matched in the sentence" (*I*, p. 239). This does not mean that linguistics is itself the system by which Barthes describes narrative, for the sentence is the largest unit that linguistics can describe. Since narrative is an organization of sentences, and since it is by means of this organization that "it is perceived as the message of another 'language,' functioning at a higher level than the language of linguistics," it must necessarily be "the object of a second [and larger] linguistics" (*I*, p. 240).

At the center of the "theory" of narrative structure stands the linguistic concept of "the level of description." A linguist may describe a sentence on any of several levels (the phonetic, the phonological, the grammatical) which exist in a hierarchical relation to one another; but described on any one of these levels, the sentence may not be said to participate in a meaning until it is integrated into a higher level of description. (Here, by the way, is the linguistic foundation of the central principle of Barthes's criticism: his insistence that the meaning of a work does not preexist the critic's analysis of it, but rather is generated by that analysis.) True, the linguist posits a "distributional" relation of elements on the same level as well as an "integrative" relation between levels. Nevertheless, the relating of the distributed elements to one another does not in itself account for meaning. Barthes puts it this way: "a phoneme, although perfectly describable, means nothing by itself; it partakes in meaning only if integrated into a word; and the word itself must in turn be integrated into the sentence" (*I*, p. 242).

Now if narrative is a "language," it too may be described on several levels. Barthes works with only three of these in the "Introduction": the level of "functions," those bits of narrative that exist as correlates of other bits of narrative; the level of "actants," i.e., of characters considered in terms of "what they do," their actions; and the level of "narration" or "discourse." And just as the descriptive levels of language exist in hierarchical relation to one another, so do the levels of narrative: for functions make sense only as they are acted by characters, and characters in narrative exist only insofar as they are "spoken" or narrated. We understand a narrative, in other words, not only by following the unfolding of the story, "horizontally," on one of these levels, but also by passing "vertically" from one level to another. "The meaning," Barthes says, "does not lie 'at the end' of the narrative, but straddles it" (*I*, p. 243). We shall understand this idea more clearly if we look briefly at each of these levels and their relations to one another.

On the level of the functions of narrative the analyst has three tasks: the identifying of the narrative units, the terms of the various correlations; the classifying of these units; and the establishing of the rules or "grammar" by which they are linked in the narrative. According to Barthes, everything in a narrative belongs to one of four classes of functional units; everything, sooner or later, is significant: "there are no wasted units" (*I*, p. 245). Thus, the unit "James Bond saw a man in his fifties" (most of Barthes's illustrations in the "Introduction" are taken from thematically simple detective fiction—hence this one from Ian Fleming's *Goldfinger*) is functional because it fits into a gradually emerging portrait of a character; indeed, it is doubly (and immediately) functional in that it also tells us that Bond does not know this character. Barthes, first of all, groups such identified units into two general classes: "functions" proper, which are distributional units that correlate with units on their own level; and "indices" or integrative units which become significant only when seen in relation to a correlate on a higher level. Thus, the unit "he picked up the receiver," is a "function" because it refers to a consequential unit ("hanging up"); but the element "four" in "he picked up one of the four receivers," is an index since it refers to a concept or "signified" ("administrative power") at the level of character.

But each of these classes may be divided again—functions into "nuclei" and "catalyses," and indices into "informants" and "indices proper." The distinction between the first pair of terms recognizes the fact that some functions (nuclei) imitate or resolve uncertainties that further the narrative, while others (catalyses) merely "fill in" the space between these "cardinal functions." "The telephone rang" is a nucleus because it presents the logical alternatives of either answering or not answering it, alternatives that wll affect the continuation of the story differently. On the other hand, "Bond made his way to the desk . . . put down his cigarette," etc., are catalyses, merely consecutive units that "saturate" the space between the ringing phone and (now) the answering of it. The distinction between "indices proper" and "informants" is made on the basis of the specificity of their referents: the former signify implicitly, the latter explicitly. Indices refer to character traits, feelings, atmosphere; informants refer to specific elements of time and space.

But how are these different units combined in the narrative syntagm? In part, at least, the syntax of functional units is implicit in the

logic of the system of classification. Informants and indices, for instance, "combine freely among themselves" through the signified to
which they may each refer. Every reader is able to relate specific
biographical information to the more pervasive traits of a character's
personality; similarly, catalyses that fill the space between nuclei
quite naturally depend upon those nuclei. The more fundamental
question of how nuclei combine with one another is more difficult,
however. We have already observed that catalyses follow one another
in a purely chronological order. The relation between nuclei, on the
other hand, is both chronological and logical, as if the fact that one
thing comes after another means that it was caused by the other.

According to Barthes, however (and he acknowledges here a
specific debt to Lévi-Strauss), we do not account for the logic of
nuclear combinations by "chronologizing" them. Time, in fact, does
not exist in narrative; it is an illusion there. The analyst's task,
therefore, is to "'dechronologize' the narrative continuum and to
'relogicize' it"—i.e., to turn chronology into an element of the narrative's logical system (*I*, p. 251). Barthes identifies three different
efforts to establish this logic of narrative functions; he does not,
however, elucidate them for us. Instead, he presents what is
modestly called a "complementary" technique for describing the
organization of the smallest functions of a narrative, those with which
existing analyses are unable to deal. This technique is worth noticing
here because it gives us a preview, on the level of functions, of
something like the hierarchical integration that operates between the
three descriptive levels. Barthes links these trivial nuclei into name-
able units called "sequences." For example, *"extending one's hand,
shaking hands, releasing the handshake"* constitute a sequence of
nuclei that is apprehended as a "greeting"; this sequence in turn
becomes a function in a sequence of larger elements including *"drawing near, stopping, hailing, greeting, settling down together"*—this
one called "encounter"—and so on and on until we reach the limit of
the level of functions (*I*, p. 254). The meaning of this final functional
sequence derives from the level immediately above it.

It follows, then, that the meaning that we attach to a trivial function
like an extended hand derives ultimately from a character that exists,
for the analyst, on another level altogether. "It may safely be assumed," Barthes says, "that there is not a single narrative in the
world without 'characters,' or at least without 'agents'" (*I*, p. 257). But
how can one manage a systematic description or classification of such
"characters?" Certainly not, the Structuralist would insist, by refer-

ring it to some external system of classes or types taken from psychological or social observation. Again, the linguistic model has suggested the most interesting answers, for grammatical categories like subject and object, indirect object, and adjunct parallel the semantic categories of communication, desire, and ordeal. Thus, although characters are not classifiable in terms of what they are, as "beings," they are classifiable in terms of what they do, as "participants"—hence A. J. Greimas's name—"actants"—for them, and Barthes's use of the word *actions* to designate the entire second level of narrative analysis. But here, too, there is a problem raised by many stories in which two opponents compete for the same goal; which one in such a case is the subject or hero? Barthes finds a similarity between the structure of narrative and the structure of games at this point, and postulates an irreducible "double subject" that may emulate the grammatical feature of "dual person" in certain ancient languages. The key to the "actional level," he remarks, may exist in the grammatical categories of person (*I*, p. 259)—i.e., a definition of characters in terms of their relation not to the world, but to a speaker, to discourse or "narration," the third level of analysis.

As the functions of narrative presuppose characters ("actants") or agents, then, so do characters presuppose narration. A character in a story does not just exist (as an actor exists on the stage): he is spoken into existence through a narrative language or "code." In other words, the story*teller* is not the author who writes down the story— not even in any of the disguises by which conventional criticism has tried to internalize him; rather, every story is told from within itself, just as the meaning of every sentence is generated within its linguistic systems. For Barthes, the presence of the narrator in the narrative may be described in terms of two (usually intermingled) systems of signs: personal and impersonal. The latter is "the traditional mode of narrative" which, by eliminating "the present of the person who is speaking," achieves something like a purely "witnessing conscious-ness." The personal system, on the other hand, expresses "the here and now" of the narration. This distinction is not, however, strictly tied to the linguistic opposition of first-person and third-"non-person" pronouns. The pronoun of the following sentence—"He [Bond] saw a man in his fifties still young looking"—does not alter the fact that it is written in the personal system, as can be demonstrated by the substitution of an "I" for the "he." But in "the tinkling of the ice cubes against the glass seemed to awaken in Bond a sudden inspira-tion," such a substitution (". . . in me," for ". . . in Bond") is impossible—not (again) because of the implied "him," but because "seemed" signifies the absence of person.

With these systems of "the narrator's code" and certain other narrational signs (the "modes of authorial intervention," "the codings of beginnings and endings," "points of view," etc.), we come to the upper limit of the structural analysis of narrative. But if meaning on any level of the analysis depends upon its integration into a superior level, whence does narration receive its meaning? From the world, Barthes answers, from other sign systems (like those treated in *Mythologies*, for instance), the elements of which are other substances ("historical facts, determinations, behaviors") (*I*, p. 265). The level of narration plays an ambiguous role, then: both "closing" the narrative, constituting it "once and for all," and bringing it into contact with the world's systems of production and consumption, as Barthes had demonstrated in *Writing Degree Zero* and at the end of *Système de la mode*. At this point, narrative encounters what, in linguistics, is called a "situation," a "body of non-associated linguistic facts" (*I*, p. 265)—"non-associated," that is, with the "language" of narrative, but constituting nevertheless a system in its own right, and providing thus a superior "level" into which the units of the narrational code may still be integrated.

The linguistic concept of "situation" brings us back to familiar territory; Barthes uses it to differentiate between what we have come to call "classical" and "modern" literature, the latter encoding its situation in a "spectacular" way (Michel Butor's *Mobile*), the former deemphasizing this code by "naturalizing" the narrative—as a collection of personal letters, for example (Richardson's *Pamela*), or as a journal (Defoe's *Moll Flanders*). The "Introduction" concludes on another familiar note: "The function of narrative is not to 'represent,'" we read; "it is to put together a scene which still retains a certain linguistic character for the reader, but does not belong to the mimetic order in any way" (*I*, p. 271). What Structuralism brought to Barthes's work, then, was not a new theoretical position, but a new way of arriving at the old ones.

Structuralism, in the strict sense in which we (following Barthes) have been using the term, is usually said to have had its origin in Lévi-Strauss's *Tristes tropiques* in 1955, and its heyday, commemorated by the same writer's *The Savage Mind*, in 1962. And yet, even as Barthes, in the essays we have been considering, enthusiastically announced the blossoming of a Structuralist study of literature, he and it were already undergoing fundamental modifications. By 1970

Structuralism appears to have lost its original impetus as an intellectural force—though indeed it persisted as a middlebrow fashion. In that year Barthes wrote that the task which he had earlier called "the structuralist activity"—the contriving of "a great narrative structure" in which all the world's stories would be seen, a narrative *langue*— was "as exhausting (ninty-nine percent perspiration, as the saying goes) as it is ultimately undesirable," and by 1971 he was sufficiently distanced from the enterprise to speak of it as "a euphoric dream of scientificity."[13]

What accounts for this change in Barthes's critical ideology, and, by the way, in that of a number of other influential French Structuralists? In his new preface to the 1970 edition of *Mythologies*, Barthes wrote that "it is obvious that the two attitudes which determined the origin of the book [i.e., the ideological critique of the language of mass-culture, and the semiological analysis of this language] could no longer today be maintained unchanged . . ." (*M*, p. 9). What, then, occurred between the writing of "Myth Today" and Barthes's updating of its theory in an essay called "Change the Object Itself" (1971)? Not French society: the social upheaval of May 1968 only made the need for ideological criticism "brutally evident," he remarked in the new preface. The myths had not disappeared, nor had the method of analyzing them changed markedly. As Barthes explains it, the change had occurred *between* the myth and the analyst's view of it: held in the analyst's gaze, myth ("like an animal long since captured and held in observation") becomes "*a different object.*" The analyst has become a producer, the object of his analysis the production. "What has changed these fifteen years," Barthes writes, "is the *science of reading*" (*IMT*, p. 166).

Let us try yet to understand the technical implications of this change. In the *Elements of Semiology* Barthes's analysis of the sign as signifier and signified resulted in his postulating two distinct systems: one of connotation, the signified of which is revealed as a "straight" ideological intention, the other, a system of denotation which functions to make the connotation seem innocent, as natural as language. Early semiological analysis had been content merely to unmask myth, as if in locating its foundation, revealing its latent meaning, it had halted its process, destroyed the ideological signified. But Barthes and other students of semiology very quickly became critical of this sort of analysis. Its very fashionableness—and, in 1970, Barthes remarked that "any student can and does denounce the bourgeois or petit-bourgeois character of such and such a form" (*IMT*,

p. 166)—would have aroused his suspicion, for fashion, whether vestimentary or intellectual, is itself a bourgeois myth. It now became apparent that the process of signification is never halted by analysis, that the language of analysis and criticism is no more able to resist being taken over by myth than any other language. The signified revealed by early semiological analysis was transformed by that analysis into a signifier; the unmasking of the myth became the point of origin of a new myth. Saussure had placed the "subject" of language (the one who speaks, writes, reads, interprets) at the center of the language system; the subject *produces* a meaning by articulating the differences of the system. But in its zeal to identify the mythic signified, early semiological analysis turned the subject-producer into a user or consumer of language; intention or meaning thus came to preexist its articulation. The subject became the source of the meaning, and the subject had moved outside the process.

Barthes observes that semiology (in 1970) was in a situation similar to that of Freudian analysis, which began by overemphasizing the latent meaning of the dream-sign and oversimplifying the subject's (or dreamer's) relation to it. But modern theory (in particular, the work of Jacques Lacan) is in the process of *re-placing* the subject, and, Barthes suggests, the subsequent study of cultural languages must make a similar effort. As Rosalind Coward and John Ellis have explained, "meaning disseminates itself in the dream according to the position of the subject (its sociofamilial contruction) and the arrangement of the signifying chain in relation to this position."[14] It is in his next work, *S/Z* (1970), that Barthes fully accepts the complexity of the subject in the process of signification.

CHAPTER 5

Writing Our Reading

O N THE FIRST page of *S/Z* (1970) Barthes epitomizes the ambitions of the first analysts of narrative (and, we might add, of Structuralists in general) as follows: "we shall . . . extract from each tale its model, then out of these models we shall make a great narrative structure, which we shall reapply (for verification) to any one narrative."[1] A literary structure, then, is a general model that reflects the common features of a specific class of individual texts. These recurring features probably vary with one another; but it is their general similarity that makes their particular differences significant. A structure, in other words, tends to "equalize" the texts it reflects, i.e., make them equal to one another. In *S/Z* Barthes proposes an alternative vision of literature: the literary work *in its difference*. Difference from what? Not from other texts; Barthes is not thinking of what gives a text its unique identity, but of the text's way of differing from itself. Whereas the Structuralist reads many different texts in order to arrive at their sameness, Barthes now recommends *re*reading the same text to arrive at its "difference." At the end of the preceding chapter we noticed Barthes's reference to a change in the Structuralist "science of reading"; once its signified had been identified, contemporary myth became a "different object" under our scrutiny—just as a rare animal in the zoo changes under our continued observation. We perceiving subjects produce this difference in the object. So it is by rereading a text that we cease to be its consumers and become producers of difference in it.

I *Reading and Writing*

S/Z is an essay of criticism-by-rereading, an essentially revolutionary activity, as Barthes defines it early in the book:

Rereading, an operation contrary to the commercial and ideological habits of our society, which would have us 'throw away' the story once it has been

79

consumed ('devoured'), so that we can then move on to another story, buy another book, and which is tolerated only in certain marginal categories of readers (children, old people, and professors), rereading is here suggested at the outset, for it alone saves the text from repetition (those who fail to reread are obliged to read the same story everywhere). (*S/Z* pp. 15–16)

To read a text only once (i.e., a "first time") is to read what we have already read, to find again what has been left in us by other texts that we have already read: the "'I' [or subject]which approaches the text is already itself a plurality of other texts," Barthes believes (*S/Z*, p. 10). To think that there is "a beginning of reading, as if everything were not already read," is an illusion, then; in a sense, "there is no *first* reading" (*S/Z*, p. 16). We find in a text what we have learned to find in it; that is how we are able to "understand" it at all. But a second reading—one, for example, "which places behind the transparency of suspense . . . the anticipated knowledge of what is to come in the story" (*S/Z*, p. 165), releases the text's signifying energy. Rereading does not help us to further understand the text, to master it by reaching "some ultimate signified" or meaning; it does just the reverse, multiplying the signifiers so that the text disseminates a plurality of meanings which makes the closure of it more and more difficult.

Actually, the "second reading" that Barthes practices in *S/Z* is not a literal second reading, but an *immediate* rereading, a reading of a text "as if it had already been read" (*S/Z*, p. 15). "Has it never happened to you," Barthes explained in *Figaro littéraire*, "to stop constantly while reading, not for lack of interest, but, on the contrary because of a flood of ideas, of stimulations, of associations?"[2] It is this sort of "fascinated, loving" reading that Barthes speaks of as "rereading," and it is this that he attempts to write in *S/Z*.

Habitually, the act of reading is a consumption, a using up of a text in order to be finished with it. Nevertheless, the consuming reader remains respectfully submissive to what he reads; his purpose demands "a kind of idleness" on his part: "he is intransitive . . . in short, *serious*," Barthes says (*S/Z*, p. 4). "Rereading," on the other hand, is playful work, a "man-handling" of a text that interrupts its "natural" flow, breaks it up so that it becomes "plural" (i.e., "the same and new"); it is reading without respect for *the* text since *it* produces *a* text. "Rereading," in this sense, is like writing: the rereader "writes" his reading. In *Critique et Vérité* Barthes argued that "the writer and the critic meet in the same difficult situation, facing the same object: language" (*CV*, p. 47). In *S/Z* he makes this idea the controlling principle of his critical project, a commentary on a short story by

Balzac. Whereas conventional critical evaluation classifies a text as complex or simplistic, sincere or insincere, original or trite, Barthes classifies it as either "writerly" or "readerly." The writerly text (as we "reread" it) is *"ourselves writing,"* before some system of meaning (an ideology, the rules of a genre, or an interpretive hypothesis) singularizes its plurality—makes it mean *something*. Such a text, says Barthes, "is the novelistic without the novel, poetry without the poem . . . production without product, structuration without structure" (*S/Z*, p. 5). The value that Barthes seeks in literature is pleasure, and the pleasure of a literary test is measured in the sort of productive activity ("rereading") we have been trying to define. "What evaluation finds," he says, "is precisely this value: what can be written (rewritten) today: the *writerly*" (*S/Z*, p. 4).

In point of fact, however, there are no writerly texts in any literature—there is no written language that does not, sooner or later succumbing to ideology or genre or criticism, mean one thing rather than another. The most writerly text, (i.e., the most plural text) would be the least written to begin with: one may think of it as the world itself, an infinitude of signifiers at play. "The writerly text is not a thing," says Barthes (*S/Z*, p. 5); it is not a product or a *re*production: it is the element of "play" in a text. The writerly, then, like the zero-degree of "writing," is an unrealizable ideal, experienced in reading only fleetingly or perhaps accidentally. The mass of our literature is readerly—works that can be read, and then accepted or rejected—but not "written" (we would not care to write them), "classical" works that reproduce an already existing meaning.

But there are degrees of readerliness. The more readerly (here we might more understandably say "readable") a work is, the less plural it is—the more written when the reader takes it up; the less readerly, or more plural, or less written a work, the more difficult we say it is—i.e., the more like a writerly text without being one. We may in fact trace the outline of a hierarchy of texts in Barthes's remarks. At the top stands the "multivalent text," completely and integrally plural, and thus "reversible" and "frankly indeterminable," the writerly ideal itself, though Barthes regards the writerly as the (unattainable) goal of what he calls "modern writing." Next come the "polysemous texts," "classical" readerly works in which various structures of meaning may be traced, making their "plural" proportionally "incomplete" or, as he says, "more or less parsimonious." Finally, there are the univocal texts, those in which language is used practically, as an instrument of communication. Now the critic can do little with works at either end of this scale. Criticism presupposes a *read* work; it is a language "consequent" to a work. But the more plural a work is, the less capable one is of finishing it; since it is indeterminable, one is always "rereading" it. "The writerly text is a perpetual present," Barthes says; it thus "demolishes criticism" (S/Z, p. 5). On the other hand, criticism of the single-voice work is simply superfluous, a saying-again of what the work was written to say. Criticism finds its proper place between these two extremes, in the range of "the more or less parsimonious" plural. Its job is the "differentiation" of this mass, a measuring, as Barthes puts it, "of the *more or less* each text can mobilize" (S/Z, p. 5).

How does Barthes "interpret" or measure the moderate plurality of a literary work? Not, certainly, by drawing forth one or more covert but complete meanings in a text, and then attempting to justify one of them as the denotation—to demonstrate, that is, the "naturalness" of its priority with respect to the other "connotative" meanings of the work. That is the aim of conventional interpretation which, as a professional activity, may be thought of as a contest in assigning meaning-priorities to a work. To Barthes's way of thinking, this activity is an effort to "finish" the work once and for all, legally to execute it in the name of the one-and-only meaning that will memorialize it. "Denotation," he says, "is not the first [i.e., the primary or preeminent] meaning, but pretends to be so; under this illusion, it is ultimately no more than the *last* of the connotations (the one which seems both to establish and to close the reading) . . ." (S/Z, p. 9). Barthes, we know, has always maintained that literature (the "classical," readerly work) is a connotation system that uses language to naturalize an intentional signified. Conventional interpretation innocently accepts this myth; that is, it accepts the naturalized signification (a connotation) as denotation. The readerly work, then, is written to be closed by interpretation—a realist text, for instance, pretends to mean only what its words denote—and the reader innocently complies with this pretense.

But suppose, in order to learn how this pretense works, we decide not to comply with it. Suppose we were to collect a number of different interpretations of a work and *redistribute* them over the work so that no single interpretation would have ascendency over another—refuse, in other words, to determine a denotation, and frankly admit that every meaning found in the work is a connotation. In thus reconstituting the textual *difference* of the work, we would be making connotation the measure of the work's incomplete plurality; we would be dealing with it at that point in the reading process *just before* the reader joins in the pretense that the work does have a specific meaning, and we would be able to establish the rationale that underlies the pretense. This, in effect (though not in actual practice) is Barthes's aim in *S/Z*.

Barthes selected Balzac's "Sarrasine" as the object of this analysis because it is a Realist work and it is in realism that the meaning (the sense of the real) produced in reading seems most like a finished product to begin with, the reader's complicity in the pretense being least noticeable here. Realism constitutes a challenge for Barthes because its survival has been attributed to its supposed singularity, its truth, not to its plurality. It presents itself as a simple denotation system: on the one hand there is the world, society, the individual (preexistent signifieds); on the other hand there is language, a collection of signifiers assumed to stand for these concepts. Such a relationship is not what we have come to know as signification, a process in which signifiers and signifieds are caught up in mutual self-production; it is merely representation, mimesis, an illusion in which the signifier becomes transparent and only the signified appears to remain. Demystifying this process as connotation has long been a favorite pastime of Barthes. A recent instance is his short essay called *"L'Effet de reél"* ("the reality-effect"), published in 1968, in which he finds an exemplary illustration of the working of connotation in the "realistic detail." Take, for example, Michelet's observation that, while Charlotte Corday's final portrait was being painted, "after an hour and a half, someone tapped softly at a little door behind her." This detail has no explicit meaning in the narrative: delete it, and the meaning of the narrative remains the same. As Barthes explains it, "it is the very deficiency of signified as opposed to referent which becomes itself the signified of realism": it is the indifference of the detail that makes it seem real—or, quite another thing, that makes it in fact *realistic*. What is signified is not the content of reality, but "the category of the 'real.'"[3]

The explanation of this paradox consists in the fact that our sense of the real is strongly literary, and we expect this literary version of the real to be reenforced. Whether or not highly charged moments in life are marked by soft tappings on little doors is not the point: it is sufficient that they have been so marked in literature. In other words, the world has become a sort of book for us, and every subsequent attempt to refer to the world is in fact a reference to the books that have already coalesced around it. According to Julia Kristeva, who has given the name *intertextuality* to this phenomenon, "every text takes shape as a mosaic of citations, every text is the absorption and transformation of other texts."[4] This concept of the intertextual—a dimension of citations or quotations (or, as Barthes calls them, "codes") of the already-read—is central to the analysis of the readerly in *S/Z*. "What we call 'real' (in the theory of the realistic text)," Barthes says, "is never more than a code of representation (of signification) . . ." (*S/Z*, p. 80).

The point is that the real itself cannot be put into words. We cannot, for example, explain or describe beauty (which, Barthes notes, can only say *"I am what I am"*) except in the form of a citation: thus Marianina (a character in "Sarrasine") is said to embody "the fabled imaginings of the Eastern poets! Like the Sultan's daughter, in the story of the Magic Lamp, she should have been kept veiled" (*S/Z*, p. 32). Beauty is not described here: it is *referred to* a cultural code (specifically, a literary code) which says to us "the beautiful." Realism, then, "consists not in copying the real but in copying a (depicted) copy of the real" (*S/Z*, p. 55). So "secure" are many of these codes (that of represented beauty, for example) that they can be used· as a support for other codes. Why, for instance, do we accept as necessary in literature the relation between beauty and love—as in the commonplace "To see her thus [i.e., so lovely] was to adore her" (lexia 326)—when "real life" presents so many violations of this law. Not, as we have just seen, because of any power of described beauty. It is due to the sheer abundance of the cultural references of beauty—hence to the "naturalness" with which it is signified. "The love established by this beauty is brought under the *natural* rules of culture," Barthes says (*S/Z*, p. 143).

We shall say, then, that the "origin" of the meaning *beauty* in the language just quoted is a code of culture, or literature, or beauty (its name is not important to Barthes). But insofar as I am familiar with this code, I grasp its sense: I have *read* the passage. But can there not also be a sense of something else in this language, something more difficult to pin down, less determinate than the sense of beauty just mentioned? Is it a sense of *danger* (since veils, by concealing, serve also as a sort of shield or protection, and Marianina "should have been kept veiled")? Or is it a sense of *sacrilege?* In looking at her unveiled is one brought too close to a spiritual mystery? I cannot say for certain. Still another reading of the passage might take me in an altogether different direction. My uncertainty is due to the fact that no code offers itself as an authority for this additional sense. I am left with an indeterminate semantic residue and a vague uncertainty that

I have indeed read the passage. If in fact there is such a residue of unresolved meaning, we will have touched upon the "plural" of Balzac's text. "The more indeterminate the origin of the statement," Barthes says, "the more plural the text" (*S/Z*, p. 41). In a Realist work like "Sarrasine," this plural is incomplete; the signifiers are given only a limited freedom of play. Even so, there is considerable semantic "noise." The point is that although the messages of the text are broken, "caught in a system of interferences," this noise is not on the whole confused, not "unnameable." Realism calls upon only "realist knowledge" to support itself, and in doing so manages to make this very appeal seem natural, an apparent imitation of reality.

As read in Barthes's analysis, however, Balzac's tale is not a typically Realist work. The latter, we have seen, postulates an identity of the signifier and signified; *behind* the appearance, the painting, the written text, stands the truth, a plenitude of meaning—what for the "modern" writer and critic is only an emptiness. "Sarrasine" is not only an illustration of the mechanism (connotation) by which that "truth" or meaning is made to seem "natural"; it also dramatizes and thus calls into question the very assumptions on which this mechanism is based. It is, therefore, a "limit text."

We can perhaps suggest this self-limiting function of the analyzed text with a brief summary of Balzac's plot. "Sarrasine" is a story about the telling of a story. The narrator, after a party given by the wealthy Lanty family, agrees to reveal to the woman he has taken to the house (in exchange for a night with her) the secret of a mysterious old man she sees there. His story concerns the passion of a sculptor, Sarrasine, for a famous and beautiful opera singer, La Zambinella, who is in fact a castrated man or *castrato*. When Sarrasine discovers this truth, he tries to kill La Zambinella, but is killed himself by the protector of the latter. The old man at the party is in fact this *castrato* and the source of the Lanty wealth. So appalled by the horror of this story is the woman to whom it is told that she reneges on her bargain with the narrator, and Balzac's story ends. The point we wish to make here is that "Sarrasine," a Realist story, demonstrates the fallacy of the Realist aesthetic. As we watch the sculptor try to capture the "truth" (in his sense) behind La Zambinella's beauty, the Realist "plenitude" supposed to lie behind appearance, we see him come closer and closer to the void which is the condition of the *castrato*, the emptiness which from a modern point of view, lies behind all appearance. Realism, Barthes argues, does not begin with "reality," but with the "already written real," with a connoted "reality," "a prospective code" (*S/Z* p.

167), and Sarrasine is a "great devourer of connotations." Thus, when
La Zambinella asks, "in a soft, silvery voice," "'And if I were not a
woman?'" the sculptor ignores what is asserted (I am not a woman)
and understands what is suggested by a "soft, silvery voice" (*S/Z*, p.
166). The Realist impulse to *go behind* the appearance, to accept the
code of representation as reality leads to a failure, and "Sarrasine,"
Barthes demonstrates, is the "emblem" of this failure (*S/Z*, p. 122).

II   *The Five Codes*

We are given Balzac's story literally twice in *S/Z:* once at the end of
the book, just "as it came from the printer," for "those who like a good
story"; and again in 561 numbered fragments calles *lexias*, in-
terspersed with commentary and digressions of critical invention and
reflection. Whereas conventional interpretation, having first read a
text and decided upon its meaning, represents it in what it regards as
the most efficient manner, citing the text only where it bears upon the
meaning and in the order that will make it most intelligible, *S/Z*
confronts the text, as it were, for the first time, considering each and
every word *as it comes* in the text. Barthes, in other words, does not
begin with either a meaning to be expressed or a critical system;
rather than *re*present Balzac's story, he *pre*sents it, and his "gradual"
reading of it becomes the source as well as the object of the critical
principles of his commentary. By cutting up the text, Barthes first of
all liberates his reading from the limitations of those "natural" structural units of the readerly work: the temporary closures of chapter,
episode, paragraph, or even sentence division which reassure the
reader of a final closure to come. Barthes wishes to deny the "naturalness" of reading, to interrupt the "natural" flow of sentences, and the
breaking of the text into lexias is a denaturalizing act, a way of working
"a maximum of disintegrative violence and a minimum of integrative
violence."[5] Detained by this denaturalized isolation of the lexias, the
reader is able to experience the connotative energy of the signifiers.

Is a title, for instance—even in its conventional isolation on the first
page—any more significant than a proper name, a means of designating or identifying? But remove it from its conventional place, and it
becomes interesting—it is able to function more freely as a signifier.
Just how interesting (in this case) is not known until the middle of the
book (digression XLVII), where the name *Sarrasine* is taken up a
second time. Here, Barthes tells us that in "customary French
onomastics," the name "*SarraSine*" would be "*SarraZine*." Taken at

its connotative value, this Z is "the letter of deviation" and, since it is also the first letter of Zambinella, "the initial of castration." In Barthes's reading of the story Sarrasine is ultimately "castrated" himself by the knowledge of Zambinella's castration; hence the subdued Z in the middle of his name. Hence, too, the title of Barthes's book, *S/Z;* the slash between the letters is the mirror by which we see the inverted difference which is the site of this meaning.

"Sarrasine," the title of Balzac's story, is the first lexia in Barthes's analysis; his commentary on it and on the first sentence of the story (lexias 2 and 3) constitutes an epitome of *S/Z* and provides, therefore, a convenient introduction to the book. The "first-time" reader of Balzac's story does not attach the name in the title to a sculptor until much later in the text (lexia 153). Nevertheless, the title is a signifier, and its function is to pose a question: *Who or what is Sarrasine?* "Query," we might say, is a connotation of the lexia "Sarrasine." Thus Barthes establishes that units of discourse "whose function it is to articulate in various ways a question, its response, and the variety of chance events which can either formulate the question or delay its answer; or even, constitute an enigma and lead to its solution" make up what he calls a *hermeneutic code* (*S/Z*, p. 17) with which all readers, merely through the experience of reading, are familiar. The reader, we have said, is himself "a plurality of other texts, of codes which are infinite" or whose origin is lost (*S/Z*, p. 10); the reader is a repository of the *already* read, the *already* experienced, and the code, Barthes says, "is the wake of that *already*" (*S/Z*, p. 20).

Answers (assuming, of course, they are efficient ones) *close* questions, and the hermeneutic (the word means "interpretive") code provides an important incentive to the consumer of the readerly work. But Barthes, who aims to demonstrate plurality, and whose interest is therefore in the means of keeping questions open, unanswered, for as long as possible, stresses the "essentially reactive" structure of this code. Indeed, the hermeneutic is "the Voice of Truth"; but expectation, Barthes argues, is "the basic condition for truth," and "truth, these [readerly] narratives tell us, is what is *at the end* of expectation" (*S/Z*, p. 76). Thus, the hermeneutic code works to prolong expectation.

The sequence of lexias 14–18 illustrates the process. The *theme* or subject of an enigma is first of all introduced (but not formulated): "'These people [the Lantys] must have a huge fortune . . .'" (lexia 14)—the narrator, from his concealed window recess, overhears this in the conversation of two guests. Lexia 15 provides two more terms of the code: the *proposal*, which tells us "There is an enigma"—"'You mean you don't know [where their fortune came from] . . .?'"; and the *avoided* (or *suspended*) *answer*, which prevents closure of the enigma and the story—"They lowered their voices and walked off to talk in greater comfort on some isolated sofa." Only in lexia 17 is the enigma at last formulated: "Nobody knew . . . from what business, what plunder, what piratical activity, or what inheritance derived a fortune estimated at several millions." But we still have no *disclosure* or solution, the final term of the code: that does not come until lexia 549. Barthes thinks of the encoding of an enigma as the construction of a sentence, an "organism" that is both reducible to the unity of a subject and a predicate, but—between these two points, before this unity is achieved—also infinitely expandable. Thus, between the "thematization" of an enigma and the predication of its disclosure may come a large variety of delaying expansions, the "morphemes" of the hermeneutic "sentence"—"hermeneutemes," in other words: the *snare* ("a kind of deliberate evasion of the truth"), the *equivocation*, the *partial answer*, and *jamming* (an "acknowledgement of insolubility").

We have said that the first-time reader does not know that "Sarrasine" is the name of a sculptor until much later in the story. Nevertheless, Barthes maintains, the title does connote a "character" or, to be more precise, a *characteristic* which, when combined with other related characteristics, creates a "character," a connoted signified. In French, the final *e* of a proper name is taken as a "specifically feminine linguistic property"; *Femininity*, in other words, is a semantic unit or *seme* of the signifier "Sarrasine." But the aim of reading, according to Barthes, is not so much the definition of this meaning by naming it, as it is the following of its "movement" from one related characteristic to another, while at the same time holding on to them in order to create "some constant form" that "*doesn't [fully] take*" (*S/Z*, p. 93). Barthes calls this practice "thematics," and he believes that our ability to follow these "flickers" of meaning to their nucleus is another sort of decoding; we are dealing here with a *semic* code, then, the "Voice of the Person," although it may also connote "ambiances, shapes, and symbols." For the author of the readerly work, the trick consists in making the signified "come forth" while avoiding any mention of it. Thus, in telling us that he is attending a party (lexias 2 and 3), and that the clock of the Elysée Bourbon has just struck midnight (lexia 4), the narrator has broken a signifier into "particles of verbal matter which make sense only by coalescing" as the connotated signified *Wealth*. The beauty of the technique is that the connotation is "naturalized" by perfectly "regular" sounding language.

The first sentence of the story is divided into two lexias: "I was deep in one of those daydreams" (lexia 2), and "which overtake even the shallowest of men, in the midst of the most tumultuous parties" (lexia 3). We may see here that lexic division is entirely a matter of convenience. A lexia is merely "the best possible space in which we can observe meanings" (*S/Z*, p. 13), a spot in the text that exhibits some density of connotation. The only rule is that we create a space in which at least one, but no more than four, meanings may be enumerated. Barthes reveals the plurality of the readerly work by approaching it *as if* for the first time. Of course, this is not the case; the sort of "microanalysis" attempted in *S/Z* would be impossible on a first reading. But while Barthes's knowledge of the subsequent "facts" of the story may sensitize him to connotative possibilities early in the text, it is not permitted to determine an interpretation of the work: the knowledge is inclusive, not preclusive.

Barthes, for example, comes to "Sarrasine" knowing that Balzac characteristically develops his stories by means of rhetorical oppositions and antitheses, and he is therefore constantly on the lookout for them. In the opening paragraph the narrator tells us that he was seated in a window recess of the Lanty mansion from which he could contemplate both a dark, cold, silent garden and a bright, warm, noisy ballroom. Now antithesis, Barthes reminds us, is the province of symbol; whenever two items are opposed, a groundwork is established for substitution and variation. Balzac's narrator, the meeting-point or mediator of these particular oppositions, fancifully indulges in this substituting tendency: "on my right," he comments in lexia 12, "the dark and silent image of death; on my left, the seemly bacchanalias of life"; and in lexia 13 he adds: "With my left foot I beat time, and I felt as though the other were in the grave." The narrator of this very readerly story has already begun to structure this symbolic grouping, to determine the movement of these oppositions in a particular direction. Barthes leaves them undetermined; "the main task," he says, "is always to demonstrate that this field [i.e., the "field of symbol," as he prefers to call the symbolic code] can be entered from any number of points, thereby making depth and secrecy problematic" (*S/Z*, p. 19).

Barthes does, however, point out three principal entrances to this field: "the route of antithesis" (an introduction to which appears in the antithetical elements of the word "daydream" in lexia 2), "the route of castration," and "the economic route." In all three, there is a "transgression" of meaning: in antithesis, because there is a bringing together of terms whose meaning keeps them separate; in castration, because there is a negation of sexual difference; and in money (Barthes means bourgeois money), because it has been removed from its origin (and no longer determines a specific quantity of work)—it has become, in other words, a sign, and is therefore subject to an interminable exchange between its signifier and signified. Remove the wall which separates and gives meaning to things, and they become problematic.

Barthes identifies another code in the second lexia, a code of actions to which he gives the Aristotelian name for "the ability rationally to determine the result of an action," *proairesis* (*S/Z*, p. 18). Like the hermeneutic code, the proairetic is a linear code; its elements, syntagmatically arranged, impel the reader forward, to the end of the readerly text. Here, however, the readerly momentum is incited not by a quest (the need to answer or solve a riddle), but by a need to name. Actions, experience teaches us, have consequences, and, as readers, we have learned (Barthes makes the Aristotelian proairesis more an empirical than a rational ability) that a particular element in a story will constitute a sequence with another when we attach a generic name to it. To read a narrative, then, is to proceed from name to name. Thus, in the second lexia, "I was deep in . . ." is *to be absorbed*, a state, Barthes says, that "already implies . . . some event which will bring it to an end—i.e., *to be roused by a conversation*, which takes place in lexia 14.

Lexia 3, the remainder of the first sentence of the story (". . . which overtake even the shallowest of men, in the midst of the most tumultuous parties"), includes both a second instance of the semic code—a party given in a fashionable section of Paris constitutes the signifier *Wealth*—and an instance of the "cultural" or "reference" code, a general designation for a variety of voices which give the discourse "a basis in scientific or moral authority" (*S/Z*, p. 18). Balzac's first sentence refers to a body of "accepted" knowledge, "a kind of scientific vulgate," as Barthes puts it. What, for example, do we know about tumultuous parties? That they are ultimately the most boring. Hence the proverbial law: *"Tumultuous parties: deep daydreams"* (*S/Z*, p. 18). There is a proverbial ring to many of the utterances of culture, the most natural sounding voices of the "classical" text. And yet, these codes are "entirely derived from books"; by that "swivel characteristic of bourgeois ideology, which turns culture into nature, [they] appear to establish reality, 'Life'" (*S/Z*, p. 206).

Thus, lexia by lexia, Barthes produces his "reading" of "Sarrasine," lingering for as long as is necessary to mark and classify the forms (or codes) by which various "senses" or meanings are set in motion. The analysis, in other words, concerns itself not with the product, but the process of signification, not with structure, but with "structuration." Another way to put this is to say that the analysis is a *producing of a text*. We must understand here that Barthes uses the word *text* in a special sense. It does not refer to the unified object of reading (as in "Please turn to chapter ten of the text"); such objects are "works" in his critical vocabulary. A *work* is a product; it originates with an "author" *(écrivant)*, and closes on a signified or meaning. A *text* is not an object at all ("the work can be held in the hand," Barthes explains: "the text is held in language"); "*text is experienced only in an activity of production*" (*IMT*, p. 157); it is the field in which signifiers *play*, and there is no end to their play. Text must therefore be identified as an imagined space where the process of its production occurs, i.e., as the network created by the codes through which the text-to-be passes. Barthes uses the word *writer (écrivain)*—a generalized term in comparison to the paternalistic "author"—when he speaks of *text*, for *writing* implies an interest in language for its own sake rather than in the particular end to which a *user* (a speaker or "author") puts it. But since a text is not a product, its production does not end with the efforts of its writer; its production is repeated again and again— and no doubt repeated differently—by each of its readers. A text, Barthes says, is "articulated with society, [with] History."[6] Hence the importance of the codes, those "associative fields" comprised of the messages of other texts.

III   *To Read the "Text"*

It appears that Barthes has always been moving toward these conceptions of *text* and *code* and intertextuality. From the beginning we have noticed his tendency to distance the writer from what he writes. Who or what produces the sense of literature? Neither an author nor a narrator, Barthes argued in *Writing Degree Zero*, but a "writing" (an *écriture*), i.e., a set of conventions common to a particular era or genre or social group which contributed its meaning to a work without an author's knowing it (the "classical") or in spite of his effort to remain free of it (the "modern"). Lost along with the author as the origin of meaning was the concept of the work as the location of meaning. The essays of the mid-1960s reflect Barthes's interest in the modern speech habit of using the verb *to write* intransitively, as in answering the question: "What is so-and-so-doing?" one might say: "Oh, he's writing." Not: "he's writing a novel"—simply "writing." Thus, in the last of the *Collected Essays,* a series of responses to a questionnaire in *Tel Quel* (1963), Barthes concluded: "to write (in the curiously intransitive sense of the term) is an act which transcends the work; to write is precisely to be willing to see the world transform into dogmatic discourse a language one has nevertheless chosen (if one is a writer) as the depositary of a meaning; to write is to permit others to conclude one's own discourse, and writing is only a *proposition* whose answer one never knows" (*CE,* pp. 278–79). In a paper read at Johns Hopkins University in 1966, Barthes modified this linguistic example, arguing now that the critical distinction to be made in the use of the verb *to write* concerns the opposition not of transitivity and intransitivity, but of particular forms of the active and middle voice. Traditionally, he argues, the verb *to write* was active, implying an action accomplished "outside the subject" or speaker since the subject is unaffected by the action; but today (and this in turn is illustrated in modern writing), this verb frequently assumes a middle state; "the subject affects himself in acting"; he "is immediately contemporary with the writing, being effected and affected by it."[7]

In *S/Z* the problem of writing has become a concern with the reader rather than the writer. The older institutional sense of "writing" is now conceived of as a field consisting of the fragments of all that has ever been read. This intertextual dimension of the codes is like a dictionary; we look to it for the meaning of a word, and find that meaning given in other words whose meanings are given by still others. To write, then—even to attempt to "express oneself"—is to appeal to this dictionary. But if "writing" has stilled the voice of the author, if the only voice that speaks is one or more of the codes, then the role of the reader and the critic must change; so Barthes had argued in his debate with Raymond Picard. Because "authors" begin with signifieds or meanings, interpretation has traditionally been a search for the author, the supposed point of origin of the text: find the author, and "explain" the text, for the author "impose[s] a limit on that text . . . furnish[es] it with a final signified," in short, closes it (*IMT,* p. 147). But remove the author—and with him the text as traditionally conceived—and interpretation becomes futile.

In an essay called "The Death of the Author," published in 1968, Barthes defines writing as the "neutral, composite, oblique space where our subject slips away, the negative where all identity is lost . . ." (*IMT,* p. 142). The "voice" of the "work" has become the plurality of voices of the text, no one of which sounds more important or authentic than another. The point of origin is no longer the writing, but the reading: thus, for Barthes, the critic writes his reading. "There is one place," he says, "where this multiplicity [of voices] is focused and that place is the reader, not, as was hitherto said, the author. . . . a text's unity lies not in its origin but in its destination" (*IMT,* p. 148). In *S/Z* this "written-reading" is described as a braiding process: "The grouping of the codes, as they enter into the work, into the movement of the reading, constitute [sic] a braid (*text, fabric, braid:* the same thing); each thread, each code, is a voice; these braided—or braiding—voices form the writing" (*S/Z,* p. 160). As far as "Sarrasine" is concerned, writing is active—"it acts for the reader"; but this writing proceeds from a *"public scribe,"* not from an author—from "a notary institutionally responsible for registering at his [reader's] dictation the summary of his interests, the operations by which, within an economy of disclosure, he manages this merchandise: the narrative" (*S/Z,* p. 152).

This does not mean, as Picard had charged, that a literary work can mean anything a reader wishes it to mean. On the contrary, that sort of willful reading is much more likely to occur in traditional interpretation, where the critic's selective use of a work confirms his "hunch" about its meaning. For Barthes, the critic does not decipher a text—for him, there is no single voice leading to a meaning. Criticism is the unraveling of the braided voices that traverse what is read. True, the voices or codes—the beginnings of an "intertextuality" which relates a particular text to a universe of other texts—are unlimited, infinite; but that does not make an analysis that attempts to trace them unsystematic—no more than (to use Barthes's image) the "running" of a thread in a silk stocking is unsystematic. On the contrary, Barthes maintains, "the *unravelled* character of the codes is . . . the *integrating part of structuration*" and the "fundamental affirmation of textual analysis." Language, Barthes reminds us, "is at once infinite and structured."[8] Neither is the traditional reproach of subjectivity warranted here. The subject of the reader is not a personal plenitude whose foreignness corrupts the purity of the text; this "I" (just like the writer's "I") is "already itself a plurality of other texts, of codes"; its plenitude is "the wake of all the codes which constitute me, so that my subjectivity has ultimately the generality of stereotypes" (*S/Z,* p. 10).

Properly understood, subjectivity is intertextuality, and "what makes the text is the intertextual."[9]

Our partial familiarity with the ideas of text and code under the older name of "writing" (and of *intertextuality* under that of "institution") should not, however, cause us to diminish the significance of *S/Z* as a turning point in Barthes's work and in modern criticism generally. As we have already noticed, French Structuralism was undergoing revision in the pages of the journal *Tel Quel* and the works of Jacques Lacan and Jacques Derrida even as its earliest formulation was being enthusiastically received in England and America. As Julia Kristeva has said, "semiotics cannot develop except as a critique of semiotics . . . [it] discovers nothing at the end of its quest but its own ideological moves, so as to take cognizance of them, to deny them, and to start anew."[10] This critical reflexiveness of all sign-based thinking accounts for Barthes's unwillingness to update the demystification of contemporary "myths" in the 1970 edition of *Mythologies*, for his halfhearted release of the long-worked-on analysis of fashion, as well as for the remarkable departures in method found in *S/Z*. Those earlier efforts were now seen by him as a "euphoric dream of scientificity."

The early enthusiasm for Structuralism is understandable: it promised nothing less than a scientific analysis of the concept of "the human." Since all social practices take place in language, and since language is accessible to scientific study, it should be possible "to consider language as the place in which the social individual is constructed. In other words, as Coward and Ellis go on to summarize the argument, "man can be seen *as language*, as the intersection of the social, historical and individual. . . . Such a consideration can only lead to a demystification of the complex and imprecise realm of the 'human'."[11] To the extent that early semiological analysis revealed the ideological basis of all signification, Structuralism did demystify "the human." But what it only gradually came to recognize was that this demystification was itself taken over by ideology; Structuralism had begun—in typical scientific fashion—by ignoring its own linguistic being, by assuming that its analytic metalanguage was merely an instrument for unmasking hidden meanings in an object language.

Barthes had been aware of this danger as early as the *Elements of Semiology*, where he warned that every "science, including of course semiology . . . contain[s] the seeds of its own death, in the shape of the language destined to speak [or explain] it," and went on to caution the semiologist against overconfidence in exposing connotation (*ES*, p. 93). The same point is made at the end of *Système de la mode*, written, let us remember, between 1957 and 1963: "the day will inevitably come when structural analysis will pass to the rank of the object-language and be absorbed into a superior system which will explain it in turn." Barthes calls this characteristic "Heracleitean" (a reference to that pre-Socratic doctrine of a unity of language and the world determined by universal law); an inevitable moment comes in human knowledge when "by its object it is condemned to identify truth with language," and it is this "necessity which structuralism precisely tries to understand . . ." (*SM*, p. 293).

By 1967 Barthes had reached that understanding. In an essay called "Science versus Literature," published the year before he began the preliminary work for *S/Z*, he observed that the structural study of literature "will be just one more 'science'" if it does not "manage to place the actual subversion of scientific language at the centre of its programme"—that is, if it does not recognize that what it finds in literature cannot be separated from its own analytic language: "How could [Structuralism] . . . fail to question the very language it uses in order to know language?" Barthes now wondered. "The logical continuation of structuralism can only be to rejoin literature, no longer as an 'object' of analysis but as the activity of writing, to do away with the distinction derived from logic which turns the work itself into a language-object and science into a meta-language . . ."[12] The structural analysis must "write itself"; hence *the writing of reading* which is *S/Z*.

CHAPTER 6

An Erotics of Literature

I "*Jouissance*"

WE HAVE learned by now that Barthes is distrustful of smooth transitions, that he finds pleasure in the spaces created by gaps and junctures, and that when, in his reading, he deals with a work ("Sarrasine," for instance) that leaves few spaces unfilled, he creates gaps in it himself by cutting it up into fragments. The Structuralist, we will recall, also began by cutting up the text he analyzed; but for him, "dissection" was a purely functional technique, the means (together with "articulation") of deriving the significant units of a narrative *langue*. The lexias of textual analysis are also significant units, textual signifiers; they differ, however, from the units of structural analysis in that they belong to discourse, not language, and, therefore, they are arrived at without the guidance of corresponding divisions in the signified. Lexic division, we have seen, is "purely empirical." Barthes created a lexia of "Sarrasine" wherever he *felt* the text was escaping him in several directions—i.e., at the point of the shifting of two or more languages or codes. From the point of view of textual theory, cutting, interrupting the flow of discourse, creates edges—one, a conformist edge, the language as culture decrees its use, the other, a subversive edge, the violation of convention—and it is in the seam or fault created by these edges, Barthes maintains, that signification can occur. This seam is also the "site of pleasure" in the text: "Is not the most erotic portion of a body *where the garment gapes?*" he asks, "the intermittence of skin flashing between two articles of clothing . . . it is this flash itself which seduces."[1] Variations in the way two readers divide the same text do not, then, invalidate the theory of textual analysis: on the contrary, as we shall see, they constitute its validation.

It is important to reemphasize this element of free play in Barthes's criticism, particularly in view of the systematic rigor of a study like S/Z, and it is well to note that Barthes regards the period in which he was engaged in this work as "perhaps the densest and happiest of my working life," an experience that represented for him, "above everything else, a pleasure, a delight *(jouissance)* in work and writing."[2] Thus far, we have accounted for the distinctive features of Barthes's criticism on generally philosophical and political grounds; in the works since *S/Z*, however, this word *jouissance* recurs with sufficient frequency to be taken as no less a justifying (if not a motivating) principle. In his translation of Barthes's *The Pleasure of the Text* (1973) Richard Miller has tried to render the sexual connotation of *jouissance* (after all, one cannot very well use "'coming,' which precisely translates what the original text can afford"[3]) with the English word *bliss*. Some such active term is necessary since Barthes opposes *jouissance* to *plaisir* ("pleasure"), a passive state. Barthes recognizes that what he needs here is a third term which French (and English) lacks, one "that simultaneously covers pleasure (contentment) and bliss (rapture)"; without such a term, the word "pleasure" must sometimes (as in the title of the book) include "bliss," and at other times be opposed to it. "I cannot avoid this ambiguity," Barthes explains, "because I cannot cleanse the word 'pleasure' of meanings I occasionally do not want" *(PT,* p. 19).

As we discuss *The Pleasure of the Text,* we will not be able to avoid this ambiguity either. Provisionally at least, we must accept his distinction between the text of pleasure and the text of bliss. The former is "the text that contents, fills, grants euphoria . . . that comes from culture and does not break with it, is linked to a *comfortable* practice of reading: the text of pleasure is often a product of the "classical," the mythological, the readerly. The text of bliss, on the other hand, is that which "imposes a state of loss, the text that discomforts (perhaps to the point of a certain boredom), unsettles the reader's historical, cultural, psychological assumptions, the consistency of his tastes, values, memories, brings to a crisis his relation with language"; the text of bliss is often the experience of the "modern," the writerly *(PT,* p. 14). Barthes provides a second distinction drawn from psychoanalysis: "pleasure can be expressed in words, bliss cannot"; bliss "causes the letter—and all possible speech—to collapse . . . [whereas] the writer of pleasure (and his reader) accepts the letter . . . the letter is his pleasure; he is obsessed by it" *(PT,* p. 21).

A criticism of *jouissance,* one that is based upon the principle of pleasure in the text is a daring, perhaps a utopian endeavor. Traditionally, criticism has been a comfort and reassurance to its readers to the degree that it has been *serious;* light-hearted, pleasurable criticism is suspect, thought to be untrustworthy. The traditional critic's pleasure in a text, regarded as a "subjectivity," must not be allowed to taint his "reading" of the work, must be kept in its place, and that place may be the past or the future—but not the present. I may speak *about* a pleasure *(plaisir)* I have enjoyed, or *about* one I anticipate, but I simply cannot speak *about* my present bliss without changing its nature: bliss can only be experienced. (We should now be able to appreciate the sexual connotation of Barthes's term *jouissance:* one cannot speak the bliss of orgasm; one can only speak *about* its pleasure.) But is a criticism of *jouissance* possible then? Certainly not as any recognizable criticism, one that aims at ordering and explaining a work. "With the writer of bliss (and his reader) begins the untenable text, the impossible text," Barthes writes. "This text is outside pleasure, outside criticism, *unless it is reached through another text of bliss:* you cannot speak 'on' such a text, you can only speak 'in' it, *in its fashion,* enter into a desperate plagiarism, hysterically affirm the void of bliss (and no longer obsessively repeat the letter of [mere] pleasure)" *(PT,* p. 22).

II *Japan as Text*

We may perhaps come closer to the pleasure that Barthes finds in emptiness by looking for a moment at a book he published in 1970 called *L'empire des signes.* The "empire of signs" is Japan, a country Barthes visited in 1966, but less, he says, as a tourist than as "a reader." The point is that Japan is for him "the country of writing" *(écriture,* not *écrivance),* the country in which he has encountered "the sign-work closest to his own convictions or phantasms, [and] . . . farthest from the loathing and irritation and denial that the Occidental semiocracy stirs in him."[4] Barthes's "loathing" or "disgust" or "nausea" is by now a familiar strain; it is aroused by the duplicity of Western modes of signification; by the priority they accord to meaning (signifieds), and by their preference for the hidden interiors over the visible exteriors of signs. All this is reversed, Barthes tells us, in Japan, which is a land of signifiers, not signifieds. The observation applies not only to Japanese calligraphy. Barthes thinks of all Japan (Japan as culture) as a "system," a language; what he encounters there, then, are things in *their written situation,* present only as surfaces, without secrets, signifying nothing—gratifying simply in themselves, like the Zen *satori (ES,* p. 99).

The wrapping of a Japanese parcel, for example, is not "the transitory accessory of the transported object"; it "becomes itself the object; the envelope itself is consecrated as a precious thing, however gratuitous; the packet is a thought" (*ES*, p. 61). Barthes finds a similar preoccupation with surface in the *haiku*, which is not, as Western readers believe, an exercise in concision (i.e., "of shortening the signifier without diminishing the density of the signified); just the opposite is true: the "technical" pains that the *haiku* demands of its writer (a "solicitude" that is inconceivable in the West, Barthes maintains) prevents the interiorization of meaning. "The *haiku* is not a rich thought reduced to a brief form," he says; it is "a brief event that finds in a stroke its just form"; its rhetoric functions to create a disproportion between the signifier and the signified—another Western impropriety (*ES*, p. 101). Japan is filled with such *haiku* forms: the flowerless gardens of neatly raked sand and rocks (no messages there!), the city of Tokyo itself, the map of which depicts a center, but a center that is empty, merely a hole—the residence of an emperor whom no one sees, i.e., whom no one knows: "a sacred nothing" (*ES*, pp. 44–46); the elaborate ritual of bowing which is unencumbered by a respect for any inner personality (*ES*, pp. 85–90). Barthes finds even an "anatomical calligraphy" of the Japanese face. "The Occidental eye [deep-set in its socket] is subject to a whole mythology of the soul"; the Japanese eye, flush to the face, is "the empty form of pleasure," a *gap* between two edges (*ES*, p. 134–38).

L'empire des signes may be Barthes's most appealing (it is unquestionably—in its superb printing by the house of Skira—the most beautiful) presentation of his post-Structuralist thought. Persuasiveness, however, does not guarantee "truth." What would an expert on Japan say about the book? Does it matter that the claim that the *haiku* does not "mean" anything is made by one who cannot read Japanese, or that the "language" he does "read" is, on the grounds of common sense, untenable since it is at once intelligible and meaningless? For Barthes, such questions miss the point. It is his ignorance of the superficial structure of Japanese that allows him to descend to the deeper, untranslatable system he calls "Japan"; his foreignness is the fulfillment of a "dream": "to be aware of a foreign (strange) language and yet not to understand it" (*ES*, p. 13). Barthes's "Japan" cannot be understood in the way one understands Japanese; its signs are empty; they signify nothing—not even *an absence of meaning*. The reading of "Japan," then, is literally a dream, since, for Barthes, "Dreaming allows for, supports, releases, brings to light an extreme delicacy of

moral, sometimes even metaphysical, sentiments, the subtlest sense
of human relations, refined differences, a learning of the highest
civilization, in short a conscious logic . . . dreaming makes *everything in me which is not strange, foreign,* speak" (*PT,* pp. 59–60). In
other words, *L'empire des signes* is itself a text of *jouissance.*

III   The Pleasure of the Text *as a Text of "Pleasure"*

Barthes's *Pleasure of the Text* is another instance of this sort of text,
one that speaks *in* rather than on bliss. Consider the form of the book:
a succession of forty-six fragmentary essays or, as he calls them,
"phylacteries," arranged alphabetically (i.e., arbitrarily) by index
terms ("Affirmation," "Babel" to "Voice") in order to avoid coherence, which promises, in readerly fashion, the *pleasure* of closure.
(An index is itself a text, Barthes has said, a second text which is the
"remainder" of a first text; it is "what is wandering (interrupted) in the
rationality of the sentences of the first."[5] Thus, what is intelligible in
The Pleasure of the Text (and this is also its bliss) is each of its moments
or fragments, not their duration in a temporal-logical connection with
one another, an observation Barthes had also made in *Mythologies* in
discussing the pleasure of watching wrestling matches. Or consider
(as if one had to be told to) the language of the book, its diction. Here
is a bit from the section indexed "War" (i.e., the war of languages):

> Still far too much heroism in our languages; in the best—I am thinking of
> Bataille's—an erethism of certain expressions and finally a kind of *insidious
> heroism.* The pleasure of the text (the bliss of the text) is on the contrary like a
> sudden obliteration of the warrior *value,* a momentary desquamation of the
> warrior's hackles, a suspension of the "heart" (of courage). (*PT,* p. 30)

The point here is not that Barthes is an indulgent stylist or that he
has not forgotten his early medical studies ("erethism," "desquamation"), but that he has managed to transmute the state of his language
(from a transparent instrument of communication to an opaque substance), to place language "outside origin and outside communication." He has made it a writing. A word, if it is sufficiently unexpected
("hackles") or extravagant ("desquamation")—if it is "succulent in its
newness," as Barthes puts it—sets itself apart from its neighbors, and
thus becomes "erotic." Nausea occurs whenever the liason of two
important words *follows of itself,*" he says. "And when something
follows of itself, I abandon it: that is bliss" (*PT,* p. 43). Or finally,

consider again the ambiguity of the terms *pleasure* and *bliss:* "there will always be a margin of indecision about them," Barthes happily acknowledges; thus their meaning will be "precarious, revocable, reversible, the discourse incomplete." The writer of *jouissance* takes as his motto: *"never apologize, never explain";* and the reader who is tolerant of logical contradiction and self-contradiction, who accepts "the cohabitation of [different] languages *working side by side* gains access to bliss." "The text of pleasure [or is it the text of bliss?] is a sanctioned Babel" (*PT*, p. 3–4).

Let us take another look at this Babel of languages in the text of *jouissance.* We have said that such pleasure is found in the fault created by two "edges," a conformist and a subversive edge. The "cut" is in fact a "redistribution"of language; the edges, then, are different codes or languages. Pleasure does not emanate from one or the other of these; "neither culture nor its destruction is erotic," Barthes explains; "it is the seam between them . . . which becomes so" (*PT*, p. 70). This is why we should not think of bliss as an effect of style; it occurs always *in the space between* language, in that instant of a revoked decorum, for example, which is neither decorous nor its revocation, nor quite the blending of the two. Bliss is the realization of the impossible, like that "purely *novelistic* instant so relished by Sade's libertine when he manages to be hanged and then to cut the rope at the very moment of his orgasm, his bliss" (*PT*, p. 7).

Given this hazardous mode of existence of *jouissance* and, for Barthes, the equally hazardous job of invoking it again in another text of bliss, it should not be surprising that the reader of *The Pleasure of the Text,* expecting a gradual sharpening of thought, definition, classification—the signifieds of criticism—experiences a disappointment, a sense of loss. This effect is not due to a weakness of the book; it is its bliss. But what Barthes has left open, some of his readers have closed. As Jonathan Culler has observed, the distinction between the text of pleasure and the text of bliss "has been so central to structuralist work on the novel that . . . it threatens to establish a distorted opposition which would seriously hamper our work on the novel."[6] The distortion to which Culler refers is a consequence of disregarding the ambiguity of the distinction, the site of its bliss, of attempting to make an absolute classification of its terms. Such a reader considers himself the "confidant," perhaps even the advocate of Barthes's pleasure. But this is a sure way to miss it, Barthes says; one must instead become the "voyeur" of his pleasure: one must "observe clandestinely" the critic's pleasure; one must "enter perversion";

then, to such a voyeur, the criticism becomes "a text, a fiction, a fissured envelope" (*PT*, p. 17). The "argument" of *The Pleasure of the Text* is not, in other words, the content of the book; it is the quality of our experience in reading it. Barthes's writing doubles the pleasure or "perversity" of the texts he speaks of (perversity because "pleasure" in writing is *without function*"); our pleasure in reading Barthes trebles it (*PT*, p. 17).

The temptation to reduce Barthes's blissful ambiguity to a merely comfortable classification (e.g., bliss exists *only* in "modern" texts; "classic" works give us *only* pleasure) is strong because we can in fact trace the structure of such a classification in *The Pleasure of the Text*, also perhaps because we know that Barthes has been an enthusiastic champion of Modernism. Barthes even articulates this interpretation of his text: ". . . if I say that between pleasure and bliss there is only a difference of degree, I am also saying that the text of bliss is merely the logical, organic, historical development of the text of pleasure; the avant-garde is never anything but the progressive, emancipated form of past culture . . ." (*PT*, p. 20). But the structure of this classification inverted is also present in the text, and let us not forget that Barthes spoke of his work on Balzac's "Classic" story as an experience of *jouissance*. This interpretation is also articulated in *The Pleasure of the Text:* ". . . if I believe . . . that pleasure and bliss are parallel forces, that they cannot meet, and that between them there is more than a struggle: an *incommunication*, then I must certainly believe that history, our history, is not peaceable and perhaps not even intelligent, that the text of bliss always rises out of it like a scandal (an irregularity) . . ." (*PT*, p. 20).

These two interpretations are absolutely contrary to one another, yet coexistent in *The Pleasure of the Text*. If one of them *pleases* me more than the other, I must be prepared, if I am to experience the bliss of Barthes's text to lose it when it collides with its contrary. The reader or "subject" who can keep in his hands "the reins of [both] pleasure and bliss is an anachronic subject, for he simultaneously and contradictorily participates in the profound hedonism of all culture . . . and in the destruction of that culture: he enjoys the consistency of his selfhood (that is his pleasure) and seeks its loss (that is his bliss)" (*PT*, p. 14). Barthes's witty description of his critical position (in 1971)—"the rear-guard of the avant-garde": continuing, that is, to like what he knew was dead[7]—locates himself at this precise point of critical vantage.

To assent to what Barthes is saying in *The Pleasure of the Text* (to assent, that is, as one does to the arguments of academic criticism), the reader no doubt requires some examples at this point. This is asking for the impossible, however. The text, as Barthes conceives of it, is not an object, something that can be relocated in criticism, but an *"absolute flow of becoming,"* like that tree which Nietzsche says "is a new thing at every instant" (*PT*, p. 61). Barthes has no illusions about the "institutional future" of such a criticism of *jouissance;* it will foster no academic concentration, no courses or textbooks. The theory of the text can produce "only theoreticians or practitioners, not specialists" (*PT*, p. 60). Even if one were able to bring together all the texts that have ever given pleasure to someone, "it is to be feared that such a labor would end *explaining* the chosen texts," reducing bliss (in both the text and the reader) to pleasure (*PT*, p. 34). Barthes avoids this danger by *asserting* rather than attempting to reproduce some pleasures (*jouissances*) of the text—but this is done "always in passing, in a very precarious, never regular fashion," merely a *circling* of *jouissance* (*PT*, p. 34). Let us look at a few of these assertions.

The bliss of Severo Sarduy's *Cobra* is asserted as follows: "a kind of Franciscanism invites all words to perch, to flock, to fly off again: a marbled, iridescent text; we are gorged with language, like children who are never refused anything or scolded for anything or, even worse, 'permitted' anything" (*PT*, p. 8). Notice the contradictions here: Sarduy's words perch and flock, but fly off; his text is absolutely permissive, yet withholds all permission. Barthes concludes this remark by saying that "the verbal pleasure [of *Cobra*] chokes and reels into bliss." It is linguistic indulgence and linguistic surfeit (a condition which Barthes's language at times shares with Sarduy's) which constitute the edges between which bliss is experienced. It is this very "two-edgedness" of *Cobra* that protects it from the death-dealing of critical interpretation.

Barthes's texts of bliss manage to escape even such sympathetic criticism. Barthes observes that there are readers "who want a text . : . without a shadow," without ideological contamination, a purely "modern" work, that is; but such readers want "a text without fecundity, without productivity, a sterile text," one that may be reduced to an explanation of its strategy—a text of pleasure, in other words. The text of bliss "needs its shadow . . . a *bit* of ideology, a *bit* of representation, a *bit* of subject" (*PT*, p. 32), even if it must create it itself. In another avant-garde text, Phillippe Soller's *Lois*, for example, "ev-

erything is attacked": "ideological structures, intellectual sol-
idarities, the propriety of idioms," syntax itself; the book is often
nothing more than "a powerful gush of words": a pleasure, perhaps,
but not a bliss—not until another language ("that of (decasyllabic)
meter, of assonance, of plausible neologisms, of prosodic rhythms, of
(quoted) truisms") is deliberately set in its path (*PT*, p. 8).

In "modern" texts bliss is earned at a higher cost than in "classical"
texts, for if bliss depends upon a break with "the consistent language," then the "modern" text, which usually starts from a subversion of consistency, must guard against becoming consistent in its
subversiveness, must break with itself in order to create that "site of
loss" in which Barthes locates bliss. The "modern" writer, in other
words, may have to create the substance of both of the needed edges
of bliss. For the "classical" writer, however, the substance of one edge
is always provided, and if he is sufficiently conscious of this language
the opportunity to break with it (to "edge" it) is always present. Thus
Barthes describes Flaubertian bliss as "a way of cutting, of perforat-
ing discourse *without rendering it* meaningless," and concludes:
"never have the two edges of the seam been clearer and more
tenuous, never has pleasure *(jouissance)* been better offered to the
reader" (*PT*, p. 9).

But Flaubert is probably a special case (it is difficult to tell in fact
whether Barthes cites him here as a "classical" or a "modern" writer).
The edges of "classical" narrative (Barthes mentions the novels of
Zola, Balzac, Dickens, Tolstoy) are in general not as deep as those we
have so far noticed; it is the reader who creates them in the varying
pace of his reading: "we boldly skip certain passages ["descriptions,
explanations, analyses, conversations"] in order to get more quickly
to the warmer parts of the anecdote" (*PT*, p. 11). Thus it is the
alternation of what is read and what is not read that constitutes the
edges of such narratives—their pleasure. Nevertheless, there is a
bliss that is "the formidable underside" of all writing. Barthes backs
up this assertion by giving a new twist to an argument of ideological
analysis we first met in *Writing Degree Zero*. Since the "official"
language at any time (the "sociolect," or "encratic" language) is one
that is "produced and spread under the protection of power," it is a
langue that alienates. Literature, Barthes argues, is always written
by "a socially disappointed or powerless group" which escapes alienation by *retreating ahead* of this language, i.e., by refusing to repeat its
"stereotypes," thus reproducing "in historical terms the bliss re-
pressed beneath the stereotype," and making possible an eruption of

bliss "across the centuries, out of certain texts that were nonetheless written to the glory of the dreariest, of the most sinister philosophy" (*PT*, pp. 39, 40–41).

IV *The Text as Body*

Barthes's reference to dreary and sinister philosophies may quite possibly be a recollection of the studies he had made of the Jesuit saint Ignatius Loyola, of the utopian social reformer François Fourier, and of the libertine Marquis de Sade, which he published together under the title *Sade/Fourier/Loyola* in 1971. A most heterogeneous trio: nevertheless, Barthes makes the claim that there is in all three "the same sensual pleasure in classification, the same mania for cutting up ["the body of the victim," "the human soul," "the body of Christ"], the same erotic, fantasmatic fashioning of the social system."[8] Each, that is, was the founder of a language, a "logothete." Since three of the four essays in *Sade/Fourier/Loyola* were originally published between 1967 and 1970, and the fourth ("Sade II," which foreshadows the fragmented mode of writing "in bliss" encountered in *The Pleasure of the Text)* appeared there for the first time, the book has a transitional character. Like the Structuralist works that preceded it ("Introduction to the Structural Analysis of Narrative" and *Système de la mode)*, it sets forth the outlines of three *langues* drawn from the *paroles* of Sadian erotics, Fourierist "passion," and Ignatian "indifference"; but now these languages are viewed in the light of the semiological definition of the text.

"Nothing," Barthes states in the preface to the book, "is more depressing than to imagine the Text as an intellectual object (for reflection, analysis, comparison, mirroring, etc.)"; it is "an object of pleasure"—"any form of text is always only the ritual that orders pleasure" (*SFL*, pp. 7, 5). The subject (of the author, of the reader) has been reintroduced here, and with him his *jouissance*. This does not mean, of course, that Barthes's concept of *jouissance* is identifiable with the ecstatic vision of the saint, the enthusiasm of the reformer, or the vicarious thrill of the pornographer. "The text of bliss is never the text that recounts the kind of bliss afforded literally by ejaculation," he wrote in *The Pleasure of the Text* (p. 55); pornographic books do not represent "the erotic scene," but "the preparation for it, its ascent; that is what makes them 'exciting'": they are "books of Desire, not of Pleasure" (*PT*, p. 58). The pleasures (in the all-inclusive

sense) of the texts of Sade, Fourier, and Loyola are not the pleasures
(in the narrow sense) of sadism, utopia, and religion, "but merely
their happiness of writing": "I listen to the message's transport, not
the message," Barthes explained (*SFL*, p. 10).

And yet it is the presence of what Barthes can only call "body" in
these texts that is important for the theory of *jouissance* set forth in
The Pleasure of the Text; it is as "body" that the subject, after its
Structuralist alienation, is readmitted into this criticism: "What we
are seeking to establish," Barthes writes here, "is a theory of the
materialist subject" (*PT*, p. 61)—hence the subject as body. For
Barthes, "body" and "text" are equivalent; their relationship becomes clear when we think of *body* as a metaphor. According to
Barthes, we have at least two bodies, i.e., two sorts of texts; one is the
body that science deals with, corresponding to the "objective" text
(the "pheno-text") of traditional criticism; the other ("utterly distinct
from the first") is the body that psychoanalysis has exhibited, the
"body of bliss," which consists "solely of erotic relations"; this erotic
body corresponds to the text of bliss (the "geno-text") which consists
of nothing more than "the open list of the fires of language (those
living fires, intermittent lights, wandering features strewn in the text
like seeds . . .)" (*PT*, pp. 16–17). At the expense of Barthes's own
blissful description here, we shall say it is the text of edges and seams.
First of all, then, the body-text equivalence is a way of differentiating
two sorts of reading: reading for knowledge (which depends upon a
text that provides us with "names" (meaning); and reading for pleasure (which depends upon a text that is "fragmented into practices,
into words which are not Names," or which have deferred their
signifieds) (*PT*, p. 45).

But there is another sense in which the body and the text are
equivalent, one which emphasizes the material presence of body *in*
the text of bliss. At the end of *The Pleasure of the Text* Barthes asks us
to imagine a sort of "vocal writing," a "writing aloud," the language
of which would be "lined with the flesh" of the subject. The "reader"
of such a text would attend to the "grain of the throat . . . the
voluptuousness of vowels, a whole carnal stereophany." The text
Barthes is speaking of there is not an oral presentation of a written
work, or a passage of writing that manages to reproduce the sounds
and rhythms of speech; it is the "articulation [in writing] of the body,
of the tongue, not that of meaning, of language." We come closest to
this text of the body, Barthes reminds us, in the cinema—in "the
sound of speech *close up.*" Probably everyone has been taken by the

materiality and sensuality of this cinematic sound, by what Barthes has characterized as the "whole presence of the human muzzle" (*PT*, pp. 66–67). In just this way, we are seized by the "grain" of writing when we experience the pleasure of a text.

We may make still a third application of the body-text metaphor. To experience the material pleasure of a text is not, we have seen, to be a consumer, but a producer of that text. The pleasure of the text, then, is the pleasure of the reader *in* the Text, and the "textual Body" is his body. What I encounter in the text that gives me pleasure is "my 'individuality,'" according to Barthes, i.e., "the given which makes my body separate from other bodies": and when, in "producing" the text of pleasure, "I write myself as a subject," it is "my body of bliss I encounter" there (*PT*, pp. 62–63). Indeed, Barthes suggests that the pleasure I experience in the text I produce may be the pleasure I derive from imagining myself as individual (*PT*, p. 62). This idea is worked out in bewildering complexity in *Roland Barthes*, where the reader-author literally creates a fictive identity as he writes himself as a subject; but it is also implicit in remarks made in the preface to *Sade/Fourier/Loyola*. What, after all, does it mean to find pleasure in one of these texts? According to Barthes, the deepest pleasure is achieved when a book "transmigrates into our life," when "the Other's writing . . . succeeds in writing fragments of our own daily lives"—only then, he adds, can we "truly say there is a Text." We take pleasure in the Sadian text—i.e., the Sadian language—not, of course, by practicing sadism ourselves (anymore than "speaking Ignatian" means praying with Loyola), but by "bringing into our daily life the fragments of the unintelligible . . . that eminate from a text we admire . . . because it hangs together well" (*SFL*, p. 7)—that is, we recognize it as "a language truth."

A new word, a coined word, one that we have never heard or seen before (Barthes's writing is filled with them), has no content for us; nevertheless, we still recognize that it is a word; neologism, Barthes has observed, "is an erotic act" (*SFL*, p. 81). To say, then, that Sade, Fourier, and Loyola were founders of languages does not mean that they devised codes which enabled them to say what they could not say before; that would imply that their languages were limited— "finished" instruments of communication. Barthes find pleasure in these logothetes, these texts, for precisely the opposite reason: for *persisting* in the elaboration of the language, for "unlimiting" it; Sade, Fourier, and Loyola "are founders of language, and only that . . . precisely in order to say nothing, to observe a vacancy" (*SFL*, p. 6).

Barthes calls this persistence the "theatricalization" of language, since, thanks to it, a Sade, a Fourier, or a Loyola ceases to be a sadist, a utopian, or a saint, and becomes instead merely "a sceneographer . . . who disperses himself across the framework he sets up and arranges *ad infinitum*" (*SFL*, p. 6). According to Barthes, I do the same thing when I "live" the pleasure of these texts: I "produce" the text in the theater of my daily life, against the background of my own social habitat; I distribute in my "interior time" moments of the textual language I produce (*SFL*, p. 8).

What the reader "lives" in experiencing the pleasure of the text is a fantasy—"a kind of fantasmatic order" (*SFL*, p. 8). It should not, at this point, come as a surprise that Barthes's theory of reading has become, since *S/Z*, explicitly psychoanalytic. Reading has become for him a neurotic act; what else can we call a practice that "splits" its subject—causes him, on the one hand, to enjoy "the consistency of his selfhood" and, on the other, to seek its loss, and in which the text that he reads is "hallucinated" by him? But ordinary reading—that complicity in duplicity which Western ideology promotes—is also an aberration: that reduction to a single meaning which, after his analysis of "Sarrasine," he identified as a *castration* (with all its psychoanalytic implications) of the reader.

Barthes in fact gives us a psychoanalytic classification of readers' pleasures in terms of their relations to texts; the obsessive, the fetishist, the paranoiac, and the hysteric. We have encountered the first of these types in the literalism of the traditional critic, whose obsession with "the letter"—i.e., with language—causes him to repeat the language of the text in his own language. Barthes's relation to the text, by his own diagnosis, is fetishist; he has given up the elaboration of comprehensive structures for a sort of play with the discontinuous and the fragmentary; here, too, perhaps, is the explanation of his preoccupation with the body—or, more precisely, with some *piece* of the body, the definition of a fetish. But is there not something perverse in this deliberate cultivation of a neurosis? Indeed there is; Barthes is not afraid to describe his recent writings as "perversions." The justification for this practice is that the perversion replaces a madness. Neurotic fetishism and its consequent fantasies are necessary, Barthes seems to be saying, as a sort of therapy against the castrating tendencies of Western ideolects. In the "utopia" of signs that Barthes dreams of, such radical therapy would not be necessary. Even in Japan, Barthes's semiological asylum or half-way house between utopia and the Western Semiocracy, fetishism is unnecessary. (We can see this in his comparison of "modern" Western theater and the Japanese puppet theater Bunrake.[9]) In the West, however, every writer's motto needs to be: *"mad I cannot be, sane I do not deign to be, neurotic I am"* (*PT,* p. 6).

CHAPTER 7

Barthes as Text

I Roland Barthes *by Roland Barthes*

R EADERS expecting autobiography in a book by Barthes called
Roland Barthes (1975) are likely to be disappointed—at least if
one takes "autobiography" to mean a writer's narration of and commentary on his own life. True, such a reader will find the book rich in
"personal detail." There are pictures of Barthes as a child and a young
man, of his parents and relatives, and of the cities and streets in which
he has moved. He will learn that Barthes was born a Protestant, that
he suffered early from tuberculosis and suffers now from migraine
headaches, that he is left-handed, paints, plays the piano, smokes a
good deal. He is even confided with a list of things Barthes likes
("too-cold beer, flat pillows . . . all kinds of writing pens . . . realistic
novels . . . Pollock . . . all romantic music . . . the Marx Brothers
. . .") and doesn't like ("women in slacks, geraniums, strawberries
. . . Miro, tautologies, animated cartoons . . . Satie, Bartok . . ."—
RB, pp. 116–17), and with a schedule of his daily activities while on
vacation in the country. Not even Samuel Pepys is, at a stretch, this
rich in triviality.

But that is just the point: Barthes's details are not intended to
produce an image. Normally, biographical discourse comes about in a
sort of "connect the dots" procedure; selected points of importance,
critically "spaced," are joined by lines of biographical significance,
tracing a preexisting image. Barthes's procedure is just the reverse of
this: the things he likes and doesn't like, he says, are "of no importance to anyone"; no image or structure determined their selection:
they "mean" only that *my body is not the same as yours* (*RB*, p.
117). The body is not imagined in Barthes; only a "listless blur" is
produced by the details, "an Anarchic foam of tastes and distastes" to
which our response must be both "complicity" and (if we happen to
be lovers of strawberries and Satie) "liberal" toleration of a contrary
taste. Barthes's aim is *to write* the body.

We know that Barthes has always been critical of the biographical genres, at least as these are conventionally produced, and his judgment on one of their subspecies is stated succinctly in this book: "Self-commentary? What a bore!" (*RB*, p. 142). Common sense tells us that in order to write *about* a "subject," we must first "fix" that subject, assign it a space that "defines" it. But Barthes, drawing now upon the psychoanalytic theories of Jacques Lacan, rejects this view; the subject, he believes, must be conceived of as *a process,* and that process is the process of signification: *"the subject is merely an effect of language"* (*RB*, p. 79). And what of "the literary subject," the author of and in a book? Barthes asks "Can one . . . begin to write without taking oneself for another? . . . I begin producing by reproducing the person I want to be. This first want . . . establishes a secret system of fantasies which persist from age to age, often independently of the writings of the desired author" (*RB*, p. 99). According to such a view, every writer must approach "his own" work as a person other than the one who wrote it—as simply another reader. That is precisely what Barthes is doing in *Roland Barthes*—and then (in case we have still not caught on) goes on to do a second time in a review of *Roland Barthes* called *"Barthes puissance trois"* [Barthes to the Third Power].[1]

It will help, then, in understanding *Roland Barthes,* if we begin by thinking of two Barthes: one is the subject who wrote this book, its author; the other, we must say, is both the object of *this* Barthes's study (appearing as a variety of pronominal "persons" or as "R.B.") and also the subject (or subjects) of the texts that the first Barthes "reads" in order *to rewrite.* The second of these Barthes can only be regarded as a plurality, a composite of works and of physical and emotional states; he is what we have now learned to call the "textual body." To keep things straight, we too shall refer to this textualized Barthes as "R.B." *Roland Barthes,* then, is Barthes's "rewriting" of R.B., much as *S/Z* is a "rewriting" of *Sarrasine.* Indeed, Barthes prefaces his book with a holograph note reminding us that "it must all be considered as if spoken by a character in a novel" (*RB*, p. 1).

Roland Barthes falls into two distinct parts: first, an "image repertoire" consisting of thirty-seven pages of photographs with captions (of Barthes from age eight to twenty-seven and of his world in those years), and second, after five pages of transition, a "repertoire of writing," an arbitrary (roughly alphabetical) arrangement of verbal fragments (similar to the "phylacteries" of *The Pleasure of the Text*), loosely related to the man and his works—i.e., to the "body." We know, from Barthes's analysis of a realistic story like *Sarrasine*, what he thinks of the *represented* body; we know that the only body that interests him is that which he calls "the erotic body," the textual body that implants its own desire in its reader. Now, since Barthes produced no "texts" in his first twenty-seven years, it is impossible for him to "rewrite" this body, and his "only biography" of this "unproductive life" must be a narrative of images (photographs), "figurations of the body's pre-history—of the body making its way toward the labor and the pleasure of writing" (*RB*, p. 3). The image repertoire of the book closes with Barthes's departure from the Sanatorium des Étudiants in 1942, marked by a photograph of his fever chart for March and April ("a farcical way of writing one's body within time," he notes), and by a portrait of himself at age twenty-seven, contrasted with another taken at age fifty-five. Apropos of the earlier portrait, Barthes supplies the following mock-dialogue: "'But I never looked like that'—How do you know? What is the 'you' you might or might not look like? . . . Where is your authentic body? You are the only one who can never see yourself except as an image . . . even and especially for your own body, you are condemned to the repertoire of its images" (*RB*, pp. 35–36).

Barthes, we know, does not much like images—they are part of the bourgeois obsession with naming and adjectivizing things—and he is particularly "troubled by any image of himself." (In this connection he cites as "a triumph of civilization" and "the truly dialectical form of erotic discourse," his imagelessness in the un-Westernized society he encountered in Morocco—*RB*, p. 43.) But the photographs that comprise the image repertoire of this book manage to escape this general condemnation; the reason is that they were chosen by Barthes because of the mysterious "fascination" they hold for him. That three-year-old in the large sombrero on a beach at Ciboure (in whom the author reads "quite openly the dark underside of myself"), or the four-year-old in bangs and a skirt identified as a contemporary of Proust's!—these are not images of Barthes for any reader; indeed, they can be such for Barthes alone, and for reasons he cannot explain: at best, they are images of only a "disturbing familiarity," he says, "both highly indiscreet (it is my body from underneath which is presented) and quite discreet (the photograph presented is not of 'me')" (*RB*, p. 3). The photographs in the book are redeemed, then, by their candid imaginariness. We might say that they have been *denaturalized*, since they no longer serve as an "alibi" of "reality." They are simply a source of pleasure for Barthes—"without my knowing why," he says, adding as a further warning to the reader that "what I shall say about each image will never be anything but . . . imaginary" (*RB*, p. 3).

But the problem of the imaginary—the difficulty of resisting the temptation to say to the reader "This is R.B." (or to oneself "This is me")—this intrusion of the "individual" (i.e., the imaginary) does not end with the "image-repertoire" of the book. Even though, as Barthes says, the Text takes his body "far from my imaginary person," and even though, to display the repertoire of writing, the Text cannot be "validated [or] justified by the representation of an individual," he cannot, simply by willing it, succeed completely in ridding his writing of the imaginary.

This difficulty is pointedly addressed in an interesting fragment called "The image-system of solitude," in which Barthes observes that R.B. feels now that he "writes more openly" than he formerly did, outside "the aegis of a great system"; "nothing sustains him" now except those "patches" of language that constitute an inter-text. "He [R.B.] says this," we are told, "without the infatuation which may accompany all declarations of independence . . . but rather in order to account to himself for the feeling of insecurity which possesses him today and . . . the vague torment of a *recession* toward . . . the old thing he is when 'left to himself.'—So you make a declaration of humility," Barthes remarks; "you still don't escape the image-system for all that . . . by a reversal you had not forseen and which you would readily overlook, you attest to the accuracy of your diagnostic: indeed, you *retrogress*" (*RB*, p. 102). The "great systems" of his past have merely been replaced by a psychological image-system. The imaginary in the form of some image-system of R.B. (*R.B. as a preexisting signified*) steals into the writing in spite of the author's efforts to banish it—by way of the reader if by no other, and in this book that means by way of Barthes the author. Barthes is acutely aware of this impasse: at the end of the fragment just cited, he comments, "But in saying as much, I [i.e., Barthes, the author] escape . . . etc. (the ladder continues)." The parenthesis, of course, makes the claim to have escaped ironical. Barthes's efforts to escape the imaginary, like R.B.'s, merely "project the image further along"—leave us with a more singular and more "natural" image: *the one who wishes to flee the imaginary.*

The only defense against this unsought return of the image is for the author to take complete charge of it from the beginning. "The vital effort of this book is to stage an image-system," Barthes writes, and "to stage" means "to arrange the flats one in front of the other, to distribute the roles, to establish levels, and, at the limit: to make the footlights a kind of uncertain barrier" (*RB*, p. 105). In *Sade/Fourier/ Loyola* Barthes had said that by "theatricalizing" (i.e., by "unlimiting") his language, Sade ceased to be a sadist and became a "scenographer," one "who disperses himself across the framework he sets up and arranges *ad infinitum*" (pp. 5–6). For a similar purpose, Barthes theatricalizes the Barthesian language—breaking it into fragments that are presented from alternating points of view ("I," "he," "you," "R.B.") and chronologically disarranging them (thus, the final fragment in the book speaks of "this August 6," the date on which Barthes indicates that he *began* writing it; a third of the way through (p. 65), we read, "by magic, this fragment [entitled "Friends"] has been written last, after all the others, as a kind of dedication (September 3, 1974)."

The result is that the image of Barthes (as well as the image of R.B.) is made to "drift" like a character out of Robbe-Grillet. (Again: "It is all to be considered as if spoken by a character in a novel.") What R.B. has done with the writings of others, Barthes now does with the writings of R.B., and expects us to do with *Roland Barthes:* only in this way can the imaginary be kept at bay, prevented from *closing* in an image of deathly clarity. Barthes makes this point in an interesting observation of R.B.: "What he listened to, what he could not keep from listening to, wherever he was, was the deafness of others to their own language: he heard them not hearing each other. But . . . did he never hear his own deafness? He struggled to hear himself, but produced in this effort no more than another aural scene, another fiction. Hence to entrust himself to writing: is not writing that language which has renounced producing *the last word*, which lives and breathes by yielding itself up to others so that they can hear you?" (*RB*, p. 107).

It is this abhorrence of "the last word" that makes *Roland Barthes* so different from conventional critical discourse, for criticism normally aspires to be the last word: the definitive placing of an author, the interpretation which will make its predecessors obsolete and any successor unnecessary. For Barthes, the last word is always an end, closure, a death. Take, for instance, what he has now come to call the *"doxa,"* i.e., "public opinion," a "last word" insofar as it is accepted as *the way things are, what needs no further comment: "Doxa* is the wrong [critical] object," he writes, "because it is a dead repetition, because it comes from *no one's* body—except perhaps, indeed, from the body of the Dead" (*RB*, p. 71). To free oneself from a *doxa,* one must react *against* it, postulate a *para*-dox. But then the paradox becomes the "last word," becomes a new doxa, necessitating a new paradox, and so on and on.

From the vantage point of *Roland Barthes* we may see R.B.'s critical career as a succession of these reactive strategies. To begin with, the *doxa* was the "false Nature" of cultural representation, to which *Mythologies* reacted with its paradoxical "demystification." Then as demystification became "immobilized in repetition"—i.e., became "doxologized"—it was displaced by a "semiological science" *(Elements of Semiology)*, which in turn became encumbered with a "repertoire of images." Against this semiological science was set Structuralism, distinguished now from its predecessor as "the science of the semiologists" ("Introduction to the Structural Analysis of Narrative," *Système de la mode);* and in reaction to its ("often very grim") "rational image-repertoire" has come the theory of the Text, "the texture of desire" and "the claims of the body" *(L'Empire des signes, S/Z, The Pleasure of the Text,* and *Roland Barthes* itself). The Text "is where I am now," the author of *Roland Barthes* writes (p. 71)—in one of the rare instances in which the writing subject ("I") merges with the "writable" object ("R.B."). But the theory of the Text must not be allowed to become the last word either; the Text, too, we read, "risks paralysis: it repeats itself, counterfeits itself in . . . testimonies to a demand for readers, not for a desire to please . . . Where to go next?" asks Barthes at the point in the present writing at which what is to follow is not yet known and the danger of a repeated structure again becomes critical.

As far as the text of *Roland Barthes* is concerned, the question "Where to go next?" is equivalent to "How to avoid writing the last word?" or, more precisely, "How to avoid repetition?"Even Barthes's "last word" on Roland Barthes will be a repetition of "the body of the Dead." The question, then, is a major concern of the book. Immediately after posing it, Barthes supplies a list of "distractions" to which an "embarrassed" writer is subject (". . . cut my nails, eat a plum, take a piss . . ."), physical acts which he consolidates under the rather puzzling term "cruising." *Cruising,* we are told, "relates to that passion which Fourier called the Variant" (hence the living body's defense against dead repetition), and which, in *The Pleasure of the Text,* Barthes defined as the *body's seeking out of a reader,* the creation of "a site of bliss" *(PT,* p. 4).

We have said that for Barthes the aim of writing is pleasure—for the writer as well as the reader; but it is also a perversion since the highest pleasure, "bliss" (as he understands it), is always constituted in loss; for Barthes, permanence is stagnation, fullness nausea. This does not mean that his writing does not say something: it does; but it speaks it "lightly" (a word that occurs frequently in *Roland Barthes*), ambiguously, elliptically, "aslant"—i.e., parenthetically, or written *in the margin*. Barthes, then, describes the progress of *Roland Barthes* as a double movement: a *"straight line* (advance, increase, insistence of an idea, a position, a preference, an image)" and a *"zigzag* (reversal, contradiction, reactive energy, denial, contrariety, the movement of a Z, the letter of deviance)" (*RB*, pp. 90–91). Indeed, the operations by which this second movement is executed are "sufficiently formal and repeated" for Barthes to regard them as "figures" or signs, and to claim, therefore, that his text is "readerly"; *"I write classic,"* he says (*RB*, p. 92).

These figures of Barthesian "production"—quite apart from *what they say*—are in themselves a matter of interest to Barthes, and therefore should also be to every reader of him. If the figures place meaning in jeopardy, they are for that reason also the sites of pleasure in the text. Take for instance "amphibology" or ambiguity: "Each time he encounters one of these double words, R.B. . . . insists on keeping both meanings ['subject,' for example, which designates both the subject of an action (a grammatical subject) and the object of a discourse (its 'subject matter')] . . . so that one delights, semantically, in the one by the other" (*RB*, p. 72). A similar effect results from his habit of *cutting off* a word at its root, of allowing it to speak its etymology. Thus "the word is seen as a palimpsest: it then seems to me that I have ideas *on the level of language*—which is quite simply: to write" (*RB*, p. 85)—*to write* in Barthes's sense, that is: to produce *écriture*, the product of a body, rather than *écrivance*, the stereotype, which always occurs *"where the body is missing"* (*RB*, p. 90).

Barthes frequently speaks of the fragment itself as one of these figures, a formal means of "interruption and short-circuiting" (*RB*, p. 93). We have several times noticed this preference for writing in brief fragmentary bursts rather than in sustained argument: one thinks of the "brief scenes" of *Mythologies* (and later of *L'empire des signes*), of the occasional insights comprising the *Critical Essays*, the lexias of *S/Z*, the "phylacteries" of *The Pleasure of the Text* and (most recently) *A Lover's Discourse*, which is explicitly subtitled *Fragments*. Barthes now points out that R.B.'s earliest text (1942) was also fragmentary, a study of André Gide's *Journal* (more fragments), citing as justification of this "choice" of "pulverized discourse" Gide's dictum that "'incoherence is preferable to a distorting order'" (*RB*, p. 93).

Though Barthes is careful to speak of this fondness for the fragment as a "choice," it becomes clear in *Roland Barthes* that this choice is not psychologically unmotivated. We find, with Barthes's help, the same "choice" appearing in his efforts at painting, characterized as "*'tachiste'* daubing," and at sketching, in which, we are told, he is unable to represent "the masses," but works with individual details—"whence unexpected 'conclusions.'" "I proceed by addition, not by sketch," he observes (*RB*, pp. 93–94). In his writing this additive procedure appears as a technique of doubling one phrase with another, as if "he could not get it over with" (*RB*, p. 58), or did not wish to reach an end. Here, for example, is one of Barthes's fragments on R.B.'s fragments: "Liking to find, to write *beginnings*, he tends to multiply this pleasure: that is why he writes fragments: so many fragments, so many beginnings, so many pleasures (but he doesn't like the ends: the risk of the rhetorical clausule is too great: the fear of not being able to resist the *last word*)" (*RB*, p. 94). The fragment, in other words, is the "site" of pleasure (*jouissance*) in Barthesian discourse; separated from what comes before and after, it frustrates closure, places the imaginary at its farthest remove: it "implies immediate delight; it is a fantasy of discourse, a gaping of desire" (*RB*, p. 94).

What we "read" in *Roland Barthes*, then, are the fragments of the Barthesian textual body, the body of bliss. In this connection, Gregory Ulmer has pointed out that Barthes has identified as the emblem of his most recent writings the strange "reliquaries" of Bernard Réquichot, a little-known artist whose works consist of boxes containing diverse objects like pieces of bone and cloth, shells and feathers, embedded in thick paint, squeezed directly from the tube. These productions, according to Barthes, are like "open torsos displaying 'the magma of the body.'"[2] Barthes is also fascinated by certain drawings and designs of Réquichot's, consisting of nothing but unintelligible script, representing for the artist a "total impasse, the impossibility of communication" which, he observes, led to the artist's suicide.[3]

Barthes's pleasure in this sort of thing (which he admits is "perverse," a sort of fragment-fetish) is at first difficult to understand. For Ulmer, it is a tracing of "the sinister pattern of the death drive": "what was a process of despair for Réquichot is bliss for Barthes."[4] True, the Text is "the destroyer of all subject" (i.e., of the author identified by history and courses of literature); but the process does not end with the death of this subject: "the pleasure of the Text also includes the

amicable return" of another form of the subject (*SFL*, p. 8). We have
seen that for Barthes, the deepest pleasure is achieved when a book
"transmigrates" into the life of the reader, i.e., when the author (no
longer as a unity) reenters our lives as a cluster of fragments, "a mere
plural of charms." For Barthes, it is the unfragmented author, em-
balmed and memorialized by our institutions, that is truly dead,
unlovable; the fragmented author, the subject dispersed, "somewhat
like the ashes we strew into the wind after death," is "a subject to
love": "the theme of the *urn* and the [grave] stone, strong, closed
objects," is thus contrasted with "*bursts* of memory" and "the erosion
that leaves nothing but a few furrows of past life" (*SFL*, p. 9).

Immediately following the preceding quotation from *Sade/
Fourier/Loyola*, Barthes recommends to a future biographer of himself the technique of *author dispersal* we have just been describing:
"were I a writer, and dead," he writes, "how I would love it if my life,
through the pains of some friendly and detached biographer, were to
reduce itself to a few details, a few preferences, a few inflections, let
us say: to 'biographemes' whose distinction and mobility might go
beyond any fate and come to touch . . . some future body, destined to
the same dispersion"; the result, he goes on, would be something like
a silent film in which the flow of images would be "intercut . . . by the
barely written darkness of the intertitles, the casual eruption of
another signifier" (*SFL*, p. 9). In *Roland Barthes*, once we allow for
its prematurity and the artificial distancing of its writing, Barthes
himself has given us this anticipated biography.

CHAPTER 8

"And Afterwards"

TO CONCLUDE is to close, to move toward and eventually reach a last word, the end or "death" which Barthes—first on ideological grounds, then because of intellectual and, finally, sensual necessity—has made a career of trying to defer. How, then, are we to conclude our own study of this writer who, in his present posture, prevents our reducing him to the summarized content of his works, and for whom we must rid our minds of the very notions of content and of the work? Barthes is a producer of Texts, and a Text is the cause of pleasure in a reader, not, in the usual sense, an object of his understanding. But Barthes is also, of course, a reader (i.e., a re-writer) of other texts, and in this respect he too is concerned with the problem of coming to an end and may, therefore, help us to arrive at our own. The title of his third and (incidentally) last essay to date on Robbe-Grillet—"The Last Word on Robbe-Grillet?" (1962)—is a vivid reminder of the problem: a confident assertion withdrawn by a question mark. We probably expect traditional criticism to claim to offer the last word, and Barthes to deny that claim. But that is not the case here, as (speaking literally now) the last words of his essay imply: "Perhaps all literature is in this anaphoric suspension which at one and the same time designates and keeps silent" (*CE*, p. 204). In other words, Barthes's essay lacks the finality of even an outright denial of critical finality.

But even this attempt to conclude by suspending meaning is for Barthes a closure—"the last closure," as he says at the end of *S/Z* (p. 217). It is important to notice that Barthes's relation to Balzac's "classical" (i.e., "closed") story parallels that between the Marquise and the narrator. The latter's story of the *castrato's* tragedy is also "classical"—it closes on a meaning: "'In telling this story,'" he concludes, "'I have been able to give you a fine example of the progress made by civilization today'" (lexia 557). But in the final sentence of "Sarrasine," the question of meaning is reopened—placed in suspen-

119

sion: "The Marquise remained pensive," we read, and Barthes goes on to comment that "the Marquise can think of many of the things that have happened or that will happen, but about which we shall never know anything: the infinite openness of the pensive (and this is precisely its structural function) removes this final lexia from any classification" (p. 216). The Marquise, we might then say, is Barthes's ideal critic, the site of "some ultimate meaning" that is kept "free and signifying"—a reader for whom the narrator's story is not finished. Unfortunately the reader of Balzac's story cannot leave matters that way. The Marquise's pensiveness suspends meaning, but closes the discourse; although Barthes cannot "read" this lexia in one of the five codes he has postulated, he must recognize that pensiveness is itself a code, "a sign of nothing but itself . . . expressivity." The critic cannot maintain the Marquise's silence.

The importance for Barthes of avoiding the critical "last word," of producing a criticism of the signifier rather than the signified, appears again and again on the last pages of his books and essays—that point in discourse at which the signifier will close upon itself unless extreme measures are taken. Barthes takes these measures in his most recent works where we encounter a discourse which puts off conclusion by beginning over and over again, a discourse of fragments. To be sure, the strategy of *Roland Barthes, The Pleasure of the Text,* and "Sade II" (in *Sade/Fourier/Loyola*) is not merely a break with a conventional code. Such a break would be a violence and, as Barthes observes at the end of the last-mentioned work, "to return violence [for the violence of a worn-out code, a conclusion, for instance] is still to speak the same code" (*SFL,* p. 171). What Sade recommends to us, he argued there, is a "principle of tact" which "subverts" the old and constitutes an utterly new language.

In *Roland Barthes* the same point is made in a quotation from Brecht which Barthes introduces under the heading "Program for an avant-garde": "'The world has surely become unhinged, and only violent movements can put it all back together. But it may be that among the instruments for doing so, there is one—tiny, fragile— which requires to be wielded delicately'" (*RB,* p. 107). Barthes tries to realize this tact and delicacy in the fragment, a way of speaking "lightly"—as music speaks. The "organization" achieved in placing one fragment after another is not a *development,* but the articulation of a "tone": "each piece is self-sufficient, and yet it is never anything but the interstice of its neighbors" (*RB,* p. 94). And what of the final fragment? We have noted that the last fragment of *Roland Barthes* was the first one written, a celebration of the conditions of *opening:* "the countryside, the morning of a splendid day: sun, warmth, flowers, silence, calm, radiance. Nothing stirs, neither desire nor aggression; only the task is there, the work before me, like a kind of universal being: everything is full. Then that would be Nature? An absence . . . of the rest? Totality? (*RB*, p. 180). Totality, the sum of things, is normally the condition that determines an end. For Barthes, it designates the work *before* him, a never-to-be-completed "task." Thus, the last fragment of the book proposes the task anew.

There is, of course, nothing unconventional about concluding a present project with the proposal of a future project; this is a "classically" coded way of concluding and one to which Barthes, in his early works, occasionally resorted: *Writing Degree Zero*, for instance, ends with a vision of a future "Utopia of language," and "Myth Today" (the long essay at the end of *Mythologies*) and *Elements of Semiology* both defer their conclusions to further developments in semiological research. But the project proposed at the end of *Roland Barthes* is not a different project; it is the project that, until just now, has been going on. For Barthes, it is a song that will be sung again, but with different words.

Barthes devised another means of avoiding closure in *Roland Barthes:* that is by following one "conclusion" with another, the sequent, then, negating its predecessor. Thus two pages after the final fragment, we are given the "Biography," a list of dates (spanning the period from R.B.'s birth in 1915 to 1962—unfinished, then!) and their noted significance. At the end of the list, Barthes identifies what we will have read as "A life: studies, diseases, appointments," but then adds a further comment: "And the rest? Encounters, friendships, loves, travels, readings, pleasures, fears, beliefs, satisfactions, indignations, distresses: in a word, repercussions?—In the text—but not in the work" (*RB*, p. 184). There are two pairs of oppositions in this note: one opposes the diachronic, objective details of R.B.'s life (listed in the "Biography") to the synchronic affectivities ("repercussions") that persist in the subject; the other opposes "the text" to "the work," i.e., the "text" as R.B. and the "work" (or works) that R.B. has produced. In an essay called "From Work to Text" (1971), Barthes gave us the other side of this statement: "there is a reversion of the [author's] work on to the [author's] life (and no longer the contrary); it is the work of Proust, of Genet which allows their lives to be read as a text" (*IMT*, p. 161). Barthes's works, then, have a place in his biography; on the other hand, the works, along with the "repercussions," constitute a sort of intertext in which the text is held. Something like this is perhaps the most final thing we can say of Barthes here, now that we have read his texts: Barthes has become an intertext for us.

As a critic whose works are also Texts, Barthes occupies a unique and somewhat paradoxical position in modern criticism. Traditionally, the economy of the critical community has been as carefully balanced as that of those Scilly Islanders who are said to have earned a precarious livelihood by taking in one another's washing rather than trying to compete with the laundry trade of the mainland;[1] critics, that is, write for other critics, through the agency of scholarly journals and university presses: there is the commercial trade for all the others. Such criticism, Barthes would say, is the object of a "consumption"; its destiny is either annihilation or assimilation, a wasting away in the toils of polemic or an immortality of influence. But a Text—even a critical Text—is not consumed; having little communicable content, it is neither refutable nor assimilable; it is bound, says Barthes, to *jouissance*, a highly dangerous sort of *laissez faire*.

But then Barthes's orthodoxy has always been suspect; from the beginning, his practice has trangressed the *doxa*. Was not his early book on Racine regarded by Picard as a threat to the stability of an established critical economy? That was how Barthes, at the end of "The Two Criticisms," interpreted the intensity of the academic reaction to the *nouvelle critique:* university criticism, he wrote, "requires an ideology articulated around a technique difficult enough to constitute an instrument of selection; positivism affords it the obligation of a vast, difficult, patient knowledge; immanent criticism—at least, so it seems—requires, in the work's presence, only a power of astonishment, a power not easily measurable" (*CE*, p. 254). To ask only that the critic be capable of astonishment, that his reader merely provide a site of bliss for the critical text is to trade with the mainland and to upset the economic balance of the critical community.

Who now engages in critical controversy with Barthes? disputes his interpretation of Balzac as Picard disputed his Racine?[2] Picard himself has become silent on the matter, not necessarily because he has had second thoughts on Barthes's or his own reading of Racine, but because it is now patently clear that Barthes is playing the game by other rules, that he does not even stand where an adversary is supposed to stand to receive the blows of the hero. For the same reason—because he has shifted the ground of his criticism from the work to the Text—it is difficult to find a Barthesian school of criticism today. Of course, Barthes's semiological and Structuralist writings have had a profound effect on literary studies. But Barthes himself has moved beyond these positions—indeed *impels* himself beyond any influence his current practices might have. "Each phase [in R.B.'s career] is reactive," we read in *Roland Barthes:* "the author reacts either to the discourse which surrounds him, or to his own discourse, if one and the other begins to have too much consistency, too much stability" (*RB*, p. 145). Since each succeeding phase is a reaction to its predecessor, the sequence may be explained in psychoanalytic terms (as "a perversion drives out a neurosis," so the "minor scientific delirium of the *Elements of Semiology* and *Système de la mode* replaces "the political and moral obsession" of *Writing Degree Zero* and *Mythologies*).

Practically speaking, however, Barthes's phases may also be explained in terms of his reading ("I had just read Saussure and as a result. . ." he noted in the preface to *Mythologies* (p. 9); and, bearing on his most recent phase: "I had my head full of Nietzsche, whom I had just been reading . . ." [*RB*, p. 107]). But Saussure or Nietzsche is not regarded as an "external" or "anterior" influence; each is an intertext, "a music of figures, metaphors, thought-words," as Barthes defines it—"it is the signifier as *siren*" (*RB*, p. 145). Barthes today is such an intertext. His value for modern critics consists not in an influence of meanings or signifieds that they may draw from him and reproduce in their own writings, but in the fact that he induces them to influence themselves in reading him (*RB*, p. 106).

Barthes's importance for literary criticism, then, consists less in his individual literary pronouncements than in the example of his practice in which we see that no criticism manages to escape the problematics that it exists to make plain. In perhaps no other critic are we made more aware that the critical act is an act of writing, guided not by the meaning of the object, but by the desire of the subject, and involved, therefore, in the fate of all writing in the world. Barthes writes a text, and the world returns it a work; he disperses himself in a series of texts, and the world reunites him in an *oeuvre*. The temptation (to succumb to the infatuation of his own image-repertoire) is felt even as *he* writes: "I delight," he confesses in *Roland Barthes*, "continuously, endlessly, in writing as in a perpetual production, in an unconditional dispersion, in an energy of seduction which no legal defense of the subject I fling upon the page can any longer halt. But in our mercantile society, one must end up with a work, an *oeuvre* . . .

While I write, the writing is thereby flattened out, banalized, made guilty by the work to which it must eventually contribute." How, then, may he write? *"Blindly,"* he answers. "At every moment of the effort, lost, bewildered, and driven, I can only repeat to myself the words which end Sartre's *No Exit:* Let's go on" (*RB*, p. 136). And, of course, Barthes has gone on, text following text with the disturbing frequency of "conclusions" in *Roland Barthes*—and there is still one more of these to mention. In a holograph note on the last page of the book Barthes writes "And Afterward?—What to write now? Can you still write anything?—One writes with one's desire, and I am not through desiring."

It is a pleasure not to have had to speak of Barthes's *last* text, i.e., his final text, here,[3] and that may be a pleasure this most hedonistic of modern writers plans to leave in perpetuity to his readers. Barthes fancies that he has not yet written any books, only "introductions" to some "'real' book," never, in fact, to be written, always only introduced, infinitely expandable and indefinitely postponed. The beauty of this plan is that the introductions themselves need not be written in order to "live," may exist in suspension, in thought, ready to "fulfill themselves, partially, indirectly, *as gestures*, through themes, fragments" (*RB*, p. 173). One of these "introductions," a projected "inventory of the language of love" (mentioned under the heading "Later" in *Roland Barthes*), has engendered Barthes's most recent text, *A Lover's Discourse: Fragments* (1977). It seems fitting that we leave it undiscussed here, allow it to remain an introduction.

Notes and References

Chapter One

1. The authority is Frank Kermode, as quoted by John Updike in a review of Barthes's *S/Z* in *The New Yorker* (November 24, 1975), p. 189.
2. Roland Barthes, "What Is Criticism?" in *Critical Essays* (hereafter parenthetically identified as *CE*), trans. Richard Howard (Evanston, 1972), p. 259.
3. Roland Barthes, "Style and Its Image," in *Literary Style: A Symposium,* ed. Seymour Chatman (New York: Oxford University Press, 1971), p. 10.
4. Dorothy Lee, "Lineal and Nonlineal Codifications of Reality," as quoted by Terence Hawkes, *Structuralism and Semiotics* (Berkeley, 1977), p. 32.
5. Roland Barthes, *Critique et Vérité* (Paris, 1966), p. 70 (hereafter parenthetically identified as *CV*). The translation is mine.
6. Gerald Bruns, *Modern Poetry and the Idea of Language* (New Haven: Yale University Press, 1974), p. 99.
7. Roland Barthes, *On Racine* (hereafter parenthetically identified as *R*), trans. Richard Howard (New York, 1964), p. 163.
8. Roland Barthes, *Roland Barthes* (hereafter parenthetically identified as *RB*), trans. Richard Howard (New York, 1977), p. 131.
9. Jonathan Culler, *Structuralist Poetics* (Ithaca, 1975), p. ix.
10. John Sturrock, "Roland Barthes," *The New Review* (1974), p. 14.
11. Mark Poster, *Existential Marxism in Postwar France* (Princeton: Princeton University Press, 1975), p. ix.
12. Roland Barthes, *Michelet* (Paris, 1975), p. 5. My translation.
13. Ibid., p. 82.
14. Poster, *Existential Marxism,* p. 386.
15. "Interview: Claude Lévi-Strauss," *Diacritics,* I (1971), 45.

Chapter Two

1. "Preface" to *Writing Degree Zero,* trans. Annette Lavers and Colin Smith (New York, 1968), p. x. Subsequent references to this book (identified as *W*) will be made parenthetically in the text.

2. Jean-Paul Sartre, *Literature and Existentialism,* trans. Bernard Frechtman (New York: The Citadel Press, 1965), pp. 21–22.

3. Ibid., p. 13.

4. Roland Barthes, *Mythologies* (hereafter parenthetically identified as *M*), trans. Annette Lavers (New York, 1972), p. 9.

5. *Structuralist Poetics,* p. 134.

6. Ferdinand de Saussure, *Course in General Linguistics,* trans. Wade Baskin (New York, 1959), pp. 65–67.

7. Maurice Merleau-Ponty, *Signs,* as quoted by Bruns, p. 98. See note 6 in Chapter One.

8. Quoted from the text of "Sarrasine" included in Barthes's *S/Z,* trans. Richard Miller (New York, 1974), p. 221.

9. Roland Barthes, "To Write: An Intransitive Verb?" in *The Structuralists: From Marx to Lévi-Strauss,* ed. Richard and Fernande De George (New York, 1972), p. 162.

10. Roland Barthes, "Science Versus Literature," in *Introduction to Structuralism,* ed. Michael Lane (New York: Basic Books, 1970), p. 414.

11. Jean-Paul Sartre, *Being and Nothingness,* trans. Hazel E. Barnes (New York: Philosophical Library, 1956), pp. 55–56.

12. "To Write: An Intransitive Verb?" p. 162.

13. Ibid., p. 163.

14. *Two Novels by Robbe–Grillet: Jealousy & In the Labyrinth,* trans. Richard Howard (New York: Grove Press, 1965), p. 141.

15. "Science versus Literature," p. 411.

16. "To Write: An Intransitive Verb?" p. 162.

17. Ibid.

18. Ibid.

19. Fredric Jameson, *The Prison–House of Language* (Princeton, 1972), pp. 155–56.

20. Sartre, *Literature and Existentialism,* p. 26.

21. This passage and the "philosopher's stone" analogy in the following paragraph are taken from an essay by Barthes called "The Zero Point of Writing" included in Maurice Nadeau's *The French Novel Since the War* (New York: Grove Press, 1967), p. 168. Though Nadeau's acknowledgement is to the Hill and Wang edition of *Writing Degree Zero* cited above, these phrases are not to be found there. As the essay is substantially different in other respects, I assume that Nadeau's source was one of Barthes's original *Combat* articles.

Chapter Three

1. Raymond Picard, *New Criticism or New Fraud?* trans. Frank Towne (Pullman, Wash., 1969), p. 18.

2. Ibid., p. 36.

3. Roland Barthes, *Elements of Semiology,* trans. Annette Lavers and Colin Smith (New York, 1968), p. 89. Subsequent references to this book (identified *ES*) will be made parenthetically in the text.

4. Picard, p. 20.

5. Ibid., p. 21.

6. *Course in General Linguistics,* pp. 14–15.

7. *Current Issues in Linguistic Theory,* as quoted by Jonathan Culler in *Ferdinand de Saussure* (Harmondsworth: Penguin Books, 1976), p. 88.

8. Ibid., p. 89.

9. David Crystal, *Linguistics* (Harmondsworth: Penguin Books, 1971), p. 104.

Chapter Four

1. Claude Lévi-Strauss, "A Confrontation," as quoted by Poster, *Existential Marxism,* p. 310.

2. Culler, *Ferdinand de Saussure,* p. 81.

3. Saussure, *Course in General Linguistics,* p. 10.

4. *Ferdinand de Saussure,* p. 81.

5. Saussure, p. 10.

6. Rosalind Coward and John Ellis, *Language and Materialism* (London, 1977), p. 12.

7. Roland Barthes, *The Eiffel Tower and Other Mythologies* (hereafter parenthetically identified as *ET*), trans. Richard Howard, (New York, 1979), p. 8.

8. Terence Hawkes, *Structuralism and Semiotics,* p. 27.

9. Roland Barthes, "The Struggle with the Angel," in *Image, Music, Text,* trans. Stephen Heath (New York, 1977), p. 126. Subsequent references to essays in this volume (identified *IMT*) will be made parenthetically in the text.

10. Robert Scholes, *Structuralism in Literature* (New Haven, 1974), p. 158.

11. Roland Barthes, *Système de la mode* (Paris, 1967), p. 8. (My translation.) Hereafter this work will be parenthetically cited as *SM*.

12. Roland Barthes, "An Introduction to the Structural Analysis of Narrative," trans. Lionel Duisit, *New Literary History* 6 (1975): 241. Subsequent references to the "Introduction" (identified *I*) will be made parenthetically in the text.

13. Quoted in Coward and Ellis, p. 25.

14. Ibid., p. 8.

Chapter Five

1. Roland Barthes, *S/Z,* trans. Richard Miller (New York, 1974), p. 3. Subsequent references to this book will be made parenthetically in the text.

2. *Figaro littéraire* (March 9–15, 1970), quoted by Hugh Davidson in "Sign, Sense, and Roland Barthes," *Approaches to Poetics,* ed. Seymour Chatman, Selected Papers from the English Institute (New York: Columbia University Press, 1973), p. 38.

3. Quoted by Fredric Jameson, "The Ideology of the Text," *Salmagundi* 31–32 (1975): 210–11.

4. Quoted in Culler, *Structuralist Poetics,* p. 139.

5. Barbara Johnson, "The Critical Difference," *Diacritics* 8 (1978): 5.

6. Roland Barthes, "Textual Analysis of a Tale by Edgar Poe," trans. Donald G. Marshall, *Poe Studies* 10 (1977): 2.

7. "To Write: An Intransitive Verb?" pp. 164, 166.

8. "Textual Analysis of a Tale by Edgar Poe," p. 3.

9. Ibid.

10. Quoted in *Structuralist Poetics,* p. 245.

11. Coward and Ellis, p. 1.

12. *Introduction to Structuralism,* ed. by Michael Lane, p. 413.

Chapter Six

1. Roland Barthes, *The Pleasure of the Text,* trans. Richard Miller (New York, 1975), pp. 9–10. Hereafter references to this book (Identified *PT*) will be made parenthetically in the text.

2. From an interview in *Les lettres francaises* (May 20, 1970), quoted by Davidson, pp. 37–38.

3. The quoted phrase is from Richard Howard's prefatory note to the book, pp. v–vi.

4. Roland Barthes, *L'Empire des signes* (Geneva, 1970). The quote is from Barthes's blurb on the jacket of the book. Hereafter, references to this book (identified *ES*) will be made parenthetically in the text. The translations are my own.

5. *Roland Barthes,* trans. Richard Howard (New York, 1977), p. 93. Subsequent references (identified *RB*) will be made parenthetically in the text.

6. *Structuralist Poetics,* p. 190.

7. From an interview in *Tel Quel,* quoted by Michael Wood in "Rules of the Game," *New York Review of Books* (March 4, 1976), p. 31.

8. Roland Barthes, *Sade/Fourier/Loyola,* trans. Richard Miller (New York, 1976), p. 3. Subsequent references to this book (identified *SFL*) will be made parenthetically in the text.

9. See Barthes's essay "Lesson in Writing," in *IMT,* pp. 170–78.

Chapter Seven

1. Barthes's review was published in *La quinzaine littéraire* (March 1–15, 1975).

2. Gregory L. Ulmer, "Fetishism in Roland Barthes's Nietzschean Phase," *Papers on Language and Literature* 14 (1978): 339.

3. Ibid., p. 340.

4. Ibid.

Chapter Eight

1. They are mentioned in Robert Graves's foreword to *Poems: 1938–1945* (New York: 1946).

2. Our point is that, in dealing with the Text rather than the work, Barthes has shifted the grounds of critical controversy, and that he now provokes few attacks from critics who are (as Picard seems to have been) unaware of this shift. Still, there is a note of the Picardian absurd in Michael Riffaterre's interesting critical review of *Sade/Fourier/Loyola* in "Sade, or Text as Fantasy," *Diacritics* 2 (1972): 2–9.

3. Since this was written, the last text has, sadly, come to pass: characteristically, it is *another* text (i.e., a new one), "Deliberations," an essay on keeping a journal.

Selected Bibliography

PRIMARY SOURCES

1. Books by Barthes

A Barthes Reader. Edited by Susan Sontag. New York: Hill and Wang, 1980.

Critical Essays. Translated by Richard Howard. Evanston: Northwestern University Press, 1972.

Critique et vérité. Paris: Seuil, 1966.

The Eiffel Tower and Other Mythologies. Translated by Richard Howard. New York: Hill and Wang, 1979.

Elements of Semiology. Translated by Annette Lavers and Colin Smith. New York: Hill and Wang, 1968.

L'empire des signes. Geneva: Skira, 1970.

Image, Music, Text. Selected and translated by Stephen Heath. New York: Hill and Wang, 1977.

A Lover's Discourse: Fragments. Translated by Richard Howard. New York: Hill and Wang, 1978.

Michelet [par lui-meme]. Paris: Seuil, 1954. *Écrivains de toujours* series.

Mythologies. Selected and translated by Annette Lavers. New York: Hill and Wang, 1972.

New Critical Essays. Translated by Richard Howard. New York: Hill and Wang, 1980.

On Racine. Translated by Richard Howard. New York: Hill and Wang, 1964.

The Pleasure of the Text. Translated by Richard Miller. New York: Hill and Wang, 1975.

Roland Barthes. Translated by Richard Howard. New York: Hill and Wang, 1977.

Sade/Fourier/Loyola. Translated by Richard Miller. New York: Hill and Wang, 1976.

Système de la mode. Paris: Seuil, 1967.

S/Z. Translated by Richard Miller. New York: Hill and Wang, 1974.

Writing Degree Zero. Translated by Annette Lavers and Colin Smith. New York: Hill and Wang, 1967. Introduction by Susan Sontag.

2. Uncollected Essays by Barthes

"L'éffet de reel." *Communications* 11 (1968): 84–9.

"Science versus Literature." *Times Literary Supplement* (London), 28 September, 1967, pp. 897–98.

"Textual Analysis of a Tale by Edgar Poe." *Poe Studies* 10 (1977): 1–12. Translated by Donald G. Marshall.

"To Write: An Intransitive Verb?" In *The Structuralists: From Marx to Levi-Strauss,* edited by Richard and Fernande De George, pp. 155–67. New York: Doubleday and Co., 1972.

SECONDARY SOURCES

"Bibliography of Roland Barthes." *Tel Quel* 47 (1971): 126–32. Complete list of Barthes's books and articles published from 1942 to 1971.

COWARD, ROSALIND, and ELLIS, JOHN. *Language and Materialism.* London: Routledge & Kegan Paul, 1977. Treats Barthes's semiology and *S/Z* from a Marxist point of view.

CULLER, JONATHAN. *Structuralist Poetics.* Ithaca: Cornell University Press, 1975. Still the best introduction to modern critical theory and practice.

DAVIDSON, HUGH M. "Sign, Sense, and Roland Barthes." In *Approaches to Poetics,* edited by Seymour Chatman. New York: Columbia University Press, 1973. A useful introduction to Barthes's critical ideas and their difference from American "new criticism."

DOUBROVSKI, SERGE. *Pourquoi la nouvelle critique?* Paris: Mercure, 1966. The fullest, most lucid treatment of the Picard-Barthes controversy by one on Barthes's side.

FUNT, DAVID. "Roland Barthes and the *Nouvelle critique.*" *Journal of Aethestics and Art Criticism* 26 (1967–68): 329–40. An early and sympathetic treatment of Barthes's work up to *Critique et vérité.*

HARARI, JOSUÉ V. "The Maximum Narrative: An Introduction to Barthes's Recent Criticism." *Style* 8 (1974): 56–77. Focuses on *S/Z.*

———. "Critical Factions/Critical Fictions." In *Textual Strategies: Perspectives in Post-Structuralist Criticism,* edited by Josué V. Harari. Ithaca: Cornell University Press, 1979. A valuable introduction to the critical context of Barthes's later work.

HAWKES, TERENCE. *Structuralism and Semiotics.* Berkeley: University of California Press, 1977. A sound, elementary survey of the subject. Valuable bibliographical material.

JAMESON, FREDRIC. *The Prison-House of Language.* Princeton: Princeton University Press, 1972. An important study of the linguistic basis of structuralist theory. Advanced.

JAYNE, EDWARD. "Zero-Degree Form: The Anti-Dialectics of Roland Barthes." *The Minnesota Review,* Fall 1979, pp. 52–70. An interesting account of Barthes's struggle to avoid philosophical commitment.

JOHNSON, BARBARA. "The Critical Difference." *Diacritics* 8 (1978): 2–9. A lucid account of the theory of reading in *S/Z.*

JOSIPOVICI, GABRIEL. *The World and the Book.* Stanford: Stanford University Press, 1971. Chapter 11 deals with Barthes in his relations with Picard.

KERMODE, FRANK. "The Use of the Codes." In *Approaches to Poetics*, edited
    by Seymour Chatman, pp. 51–79. New York: Columbia University
    Press, 1973. One of the rare instances of an English critic using Barthes's
    critical techniques on English novels.
NICHOLS, STEPHEN G. "Roland Barthes." *Contemporary Literature* 10
    (1969): 136–46.
PICARD, RAYMOND. *New Criticism or New Fraud?* Translated by Frank
    Towne. Pullman: Washington State University Press, 1969. A "univer-
    sity" critic looks at Barthes and the *nouvelle critique*.
RIFFATERRE, MICHAEL. "Sade, or Text as Fantasy." *Diacritics* 2 (1972): 2–9.
    A critical review of Barthes's *Sade/Fourier/Loyola*.
SAUSSURE, FERDINAND DE. *Course in General Linguistics*. Translated by
    Wade Baskin. New York: Philosophical Library, 1959. Required reading
    for any understanding of Barthes.
SCHOLES, ROBERT. *Structuralism in Literature: An Introduction*. New Ha-
    ven: Yale University Press, 1974. The first impotant treatment of the
    subject by an American writer.
SONTAG, SUSAN. *Under the Sign of Saturn*. New York: Farrar, Straus,
    Giroux, 1980. A fine personal tribute.
STURROCK, JOHN. "Roland Barthes." *The New Review* 2 (1974): 13–20.
    Perhaps the most readable account of Barthes's work prior to *S/Z*.
TODOROV, TZVETAN. "Reflections on Literature in Contemporary France."
    New Literary History, 10 (1979): 511–31.
ULMER, GREGORY L. "Fetishism in Roland Barthes's Nietzschean Phase."
    Papers in Language and Literature 14 (1978): 334–55. An interesting, but
    difficult analysis of Barthes's latest writing.
———. "The Discourse of the Imaginary." *Diacritics* 10 (1980): 61–75. Dis-
    cusses *A Lover's Discourse* and *Roland Barthes* as examples of a "new
    genre." A valuable contribution.
UNGAR, STEVEN. "RB: The Third Degree." *Diacritics* 7 (1977): 67–77. Dis-
    cusses the importance of the "body" in Barthes's recent work.
VELAN, YVES. "Barthes." *Modern French Criticism*. Edited by John K.
    Simon. Chicago: University of Chicago Press, 1972. Criticism of Barthes
    by one of his own kind. Contains a bibliography of articles about
    Barthes.
WOOD, MICHAEL. "Rules of the Game." *New York Review of Books*, March
    4, 1976, pp. 31–34. Interesting review of five of Barthes's books in
    translation.

Index

Bachelard, Gaston, 47, 53

Balzac, Honoré de, 21, *35–37*, 39, 40, 41, *66*, 81, 83, 90, 102, 104, 119–20, 122; "Sarrasine," 21, *35–36*, 66, *83, 84–86, 87, 89–91,* 93, 96, 108, 111, 112, 119

Barthes, Roland, on "bad faith," 37, 38, 41, 51, 54; on the bourgeois, 23, 29, 34, 36, 37, 38, 42, 43, 45, 46, 59, 77–78, 90, 91, 112; on the "classical," *36–37,* 38, 39, 40, 41, 42, 43, 45, 53, 59, 76, 81, 82, 89, 91, 92, 97, 102, 104, 116, 119, 121; on "connotation," *52,* 54–55, 68, 69, 70, 77, 82, 83, 85–89; on denotation, 67, 68, 77, 82, 83; on *écriture,* 24, *25,* 36, *44,* 45, 98, 116; on Existentialism, 17, 23, 51, 58; on *jouissance,* 97–98, 100–106, 117, 122; on literature as an institution, 25, 28, 29, 36, 41, 45, *55–56,* 94; on Marxism, 17, 19, 47, 58; on metalanguage, *34,* 50, *51–52,* 68, 69, 95; on the "modern," 14, *36,* 37, *39–44,* 51, 59, 76, 81, 85, 92, 97, 102, 103, 104, 109; on "myth" *28–34,* 35, 36, 44, 45, 50, 51, 52–53, 67, 78, 79, 82, 94, 97; on the natural, 16, *26,* 28, 29, 32, 33, 34, 36, 39, 50, 62, 69, 71, 80, 82, 84–85, 86, 91, 113, 115, 121; on the *nouvelle critique,* 12, 19, *47–48,* 49, 53, 55, 122; on psychoanalysis, 19, 21, 47, 53, 58, 97, 106, 108, 111, 123; on the "readerly," *81–82,* 86–90, 97, 100, 116; on the realistic, 36, 43, 51, 59, 71, 82, *83–86;* on the relation between critic and literary text, 12–13, 14–15, 92–93, 107; on the relation between criticism and literature, 12, 51, 53–56, 93; on semiology, 24, *28–34,* 52, 60, 67–69, 77–78, 94, 105, 108, 115, 123; on Structuralism, 20, 21, *58–67,* 75,

76, 105, 115, 123; on structuration, 81, 91, 93; on the subject, 14, 49, *56,* 61, 78, 79, 80, 92, 93–94, *105–108,* 111, 116–118, 121, 123; on textuality, 21, *91–94,* 96, *105–108, 111–13,* 115, 117, 119, 121–123, 129n2; on the "writerly," 81, 97; on "writing," *25–27,* 28, 29, 34, 36, 39, 40, 41, 42, 43, 45, 51, *91–92,* 94; on the zero-degree, 14, 44–45, 81

WORKS: BOOKS

Critical Essays, 19, 92, 116

Critique et Vérité, 19, 48, 50, 56, 80

Eiffel Tower and Other Mythologies, The, 62,

Elements of Semiology, 20, 21, 52, 62, 66, 67, 68, 69, 77, 94, 115, 121, 123

L'Empire des signes, 21, *98–100,* 115, 116

Lover's Discourse, A, 116, 124

Michelet par lui-meme, 15, 17, 18

Mythologies, 17, 20, 24, *28, 29,* 31, 36, 37, 44, 51, 60, 62, 67, 68, 76, 77, 94, 100, 115, 116, 121, 123

On Racine, 19, 21, 48, 53

Pleasure of the Text, The, 22, 97, *100–103,* 105–106, 111, 115, 116, 120

Roland Barthes, 15, 16, 17, 22, 107, *110–11, 114–18,* 120–21, 123, 124

Sade/Fourier/Loyola, 21, *105,* 107, 114, 118, 120, 129n2

Systéme de la mode, 20, 66, *68,* 71, 76, 94, 95, 105, 115, 123

S/Z, 21, 66, 78, *79–80,* 83, *86–87,* 89, 92, 93–95, 96, 97,·108, 111, 115, 116, 119

Writing Degree Zero, 13, 16, 17, *21, 23, 27, 28,* 29, 34, 37, 39, *42, 44, 45,* 49, 51, 59, 71, 76, 91, 104, 121, 123

Twayne's English Authors Series

Sylvia E. Bowman, *Editor*

INDIANA UNIVERSITY

William Wordsworth

WILLIAM WORDSWORTH

By RUSSELL NOYES

Indiana University

Twayne Publishers, Inc. :: New York

To Vernice

Preface

T HE AIM of this book is to examine critically those poems of Wordsworth that have endured the sifting of time. The life of the author, the sources and analogues of his poems, the circumstances and progress of their composition, and other information useful to this central purpose are given. Biographical and other pertinent facts are presented in chronological sequence as they unfold in a meaningful pattern to show Wordsworth's development and achievement as a poet.

Thus Chapter 1 opens with a picture, given to us by Wordsworth himself, of a babe in arms being nurtured by the "ceaseless music" of the Derwent River. The chapter continues with an account of the gifts received from his mother and father, and of the ministering gentleness of his sister. It tells of the young boy's driving power and stubborn energy and of his awesome experiences in solitary places. It fills in important events in his schoolboy days at Hawkshead and his friendships there. So the story moves forward to life at Cambridge, to summer vacations including the momentous tour of the Alps with Jones, to London after college, to France and the revolution and his involvement with Annette Vallon, to London again in the throes of doubt and despair, finally to Racedown with Dorothy and the poet's slow recovery. Out of the pattern of these circumstances one sees the poet moving from early experimentation and imitation in *The Evening Walk* and *Descriptive Sketches* to *Guilt and Sorrow* and *The Borderers* until his way is cleared and his art is matured in "The Ruined Cottage."

Subsequent chapters carry forward the account of Wordsworth's poetic advance. Attention is paid to the prose only insofar as it opens up his poetic intentions and sheds light upon those accomplishments. Chapter 2 tells of the friendship of Wordsworth and Coleridge and their history-making collaboration in the creation of *Lyrical Ballads*. Chapter 3 tells of the potent release of creative energy stirred by recollection, while the poet was in Germany, that resulted in the new kind of poetry that went into the second volume of the *Lyrical Ballads* (1800). Chapter 4, central in many ways, offers an account of the origin and composition of *The Prelude*, Wordsworth's masterpiece, of its themes and ideas, and of its language, structure, and style. Chapter 5 tells of crucial happenings in Wordsworth's life during the years 1802 to 1807 and how *Poems in Two Volumes* (1807) reflect them. Chapter 6 offers an account of Wordsworth's once highly esteemed, but now neglected, *The Excursion*; this chapter also has something to say about the reasons for the poet's fading powers and about the poems of his later period. The final chapter summarizes Wordsworth's shortcomings and excellences and evaluates his achievement as a great, original genius.

More has been written about Wordsworth than any other English author except Shakespeare. Many of the books and articles about him are, or course, excellent and of great usefulness to the beginning student as well as to the expert. The most worthwhile among them are cited in the Selected Bibliography with evaluations that should be helpful. Wordsworth has been reappraised by each generation of readers beginning with his own, and controversy is still whirling about him on a number of issues. His genius is of such magnitude that it raises more questions than one can expect to be settled. In his own day, the "simple" Wordsworth was ridiculed for his simpleness, but he is now acclaimed by some for that very quality. In his lifetime he was censured by Keats for the limitation of what Keats called the "egotistical sublime"; but, among Wordsworth's defenders, his reach to the sublime, though intimately personal, did not limit him from translating the power of vision to an encompassing love of his fellow men.

To Shelley and Browning, Wordsworth was the "lost leader," a renegade to his earlier republican faith, but Mary Moorman and others have undertaken to put that once fashionable platitude about the poet out of style. Over the years a wide divergence of opinion has also prevailed about the character and value of Wordsworth's mystic faith and his teaching about Nature. Scholars like J. W. Beach and Basil Willey are among the skeptics, but Alfred N. Whitehead has made a spirited defense of Wordsworth's natural philosophy as viewed in our scientific age. Today, new insights are being offered about the psychology of Wordsworth's creative imagination. And so the search for meaning and understanding goes forward.

Preface

My pursuit of meaning in Wordsworth's poetry has continued in and out of the classroom for more than three decades. The results of this long search are presented in these pages. Acknowledgment of my debt to published scholarship may be understood to include those works listed in the Selected Bibliography, but some books and articles that have been of unusual importance or influential in points of interpretation are singled out for special mention in Notes and References. I wish especially to acknowledge the stimulus and challenge over the years of students in my classes, both undergraduate and graduate, who have called for and in a considerable measure helped to shape clarity and insight into meaning wherever it is found in this study.

For kind permission to reprint portions of critical commentary made by myself on some half-dozen of Wordsworth's poems first appearing in *Wordsworth and the Art of Landscape* (1968) I wish to thank the Indiana University Press. For most excellent editorial criticism and advice I am grateful to Professor Sylvia Bowman.

My greatest obligation is to my wife, Vernice Lockridge Noyes, who has been a sympathetic and discerning critic of my labors, and who has typed this manuscript.

RUSSELL NOYES

Indiana University

ABOUT THE AUTHOR

Russell Noyes is a distinguished scholar in the field of the English romantic poets and of Wordsworth in particular. He received his doctorate from Harvard University and has taught English at the University of Massachusetts, Boston University, and Harvard University. At present he is Professor of English at Indiana University where he served for ten years (1941-51) as Chairman of the department. He has contributed numerous articles on English romanticism to scholarly journals and is the author of *Drayton's Literary Vogue, Wordsworth and Jeffrey in Controversy,* and the widely used textbook, *English Romantic Poetry and Prose.* His latest book, *Wordsworth and the Art of Landscape* has received recognition for being one of the best designed and most scholarly books published in the mid-west in 1968.

Contents

Chronology

1770 April 7, William Wordsworth born at Cockermouth in Cumberland; second son of John Wordsworth, a lawyer, and Anne (Cookson).

1778- Mother died and the family dispersed; Wordsworth sent to
1787 lodge with Ann Tyson in Hawkshead where he attended the village grammar school. His schoolmaster, William Taylor, encouraged him to write verses.

1783 Father died, leaving his five children in the guardianship of their uncles.

1787- Attended St. John's College, Cambridge. Spent two summer
1791 holidays in the Lake Country and a third (1790) in a walking tour with Robert Jones through France and Switzerland across the Alps into Italy.

1791 Bachelor of arts degree at Cambridge without distinction and without plans for the future; in London; to France (November).

1792 At Orléans (winter and fall), affair with Annette Vallon, who bore him a daughter, Caroline; at Blois (spring and summer), met Michel Beaupuy and became a complete convert to French republicanism. Returned to England (December).

1793 *An Evening Walk* and *Descriptive Sketches* published; walking tour over Salisbury Plain and into Wales (visited Tintern Abbey in the Wye Valley).

1794 Unsettled; moved about living with relatives and friends.

1795 Bequest of £900 from Raisley Calvert enabled Wordsworth to establish a home with his sister Dorothy at Racedown farmhouse in Dorsetshire. Plunged into extensive reading of modern European literature.

1796- Composed *The Borderers*, a five-act drama, and "Margaret;
1797 or The Ruined Cottage."

1797- Settled with Dorothy at Alfoxden, a country estate near
1798 Nether Stowey, in Somersetshire, where Coleridge lived.

Close communion of spirit with Coleridge resulted in the *Lyrical Ballads*. Revisited the Wye Valley and Tintern Abbey with Dorothy.

1799   In Goslar, Germany, during a bitterly cold and lonely winter, but poetically productive. Wrote the Lucy poems and books I and II of *The Prelude*. Settled with Dorothy at Dove Cottage, Grasmere, their principal residence until 1808.

1800   A productive year: the great fragment of *The Recluse*, *Michael*, and many other poems. Coleridge settled nearby at Keswick; frequent intercourse between Wordsworth and Coleridge.

1801   Unproductive interval; Wordsworth's creative power in temporary subsidence.

1802   Year opened with a resurgence of productive energy, which continued with few and short interruptions until 1807. Composed part of the great "Ode: Intimations of Immortality," many of his best sonnets, and numerous fine lyrics. In late summer, journeyed with Dorothy to Calais; spent a month visiting with Annette and Caroline. Married Mary Hutchinson (October 4).

1803   Tour of Scotland with Dorothy resulted in a series of poems. Spent a week with Walter Scott. Friendship and patronage of Sir George Beaumont began in this year and continued until Sir George's death in 1827.

1804   Re-engaged in the composition of *The Prelude* (completed in 1805).

1805   His brother John drowned in the wreck of his own vessel, the *Abergavenny*.

1807   *Poems, in Two Volumes* published; savagely attacked in *Edinburgh Review*.

1808   Moved to Allan Bank, Grasmere.

1809   *The Convention of Cintra*, a political tract, published.

1810   Became estranged from Coleridge (reconciled in 1812). "A Description of the Scenery of the Lakes" published.

1813   Appointed Distributor of Stamps for Westmoreland. Moved to Rydal Mount.

1814   *The Excursion* published.

1815   *Collected Poems* and *The White Doe of Rylstone* (written in 1807) published.

1819   *Peter Bell* (written in 1798) and *The Waggoner* (written in 1805) published.

1820   *The River Duddon*, a series of sonnets, published.

1822   *Memorials of a Tour of the Continent* and *Ecclesiastical Sketches* published.

1835   *Yarrow Revisited, and Other Poems* published.

1839   Honorary doctorate at Oxford greeted with acclamation.

1842   *Poems Chiefly of Early and Late Years* published. Resigned as Stamp Distributor and received a pension of £300 per annum from the Civil List.

1843   Succeeded Robert Southey as poet laureate.

1850   April 23, died at Rydal Mount; buried in Grasmere churchyard. *The Prelude*, revised in 1839, published posthumously.

CHAPTER 1

The Making of the Poet

I *Childhood at Cockermouth*

Wordsworth's poetic life began, he tells us in *The Prelude*, on the banks of the Derwent in Cockermouth, when, even as a babe in arms, the river was an influence stretching back beyond the gates of conscious memory, a presence which

> ...lov'd
> To blend his murmurs with my Nurse's song,
> And from his alder shades and rocky falls,
> And from his fords and shallows, sent a voice
> That flow'd along my dreams.

The sound of running water, he often felt, was almost part of his own being, and in aftertime he thanked the Derwent for this first gift of "ceaseless music." At five years of age he was bathing in that stream and making sport long summer days along its banks, "a naked savage" filled with a mysterious happiness.

Within his spacious home on High Street his mother gave him the priceless gift of tenderness and love. Wordsworth in after years attributes, in *The Prelude*, to the mother the archetype from which springs the happiness of the child's intercourse with the universe: "From this beloved Presence, there exists/A virtue which irradiates and exalts/All objects through all intercourse of sense." His own mother first introduced him to Nature; and, when her presence was withdrawn, the boy transferred to Nature the affection and devotion which he had felt for her. To his father, he owed one great debt: Mr. Wordsworth cared for English poetry and encouraged his son William to learn by heart "large portions of Shakespeare, Milton, and Spenser."

The boy Wordsworth had a driving power and a stubborn energy. He was, he tells us, "of a stiff, moody, and violent temper." He once struck his whip through a family portrait, after first daring his brother Richard to do so. And once, in a frenzy, he went up to the attic of his grandfather's house with the intention of killing himself with one of the foils kept there. His mother said he was the only one of her children about whose future she was anxious; he, she said, would be remarkable for good or ill.

In *The Prelude* Wordsworth tells of numerous strange and awesome experiences when fear, shooting across the "coarser pleasures" of his boyhood and their "glad animal movements," became a potent ministrant in shaping his poetic mind. The earliest of these "spots of time," which may serve as representative of others, occurred when he was only five years old. When he was riding with his father's servant near Penrith Beacon, he somehow became separated from his guide. Uncertain where he was, he dismounted and led his pony to a hollow, where he found an old moldering gibbet post and at its foot some initials carved in the turf. He recognized the spot as that upon which a murder had been committed; and, as was the fashion of the times, where the murderer had been hanged. At once he fled up the hill, half-faint with terror, till he reached the beacon summit, where he saw a girl carrying a pitcher on her head and forcing her way with difficulty against the wind.

> It was, in truth,
> An ordinary sight; but I should need
> Colours and words that are unknown to man
> To paint the visionary dreariness [of that scene.]

Through this adventure in that wild and haunted place, and others like it to follow, the child, not yet six, felt the imaginative awe in the presence of mystery which solitude and solitary things habitually evoked in the man.

Counterbalancing his wildness and turbulence, and supporting the tenderness of his mother, was the gentleness of his sister Dorothy. In the poems celebrating the early years of his life, Wordsworth keeps returning to the softness of her nature. When they together discovered by chance a sparrow's nest, "She looked at it and seemed to fear it;/Dreading, tho' wishing, to be near it." When, in their childish play, together they chased the butterfly, he rushed like a very hunter upon the prey, "But she, God love

her! feared to brush/The dust from off its wings." Dorothy brought
to her brother in later years the gentleness he acknowledged was
hers when they were children; she brought, too, other gifts com-
pounded upon it:

> She gave me eyes, she gave me ears;
> And humble cares, and delicate fears;
> A heart, the fountain of sweet tears;
> And love, and thought, and joy.
> > "The Sparrow's Nest"

II   *Schoolboy at Hawkshead*

Wordsworth's eight years at Hawkshead, from his tenth to his
eighteenth year, contributed riches to the formation of his poetic
mind. He attended the grammar school for seven or eight hours a
day, but the rest of his existence seems to have been entirely free.
Joyously he gave himself up to the amenities which surrounded him.
He joined his schoolmates in gregarious sports indoors and out, but
the adventures which made the deepest impression upon him were
those he experienced by himself. When, alone, he snared wood-
cocks, plundered the raven's nest, or reaped the harvest of hazel
nuts. Alone, he wandered through the hollows and over the cliffs,
embarked by boat upon the surface of the lakes, and followed the
rivers to their sources on the lonesome mountain peaks. Swiftly
the whole of the countryside became his inheritance. All scenes
"beauteous and majestic," became "habitually dear, and all/Their
hues and forms were by invisible links/Allied to the affections."

In his fourteenth year Wordsworth first became conscious of loving "words in tuneful order"; he "found them sweet/For their
own sake, a passion and a power." His schoolmaster, William
Taylor, encouraged him in the writing of poetry; and he composed,
at Taylor's request, lines celebrating the bicentenary of the school's
founding. This exercise put it into his head "to compose verses
from the impulse of my own mind." Taylor seems to have had a
taste for poets like Thomas Gray, William Collins, Thomas
Chatterton, and James Beattie—poets that quickly became the
favorites of the young Wordsworth.

Of what survives of Wordsworth's youthful verse one poem stands
out: "The Vale of Esthwaite," which he describes as a "long poem

running on my own adventures and the scenery of the country in which I was brought up." Essentially a topographical poem, written in the eight-syllable meter of Milton's "L'Allegro" and "Il Penseroso," it describes Esthwaite valley and surrounding places, with an intermingling of Gothic passages after the fashion of the day. What distinguishes the poem as an unusually promising one is the vivid recording of many directly observed images of the land-scape. Wordsworth in his seventy-third year told Miss Fenwick, when he was dictating notes about *An Evening Walk*, that he recollected the time and place where most of them were noticed. Wordsworth mentioned as an example the instance of the shepherd dog barking and bounding among the rocks to intercept the sheep, an action of which he was eyewitness for the first time while crossing the Pass of Dunmail Raise. Also he recalled distinctly, he said, the very spot where the image of the darkening boughs and leaves of the oak tree, "fronting the bright west," first struck him: "It was in the way between Hawkshead and Ambleside and gave me extreme pleasure." He also remarked that "The moment was important in my poetical history; for I date from it my consciousness of the infinite variety of natural appearances which had been unnoticed by the poets of any age or country, so far as I was acquainted with them, and I made a resolution to supply, in some degree, the deficiency."[1]

III   *Cambridge and* An Evening Walk

In the autumn of 1787 Wordsworth exchanged the hardy simplic-ity of Hawkshead for the comparative luxury of life at St. John's College, Cambridge. At the time of his entrance, Cambridge was a place of idleness and intellectual languor. Wordsworth was thrilled at his arrival, but from the first the lectures and examinations failed to interest him. He loved companionship and moved easily "into the weekday works of youth" that surrounded him, drifting aim-lessly and reading "lazily in lazy books." But he possessed also an inner integrity, one greater than that of the world he was living in, that left a strangeness in his mind, a feeling that he "was not for that hour,/ Nor for that place."

For his first summer vacation Wordsworth returned to Hawkshead and soon discovered that his year's absence had wrought great changes in himself. He now began consciously to look at both Man and Nature with a "humanheartedness" so new that it felt like the dawn of another sense. He looked with "clearer knowledge" upon the simple dalefolk he had known as a schoolboy—the quiet woodman, the shepherd on the hills, and even his old dame nodding over her Bible. A lonely encounter with a vagrant soldier met at nightfall upon the highway, who was in need of his help and whom he left in comfort, made a solemn impression upon him that banished all thoughts of frivolity from his mind and gave a new direction to his approach to "the problem of humanity."

The climaxing event of this summer, and one of the most momentous of his life, came to Wordsworth as he returned home at dawn from a night of "dancing, gaiety, and mirth." On his two-mile walk home he had reached some high ground just as the sun was rising, and the wondrous beauty of the morning broke upon him. The shock of sudden removal from excited companionship with "spirits upon the stretch" into brooding solitude caused his mind to leap forward into full communion with the beauty before him:

> Magnificent
> The morning was, in memorable pomp,
> More glorious than I ever had beheld.
> The Sea was laughing at a distance; all
> The solid Mountains were as bright as clouds,
> Grain-tinctured, drench'd in empyrean light;
> And, in the meadows and the lower grounds,
> Was all the sweetness of a common dawn,
> Dews, vapours, and the melody of birds,
> And Labourers going forth into the fields.
> —Ah! need I say, dear Friend, that to the brim
> My heart was full; I made no vows, but vows
> Were then made for me; bond unknown to me
> Was given, that I should be, else sinning greatly,
> A dedicated Spirit.
>   (*The Prelude*, Book IV)

His "moment at sunrise" was not a conscious dedication by Wordsworth to the vocation of poet. The bond given to him was "unknown." Nevertheless, events proved it to be a prophetic blessedness that sustained him for many years.

On his return to college Wordsworth was less attracted to "indolent and vague society," and he withdrew into his own life of feeling and of thought. Authorship now seemed less presump-

tuous; and, during his second and third winters at Cambridge, it
became his practice, he says, to retire after dark into the college
garden where he paced up and down its "Groves and Tributary
walks" in the throes of poetic composition. During his second summer vacation he visited Dorothy at Forncett, where she was living
with her uncle William Cookson, and made various wanderings on
foot through the north of England. For the last month of his
holiday (from mid-September to mid-October) he stayed at Hawkshead where he continued and probably completed *An Evening
Walk*, a poem of nearly four hundred and fifty lines.

   An Evening Walk, a topographical poem in heroic couplets, was
offered to the reading public as an album of beautiful landscape
scenes, chiefly of several Wordsworthian rambles around Lake
Windermere. The scenery is described in accordance with the
principles of the "picturesque" school of topographical poets, such
as Erasmus Darwin and William Rogers, and of the famous delin-
eator of "picturesque" scenes, William Gilpin. *An Evening Walk*
borrows many images from "The Vale of Esthwaite" and continues
Wordsworth's resolution, begun in that poem, to supply in poetical
form an abundant variety of directly observed natural appearances.
Wordsworth's scenes are rooted in reality; the village murmurs
arise from his own Hawkshead.[2] However, Wordsworth reminds
his readers that "the plan of his poem has not been confined to a
particular walk or place"; for he was "unwilling to submit the
poetic spirit to the chains of fact and real circumstances."

   The poem is structured on the picturesque variations of landscape as revealed by the gradations of evening light—sunset, twilight, and moonlight. Human and animal inhabitants are not
excluded; the shepherds and dogs, the muleteers and their trains,
the peasant and his horse, and the majestic swans—all enhance
the pastoral scene. The swans, in particular, reflect the idyllic character of their natural surroundings. The swan's bower, "where leafy
shades fence off the blustering gale," is described in terms paralleling a peaceful shepherd's cottage. Contrasted to the idyllic life of
the swan and her brood is the beggar woman and her starving children who are at the mercy of cruel storms and freezing weather.
She serves as a humanitarian figure reflecting Wordsworth's newly
awakened interest in the sufferings of the poor.

   But the social accent in *An Evening Walk* hardly ruffles the placid
surface of its sequence of picturesque descriptions. Having ex-

pressed his sympathy for innocence in distress, Wordsworth returns to his description of the charms of evening and concludes his poem with its finest passage in which he joins Man and Nature in a magnificent manipulation of the images of sound. *An Evening Walk* is the work of a young poet: the imagery is overloaded and often obscured by the affectations of manner and style. But, for all its faults, the poem has a freshness, vitality, and an accuracy in its images that is derived from personal observation. These qualities mark the poem as a work of genius.

IV   *Tour of the Alps, France, and* Descriptive Sketches

During the long vacation between Wordsworth's junior and senior years at St. John's College, when he should have been studying for his comprehensive examinations, he left for a walking tour of France and Switzerland with his classmate Robert Jones. His main reason for going was to indulge his passion for natural scenery especially among the magnificent Swiss Alps: "Nature then was sovereign in my heart,/And mighty forms seizing a youthful Fancy/ Had given a charter to irregular hopes." He entered France on the anniversary of the storming of the Bastille and found himself plunged into the flood of revolutionary zeal to which he abandoned himself: "Bliss was it in that dawn to be alive,/But to be young was very Heaven!"

Still Wordsworth was not touched, he says, by the revolution with "intimate concern." He seems to have been carried away with the abstract ideal of liberty, which would soon have evaporated had not the essentially practical Wordsworth seen that the ideal was grounded in reality. When the tour of the Alps was completed, he returned to Cambridge and in February took his degree without distinction. After some months in London, he returned to France with the professed intention of perfecting his French as qualification for a tutorship. At this time, the transformation of the enthusiast for Nature into the full-fledged enthusiast for revolution was soon accomplished.

By a noteworthy chance Wordsworth came to know Captain Michel Beaupuy, one of a band of military officers with republican sympathies stationed at Blois. Beaupuy fed Wordsworth's mind with revolutionary philosophy and showed him the sufferings of the poor under the old regime. When they chanced one day to meet a hunger-bitten girl dragging a heifer and when Beaupuy, in agita-

tion, cried out, " 'Tis against *that*/That we are fighting," Wordsworth saw the need for the revolution. "Then I became a patriot,"
he said, "and my heart was all/Given to the people, and my love
was theirs." He nearly joined the Girondists (a party of moderates)
when he was in Paris, but he was recalled to England by lack of
funds and perhaps by pressing personal claims. For Wordsworth
had been swept away by other tides. When he was in Orléans he
had fallen blindly, passionately in love with a dark-eyed French
girl, Annette Vallon, who responded to his love and bore him a
daughter. His sudden return to England seems to have been partly
forced upon him by the necessity of securing funds for their support. He seems to have desired to rejoin Annette; but, when war
broke out, return was impossible.

During his residence in France Wordsworth was at work on
Descriptive Sketches, a poem in heroic couplets based on his Alpine
tour of two years earlier with Jones. A loco-descriptive poem of some
eight hundred lines, it recounts, in a crowded sequence of sketches,
the esthetic pleasures of the pedestrian traveler in the Swiss and
Italian Alps. When Wordsworth was on his tour, he wrote Dorothy
that he was "a perfect enthusiast" in his admiration for Nature in
all her forms. In the poem, however, the original feeling of unre-
strained enthusiasm is curiously colored by a newly acquired mood
from his second visit to France. Wordsworth casts the poet in the
role of a melancholy wanderer seeking refuge from love's misery,
in all probability a transference of symptoms agitating the lover of
Annette. Sections of the poem that describe the scenery of the
Italian lakes follow the vogue of the then-popular travel poetry.
In the scenes describing Lake Como, for example, there is a well-
conducted, harmonious time sequence (that reminds one of *An
Evening Walk*) in the passage from sunset to twilight to starlight
and the next morning in the progress of the rising sun. However, it
should be noted that there are two types of landscape featured in
Descriptive Sketches: one is a mild beauty represented by the
"delicious scenes" of the Italian lakes; the other, the more awesome
beauty of the Alps mountains.

In the high Alps Wordsworth was confronted by Nature on a
scale mightier and more awe-inspiring than he had hitherto ever
dreamed of—and evocative of sensations that approached sublimity.
Many scenes vexed his sight and many overwhelmed him; his
imagination sought helplessly for an inner vision to rest upon. When

he tried to put into words his impressions of the Alps in *Descriptive Sketches*, he leaned heavily upon the writings of two earlier travelers to Switzerland, William Coxe and Ramond de Carbonniéres. He used Ramond for scenic details and for vocabulary; but, over-all, the Frenchman was not much more than a crutch for Wordsworth to lean on. Boldly, Wordsworth widened the contrasts and multiplied the *locus* of life. Through personification and animism he made a separate (visual) entity of nearly everything his glance encountered. Few single "prospects" satisfied him; he spread the swift interchanges of seasons, times, and landscapes over Nature as a whole. Not until ten years later in *The Prelude*, Book VI, did he express at last the harmonizing vision of the idea of Nature that was haunting his mind. But, as Hartman observes, the distance between *The Prelude*, written in Wordsworth's maturity, and *Descriptive Sketches* is enormous.[3]

On the tour with Jones, Wordsworth took pleasure in meditating upon scenes of domestic felicity among the cottagers and upon the freedom of the shepherds in their mountain haunts. But in *Descriptive Sketches* these sentimental reflections are vigorously transposed into Wordsworth's beliefs in the manifold blessings of the republicanism that he had adopted after his summer with Beaupuy. In the poem, he abandoned his disguise as a leisurely and observant pedestrian traveler; and he heightened his scenic descriptions with militant vignettes of "social suffering," tributes to noble statesmen-warriors, and a salute to traces yet remaining in republican Switzerland of a bygone Golden Age. He ended the poem with a vehement prayer that France might ride "Sublime o'er Conquest, Avarice, and Pride"—that she might defeat all enemies of the Republic.

When *Descriptive Sketches* was published in London, a few months after the execution of the king, its fiery defense of revolutionary freedom stirred the anger of reviewers. However, most readers in the London of 1793 appear to have been indifferent to its subject or discouraged by its inflated obscurities. Coleridge alone recognized occasional flashes of splendor.

V *Ardent Republican: "Letter to the Bishop of Llandaff" and "Guilt and Sorrow"*

Wordsworth returned to England in December, 1792, "a patriot of the world." For him, the French Revolution was not simply the struggle of a poor people to be free but the dawn of a new day for all mankind. He explains in *The Prelude* that, to him, coming from his free world of shepherds, farmers, and Cambridge students, the revolution seemed nothing out of the natural order. It was the rightful gift to all men of what was already their precious heritage— freedom and equality between man and man. His deep, ingrained love of England, its very soil and its people, had extended itself to France; and personal love had sealed the bond. Then, suddenly in February, 1793, England declared war on France; and he was thrown into agonizing mental conflict. He "felt the ravage of this most unnatural strife" in his own heart.

Wordsworth did not yield to despair at once; he wrote a blistering defense of the revolution in reply to a recanting bishop, Watson of Llandaff, who formerly had supported the event. Wordsworth's document, entitled "A Letter to the Bishop of Llandaff on the Extraordinary Avowal of his Political Principles . . . by a Republican," was never finished and remained unpublished, probably because his publisher Johnson, though a friend of radicals, knew the danger of possible prosecution by the government. For Wordsworth's letter is a direct attack on monarchy, and on the constitution of "Kings and Lords and Commons . . . who have constitutionally the right of enacting whatever laws they please, in defiance of the petitions or remonstrances of the nation." Wordsworth repudiates the bishop's smug satisfaction with things as they are and speaks out, often with an edge of sarcasm, on the extremes of poverty and riches, the prevalent injustices of English law courts, the curse of hereditary nobility that breeds insolence and wickedness, and disastrous war instigated by royalty that heaps its misery upon the poor. But the interest in the pamphlet lies not so much in the ideas expressed, which were not startlingly original, as in its burning sincerity. Wordsworth, genuinely aroused, pressed his attack, as Émile Legouis rightly says, with "almost religious fervor."

Wordsworth's stay in London was terminated when a wealthy school-fellow, William Calvert, invited him to be his companion on a tour of southern England. They spent a month at the Isle of Wight and were on their way north when Calvert's horse, which was not used to carriage duty, dragged the occupants and their vehicle into a ditch and broke it to shivers. Wordsworth and Calvert both escaped unhurt, but they decided to end the tour. Calvert mounted the horse and rode off to the north of England, leaving Wordsworth alone in the middle of the vast, uninhabited Salisbury Plain over which he wandered for two or three days. One of the places his wanderings took him was to Stonehenge near which, in a mood of exaltation, he had a mystical experience that may be ranked in importance with his "dedication," five years before, during his first vacation. He felt an inrush of faith, never so fully felt before, that he was one of that great company of poets possessed with a "privilege" whereby a work of his, "creative and enduring, may become/A power like one of Nature's."

In his reverie he saw a phantom pageant of the legendary past, "Saw multitudes of men, and here and there,/A single Briton in his wolf-skin vest/With shield and stone-axe, stride across the Wold." He called on darkness, and the pitch black was broken by flames and the sight of human sacrifices being offered up in the flames of the altar. In some odd way Wordsworth seems to have associated the ancient Britons of his "reverie" with the poor of his own time. As he made his way to the Vale of Clwyd in Wales by way of Bristol and the valley of the Wye, he found himself taking a new interest in tramps and beggars who were walking the roads with him. Republicanism, which he had learned from Beaupuy, now assumed a new meaning. He began to question and to watch those he met and to hold familiar talk with them. On the long solitary walk from Salisbury Plain to Wales, equality ceased to be a doctrine and became a way of life. From that time, Wordsworth determined he would be the poet of humble life.

The first fruit of this determination was a narrative poem composed mentally during his wandering, written down during the next few weeks, and revised two years later at Racedown. Eventually, again drastically altered and augmented, the poem was published in 1842 as "Guilt and Sorrow." In its least complicated form it is the story of "The Female Vagrant," which was printed in the *Lyrical Ballads* in 1798. This version records the tragic life story of a Cumberland woman, now reduced to destitution, which is told during a night storm to a traveler who has lost his way on Salisbury Plain. The traveler is clearly Wordsworth, who transfers to the poem many images of the bleak Salisbury landscape and reflections of his own depressed and disillusioned mood.

The story itself, he tells us, is a true one as told to him a year or two before by the sufferer herself. Her persecution began when a capitalizing landowner, empowered by the enclosure laws, drove her father from his hereditary farm. An interval of happiness was theirs when she married and her father came to live in her new home. But their respite from sorrow was brief: her father soon died; her husband, forced into idleness by economic pressures, joined the navy. She followed him with their three children across the Atlantic, only to suffer constant distress and finally bleak misery when, in one remorseless year, all perished.

In his revision of the poem, which was undertaken in October, 1795, and identified in manuscript as "Adventures on Salisbury Plain," Wordsworth extended the picture of injustice and painted oppressive social conditions in still darker colors. In this version, the vagrant woman's father is the prey "to cruel injuries" and persecuted with "wilfull wrong" until he is forced from his land. To the tale of the female vagrant's sufferings Wordsworth added her cruel treatment at the hospital and her homeless wandering after her release. He also added the pitiable story of an impressed sailor who was returning home after service in the American wars. Following his discharge, he was incited by a cruel fraud to commit murder. He confesses the crime to his wife, who, in the last stages of consumption, forgives him and dies in his arms. The sailor surrenders himself to justice and is publicly hanged.

Into the stories of these three desolate outcasts Wordsworth poured a bitter, unsparing indictment of the dominant class which oppresses the poor and makes them what they are. He exposed corrupt power and privilege, the calamities of war, the cruel impressment of soldiers and sailors, unfeeling charity, the forced perversions of simple hearts, and the horrors of public execution. Underlying Wordsworth's virulent attack on English society were his republican sentiments, already given forceful expression in the closing lines of *Descriptive Sketches* and in "Letter to the Bishop of Llandaff." But in "Salisbuy Plain" he faced more squarely the problem of interpreting social abuses in terms of what he saw and felt. For the first time, he created real characters drawn from the world he knew and identified himself with their experiences and their feelings.

Wordsworth also got himself into "Salisbury Plain" in another significant way. The visionary experience which he had by the pillars of Stonehenge that obliged him to draw comparisons between the barbarous age of the Druids and "the terrors of our day" spread to encompass his response to the solemn desolation of Salisbury Plain. In his representation of it, Wordsworth provided his poem with the atmosphere of mysterious awe characteristic of the Gothic school of terror. This estheticism does not, as some critics claim, divide the esthetic impulse between terror and pity; instead, it enhances what Wordsworth says in his preface to the poem were his "melancholy forebodings" over the distress and misery to which the poor are subject. As he pursued his lonely way along the bare white road almost empty of the signs of man, his loneliness quickened his imagination. With an arresting vividness he paints his desolate scenes, such as the lonely guide post on the waste momentarily revealed by lightning, or the bleakness of the landscape described by stark negations:

> No gipsy cower'd o'er fire of furze or broom;
> No labourer watch'd his red kiln glaring bright,
> Nor taper glimmer'd dim from sick man's room;
> Along the waste no line of mournful light
> From lamp of lonely toll-gate stream'd athwart the night.

What aroused Coleridge's admiration for "Salisbury Plain" when he first read it in 1796 was "the union of deep feeling with profound thought; the fine balance of truth in observing, with the imaginative faculty in modifying, the objects observed, and above all the original gift of spreading the tone, the atmosphere, and with it the depth and height of the ideal world around forms, incidents and situations, of which, for the common view, custom had bedimmed all the lustre."[4] Coleridge's claims are excessive, but they do indicate, with discrimination and accuracy, what Wordsworth's intentions in poetry were at the time and those features that would distinguish his poetry in the future.

VI *William Godwin and Godwinism*, The Borderers

Not long after Wordsworth's return from France, a change occurred in his thinking about the revolution. A year of bloody excesses under Robespierre no doubt had its effect, but the crucial factor in bringing about the change was his absorption in William Godwin's famous treatise, *Enquiry concerning Political Justice*.[5] Though Wordsworth nowhere mentions *Political Justice* in *The Prelude*, the passage in which he describes his attempts to solve all moral problems by the light of "human Reason's naked self" is

generally assumed to refer to that work.[6] *Political Justice*, which
was published in February, 1793 (nearly coincident with the out-
break of war), made an immediate and great impact upon the thinking of political liberals. "No work of our time," wrote William Hazlitt, "gave such a blow to the philosophical mind of the country."
Wordsworth recaptures in *The Prelude* the glamor of its early en-
ticement for him:

> What delight!
> How glorious! in self-knowledge and self-rule,
> To look through the frailties of the world,
> And . . .
> Build social freedom on its only basis,
> The freedom of the individual mind.

Wordsworth seems to have read *Political Justice* at the time of
its publication and almost immediately to have fallen under its
spell. At the outset, it is true, he "lent but a careless ear" to its
"subtleties"; and in his "Letter to the Bishop of Llandaff," written
in the spring of 1793, he surrendered himself only to those parts of
Political Justice which fitted in—as so much of it did—with the
"heart-bracing colloquies" of Beaupuy. In "The Female Vagrant,"
conceived and written in late summer of the same year, he stressed
the broad humanitarian aspects of Godwin's creed, such as his protests against wealth and property, his sympathy with the outcasts
of society, and his hatred of war. However, by the summer of 1794,
a year later, Wordsworth was thinking of reform and revolution
more closely in terms of the fundamental premises of Godwin's
philosophy. Godwin severely condemned revolutions because "they
suspend the wholesome advancement of science and confound the
process of nature and reason." And reform, Godwin asserted, can
only be effective when it advances step by step "with the illumination of our understanding."

An excellent example of Wordsworth's adoption of Godwin's
premises is in his prospectus of "The Philanthropist, a Monthly
Miscellany" that is expounded in June, 1794, in a letter to his friend
Mathews and that is crammed with ideas straight out of *Political
Justice* couched in the language of its author.[7] Among other things,
Wordsworth wrote, "I recoil from the bare idea of a revolution"—
a striking reversal in the thinking of the man who just a year before

in the "Letter to Llandaff" had waived aside objections to the immediate overthrow of the British monarchy. Though Wordsworth was still an enemy of his country's institutions, he now saw through Godwin's eyes that the only way to end abuses was through education and the patient appeal to "reason."[8]

In the summer of 1794 Wordsworth had a renewal of hope for France when he heard by chance, while crossing the sands of the Leven estuary, that Robespierre was dead. He tells in *The Prelude* of his tremendous emotional relief on hearing this news, being fully persuaded that once again the true ideals of the revolution would be carried on. But when France in 1795 "became oppressors in their turn" by ruthlessly invading other lands, Wordsworth turned to Godwin's philosophy of pure reason as the only support left to save him from chaos. His dependence upon Godwinian rationalism, however, was of short duration. For Wordsworth soon realized that Godwin's ideal world of pure reason was an almost complete contradiction of the solid world of man and Nature that had nourished his own beliefs. In a melancholy frame of mind Wordsworth pushed his speculations forward

> . . . till, demanding formal *proof*,
> And seeking it in everything, I lost
> All feeling of conviction, and, in fine,
> Sick, wearied out with contrarieties,
> Yielded up moral questions in despair.

From this quagmire of moral despair Wordsworth retreated to the firmer ground of "mathematics and their clear and solid evidence." But he was in dire need of further help, which by great good fortune was not long in coming.

In the autumn of 1795 an old dream of Wordsworth and his sister Dorothy to establish a home together was realized. Raisley Calvert, brother to William Calvert, had died and left Wordsworth a legacy of £900; and some new Bristol friends named Pinney had provided a handsomely furnished house rent-free, in Dorset, called Racedown Lodge. It was at Racedown that Wordsworth came to terms with himself, cast off his despondency, and re-entered the security of his true beliefs. His salvage was effected partly by a "return to Nature" and partly by the ministration of two precious human agencies, Dorothy and Coleridge. Dorothy cheered and nourished his spirit, gently reawakened his love of natural beauty, called out his compassionate instincts for the poor and simple folk of Dorsetshire, and most of all "preserved him still a poet." Coleridge, by his unstinting praise, gave Wordsworth confidence in himself just when he most needed it. But the road back was long, devious, and painful. Even the visitation of the "gentle breeze" that roused his creative powers when he set out for Racedown from Bristol and promised deliverance did not produce any startling poetic results. The first two months at Racedown were spent in revising and adding to "Salisbury Plain." Then, after nearly a year of silence, Wordsworth began his only drama, *The Borderers*, a five-act tragedy in blank verse.

The Borderers, a document in which can be read the story of Wordsworth's convalescence at Racedown and his verdict upon Godwinian ethics, reveals both an absorption in and a reaction to Godwin's doctrines. It exposes the dangers of the intellect; at the same time, it upholds the validity and worth of benevolence. The story takes place in the thirteenth century in the border land between England and Scotland, a region where there is no law "but what each man makes for himself." The action centers upon Oswald, a kind of Iago, whose apparent "motiveless malignity" is exposed. Some aspects of Wordsworth's moral crisis are revealed in the character of Oswald, but chiefly they are to be read in the actions and responses of his victim, Marmaduke. First, we need to know the story.

In his youth Oswald, a perfectly good man, "the pleasure of all hearts," went on a sea voyage to Syria. The crew persuades him, quite falsely, that the captain has initiated a foul conspiracy against his honor. In a mood of revengeful passion, Oswald insists that the captain be left on a barren island to starve to death; but he soon discovers that the crew has made him the agent of a plot to rid themselves of a master they hate. Some years later, in England, he meets Marmaduke, the "mirror of his youthful self," enjoying the love of a good woman. By some demonic urge, he is driven to recreate his own fate in this counterpart of himself. He attaches himself, accordingly, to the company of borderers commanded by Marmaduke; and, having won his confidence and affection, he proceeds to poison his mind with suspicion.

Marmaduke hopes to marry Idonea, the beautiful and innocent daughter of old blind Herbert, once a baron but deprived arbi-

> . . . obeyed the only law that sense
> Submits to recognize; the immediate law,
> From the clear light of circumstances, flashed
> Upon an independent Intellect.

Then by false reasoning, which he knows to be false, Oswald leads his victim into crime.

After completing *The Borderers*, Wordsworth wrote a remarkable prefatory essay in which he examines the psychology of such people as Oswald.[9] In this essay Wordsworth traces the process by which crime becomes attractive to "a young man of great intellectual powers yet without any solid principles of general benevolence." He sees Oswald's master passions as "pride and the love of distinction." When his happiness deserts him, after being betrayed into a great crime, he quits the world in disgust with strong misanthropic feelings. In his retirement, he weighs the motives of men, finds evil in actions usually esteemed virtuous, and sees good in actions that commonly are considered evil. His contemplations make him a moral skeptic, and "as his skepticism increases he is raised in his own esteem." Now Wordsworth seems to be reviewing in his preface, though perhaps unconsciously, his own mental problems during the past three years. He is, of course, no Oswald; but he had been betrayed, "if not into a great crime," at least into the seduction and desertion of Annette. And, like Oswald, he attempted to free his mind by adopting Godwinian doctrine.

However, it is in the character of Marmaduke, though the dramatic circumstances are wholly altered, that Wordsworth speaks about his deepest experiences. In another paragraph of his prefatory essay, he probes the motives of immoral actions and sheds some light on this point. He notes how moral sentiments are often applied to vicious purposes. In works of imagination, he says, men see the motive and the end; but hypocrisy in real life—one's own or other people's—is seldom recognized until too late. Men are betrayed before they know that an attempt is made to betray them. These observations on the seduction of Marmaduke by Oswald apply equally well to Wordsworth and his unhappy love affair with Annette. What seemed to Wordsworth at the time of his affair to be dictated by the best motives in the end was seen as a "betrayal." Subsequently, he intimately experienced guilt, remorse, and suffering such as Oswald's victim had known. And, when he realized

trarily of his rightful title and lands. But the subtle Os
bribing a crazed vagrant women, spreads the lie that
bought her daughter Idonea and pretends she is his own
he designs to pander Idonea to the lascivious Lord Clif
playing on Marmaduke's imagination with "a few swelling
and a flash/Of truth, enough to dazzle and to blind," Oswal
persuades Marmaduke in the absence of justice to murder th
ingly hypocritical old man.

In a dungeon "dark as the grave" Marmaduke is about t
Herbert dead when a resemblance in the old man's face to Id
baffles him. He looks up to pray and, beholding through a
"a star twinkling above his head," cannot bring himself to kil
Oswald is dismayed; but, with additional innuendos and pres
he gets Marmaduke to resort to the superstition of an ordeal, w
by Marmaduke abandons Herbert on a desolate moor to s
A shepherd, Eldred, whose character has been deceitfully su
discovers Herbert; but, since he cannot help the old man for
of being suspected of foul play, he leaves him to

Oswald acclaims Marmaduke for throwing off the tyrann
custom and independently performing an act guided by the
of reason. Marmaduke, however, is filled with misgivings, wl
soon turn to anguish when he learns that Herbert is innocent. W
Oswald's treachery is discovered, he is slain by the other border
Marmaduke, the once virtuous chief of the band, now crushed a
filled with remorse, begins a solitary life of wandering penance.

The Borderers, like "Salisbury Plain," is a study of some proble
in criminal psychology; but it also presents answers about hum
nature that expose the fallacies inherent in Godwinian rationalisr
Oswald is an utterly godless man in whom the springs of pity ha
dried up; having committed a great crime, he plunges into a care
of deliberate wickedness, gratifying his sense of intellectual powe
by the destruction of innocence and virtue. He is not, like the sailo
in "Salisbury Plain," a victim of social injustice; indeed, *The Bor-*
derers has little to do with social evils. The root of Oswald's deprav-
ity is his vindictiveness and innate pride; he cannot live without
enslaving others. His power, while it lasts, resides in an intellectual
eminence beyond good and evil from whence he initiates his engines of destruction. He tells Marmaduke that he has

that he was the cause of the suffering of an innocent person, his remorse, like that of Marmaduke, took the form of accusing himself and of condemning his presumption.

By writing *The Borderers*, Wordsworth purged himself from pessimism, clarified his thinking about Godwinian ethics, and exposed doctrinaire reasoning as an inadequate basis for justice and as an untrustworthy guide for human conduct. He came to realize that feelings are of primary importance and that the first duty of the individual is to love his fellow man and every living thing. Wordsworth did not mean to condemn the true intention of Godwinism but the evil abuse of it from which he believes he has escaped. Godwin at his humanitarian best he retained.

As a piece of literature, Wordsworth's drama has little to commend it. Coleridge thought it "absolutely wonderful," but it was rejected as unfit for the stage, and readers have since found it rather dull. It is interesting as Wordsworth's first developed attempt at blank verse and as revealing his patent indebtedness to Shakespeare in the Iago-like character of Oswald and in borrowings from *Macbeth*, *Lear*, and *Hamlet*. Wordsworth takes over the entire machinery of Gothic romance in the suspenseful terror of the murder scenes; and, in the character of the villain-hero Oswald, he owes much to the prideful tyrants of Mrs. Ann Radcliffe and Friedrich Schiller.

But Wordsworth was not simply reproducing the ruthlessness of fictional characters in his drama. He also had before his eyes the sinister figures of Robespierre, Jean Paul Marat, and their kind who wrought their havoc upon human happiness. They are the flesh-and-blood counterparts of Oswald, as Wordsworth himself afterward testified: "During my long residence in France, when the revolution was rapidly advancing to its extremes of wickedness, I had frequent opportunities of being an eye-witness of this process (i.e. the progressive hardening of the heart), and it was while that knowledge was fresh in my memory, that the tragedy of *The Borderers* was written."[10]

VIII *Poet of the Human Heart*: "*The Old Cumberland Beggar*" *and* "*The Ruined Cottage*"

By the time Wordsworth finished *The Borderers*, he had resolved the inner discords that plagued him since his return from France. Through the stimulating companionship of Dorothy he had redis-

covered Nature's healing power and was prepared to fuse his renewed love of Nature with a new orientation to society. He was
ready to celebrate in his poetry those aspects of Nature and humanity most likely to encourage the benevolent affections. The first
poem embodying his new vision of man and Nature was "The Old
Cumberland Beggar," completed at Racedown in 1797. Its setting
is the countryside of Cockermouth, and the beggar is one of that
confraternity the poet remembered from his boyhood, who "confined themselves to a stated round in their neighbourhoods" and
were sure of alms at various houses.

Wordsworth made the old man the subject of a poem as a protest
against the "political economists" who at that time were prosecuting
a "war against mendacity in all its forms." The politicians saw beg-
gary as a social nuisance, but Wordsworth did not want to see the
state push the beggars off the roads into the "HOUSE, misnamed
INDUSTRY." He was dead set against workhouses as a cure for un-
employment, places which in most cases were comfortless asylums
for the poor and aged. Wordsworth made his plea to let the old
beggar remain free to live and die "in the eye of Nature." His
person is hallowed by his nearness to Nature and precious because
his helplessness keeps alive the compassion of man. The horseman
stops to place the proffered coin safely within the old man's hat;
she who tends the tollgate stops her work when she sees the aged
beggar coming and lifts the latch for him; the boisterous postboy
turns his wheels aside and passes gently by: "Where'er the aged
Beggar takes his rounds,/The mild necessity of use compels/To acts
of love."

The country folk come to think of the Beggar as a constituent
part of their lives. But Wordsworth even goes beyond the common
response and underscores the benevolent interrelationship of all
creation:

> 'Tis Nature's law
> That none, the meanest of created things,
> Of forms created the most vile and brute,
> The dullest or more noxious, should exist
> Divorced from good—a spirit and pulse of good,
> A life and soul, to every mode of being
> Inseparably linked.

Charles Lamb complained that there was too much lecturing in the poem. But, if this is so, there is also in the descriptive parts an awareness of suffering among the aged that was new in poetry, at least since Shakespeare. And in the last verse paragraph (the last thirty-six lines) there is a moving defense of the old beggar as a person in and for himself. As Wordsworth does with some other vagrant, solitary figures (for example, the leech-gatherer in "Resolution and Independence" and the old soldier in Book IV of *The Prelude*), he reveals the value of the Cumberland beggar's individuality. He seems to hold within him, as Wordsworth's solitaries so often do, the "secret of inscrutable dignity." As John F. Danby says, "He has endured the accidents of experience past the point at which experience has any further power to give or to take away."[11] The old Beggar ". . . is by nature led/To peace so perfect that the young behold/With envy, what the Old Man hardly feels." In the end, he becomes something more than a social problem: he is an archetype of the inherent value of human personality, a precious proof that "all of us have one human heart."

An even better poem than "The Old Cumberland Beggar" embodying Wordsworth's new humanitarianism, if not a more light-hearted one, is the poem "The Ruined Cottage."[12] The story is a simple one. The cottage, which has recently become ruined, had been inhabited by a weaver and his wife and their two children. Their married life had begun in happiness, but became stricken by the successive seasons of blighted harvests and by the plague of war. Margaret struggled through those calamitous years with cheerful hope until Robert, her husband, fell ill of a fever. This costly illness, which consumed their small savings, was followed by a prolonged period in which Robert could find no work. In despair, he joined a troop of soldiers going to a foreign land. Margaret, left alone, tried to keep up hope; but, as time passed and she heard no tidings of her husband, her spirits drooped; she became listless and negligent. The cottage lost its neatness; weeds defaced the hardened soil of the garden; her baby died. For five long years she lingered alone in the cottage which from neglect sank into decay; at last, she became ill from exposure and died.

The narrative of "The Ruined Cottage" bears some resemblances to that of the female vagrant in "Guilt and Sorrow," but the story is told without bitterness and with a new objectivity. This objectivity is aided by the poet's use of a narrator other than himself, a "Pedlar" (later to become the Wanderer of *The Excursion*), and by setting the narrative back ten years in time. Much of the power of "The Ruined Cottage" comes from the skillful handling of the significant detail through which the poet reveals the relentless grinding down of Robert and Margaret—the blighting harvests, the prolonged and costly illness, enforced idleness, war, and desertion.

But the objective details that reveal the concomitant disintegration of Margaret and the cottage make the poem become truly great. The Pedlar on his visits to the cottage observes the significant changes that have taken place in his absence. The border tufts have invaded the garden paths they used to deck; the toadstool has sprung up by the broken arbor. Through these details and many similar ones reported without editorializing by the Pedlar, Wordsworth typifies the process of ruin which has overtaken everything human and man-made in the poem. The details are symbolic and, as such, offer a complete insight into Margaret's problem and character. The outward manifestations of decay are the signs of inner psychological disorder.

Without her husband, Margaret struggles hopelessly for survival. Her grief is compulsive and irreparable. For five tedious years "she lingered on in unquiet widowhood," "a sore heart-wasting." From the broken arbor, if a dog passed by, she would quit the shade and look abroad. Whenever a discharged soldier or a mendicant sailor passed the cottage, or a stranger horseman came by the roadside gate, with faltering voice she would question him, still hoping to learn something of her husband's fate. The poem closes with lines of acute poignancy:

>   Meanwhile her poor hut
> Sank to decay, for he was gone, whose hand
> At the first nippings of October frost
> Closed up each chink, and with fresh bands of straw
> Chequered the green-grown thatch. And so she lived
> Through the long winter, reckless and alone;
> Till this reft house, by frost, and thaw, and rain
> Was sapped, and, when she slept, the nightly damps
> Did chill her breast, and in the stormy day
> Her tattered clothes were ruffled by the wind
> Even at the side of her own fire. Yet still
> She loved this wretched spot, nor would for worlds

Have parted hence, and still that length of road
And this rude bench one torturing hope endeared,
Fast rooted at her heart; and here, my friend,
In sickness she remained, and here she died,
Last human tenant of these ruined walls.

In "The Old Cumberland Beggar" and "The Ruined Cottage" Wordsworth ceased to be a social reformer; he became a poet of the human heart. Believing now that attacks on the social order were likely to result in more harm than good, he was determined "to stress in his poetry the serene rather than the turbulent in nature, the good rather than the evil in common humanity."[13] Accordingly, he united in these poems his love of Nature with a belief in a benevolent necessity for the whole of society. Midway in "The Ruined Cottage" the Pedlar explains to the Poet, his listener, that it would be wantonness to take pleasure in recounting the sufferings of Margaret if there were not "often found/In mournful thoughts, and always might be found,/A power to virtue friendly." In the original manuscript Wordsworth closed the poem with a long reflective argument (afterward incorporated into *The Excursion*, Book IV) in which he tells how, by degrees, the painful story of Margaret became softened in his thoughts and he felt "a holy tenderness pervade his frame." So it was providentially meant that, out of all human experiences, whether of suffering or of joy, man's being should be oriented to moral goodness:

Thus deeply drinking in the soul of things
We shall be wise perforce, and we shall move
From strict necessity along the path
Of order and of good.

"The Ruined Cottage" marks a manifest advance in Wordsworth's poetic power as well as in his social thinking. He makes no use of terror or Gothic trappings to jack up an emotional response. He does not exaggerate, nor deplore, nor condemn; and at no point does he intrude a grudge against society. Instead of resentment toward the oppressors of the poor (such as he had felt in his revolutionary days), he awakens by simple, unadorned statements sympathy and love for the gentle Margaret. With this remarkably fine poem, Wordsworth's formative years as a poet ended. He entered at last into his true heritage.

Lyrical Ballads, *1798*

I *Two Poets Join Forces and* Lyrical Ballads *Is Born*

O N a memorable day at Racedown in June, 1797, Wordsworth
recited "The Ruined Cottage" to Coleridge, who hailed it "the
finest poem in our language, comparing it with any of the same or
similar length."[1] Coleridge's admiration for his new friend, as well
as for his friend's poetry, was unbounded. In a letter to Joseph Cottle, he spoke of Wordsworth with heartfelt sincerity as "the greatest
man I ever knew."[2] Wordsworth was equally drawn to Coleridge,
for each discovered in the other the fulfillment of an immediate
need. Coleridge found in Wordsworth a friend who recognized his
genius and who offered a steady hand to direct it. In return, besides the kindling warmth of unstinted admiration, Coleridge gave
to Wordsworth the vast resources of his fertilizing intellect. "He
was most wonderful," Wordsworth wrote long afterward, "in the
power he possessed of throwing out in profusion grand central truths
from which might be evolved the most comprehensive systems."[3]

Within a month after Coleridge's visit, the Racedown household
was broken up; William and Dorothy, in order to be near Coleridge,
settled at Alfoxden, a lovely Queen Anne mansion about three miles
from Coleridge's cottage at Nether Stowey. During the momentous
year that was to follow, from July, 1797, to July, 1798, the two
friends enjoyed daily companionship and almost constant exaltation
of spirits. With the fervor of highminded youth, they talked of making the world better through their poetry. They hoped in that time
of national crisis and pessimism to bring to men, disillusioned by
the French revolutionary idea, the secret they had discovered of
the principle of joy in the universe. They would preach no political
or social reform; but, in order to reach men, they would cast out
of their writing all poetic diction and return to directness, sincerity,
and basic human emotions. The older writers and the traditional
ballads would be their models.

To realize their dreams, the two poets tried several times at collaboration but never with success. From one of these attempts, however, was born the idea of the *Lyrical Ballads*. Late in the afternoon of November 13, 1797, William, Dorothy, and Coleridge began a walking trip to the Valley of Stones near Lynmouth. To defray the modest expenses of their journey, they planned to compose a ballad to be sold to *The New Monthly Magazine*. In the course of their walk that evening, they began together the composition of "The Ancient Mariner" to which Wordsworth, as he said, "made several trifling contributions." As they endeavored to proceed conjointly that same evening, their manners proved so widely different that Wordsworth withdrew from the undertaking. The practical difficulties of collaboration brought to light the fundamental differences in their mental operations, and they began to talk of a volume of poems, each working in his own manner. Coleridge gives a graphic account twenty years later in *Biographia Literaria*, Chapter XIV, of the division of labor between them:

The thought suggested itself (to which of us I do not recollect) that a series of poems might be composed of two sorts. In the one, the incidents and agents were to be, in part at least, supernatural; and the excellence aimed at was to consist in the interesting of the affections by the dramatic truth of such emotions, as would naturally accompany such situations, supposing them real . . . . For the second class, subjects were to be chosen from ordinary life; the characters and incidents were to be such as will be found in every village and its vicinity, where there is a meditative and feeling mind to seek after them, or to notice them, when they present themselves.

In this idea originated the plan of *Lyrical Ballads*, in which it was agreed that my endeavours should be directed to persons and characters supernatural, or at least romantic; yet so as to transfer from our inward nature a human interest . . . sufficient to procure for these shadows of imagination that willing suspension of disbelief for the moment, which constitutes poetic faith. Mr. Wordsworth, on the other hand, was to propose to himself as his object, to give the charm of novelty to things of every day, and to excite a feeling analogous to the supernatural, by awakening the mind's attention from the lethargy of custom, and directing it to the loveliness and wonders of the world before us.

[Both of them were to observe] the two cardinal points of poetry, the power of exciting the sympathy of the reader by a faithful adherence to the truth of nature, and the power of giving the interest of novelty by the modifying colours of imagination.

Coleridge put the finishing touches to "The Rime of the Ancient Mariner" in March, 1798, which was given first place in the new volume. He began "Christabel" with high hopes, but he got through only Part I that spring and never finished it. Wordsworth, until the first week of March, was engaged entirely in blank-verse composition; but, from early March to May, 1798, a flood tide of inspiration resulted in a number of poems written expressly for the projected volume with the theory in mind. Scholars know, incidentally, from a letter written to James Tobin on March 6 that the theory was not created afterward merely to justify the poems. Theory and poetry went hand in hand. During the summer the offerings of each poet deemed suitable for the new volume were gathered together and taken to Joseph Cottle of Bristol for publication. That glorious afterthought, "Tintern Abbey," written in September, was added later to the other pieces already set up for the press. The joint collection was entitled *Lyrical Ballads, with a Few Other Poems* and was provided with a short "Advertisement" written by Wordsworth.

II *The Intention and Originality of the New Poetry*

In his preamble Wordsworth recorded the chief points of the new poetic theory and sought to disarm readers against prejudging the experimental poems written under it. He reminds his readers that the materials of poetry are "to be found in every subject which can interest the human mind"—and as evidence there are the poets and the poems themselves. He states that the majority of the poems in the volume are to be considered as experiments. "They were written," he says, "chiefly with a view to ascertain how far the language of conversation in the middle and lower classes of society is adapted to the purposes of poetic pleasure." What Wordsworth does not say, but what one learns from the Preface to *Lyrical Ballads*, 1800, written at length to defend them (of which more later), is that he wanted to identify poetry with life—to penetrate the "lethargy of custom" and make people feel anew the primal impulses common to all mankind.

To achieve this result, Wordsworth concentrated upon the emotion to be aroused by the poem and not the poem itself; as he says in the 1800 Preface, "The feeling therein developed gives importance to the action and situation and not the action and situation to the feeling." He intended that the emotion aroused by his poems would be so powerful and of such a kind that it would reveal, as with a religious force, the workings of the human heart. By this means he hoped also to awaken and spread abroad (a wish close to his heart) a humanitarian attitude toward those born to "a poor and humble lot."

There is no trace of the talks of the two poets that resulted in the title *Lyrical Ballads;* however, they have left sufficient evidence to interpret their intended meaning. Both of them were great admirers of Bishop Percy's collection of ballads *Reliques of Ancient Poetry* (published in 1765), and Wordsworth declared in his Preface of 1815 that English poetry had been "absolutely redeemed by it." There were also broadside ballads hawked in the streets, such as "Babes in the Wood," which Wordsworth would have heard in London and which very well could have served him as models for such pieces as "Goody Blake and Harry Gill." He wrote to Francis Wrangham that some of his poems had been written with a view to their eventual circulation as broadsides and so, perhaps, to their supplanting the half-penny ballads of the time; they were "flowers and useful herbs to take the place of weeds."[4] Also in popular favor at that time were the translations of German "ballads," especially of G. A. Bürger's "Lenore" and "Die wilde Jäger." And there were approximations of all these ballads in the magazines, newspapers, and pamphlets where current poetry appeared. But in their title *Lyrical Ballads* Wordsworth and Coleridge chiefly had in mind Percy's folk ballads. In them a tragic story is narrated. On the other hand, in a lyric poem the essence is a heightened emotion. That is where "lyrical" comes into the title, for in their ballads the emphasis is not on the story or the dramatic events but on the emotions embodied in the story. The stories are reduced to their pathetic human essentials; the heartrending situations are actualized. Because of the feeling, the lyrical element, one must accept the story, willingly suspend disbelief in the supernatural happenings of "The Ancient Mariner," or be interested in such trivialities of adventure as occur in "The Idiot Boy."

Lyrical Ballads was published anonymously by J. and A. Arch, London (Cottle at the last minute having transferred his copyright), in October, 1798. Of the twenty-three poems in the volume, four are by Coleridge, including, besides "The Ancient Mariner," a conversation piece in blank verse entitled "The Nightingale" and two extracts from his tragedy *Osorio*, "The Foster Mother's Tale" and "The Dungeon." Of Coleridge's contributions only "The Ancient Mariner" was written to fulfill his assignment in the new poetic theory. However, the majority of Wordsworth's contributions, which total nineteen, were written expressly for the projected volume with the theory in mind. Those not involving the theory, apart from "Tintern Abbey," which Wordsworth himself says was composed in the loftier and impassioned strain of the ode, were poems written before 1797—"Lines Left upon a Seat in a Yew-tree," "The Female Vagrant," "Lines written near Richmond," "The Convict," and "The Old Man Travelling"—none of which show any trace of ballad literature.

All the other poems, in a variety of ways, are the real experiment wherein Wordsworth attempts to coordinate the artless art of the ballads with his own observation of the psychological processes underlying the lives of simple men. The originality of Wordsworth's contributions to *Lyrical Ballads* was in the phychological mode and power of the poems and in their language rather than in their subject matter. His figures, settings, and themes were commonplaces in the magazine poetry of the day;[5] but no other poet brought to them such an eye for precise observation, such an ear for the vernacular, or such a heart and mind for probing deeply the essentials of man's being.

One of the most precious gifts that Coleridge brought to Wordsworth was his championship of the associational psychology of David Hartley. This psychology was not new to Wordsworth, but Coleridge's enthusiasm for it quickened Wordsworth's interest in it and sharpened his perceptions. With Hartley as his guide, Wordsworth turned his back on his personal life and, as has been said, "made something of a strenuous voyage of discovery—a sort of arctic expedition—into a region where life was reduced to its elements, the outward trappings at their simplest."[6] His intention above all in *Lyrical Ballads*, as he stated in the 1800 Preface, was to make incidents and situations chosen from common life "interesting by tracing in them . . . the primary laws of our nature: chiefly, as far as regards the manner in which we associate ideas in a state of excitement." What he did was to turn tragic themes into psychological studies so that the feeling developed could give importance to the action.

To support his aim, Wordsworth deliberately imitated the speech of the lower classes, with all its peculiarities of vocabulary and syntax. He sometimes employed the mannerisms of uneducated speech (a feature of popular ballads), such as the repetition of pronouns after a substantive ("The doctor *he* has made him wait") or reduplication in the predicate to reveal an inattentive mind ("*It* stands erect, *this aged thorn*"). Sometimes he tried to suggest the naïveté of folk ballads through language and rhythms that were "unsophisticated to the point of doggerel." There were gains and losses from Wordsworth's conscious attempt to use "the language of the middle and lower classes for the purposes of poetic pleasure." Yet, over-all, the newness of style and the simplicity of language, despite its occasional crudeness, give an impression of poetry operating in a new dimension of freshness and depth.

On one level, Wordsworth's experiment involved poetic diction; but, at a deeper level, *Lyrical Ballads* is an experiment in modes of dramatic technique.[7] In order to mask his own passion and to identify himself with the passions that stirred his characters, Wordsworth used dramatic self-projection. Of the thirteen experimental poems, nine are dramatic or semidramatic in form. In these he used a variety of methods, picking up and laying down his masks. Sometimes he is the narrator, sometimes the characters involved, and sometimes the poet himself. By changing the voice, he can step from one frame to another and back again: the storyteller, story, and poet-manipulator are reciprocally and dramatically related. By using all the devices of language, meter, and dramatic modes available to him as a poet, he hoped to convey passion to readers not accustomed to sympathize with men in the lower levels of society whose manner and language are different from their own.

III   "*The Thorn*"

"The Thorn" carries out Wordsworth's avowed intention to trace in situations of common life "the primary laws of our nature." Like Coleridge's "The Ancient Mariner" and his own "Peter Bell" and "Goody Blake and Harry Gill," the poem is a study in mental pathology. In its own fashion, it illustrates the tremendous effect upon the imagination of a painful idea vividly impressed upon the mind. It grew out of Wordsworth's excited notice of a stunted thorn tree, which, under unusual aspects of mist and rain, was revealed to him with visionary impressiveness. He felt that if he could produce on other minds the effect that the "poetry of nature," had produced on his mind, then the great problem of the source and end of imaginative art was solved.

To commemorate his vision, he attached a tragic story to the scene; and he chose as a medium of communication to the reader a simple narrator in the person of a loquacious, retired sea captain. Wordsworth had a surprisingly specific narrator in mind; and, in a long note to the poem in 1800, he spelled out in detail his character and mental habits. He is an important link to the poem but not an end in himself. As Wordsworth describes him, he is credulous and talkative from indolence, prone to superstition, slow of faculties and deep in feelings, and has a modest endowment of imagination. He is represented as sharing his thoughts with a simple villager of less sensitivity than his own. His language is folk oriented, watered down with clichés, and encumbered with almost obsessive repetitions. But he is an honest witness. For all the self-imposed fetters under which Wordsworth labors, he handles his materials with artistic sophistication and with a high degree of effectiveness.

The narrator begins in a matter-of-fact, repetitious manner by describing the thorn tree as an "aged" and "a wretched thing" encumbered and overgrown with mosses. It becomes for the reader an emblem of the human story of Martha Ray in her misery; to the villagers, as represented by the mariner, it is an emblem of the crime of child murder. The poem continues in the same flat, repetitious language with a description of the muddy pond; then in more fanciful language presents a beauteous hill of moss and a woman who often sits beside it:

> A Woman in a scarlet cloak,
> And to herself she cries,
> "Oh misery! oh misery!
> Oh woe is me! oh misery!"

The near-banal repetitions used by the narrator in describing the thorn and the pond thwart the reader's sympathetic response and hold it in abeyance. But, when the plaintive cry of the lonely woman is repeated, the reader's emotions are releasd. To re-enforce and sustain them, Wordsworth's own passion and beauty of language break through in the next stanza:

> At all times of the day and night
> This wretched Woman thither goes;
> And she is known to every star,
> And every wind that blows;
> And there beside the Thorn she sits
> When the blue day-light's in the skies,
> And when the whirlwind's on the hill,
> Or frosty air is keen and still,
> And to herself she cries,
> "Oh misery! oh misery!
> Oh woe is me! oh misery!"

The proper conditions have now been established for the mariner to tell the poor woman's story as he has been able to piece it together. Some two and twenty years ago Martha Ray gave her company to Stephen Hill, who promised to marry her. But Stephen forsook her, though she was carrying his child, and married another. On that woeful day she lost her reason, but a villager claims her reason was restored just before her child was born. No one ever knew when or where Martha Ray gave birth to the child; but about that time some remember that she often climbed up the mountain and that at night, when the wind blew, cries were heard coming from the mountain peak. Some say they were living voices; others swear they were voices of the dead.

After the narrator has finished his story, he tells how he chanced one day in a windy rainstorm to come across Martha Ray in a scarlet cloak sitting beside the old thorn. He did not speak, but he heard her cry, "Oh misery! Oh misery!" At this point, to heighten the coloring of imagination, Wordsworth invokes village superstitions that touch the incident with mystery and awe. Some say she strangled or drowned her baby and buried it beneath the hill of moss. Some say the scarlet moss is red from the infant's blood. And some say

> . . . if to the pond you go,
> And fix on it a steady view,
> The shadow of a babe you trace,
> A baby and a baby's face,
> And that it looks at you.

At the end, attention is focused upon the thorn bound with the heavy tufts of moss that strive to drag it to the ground; and the poem closes with the repeated cries of Martha Ray reverberating in the reader's consciousness.

How successful, one may ask, was Wordsworth in adopting his new poetical theories in "The Thorn"? Coleridge objected to "a daring humbleness of Language and Versification, and a strict adherence to matter of fact, even to prolixity." He thought it was not possible "to imitate truly a dull and garrulous discourser, without repeating the effects of dullness and garrulity." Wordsworth made significant changes after Coleridge's criticism; but, in refining the narrator's language, the poet makes him more dramatically false. Wordsworth was more nearly right in the first rendering, for the narrator's very irrelevancies and redundancies force the reader to take in his full story's span and, after the reader's mind has been freed from them, to feel the shock of man's inhumanity to man. A strong feeling of compassion survives at the end. "The Thorn" just misses by a narrow margin being one of Wordsworth's great poems.

IV *"The Idiot Boy"*

"The Idiot Boy" offered a sharper challenge to current taste than any other poem in *Lyrical Ballads*. It was criticized and ridiculed on all sides, yet with Wordsworth the poem always remained one of his favorites. He composed it with great glee almost extempore. It is a poem of mixed modes being at once poignantly real and comically absurd. On the comic side, it is essentially a rustic mock-epic including a life-and-death issue, last chance of success depending upon the least likely person to succeed, frantic search and rescue of the rescuer, and finally the happy resolution of everyone's afflictions. Wordsworth, who meant for the reader to enjoy the bathos of the adventure, supports the comic mood with empty phrases and shabby rhymes: "fiddle-faddle—saddle"; "shocked her—doctor."

The whole action is a kind of parody on knight-errantry. The champion to the rescue is Johnny Foy, the Idiot Boy. The doting mother of the Idiot Boy is Betty Foy, neighbor to Old Susan Gale who lives alone. One clear March night, when the moon is up and the owls are shouting, Susan Gale falls painfully ill. There is none within a mile around to help, and Betty cannot leave her alone. So Betty mounts her idiot boy upon her pony and excitedly tells

him—directions repeated over and over—to fetch the doctor in the village. Betty proudly watches her idiot boy depart, but one can guess that he will not go far upon the right way; for he is mounted on "a horse that thinks/And when he thinks, his pace is slack."

Poor Susan and Betty wait and wait until past midnight for the doctor and his guide. When her anxiety for Johnny can no longer be withstood—"he is but half-wise"—she leaves Susan to search for him. She hastens to the village and there rouses the doctor, who sleepily and grumblingly declares he has seen nothing of Johnny. Poor Betty is so overcome with worry over her idiot boy that she completely forgets to send the doctor to Old Susan Gale. It is now three o'clock, and Betty has lost all hope. Suddenly the thought strikes her that the pony, "who is mild and good," has perhaps carried Johnny along the dell to the family woodlot.

And what has Johnny been doing all this time? Perhaps, says Wordsworth, giving his fancy reign, he is riding up the cliffs and peaks to lay his hands upon a star; perhaps, like Don Quixote (for the idiot was a "natural" like La Mancha's knight), he's hunting sheep, "A fierce and dreadful hunter he!" But, in truth, Johnny, though near the thunderous waterfall, is just sitting upright upon his mount as the pony feeds upon the grass. Good Betty Foy, when she sees him whom she loves, screams with delight; and, in her eagerness to embrace him (Wordsworth describes her action with a touch of slapstick), she almost overturns the horse. Alive with joy, she kisses and kisses again her idiot boy and tells him to never mind the doctor. Meanwhile, poor old Susan, beset by fears over what has happened to Betty and her idiot boy, rises from her bed as if cured by magic. The three are happily reunited and Johnny, when asked by Betty where he had been,

> Made answer, like a traveller bold,
> (His very words I give to you,)
> "The cocks did crow to-whoo, to-whoo,
> And the sun did shine so cold!"
> —Thus answered Johnny in his glory,
> And that was all his travel's story.

The action of Wordsworth's mock-heroic is dramatically paced and well timed. The rattling comic tempo never lets up; Wordsworth could not find a place to insert a description of the Idiot Boy without hindering the forward movement. The tone is "beautifully mock-solemn yet indulgently ready with its sympathy."[8] The reader is called upon for tenderness yet is not asked to surrender his identity. Wordsworth as narrator makes the reader aware of his masks. He assumes a colloquial personality and addresses intermittent, half-jocular remarks to his muse, to the reader, and to the characters in his tale. The result is an irony that permits identification with the anguished passion of Betty Foy; at the same time, it allows for an awareness of the exuberant delight of the poet's play of mind and turns of emotion.

Because of Wordsworth's levity of style, a derisive public mistook his basic purpose, which was to illustrate the depth of a mother's love lavished upon an object repellent to others. Coleridge, who attacked "The Idiot Boy," charged that the author had not "taken sufficient care to preclude from the reader's fancy the disgusting images of *ordinary morbid idiocy*" and that he had, as a result, produced a "laughable burlesque on the blindness of anile dotage."[9] John Wilson frankly confessed his inability to care for the poem: "I admire the talents of the *artist*, the *picture* disgusts me inexpressibly."

Wordsworth wrote a spirited rejoinder to Wilson reproaching him and others for false delicacy which showed "a certain want of comprehensiveness in thinking and feeling." For himself, he said, he often applied to idiots "that sublime expression of Scripture, that their life is hidden with God." The spectacle of a mother's unselfish love for an idiot child was for Wordsworth a realization of the mystery of original goodness. This was the divine side of the mysteriously meaningful dialogue in his comic adventure of the Idiot Boy. Without condescension or prudential morality, Wordsworth got right inside his characters and traced for his readers' edification the love which gives freely and without thought of any reward. Unfortunately, the reading public has not yet accepted Wordsworth's poem on the terms in which it was offered.

V   *"Peter Bell"*

Like "The Thorn" and "The Idiot Boy," "Peter Bell" was originally intended as one of Wordsworth's experimental poems for *Lyrical Ballads*; but it was too long for inclusion and was withheld from publication until 1819. When it did appear, it was parodied and ridiculed on all sides, though it was called by Coleridge "most wonderful and admirable." Coleridge's tribute is the more significant because he knew that "Peter Bell" was his friend's rival to "The Ancient Mariner." As Wordsworth explained in his prefatory letter to Southey, dated April 7, 1819, "Peter Bell" was "composed under a belief that the imagination not only does not require for its exercise the intervention of supernatural agency, but that, though such agency be excluded, the faculty may be called forth as imperiously, and for kindred results of pleasure, by incidents within the compass of poetic probability, in the humblest departments of daily life."

Precisely as in "The Ancient Mariner," Wordsworth's poem tells of the wanton cruelty of a man toward an animal and of the release of the man from the consequences of his crime through a gush of pity. But, whereas in "The Ancient Mariner" the consequences are magical, the sinner in "Peter Bell" is frightened into becoming "a good and honest man" by a mental process that is strictly psychological—by tricks of moonlight, echoes of an ass's bray, the cry of a boy searching for his dead father, a withered leaf, some Methodist hymn-singers, and finally a weeping woman. The poem is one of Wordsworth's most intense studies of the workings of the human mind, and it is a testament to his central faith that "Nature," even in the humblest departments of daily life, is capable of influencing for good even one of her more rebellious and insensitive children.

Though the theme of "Peter Bell" is highly serious, its form and treatment are comic. Wordsworth uses light tetrameter stanzas and a folksy diction appropriate to the narrator in his role as provincial poet. In the prologue, the poet asks to be let down among his simple neighbors to tell a tale of "The common growth of mother-earth." In all three parts of the poem, the language is pitched on the colloquial level, and the verses are spun out with bathetic wordiness. In no other poem by Wordsworth is the diction so daringly commonplace and the humor so blatantly realistic. Much of the humor was progressively toned down in succeeding revisions, but much of the comic earthiness remains in the poem to delight appreciative readers or to feed the ego of the parodists.

The hero of the story is Peter Bell, a wild rover such as Wordsworth had walked with along the river Wye. A potter by trade, he has for more than thirty years been living in the open air and traveling in sight of the grand and the beautiful. But he was brutal, immoral, and insensitive; Nature never could find the way into his heart: "A primrose by a river's brim/A yellow primrose was to him,/And it was nothing more." However, the terrors he experiences one beautiful moonlight night open the way to his regeneration.

On that night in November, Peter, while trudging along all alone beside the river Swale, took a path that promised to shorten his way. The path leads him to a quarry and, beyond it, to a meadow where he discovers a solitary ass with his head hanging over a stream of water. In his pique over missing his way, Peter determines to steal the ass. Accordingly, he leaps upon the creature's back, kicks him, and wildly jerks on the halter; but the ass will not budge. Wordsworth confesses that "he took delight in the habits, odd tricks, and physiognomy of the asses that roamed the Alfoxden woods." At this point in the action, he interjects a comical observation. Peter, fearful of being discovered in his theft, leaps from the back of the ass and cautiously looks around him. All is silent far and near— "Only the Ass, with motion dull,/Upon the pivot of his skull/Turns round his long left ear."

Peter now raises his staff and staggers the "patient, uncomplaining beast" with a cruel blow. The ass drops gently upon his knees; falls and lies upon the river's bank; and, as he does so, turns a reproachful look upon Peter. The hardhearted rover mercilessly beats the helpless creature until he lies still as death. With a curse Peter declares he will fling him into the river. Whereupon the ass sends forth a clamorous bray; and, as Peter turns to his demonic work, the ass again more ruefully lengthens out "The hard dry seesaw of his horrible bray!" A strange fear seizes Peter; he drops his staff, bends over the water, and imagines that he sees in its depths strange sights: Is it a gallows, a coffin, or a shroud? Is it a grisly idol, imp, or fiend? What he sees is a dead man's face seen through the water by moonlight.

Wordsworth is here practicing Coleridge's art of the impact of the supernatural upon simple, superstitious minds, but doing so by shedding "the charm of novelty" over the circumstances of every day. Astonishment and fear seize Peter; he looks fascinated—"he cannot choose but look"; then, with a frightful shriek, he falls back into a dead faint. The process of inward change has begun, though at first the only manifestations are terror.

Peter at length recovers from his swoon; and, encouraged by the ass, who stands beside him, he probes the stream until he dislodges and hauls to shore the drowned master over whom the ass had kept watch without food for four days. Strange pity surges through the heart of Peter, and he vows to do whatever the ass would have him do. He mounts upon the creature's back (the mounting on the ass is for Peter what his blessing of the water snakes had been for the Ancient Mariner) and is carried toward the master's home; but he is confronted on the way with a series of "severe interventions" that best serve Nature's own aims. Near the quarry's mouth a strange, piercing cry strikes Peter's ear, the likes of which he has never heard. His fear is quickened by the wild, fantastic shadows of the quarry rocks and even by the rustling of a withered leaf. When he sees the bloody wound he had inflicted on the ass's head, a ghostly agony passes through his brain. An underground explosion in the mine beneath him adds to his terror.

But, of all these sights and sounds, one is of special importance; for it coalesces with an important memory. A ruined chapel which they pass by reminds him of a similar scene in Fifeshire, where he married his sixth wife, a mere girl of sixteen. The scene, with its associated memories, turns him adrift into the past. Wordsworth now calls upon "Spirits of the Mind" (such ministrants as he himself in boyhood had felt in darkness or stormy night) to show their empire over the heart of Peter Bell. Peter has the shocking experience of seeing a vision of himself, "an unsubstantial creature," "not four yards from the broad highway"; and "stretched beneath the furze" is his poor Highland child-wife, the victim of his wickedness, dying there before him. A grievous contrition seizes Peter, which is shortly thereafter confirmed by the voice of a Methodist preacher crying aloud from a tabernacle, "Repent! repent!" When the ass leads the way to his owner's home, the widow piteously questions Peter about her dead husband; and, when the miner's orphaned boy returns and lovingly greets the ass, Peter Bell can endure no more and sobs aloud. After ten months' melancholy he became "a good and honest man."

"Peter Bell" is a very bold experiment, for one would expect such a serious subject as the regeneration of a sinful man to be treated with greater dignity. It is not surprising that the poem has seemed ridiculous to many. But, when Hazlitt visited Wordsworth at Alfoxden and heard the poet read "Peter Bell" aloud in the open air, "The comment on it by his face and voice was very different from that of some later critics! Whatever might be said of the poem 'his face was as a book where men might read strange matters,' and he announced the fate of his hero in prophetic tones."[10] Over the years, Wordsworth subdued the humor and removed several passages of satire objectionable to respected friends. But he never tampered with the tributes to the courageous ass. Nor did he ever yield his conviction of the importance of Peter's discovery "That man's heart is a holy thing."

VI *"Goody Blake and Harry Gill" and "Simon Lee"*

"Goody Blake and Harry Gill" is not strictly a lyrical ballad; that is, the feeling does not give importance to the action, but the action and situation give importance to the feeling. This poem comes closest to the kind Wordsworth told Wrangham might be written to circulate as a broadside ballad. The poet adapts the voice and idiom of a rustic commentator and projects his story in a strain of ballad homiletics, at once "sophisticated and grotesque." He took the "true story" from Erasmus Darwin's *Zoönomia*, stated as happening in Warwickshire, and located it in Dorsetshire where he had come to know firsthand the acute suffering among impoverished peasants during the severe winter.

The poet quickly engages the sympathy of the reader for Goody Blake, a poor old dame who lives alone in an unsheltered cottage. Sometimes, when the frost is past enduring and her poor old bones ache from the cold, this *canty* dame leaves her meager fire to break sticks from the hedge of the lusty drover, Harry Gill. The climax comes when, long suspecting her trespasses, Harry, one frosty night, watches to seize old Goody Blake. But he becomes the victim of his own folly; when he seizes and threatens her, she kneels and prays:

> She prayed, her withered hand uprearing,
> While Harry held her by the arm—
> "God! who art never out of hearing,
> O may he never more be warm!"
> The cold, cold moon above her head,
> Thus on her knees did Goody pray;
> Young Harry heard what she had said:
> And icy cold he turned away.

Harry piles on three riding coats and pins blankets about him, "Yet still his jaws and teeth they chatter." Never will Harry Gill be warm again.

In the fulfillment of the curse, the borderland between magic and psychology is bridged. Wordsworth stated in the 1800 Preface that he wished in "Goody Blake and Harry Gill" to draw attention "to the truth that the power of the human imagination is sufficient to produce such changes in our physical nature as might appear almost miraculous." Goody's curse is made the clear agent of rightful destruction. Though Goody Blake is caught stealing, the moral law supports her in inflicting Harry Gill with perpetual cold. To bear home his moral, the poet closes with a wry twist of ballad piety: "Now think, ye farmers all, I pray/Of Goody Blake and Harry Gill!"

In "Simon Lee, the Old Huntsman," a poem about one of Wordsworth's neighbors near Alfoxden, the feelings do give importance to the action; hence, it is a true "lyrical ballad." In his youth Simon Lee had been a merry huntsman to the Squires of Alfoxden; no one could outrun him or surpass him in the chase. But in old age he was bereft of health and he suffered neglect and poverty. He had become so enfeebled that one day, when Wordsworth was passing by, Simon was incapable of coping with the single root of an old tree. The poet, who proffered his help, easily severed the root with a single blow of the ax; and tears of thanks poured forth from the grateful old man. The incident of the root-cutting is told with matter-of-fact faithfulness, even a trace of humor; but the moral lesson is pronounced in prophetic tones:

> —I've heard of hearts unkind, kind deeds
> With coldness still returning;
> Alas! the gratitude of men
> Hath oftener left me mourning.

No one of the ballads was more often laughed at than "Simon Lee," chiefly because of the extreme rudeness of style. The language is prosy and shockingly realistic: "His ancles they are swoln and thick;/His legs are thin and dry." Wordsworth's art is unpretentious, yet it is still effective. If one can reject the temptation to laugh or to be sentimental, he will find that the poet has prepared him carefully for the vindication of the feelings of benevolence and gratitude.

VII   *Three "Complaints"*

"The Mad Mother," "The Complaint of a Forsaken Indian Woman," and "The Last of the Flock" are "complaints." The complaint is a ballad form in a pattern already set by Percy and especially adapted to Wordsworth's purposes; for the story is told, as in a dramatic monologue, by the person most deeply concerned and the speaker's feelings are made a significant part of it. Each of these three ballads is set up in ten line stanzas with the meter made "more lyrical and rapid" in order to engage the reader's sympathy. In the finest of the complaints, "The Mad Mother," Wordsworth drives deep into the piteous incoherence of her derangement; as Coleridge so admiringly put it, "in which from the increased sensibility the sufferer's attention is abruptly drawn off by every trifle, and at the same instant plucked back again by the one despotic thought. . . ." The circumstances, Wordsworth tells us, were based on a story told him by "a lady in Bristol" who had herself seen such a woman as he described.

"The Complaint of a Forsaken Indian Woman," taken from an account the poet had read in Hearne's *Journey from Hudson Bay,* was avowedly written to "follow the fluxes and refluxes of the mind . . . by accompanying the last struggles of a human being at the approach of death, cleaving in solitude to life and society." The eddying of thought and a very fine use of a double refrain create a wonderul artistic effect, but a sophisticated sentimentalism makes this tragic ballad less appealing to most readers than "The Mad Mother." The third of Wordsworth's complaints, "The Last of the Flock," based on an incident that occurred in the village of Holford, close by Alfoxden, is far more homely and prosaic than the other two complaints, though Wordsworth would not have felt it less pathetic. It centers on the anguish of a shepherd who was forced in time of need to sell his precious flock in order to keep his children from starving to death.

VIII   *Two Didactic Anecdotes*

Two didactic poems, "Anecdote for Fathers" and "We Are Seven," both spoken in the poet's own person and founded on fact, involve the questioning of children. In "Anecdote for Fathers" the child was a son of Wordsworth's friend, Basil Montagu; and the boy had been two or three years under the poet's care. Dorothy found the boy a "perpetual pleasure," but Wordsworth complained that "he lies like a little devil." The full title on its first appearance read "Anecdote for Fathers, Shewing How the Art of Lying May be Taught." In 1800 "the Art of Lying" was changed to "the Practice of Lying" in the subtitle, and in 1845 the subtitle was dropped for a Latin epigram from Eusebius which, translated, means: "Restrain your eagerness, for I shall speak falsely if you force me."

In the poem, the reader observes the vagrant wish of the child to be in a place he is not in; when the boy is questioned by his father, and when he is pushed still harder, his thoughtless wish is bolstered by still another vagrant statement which is an outright lie. Wordsworth wanted to show that a child's feelings have their own inner laws; if an adult mind, with its logical ideas of cause and effect, intrudes itself into the unthinking mind of a child, distortions and untruths result. Some persons consider Wordsworth's poem to be a conscious refutation of Godwin's belief that lying is unnatural and is only the product of an evil social system. The poet learned quite a different lesson from his "dearest boy."

"We are Seven" is founded upon a conversation the poet had with a little girl at Goodrich Castle in 1793. Wordsworth composed the last stanza first, having begun with the last line; when he needed an opening stanza to complete it, Coleridge supplied it impromptu. Wordsworth's aim in writing this poem was to show "the obscurity and perplexity which in childhood attend our notion of death, or rather our utter inability to admit that notion." He himself acknowledged, in his comments on the "Ode on Immortality," that nothing was more difficult for him in childhood than to admit the notion of death as a state applicable to his own being. In "We Are Seven" Wordsworth states that the little girl cannot accept the idea of death because of feelings of animal vivacity:

> —A simple Child,
> That lightly draws its breath,
> And feels its life in every limb,
> What should it know of death?

This feeling is different from "a sense of the indomitableness of the spirit within me" which the poet says possessed him in childhood. In either case, however, the strong sense of personal identity and the consequent impossibility on the part of the child to admit the idea of personal annihilation are the same.

Because of the cumbrous intermixture of the grotesque with the exquisite and sublime in "We Are Seven," the poem quickly became a favorite with the parodists. One of the choicest parodies is Max Beerbohm's caricature of Wordsworth holding an umbrella while cross-questioning a sad-looking urchin in the rain. But Wordsworth's poem was also very popular. There were many single copies printed surreptitiously and circulated in the way broadside ballads were. In the Lilly Library at Indiana University there is a copy of the ballad printed on a single sheet in seven different languages, one of them Japanese.

IX   *Four Nature Poems*

Among the experimental ballads there are four Nature poems which epitomize Wordsworth's faith—"To My Sister," "Lines Written in Early Spring," "Expostulation and Reply," and "The Tables Turned." They are set forth in language which is neither that of a native nor of a child but that of the poet himself. Coleridge deplored in *Biographia Literaria* Wordsworth's undue predilection for the *dramatic* form in certain of the ballads; but in these poems, except for the opening query by Matthew in "Expostulation and Reply," the poet is everywhere speaking in his own person. Moreover, the language that he uses bears a close relationship with the genius of English language at its simple best.

"To My Sister," the first of these poems to be written, celebrates with a "fine, careless rapture" the coming of spring warmth. One early March day at Alfoxden, Wordsworth felt overpoweringly the joy of spring—"Each minute sweeter than before"—and sent word to Dorothy to put on quickly her woodland dress and come forth to spend the day with him in idleness. They need no book, he urges, for "It is the hour of feeling."

> One moment now may give us more
> Than years of toiling reason:
> Our minds shall drink at every pore
> The spirit of the season.

The ethic that Wordsworth is expressing is that joy, serenity, and love itself would inevitably flow into and forth from the human heart if only it would surrender itself to the vital, joyous spirit everywhere found in Nature.

The poem "Expostulation and Reply" and its companion "The Tables Turned" were the result "of a conversation with a friend who was somewhat unreasonably attached to books of moral philosophy." The friend was William Hazlitt, who visited Wordsworth at Alfoxden at the end of May. Wordsworth felt that the book learning to which Hazlitt was then addicted, especially the cold intellectualism of Godwin, would lead men into an arid desert of mechanical rationalism. He felt that true knowledge must be founded upon experience received freshly through the senses.

Thus in "Expostulation and Reply," when Wordsworth's friend (the Matthew of the poem) reproaches the poet for sitting idle half a day on his "old grey stone" and for neglecting his book learning, Wordsworth spiritedly made reply—

> The eye—it cannot choose but see;
> We cannot bid the ear be still;
> Our bodies feel, where'er they be,
> Against or with our will.
>
> Nor less I deem that there are Powers
> Which of themselves our minds impress;
> That we can feed this mind of ours
> In a wise passiveness.

What Wordsworth is saying is that the senses furnish men with the primary data out of which they build this moral and spiritual life; hence, they must keep the senses open. In the Preface of 1815 Wordsworth places first among the powers requisite for the production of poetry "the ability to observe with accuracy things as they are in themselves, and with fidelity to describe them, unmodified by any passion or feeling existing in the mind of the describer":

> Think you, 'mid all this mighty sum
> Of things for ever speaking,
> That nothing of itself will come,
> But we must still be seeking?

In "The Tables Turned" the poet, with a light touch of extravagance, calls upon his friend to leave the "dull and endless strife" with books:

> Come forth into the light of things,
> Let Nature be your Teacher.
>
> She has a world of ready wealth,
> Our hearts and minds to bless—
> Spontaneous wisdom breathed by health,
> Truth breathed by cheerfulness.
>
> One impulse from a vernal wood
> May teach you more of man
> Of moral evil and of good
> Than all the sages can.

No one should seriously suppose that Wordsworth was here or elsewhere declaring himself an enemy of book learning. He obviously did not mean that a person was to give up reading now and forever anymore than he was to sit in permanent passiveness on an old gray stone. He was protesting against the overbearing encroachment of the "meddling intellect."

In "Lines Written in Early Spring" a sad thought intrudes itself. On a mid-April day, when the poet reclines beside the brook that runs through the grounds at Alfoxden, he feels his human soul linked with pleasure to Nature's fair works. Yet in the midst of a world that seems to be meant to be free and joyous and that appears to be so among the flowers, the birds, and the budding twigs—man alone is joyless. France at that time had ruthlessly invaded Switzerland; and Wordsworth, though surrounded with joyousness, was grieved—had "reason to lament/What man has made of man."

These four Nature poems not only express in the poet's own person the profundities of his faith, they sing with a rhythmic gaiety. The style is markedly simple; yet the simplicity is given everlasting appeal by means of lilting rhythms and repetitions. For example, the last line of each poem (except "The Tables Turned") serves through repetition as a refrain. All have oxymoronic surprises, such as, "wise passiveness," "spontaneous wisdom"; aphorisms, "we murder to dissect"; and bare precept, "Come forth into the light of things." The most notable stylistic feature is exaggeration, which has frequently been misunderstood. But it need not and should not be: when shorn of its stylistic exaggeration, the poet's basic teaching easily reveals itself. His precepts sprang from the very roots of his experience and are so universally true that they still speak through these poems to the condition of many human spirits.

X "Lines Composed a Few Miles Above Tintern Abbey"

Wordsworth and his sister left Alfoxden on June 25, 1798; and, after a week with Coleridge in Stowey, they journeyed to Bristol where Cottle was preparing *Lyrical Ballads* for the press. After a week spent working with him, William felt a longing to see once more the valleys and hills of Wales, through which he had wandered five years before. He wanted to share with Dorothy the beauteous scenes which, despite a long absence, he had never forgotten. So he took her on a four-day ramble along the Wye River, during which they visited the beautiful ruins of Tintern Abbey and proceeded as far north as Goodrich Castle before returning the way they had come from Bristol.

At one point in their wandering up the river from Tintern Abbey, William led Dorothy to a vantage point that opened to their view a magnificent prospect. There in the tranquility of a sycamore's shade the poet's mind traveled back past that day of ecstasy five years ago to the still further time of carefree schooldays and forward again through fleeting shadows to the present. To one "so long a worshipper of Nature," a multitude of memories crowded to a climax of joy in the present stillness of his mind. Feeling surged upon feeling until the tranquility of his mind gave way before "a spontaneous overflow of powerful feelings" and a poem was born. Wordsworth relates afterward that he began composing it upon leaving Tintern after crossing the Wye, and that he concluded it just as he was entering Bristol. Not a line of it was altered and not any part of it written down until he had reached the city. The full title of this now famous poem is "Lines Composed a Few Miles above Tintern Abbey, on Revisiting the Banks of the Wye during a Tour, July 13, 1798." The title is not quite accurate; for, as Wordsworth says, the poem was composed after leaving Tintern Abbey. But the prospect described is the one as seen a few miles above the abbey.

The travelers seem to have taken William Gilpin's *Tour of the*

Wye with them. In the opening stanza of "Tintern Abbey," at any rate, the landscape prospect seen from "under this dark sycamore" is described overtly in picturesque terms and the closing lines appear to owe a debt to Gilpin.[11]

> Five years have past; five summers, with the length
> Of five long winters! and again I hear
> These waters, rolling from their mountain-springs
> With a soft inland murmur.—Once again
> Do I behold these steep and lofty cliffs,
> That on a wild secluded scene impress
> Thoughts of more deep seclusion; and connect
> The landscape with the quiet of the sky.
> The day is come when I again repose
> Here, under this dark sycamore, and view
> These plots of cottage-ground, these orchard-tufts,
> Which at this season, with their unripe fruits,
> Are clad in one green hue, and lose themselves
> 'Mid groves and copses. Once again I see
> These hedge-rows, hardly hedge-rows, little lines
> Of sportive wood run wild: these pastoral farms,
> Green to the very door; and wreaths of smoke
> Sent up, in silence, from among the trees!
> With some uncertain notice, as might seem
> Of vagrant dwellers in the houseless woods,
> Or of some Hermit's cave, where by his fire
> The Hermit sits alone.

There is no lack of significant pictorial detail in this opening passage. The landscape is described with more than usual care, and it has many tactual images rendered with great clearness for the eye and the mind to rest upon. Yet there is also much that points to an inward psychical response. The waters of the river are heard "rolling from their mountain springs," but the full impression is not of a river seen or heard but of one felt in its continuing entity as it winds from its mountain home to its confrontation "inland" by the tides of the sea. Wordsworth has moved from the river of the outer physical world to a river whose existence is an inner prospect of the mind.

So, too, the "steep and lofty cliffs" before him "on a wild secluded scene" impress *"thoughts of more deep seclusion."* Additional features of the landscape describe man and Nature as mixing together, and their combining becomes significant inwardly and symbolically. The grass of the pastoral farms is "green to the very doors"; plots of cottage-ground "lose themselves in groves and copses"; hedge rows and woodlands intermingle; wreaths of smoke (man created) lose themselves among the houseless woods where men dwell. Then, somehow, the upward movement of the lofty cliffs and smoke connect the living, inhabited landscape with the quiet of the sky in an ascent that suggests a spiritual union of the whole. Wordsworth has rendered a masterful landscape in these verses, selecting and dramatizing its pictorial features; but he has also endowed it with inward symbolic significance. In his landscape of the Wye, man, Nature, and the Divine world are interfused—all exist in a mighty unity.

The landscape before him starts the ruminative process, and he thinks of all that the memory of this beautiful scene has meant to him during his five years of absence. He believes that he owes to those beauteous forms three blessings: first, sensations sweet, physical, and restorative, "felt in the blood," which pass even into his inmost mind with quieting effect; second, feelings unperceived and unremembered but which mysteriously guide him in the per- formance of kind and unselfish acts, such as the severing of the tree root for old Simon Lee; third, and crowning all, he was lifted at intervals to mystic vision whence he was enabled to "see into the life of things." It is unlikely that Wordsworth experienced this last and highest gift until perhaps a year or so before his second visit to the Wye. But restorative sensations nourished his physical and moral being often during the years of loneliness.

As he looks upon the "steep woods and lofty banks," he recalls the image of himself as he came that way five years before. He sees himself as one who then sought refuge from tormenting mental conflict by flinging himself into physical delight in Nature like one driven by insatiable thirst. But now "That time is past/ And all its aching joys are now no more/ And all its dizzy raptures." The loss, however, is compensated by "other gifts" more precious. The sounding cataracts that haunted him on his first visit and the din and turmoil in the cities which followed it have been replaced by the "soft, inland murmur" of the river and by the silent beauty of the landscape. The new-found tranquility before him induces a quietistic response within. He now has a gentler outlook on the tragedy of humanity ("Nor harsh nor grating, though of ample power/ To chasten and subdue"). And he gains a sense of Presence deeply interfused around him and in him, illimitable and united in one joyous harmony of all existence:

> And I have felt
> A presence that disturbs me with the joy
> Of elevated thoughts; a sense sublime
> Of something far more deeply interfused,
> Whose dwelling is the light of setting suns,
> And the round ocean and the living air,
> And the blue sky, and in the mind of man:
> A motion and a spirit, that impels
> All thinking things, all objects of all thought,
> And rolls through all things.

Wordsworth's return to the Wye in 1798 supplied him with a montage (the superimposition of one experience upon another) that confirmed his belief in the unity of past and present, as well as his belief in the unity of man and Nature. The chief human agency in the reconciling work was Dorothy, who was in the precise stage of development that the poet was five years before. To Dorothy still belonged the ecstatic, primitive delight in natural things that Wordsworth recognizes can no longer be his. He does not "murmur" at his own change but projects his own present into his sister's future in a warmly felt and generous prayer for her as a worshiper of Nature. Nature in its beauty is a source of joy and of healing thoughts that will minister to Dorothy in her future need as it has ministered to the poet in the past. Wordsworth's faith in Nature's power to bring comfort to his sister was a complex, intuitive belief comprised of sensation, feeling, knowledge and half-knowledge, moral awareness, and mystical insight—all united in the powerful solvent of his tenacious memory. And beautifully intertwined with the intricate network of impressions held in memory is the quality of hope, running forward and backward, opening up vistas that look toward the "Uncreated."

"Tintern Abbey" was added to *Lyrical Ballads*, then being readied for the press, and became the concluding poem in the book. It was not one of the experimental poems; indeed, it has nothing to do with them except that its language, like those of other personal poems in the volume, keeps to the high road of poetic tradition established by Shakespeare, Spenser, and Milton. Its music is impassioned, which in Wordsworth's view made it comparable to an ode. Its repetitive words, phrases, and patterns give to the flowing rhythms a wonderfully resonant and noble beauty. The poetic expression of the impact of the scenic landscape upon the innermost recesses of the poet's mind was as spontaneous as it was powerful. The poem took shape while his feelings were overflowing with excess of joy and while his faith in the power of Nature to dispel "fear or pain or grief" was still at high tide. In after years he qualified and subdued his pronouncements in "Tintern Abbey." But he never lost delight in the simple converse of Nature or his faith that all created things can bring pleasure to the sensitive person impelled by love or praise.

XI The Publication and Reception of Lyrical Ballads

Lyrical Ballads appeared anonymously on or about October 1, 1798, without a hint to reveal the presence of more than one author. Wordsworth and Coleridge craved anonymity in their venture; to insure it, they had removed at the last moment Coleridge's "Lewti," a lyric which had appeared in print in *The Morning Post* and known to be his work; and they substituted for it "The Nightingale." The secret of authorship was so well kept that neither the authors' names nor even the fact of dual authorship became generally known until announced in the Preface to the second edition.

Curiously enough, after Cottle had run off a few copies of *Lyrical Ballads* under his own imprint, he sold the edition to J. and A. Arch, a London bookseller, probably because he had become alarmed by Southey, who warned Cottle that the work would not sell. Southey, who was still estranged from Coleridge, was planning to give the new book rough handling when he reviewed it. And, sure enough, not a month had passed following publication before Southey's review appeared in *The Critical Review* of October, 1798. Southey, who claimed not sufficiently to understand the story of "The Ancient Mariner" to analyze it, dubbed it "a Dutch attempt at German sublimity." He also condemned "The Idiot Boy," Wordsworth's favorite poem: "No tale less deserved the labour that appears to have been bestowed upon this." He thought the serious pieces to be the better part of the volume, for example, "The Female Vagrant"; but he considered the experiment a failure "because it has been tried upon uninteresting subjects."

All of the reviewers followed Southey's lead in finding fault with "The Ancient Mariner." Dr. Burney in *The Monthly Review* of June, 1799, thought "The Rime of the Ancient Mariner" "the strangest story of a cock and bull that we ever saw on paper." He said the experiments were unworthy as poetry, but he admired touches of genius and wished "to see another volume by the same hand, written on more elevated subjects and in a more cheerful disposition." The only review in full and intelligent sympathy with the novel "experiment" was written by Francis Wrangham, a friend of Wordsworth; and it appeared in the *British Critic* of October, 1799. Wrangham thought that the intermediate part of "The Ancient Mariner" was too long and that the antiquated words might better be omitted entirely. But the poems of the rest of the volume, he wrote, have high merit and some of them "a very high rank of merit."

Mrs. Coleridge wrote to her husband in Germany (where he and the Wordsworths were when the volume finally was published) that the *Lyrical Ballads* were "laughed at and disliked by all with very few excepted," but her bluntness does not seem to join with the facts. The volume eventually sold much better than the authors themselves had expected, and it was liked by a much greater number of people. Four editions (added to in the meantime) were called for by 1805. As proved in the long run, the instinctive responses of young William Hazlitt, though not those of a reviewer, were prophetic of the final evaluation to be placed upon the new poems. On Hazlitt's visit to Alfoxden during the last days of May, 1798, he had free access to Wordsworth's contributions to *Lyrical Ballads* then still in manuscript. Hazlitt later recorded his impressions in "My First Acquaintance with Poets":

I dipped into a few of these with great satisfaction, and with the faith of a novice. . . I was not critically or skeptically inclined. I saw touches of truth and nature, and took the rest for granted. But in "The Thorn," "The Mad Mother," and "The Complaint of a Forsaken Indian Woman," I felt that deeper power and pathos which has since been acknowledged . . . as the characteristics of this author; and the sense of a new style and a new spirit in poetry came over me. It had to me something of the effect that arises from the turning up of the fresh soil, or the first welcome breath of Spring.

CHAPTER 3

Lyrical Ballads, *1800*

O N September 15, 1798, William, Dorothy, and Coleridge sailed from Yarmouth to Hamburg, Germany. They saw the sights and visited with Klopstock but separated at the beginning of October. Coleridge left for Ratzeburg, and the Wordsworths, for no discoverable reason, settled at Goslar, at the edge of the Harz Mountains, to spend the winter. It turned out to be one of the coldest winters on record. As a consequence, the poet and his sister found themselves isolated in a foreign country, with no books except the few they brought with them, no social amenities, and little opportunity to learn the German language, the chief purpose for which they had come.

Isolated in Goslar, the Wordsworths were thrown back upon themselves and upon thoughts of their homeland. To the poet in that alien environment fervent recollections of his childhood and other memories came with an intensity he had never before known. Exile fed the springs of inspiration; again he was possessed by the "creative breeze," and it was blowing now, not gently, but as "A tempest, a redundant energy." The result was some of Wordsworth's finest poetry, differing sharply from the Alfoxden poems, which were based for the most part upon everyday events that had transpired shortly before they were written.

Reminiscence or recollection had already appeared in "Tintern Abbey," but in the Goslar poems it was raised and intensified to the highest degree. Within the recesses of his own mind Wordsworth recovered those "spots of time"—moments that returned to consciousness out of the depths of the past—leaping "from hiding places ten years deep." A most notable list of poems composed during the frigid winter at Goslar attest to the rich new sources of inspiration released in the poet. These poems include the matchless pictures of his boyhood that later were to become part of *The Prelude*, the Lucy poems, "Lucy Gray," "The Poet's Epitaph," the Matthew poems, and "Ruth."

I *The Lucy Poems*

The five elegiac pieces known as the Lucy poems are all associated
with the stay in Germany, though one of them seems not to have
been written until April, 1801. Four are in ballad stanza and reveal
Wordsworth's interest in this form quickened by his purchase at
Hamburg of a copy of Percy's *Reliques*. In those lonely months in
Germany the love of England was firmly re-established. Out of that
nostalgic yearning and an aching memory of sufficiency now lost.
the Lucy poems had their origin. Robert Frost once said that poetry
often begins in a lovesickness or in a homesickness. The Lucy poems
seem to have begun in both:

> I travelled among unknown men,
>   In lands beyond the sea;
> Nor, England! did I know till then
>   What love I bore to thee.
>
> 'Tis past, that melancholy dream!
>   Nor will I quit thy shore
> A second time; for still I seem
>   To love thee more and more.
>
> Among thy mountains did I feel
>   The joy of my desire;
> And she I cherished turned her wheel
>   Beside an English fire.
>
> Thy mornings showed, thy nights concealed
>   The bowers where Lucy played;
> And thine too is the last green field
>   That Lucy's eyes surveyed. [1]

The Lucy that the poet mourns the loss of is a person; but one
does not know who she was—nor, indeed, if there ever was a Lucy.
It is possible, of course, to deny any particular identity to Lucy
and to hypothesize that she was a purely ideal creation existing
solely in the imagination of the poet. The name of Lucy had become
a sort of commonplace in elegiac poetry. It occurred in Percy's
Reliques in a poem "Lucy and Colin" written by Thomas Tichell
and elsewhere in poems by George Lyttleton, Edward Moore,
Thomas Chatterton, William Collins, and Samuel Rogers; Words-

worth was acquainted with most of them. It would be rash, however, knowing Wordsworth's strong tendency toward the autobiographical, to say that Lucy is entirely fictitious.

A number of candidates have been offered as her living counterpart: Annette Vallon, who is finally rejected by means of the poems (but the fact that Lucy was English and a child of Nature disposes of any possible connection with Annette); Mary Hutchinson, his future wife toward whom his heart was now returning (why then, should she be dead?); Margaret Hutchinson, her sister, whom perhaps in early youth the poet had loved and who, indeed, had died of consumption in 1796; Mary of Esthwaite, perhaps a real but unknown schoolboy love of Hawkshead days; and his sister Dorothy, for whom the strongest case can be made.

There is definite evidence that the name "Lucy" is connected with Dorothy. Lucy is Dorothy in the Glow-Worm poem ("Among all lovely things") and in the early unpublished version of "Nutting," which was written in Germany. Coleridge, who thought Dorothy was Lucy, sent Thomas Poole a copy of "A Slumber did my Spirit seal" and added by way of explanation that "Most probably in some gloomier moment [the poet] had fancied the moment when his sister might die." Bateson explained the death and sexlessness of these love poems by conjecturing that Wordsworth was falling in love with Dorothy and that he subconsciously solved the dangerous and explosive situation by symbolically killing her. But the sensational incest wish and the psychic burial theory have not found acceptance.

Lucy may have had her origin in some real person or persons, but in the poems she has been sublimated into something much more than a person. She is an ideal figure apothesizing English maidenhood and all the poet's feelings about love, women, and Nature. She is seen entirely from within the poet; at times, she seems barely human, ready to lapse back into Nature. Lucy is "a *thing* that could not feel/The touch of earthly years." There is no real difference between her living and dying, except in the consciousness of the survivor. The unresolved ingredient of the poet's thought is the agonizing search for steadfastness and permanence behind Nature as idealized in the person of Lucy. His consciousness is overwhelmed by the fateful passing of youth, beauty, and love. "But she is in her grave, and, oh,/The difference to me!"

The first poem in the "Lucy" cycle, "Strange fits of passion,"
is constructed around Lucy's cottage. The poet pictures himself
one moonlit evening as riding on horseback toward her house.
Mary Moorman reconstructs the setting as true to Racedown and the
entire poem as a personal memory of a true event in the lives of
William and Dorothy. Of greater interest than the identity of Lucy,
however, is the mental condition of the poet. "In one of those sweet
dreams I slept,/Kind Nature's gentlest boon," he says of his ride
to Lucy's cottage. His person is in an hypnotic state, a creative sleep
of the senses when the "soul" and imagination are most alive, kept
in focus by the moon and reinforced by the rhythmic repetition of
the horse's hoof beats. Then, when he rides uphill and the moon is
suddenly blotted out, the hypnotic mood is broken—

> What fond and wayward thoughts will slide
>   Into a Lover's head!
> "O mercy!" to myself I cried,
>   "If Lucy should be dead!"

In the Lucy poems, Wordsworth effectively employs metaphors
and symbols—and in none more so than in the famous "She dwelt
among the untrodden ways." This lyric in its first version as sent
to Coleridge consisted of five stanzas. It was cut to three for publication in 1800 and certainly lost nothing thereby. The middle stanza
contains the famous and beloved metaphors:

> A violet by a mossy stone
>   Half hidden from the eye!
> —Fair as a star, when only one
>   Is shining in the sky.

These metaphors and the first stanza illuminate each other. The
isolation of the violet and the star set off their beauty; they, in turn,
enhance the beauty of Lucy despite her solitude. Also the violet and
the star seem humanized by being compared to Lucy; but, at the
same time, the comparison of Lucy to the lovely but inanimate objects in Nature keeps her from being warmly human. Lucy is far
removed from, for example, Keats's fair love with ripening breast
in his "Bright Star" sonnet.

The Lucy elegies also are a triumph through understatement; especially is this characteristic in "She dwelt among the untrodden ways." Here understatement achieves its full effect in the last four words: "But she is in her grave, and, oh,/The difference to me!" Among the Romantic poets, only Walter Savage Landor could use restraint with anything like Wordsworth's dynamism, as in "Rose Alymer,"—"A night of memories and of sighs/I consecrate to thee." But a comparison of these two justly famed elegiac conclusions reveals at once that Wordsworth's has the greater power.

"Three years she grew in sun and shower" was written when at length spring had come and Wordsworth and his sister had left Goslar and were walking through the Harz forest to Nordhausen. A poem of seven six-line stanzas, it is the only one of the Lucy poems not in ballad meter. In six of the stanzas Nature undertakes to over-see Lucy's growth in her daily comradeship with the vital impulses of beauty and delight which everywhere surround her, for she is "Nature's child." Nowhere has the poet more simply and delicately described the twofold power of Nature to quicken and to calm:

> Myself will to my darling be
> Both law and impulse: and with me
> The Girl, in rock and plain,
> In earth and heaven, in glade and bower,
> Shall feel an overseeing power
> To kindle or restrain.

As Wordsworth describes the ministry of natural beauty in molding the loveliness of Lucy, the verse reaches a lyrical perfection scarcely equaled elsewhere by the poet:

> The floating clouds their state shall lend
> To her; for her the willow bend;
> Nor shall she fail to see
> Even in the motions of the Storm
> Grace that shall mould the Maiden's form
> By silent sympathy.
>
> The stars of midnight shall be dear
> To her; and she shall lean her ear
> In many a secret place

> Where rivulets dance their wayward round
> And beauty born of murmuring sound
> Shall pass into her face.

The poet's representation in this lyric of the molding discipline which Nature brings to Lucy merges with the more personal image he has given elsewhere of Dorothy responding to Nature's influence.

"A slumber did my spirit seal"—the "sublime epitaph," as Coleridge called it—consists of but two four-line stanzas. But in those eight lines Wordsworth has achieved a masterful compression of poetic power. In the cryptic first line, which summarizes the thought of the first stanza, the poet pictures himself in an hypnotic mystic sleep. His being is in sublime repose, as it was in the opening lyric of the cycle when he was approaching Lucy's cottage—"In one of those sweet dreams I slept." He is confidently self-possessed in his thoughts about his loved one; he cannot imagine Lucy's death. Then suddenly she is gone:

> No motion has she now, no force;
> She neither hears nor sees;
> Rolled round in earth's diurnal course,
> With rocks and stones and trees.

Irony, not often used by Wordsworth, pervades the first stanza of this elegy. The slumber which captivated him, but which he could not associate with Lucy—"She seemed a thing that could not feel/ The touch of earthly years"—is suddenly hers forever as she sleeps the sleep of death. She, who once seemed so alive that her lover was lulled into the fake security of thinking that she could never be without life, is now absolutely and irrevocably without motion, vitality, or feeling. She, who seemed to exist so that the passing of time meant nothing, is now become an inseparable part of the imperative cosmic forces of consuming time.

The poet is crushed by Lucy's death. Something unique has gone from his life and from the universe. There is no thought of immortality. He has been living under the assumption—supported by mystic moments of insight when slumber sealed his spirit[2]—that there is steadfastness, serenity, and permanent power behind Nature. In "Three years she grew," Nature spoke and declared her dual force: "Myself will to my darling be/Both *law* and *impulse*." Law, especially natural law, is permanent and steady; but impulse, the poet learns, is uncertain and wayward. He had been deluded by the thought of Lucy's deathlessness. When at last she is in the grave, he finds himself time's fool. For Lucy had become so completely the sublimation of existence that, with her passing, he is overwhelmed by an awareness never before realized of the mutability of all values and all existence.

The Lucy poems are sublimated love poems of sustained pathos. They are unexcelled in the use of simple language to express pure and spontaneous emotion. In addition, their symbolic import places them among the most perfect expressions of Wordsworth's sense of mutability. By them, we are made sublimely aware of the tragic realities of our frail human existence.

II *"Lucy Gray; or, Solitude," "Ruth," and "Poor Susan"*

"Lucy Gray; or, Solitude," a haunting ballad of childhood, is founded upon a true story remembered by Dorothy of a little girl lost in a snowstorm. The suggestion has been made that "Lucy Gray" should be placed in the Lucy cycle; indeed, it has been conjectured that this ballad is the starting point of all the Lucy poems. It is noteworthy that the first three and the last two stanzas do make a complete Lucy poem; and also, like others in the series, it was written at Goslar in the ballad meter.

Lucy Gray is a solitary child and belongs to the world of wild and innocent animals—the fawn, the hare, and the roe. She is associated with all that is free and lovely in the natural world; moreover, she is "The sweetest thing that ever grew/Beside a human door." One day her father, fearing a stormy night, calls upon Lucy to go to the town with a lantern to light the way for her mother through the snow. The child goes willingly, blithe as "the mountain roe"; but, when the storm "came on before its time," Lucy lost her way. The wretched parents, who searched all that night, found no trace of their little girl. Next morning they discovered the child's footmarks and traced them to the middle of the wooden plank over a stream—"And further there were none!"

In his note to "Lucy Gray" Wordsworth expresses a hope that "The way in which the incident was treated and the spiritualizing of the character might furnish hints for contrasting the imaginative influences which I have endeavoured to throw over common life with Crabbe's matter of fact style of treating subjects of the same

kind." In Wordsworth's ballad Lucy died, but no corpse was found.
Perhaps, the poet suggests, the child did not die in any natural sense;
she may have been translated into an identification with immortal
Nature. Though Lucy Gray is specially vulnerable to death, she is
also specially impervious to it. In lonesome places the "living child"
may still be seen as she trips along, or she may be heard singing
"a solitary song/That whistles in the wind."

"Ruth" was written at Goslar from memories of a story Wordsworth had of a wanderer in Somersetshire. The verse form is a six-
line stanza resembling that of Drayton's "Dowsabel," which was in
the copy of Percy's *Reliques* that Wordsworth had purchased in
Hamburg. The subject of woman's unhappy love frequently appears
in the *Reliques,* two cases of which exactly parallell that of "Ruth."

"Ruth" is a tale of courtship and desertion, in which Wordsworth
shows a further range of his awareness; he extends particularly the
boundaries of his thought about Nature's teachings. Ruth was not
seven years old when her father remarried; and the child, slighted
by her stepmother, became a solitary wanderer over the countryside. When grown to lovely womanhood, she was courted by a
young soldier just returned from the war in America. A handsome
youth, he enthralled Ruth with his stories of life among Indians and
their idyllic existence. Ruth readily accepted his proposal to make
her home with him in the wild woods of America; and they were
wed.

The youth had grown up in the eye of Nature, but in a wild land
he had been exposed to unsettling sights and sounds. From unworthy men he absorbed evil ways and himself became "the slave
of low desires." The love of Ruth had at first stirred in him higher
and better thoughts, but these soon left him. He deserted her to return to his life "with roving bands of Indians in the West." Ruth,
crazed by his betrayal and having no place to go, becomes a vagrant.
She lives in the open and begs for her food by the roadside. Left to
loneliness and neglect, the best that she can hope for is the relief
from "the engines of her pain" which madness brings her. The last
she can expect is that her body shall lie buried "in the hallowed
mould."

"Ruth" shows that in 1799 Wordsworth is not exuberantly pro-
claiming that all persons exposed to outdoor life will inevitably
become morally upright. "Wild and voluptuous nature" can have
a corrupting effect, as it did upon the fair youth from Georgia. And

Nature can be indifferent and cruel to a helpless human being, as it was to Ruth who had "sore aches" and "body wretchedness,/ From damp, and rain, and cold." Nature was not only the influence that shaped Ruth's beauty but "the tool that shaped her sorrow." Wordsworth had no illusion that city dwellers would be better off if they abandoned themselves to the raw wildness of country life.

Nor is personal responsibility in moral matters to be overlooked. The stepmother of Ruth by her cruel neglect is exposed as wholly culpable. Also the deserting husband is held up for severe condemnation. In the desertion theme, the poet may again have been expressing remorse for his treatment of Annette. The time of Wordsworth's infirmity in France was characterized by license and wildness not unlike that to which the Georgian youth was exposed in the American wilderness. In any event, Wordsworth reveals a perceptive understanding of Ruth's faithless husband—how he came to be the unstable person that he was and why he acted the way he did. He also shows poignant pathos for the abandoned Ruth. "Ruth" made severe demands upon Wordsworth's art and is of unequal quality. But he achieved in this narrative some noteworthy features already discussed, to which should be added the effective painting of the exotic splendors of North America (lines 49-84) taken from *Bartram's Travels*.

"The Reverie of Poor Susan" Wordsworth himself dated in 1836 as having been written in 1797; but he altered the date later to "1801 or 1802" (a mistake, as the poem was published in 1800). Mary Moorman wonders if he did not write the poem in Germany in 1799, for the title is an exact translation of Bürger's "Das Arme Süsschen's Traum," his favorite in the volume of Bürger's poems he purchased at Hamburg. In February, 1800, he wrote to Coleridge that he had found pleasure in reading Bürger; but he also complained of a lack of "distinct forms" and "feelings" in the German poet. "Poor Susan" is almost an answer to this defect in Bürger. Susan turns from the wearisome dullness of city life to behold, through the window of imagination opened by the song of the caged thrush, the distinct forms and images of her country home from which she has been so long separated: "A mountain ascending, a vision of trees. . . ." As she looks upon the beauteous scene before her she is restored as if by miracle, and "her heart is in heaven." But, as quickly as the vision came, it faded away. Wordsworth isolates the feeling, yet in no way sentimentalizes upon Susan or her

situation. With a deeply perceptive charity, he opens the readers'
hearts to understanding and sympathy.

III   *The Matthew Poems and "A Poet's Epitaph"*

Among the memories of his youth that flowed with delicacy and
clarity into Wordsworth's brooding mind at Goslar were those of
his schooldays at Hawkshead. These memories were lovingly recorded in the Matthew poems in which the poet establishes contrasts between youth and age that center in the schoolboy and his
schoolmaster, respectively. However, the Matthew of the poems is
not a factual representation of Wordsworth's teacher, William
Taylor, who died in his thirty-third year. Rather, he is a composite
and idealized figure having more affinities with an old traveling
packman, who became attracted to the schoolboy and was his companion in many a ramble through the hills. The characteristics of
this packman are set forth with some fullness in an unpublished
Addendum to "The Ruined Cottage."[3] He had a serene and cheerful disposition and a stock of "home-felt" wisdom which he im-
parted to his young companion in whimsical stories and comments.
All the poems of the Matthew series, including elegies left in
manuscript by Wordsworth, stress the old man's paradoxical temperament. The poem "Matthew" characteristically sets forth the
wondrous incongruity of his sighs and tears:

>   The sighs which Matthew heaved were sighs
>   Of one tired out with fun and madness;
>   The tears which came to Matthew's eyes
>   Were tears of light, the dew of gladness.

In "Two April Mornings," Matthew is "As blithe a man as you
could see/On a spring holiday," yet he uttered "so sad a sigh" it
aroused his youthful companion with whom he is out walking to
question him as to its cause. He replies that the resplendent April
morning which gladdens them brings fresh into his mind a day
just like it thirty years before. On that day he had come by chance
to stand beside his nine-year-old daughter's grave, and he was
filled with a poignant yearning for her:

> Six feet in earth my Emma lay;
> And yet, I loved her more,
> For so it seemed, than till that day
> I e'er had loved before.

When he turned to leave his daughter's grave, he met beside the churchyard yew "A blooming Girl, whose hair was wet/With points of morning dew." She was a vision of loveliness, a Lucy as it were come to life:

> A basket on her head she bare;
> Her brow was smooth and white:
> To see a child so very fair,
> It was a pure delight!

> No fountain from its rocky cave
> E'er tripped with foot so free;
> She seemed as happy as a wave
> That dances on the sea.

The fresh beauty of the living girl vividly restored the fact of his daughter's sweet loveliness. But there are things the heart cannot replace. Matthew looked at the girl before him and looked again, and he was so pierced with longing he could not wish her to be his. One of the strange facts of parental love is that a child of one's own cannot be replaced by one who is not. Years later the poet remembers this surprising ending to his old teacher's story, and in a final stanza he creates, in effect, a third April morning:

> Matthew is in his grave, yet now,
> Methinks, I see him stand,
> As at that moment, with a bough
> Of wilding in his hand.

In "The Fountain," the poet and his old teacher Matthew are seated together one beautiful morning beneath a spreading oak beside which a fountain gurgled. As they speak with open hearts, they release in friendship their inner thoughts. The fountain may be thought of as symbolizing in their dialogue the ebullient spirit

of youth; the oak, the sober wisdom of age. The boy, responding to
the joyous sound of the running water, calls upon the old man to
sing some border song or witty rhyme that suits a summer mood.
But Matthew at first disappoints the expectations of the boy. The
old man looks at the fountain and observes how thoughtlessly and
changelessly it flows. As a youthful, vigorous man, he often joyously
lay beside this spring; but, now in old age, he is saddened by the
losses he has suffered of "kindred laid in earth." He is compelled
to feel a sorrow corresponding to the joy his human relationships
once gave him. This is a "foolish strife," but it is indigenous to man
and inevitable.

When the boy exclaims that he could be a son to him, the old man
knows better: "Alas! that cannot be." Age retains so intense a
memory of love, it takes away the power to form new attachments
to replace those lost. But the sorrow must be borne; and Matthew,
being a man of glee, in the end sings "About the crazy old church-
clock,/And the bewildered chimes." Matthew has been "pressed
by heavy laws," but he has not dried up. He has kept alive the
mirth of youth to hide the sorrow of age. An energetic spirit still
bubbles like a fountain within him and feeds the laughter that hides
tears.

Matthew is a wondrously archetypal figure, particular and yet
symbolic, a village schoolmaster and yet a kind of gnomic oracle.
Paradoxes and opaque symbols subtly intertwine in the unfolding
of his character. In "The Fountain," above the "witty rhymes" one
hears the tolling paradox: "The wiser mind/Mourns less for what
age takes away/Than what it leaves behind." And, at the close of
"Two April Mornings," one sees Matthew "with a bough of wilding
in his hand," symbol at once of gaiety and sorrow.

"A Poet's Epitaph," written in Goslar, is a satiric thrust at world-
lings insensitive to a true poet's worth. Wordsworth addresses those
who would approach his grave; and he cautions the politician, the
lawyer, the divine, the scientist, and the moralist to give him wide
berth. Men who devote themselves to rational analysis and unpro-
fitable "getting and spending" are unworthy visitors. But the gallant soldier who lays aside his sword is welcome. And let the poet
"with modest looks,/And clad in homely russet brown" come near.
The picture of the poet is, of course, a self-portrait and a memorable one:

He is retired as noontide dew,
Or fountain in a noon-day grove;
And you must love him, ere to you
He will seem worthy of your love.

The outward shows of sky and earth,
Of hill and valley, he has viewed;
And impulses of a deeper birth
Have come to him in solitude.

Charles Lamb objected to "the vulgar satire upon parsons and lawyers in the beginning" and to the coarse use of an epithet, later removed, that intensified his attack upon the scientist by referring to his "pin-point of a soul." Lamb thought "All the rest is eminently good, and your own."

IV *Pastorals: "The Brothers" and "Michael"*

In early spring William and Dorothy left Goslar; and, after wandering about in Germany and briefly visiting Coleridge at Göttingen, they were back in England in May. And "right glad" they were, wrote William, "for we have learned to know its value." They headed northward to visit Mary Hutchinson at Sockburn-on-Tees, where her brother Tom had a farm. Coleridge, who joined them there, accompanied William on a walking tour of the Lakes, the chief object of which was to find a suitable place for him and his sister to live. In the exquisite valley of Grasmere William found the very cottage of Dorothy's dream and returned to Sockburn to fetch her. On a cold December day in 1799 they ended a wild winter journey at Dove Cottage, which became their home for the next eight years.

Grasmere was a peaceful spot for the poet to work but not in self-centered solitude. The brother and sister roamed the dales and hills alert with eager, questing eyes and hearts for the substance of poetry. Rural incidents such as Wordsworth had treated imaginatively in the first *Lyrical Ballads* they found near at hand, but the narrative poems resulting from them differ in several important aspects from the narratives of Alfoxden days. Two moving pastorals, "The Brothers" and "Michael," were written in the first year at Grasmere. Their focus, like that of the earlier poems, is on the psychology of passion; and the feeling developed in them gives importance to the action and situation, not the other way around. But in these pastorals there is no derangement caused by grief, as in "The Thorn" or "The Mad Mother." The passion has to do simply with the brave endurance of humble, rustic figures. And the passion is communicated not by "lyrical and rapid metre" nor in repetitious, excited utterance, as in "The Thorn," but in muted understatement. Gone, too, is the uncouth, colloquial language; in its place is a somewhat heightened, yet natural and easy, conversational tone that represented for Wordsworth a compromise between dramatic and poetic propriety.

"The Brothers" and "Michael" both have to do with man's attachment to place. At the time Wordsworth came to live at Dove Cottage, there was a decline in small properties in the Lake District. The factory system was driving the hand loom from the cottages, the loss of which spelled ruin for the proprietors. To Wordsworth, who thought that a small property was the principal support to the affections, such a loss was tragic. In a letter to Charles James Fox, the Whig possessing the greatest "sensibility of heart," Wordsworth explained that the tract of land possessed by the independent proprietors in the Lake Country "serves as a kind of permanent rallying point for their domestic feelings." A small farm is, as it were, a tablet upon which is recorded the history of a man's emotional life. Its permanent objects—its trees, its stone walls, its brooks—are bound up with memories of the past, associated with acts of kindness as in the rescue of a sheep or acts of love involving one's child.

Thus these two pastorals, Wordsworth explains to Fox, were "Written with a view to shew that men who do not wear fine cloaths can feel deeply." The protagonists in "The Brothers" and "Michael" differ markedly from such characters as Martha Ray, Simon Lee, and others in the 1798 *Lyrical Ballads*. Their feelings, unlike those of the deranged or servile characters of the earlier poems, are based upon an honest confrontation with life's tragic inconstancy. And their feelings run deep because they are held bravely under control. The protagonists are also different from the conventional representation of country persons which before Wordsworth's time had debased the extrinsic differences that separated man from man. In "The Brothers" and "Michael," the poet rejects the fanciful Arcadian characters of make-believe pastorals and establishes in their place real countrymen who are elevated to the position of statesmen by their possession of property.

"The Brothers"—"that model of English pastoral," as Coleridge called it—is based upon a story told to Wordsworth by a shepherd of Ennerdale. The tragic separation of two brothers is prefigured in the poem in terms of symbolic landscape:

> On that tall pike . . .
> There were two springs which bubbled side by side,
> As if they had been made that they might be
> Companions for each other: the huge crag
> Was rent with lightning—one hath disappeared;
> The other, left behind, is flowing still.

Leonard Ewbank, after twenty years at sea, has returned to his paternal home with the determined purpose of resuming the shepherd's life he had formerly shared with his brother. He meets and recognizes the village priest, but is unrecognized by him, and engages him in conversation. He learns that his brother, who was never so robust and hearty as himself, had one May day gone up the hills to look after the newborn lambs. Being wearied with the climb, he had stopped to rest upon a high crag and had fallen asleep there. Upon awakening, he apparently became confused and plunged to his death; for the next morning his crushed body was found on the rocks below. Leonard is so overwhelmed by the story of his brother's death that he cannot trust himself to tell the pastor who he is, but he writes him a letter that night on his way back to the seacoast to beg his understanding and forgiveness. He cannot bear now to think of returning to live in the vale where he had once been so happy.

By restrained language and tragic irony, imaginatively supported by dramatic symbolism, Wordsworth gives this simple tale a pathos that is akin to that in Greek tragedy. He convincingly makes his point that "men who do not wear fine cloaths can feel deeply."

"Michael" is a blending of two local traditions: one involves the character of Luke founded on the story of the son of an old couple who leaves home and takes to evil ways; the other centers in the person of Michael himself drawn from an old shepherd who had been seven years building a sheepfold in a solitary valley. Shepherds, Wordsworth tells us in *The Prelude* (Book VIII, 11. 215-327), had been the first men to arrest his interest and admiration. In the introductory lines to "Michael" he says that such a story as that of Michael had been known to him in boyhood and "led me on to feel/For passions that were not my own, and think . . ./On man, the heart of man, and human life." Into "Michael" he poured all his faith in the shepherd-statesmen of the fells whom in boyhood he had loved. Wordsworth stated in a letter to Poole that his aim in the poem was "to give a picture of a man, of strong mind and lively sensibility, agitated by two of the most powerful affections of the human heart; the parental affection, and the love of property, *landed* property including the feelings of inheritance, home, and personal and family dependence."[4]

At the opening of the poem, the reader is invited to turn his steps "up the tumultuous brook of Greenhead Ghyll" until he comes to a hidden mountain valley where beside the brook appears "a straggling heap of stones." These stones mark the site of a covenant. In them is symbolically merged the love of the land and the love for his son that were bound together in the heart of an old shepherd. The poet will relate his story, "a history homely and rude" for "the delight of a few natural hearts" and "for the sake/Of youthful Poets, who among these hills/ Will be my second self when I am gone."

The shepherd Michael is the grandest character that Wordsworth ever drew. He was an old man, past eighty, but stout of heart, strong of limb, and keen of mind—more prompt and watchful in his shepherd's calling than ordinary men. From confronting the challenge of Nature, he had built his strength. He had learned the meaning of all winds; and oftentimes, when others paid no heed, he heard the warning in the blasts that summoned him up the mountain. He had kept watch alone "Amid the heart of many thousand mists,/That came to him, and left him, on the heights." Over the years the fields and hills of his domain had impressed many incidents upon his mind "Of hardship, skill or courage, joy or fear." So there was built within Michael a deep and enduring attachment to the land:

> Those fields, those hills—what could they less? had laid
> Strong hold on his affections, were to him
> A pleasurable feeling of blind love,
> The pleasure which there is in life itself.

Michael was joined in his labors by a "comely matron," twenty years younger than himself; and to them an only son was born when Michael, in shepherd's phrase, had "one foot in the grave." This

son, named Luke, with two brave sheepdogs, made all their household. It was a home known throughout the vale for endless industry.
After the day's work was done, the housewife lighted a lamp by the
light of which the couple and Luke worked at domestic tasks far
into the night. The light, famous in the neighborhood, became
"a public symbol of the life/That thrifty Pair had lived." The house
itself was named THE EVENING STAR.

Michael loved his helpmate, but he loved even more the son of
his old age. While Luke was but an infant, the shepherd joyed
to have the young one in his sight when he worked in the field or
sheared the sheep near their cottage under the large oak tree, named
the CLIPPING TREE. As the child grew, Michael saw that his
son lacked no "pleasure that a boy can know." With his own hand
he cut a sapling and made it into the shepherd's staff for the boy
as a mark of new dignity. When the lad was ten, he stood against the
mountain blasts with his father and fearlessly shared the dangers
and the toil of his work. Small wonder that the objects the shepherd
loved were dearer still and that responses from the boy made the old
man's heart seem born again. When Luke had reached his eighteenth year, he was his father's "comfort and his daily hope."

So the simple household lived from day to day, when to Michael
suddenly came distressful news. Through no fault of his own, the
shepherd was called upon to pay an unlooked-for claim of nearly
half his substance. His first resolve was to sell at once "a portion of
his patrimonial fields"; but, as he thought of his lifelong diligence
to possess the land and of his purpose to hand it on to Luke to
possess "free as is the wind/That passes over it," his heart failed
him. To save the land it would be better, he thought, to have Luke
go to the city to work and with thrift quickly pay off the debt and
return. Isabel was not so sure and for a time withheld approval. The
dialogue of Michael and Isabel, with its anxious probing of Michael's dilemma, is among the finest that Wordsworth ever wrote.
The words, which come straight from the hearts of Michael and his
wife, are a poignant revelation of their glowing hopes and cautious
fears. At length, after many misgivings, Isabel agrees that Luke
should go.

Before word of his disastrous loss had come to Michael, he had
planned to build a sheepfold and for that purpose had gathered
a heap of stones in the mountain valley. To that spot on the evening before Luke left for the city the old man and his son repaired.
There Michael asked Luke to lay one stone. And if evil men are ever

his son's companions, he said, "think of me, my Son,/And of this
moment; . . . a covenant/'T will be between us." Luke stooped
down and did as his father had requested: "At the sight/The Old
Man's grief broke from him; to his heart/He pressed his Son, he
kisséd him and wept."

The next day Luke went to the city, and at first all was well; but
at length he gave himself to evil ways and was driven at last "to
seeking a hiding-place beyond the seas." The son's default is treated
briefly and quietly, for "Michael" is the story of the old shepherd.
After Luke's defection, one might think that the old man would be
crushed with grief and die. He suffered, but he did so bravely; and,
through his love of Luke, his heart was born again:

> There is comfort in the strength of love;
> 'Twill make a thing endurable, which else
> Would overset the brain, or break the heart . . .
> And to that hollow dell from time to time
> Did he repair to build the Fold of which
> His flock had need. 'Tis not forgotten yet
> The pity which was then in every heart
> For the old Man—and 'tis believed by all
> That many and many a day he thither went,
> And never lifted up a single stone.

In Michael, there is concentrated the patient strength of a man who
has lived "in the strength of nature." With strange and lonely fidelity he still looked up to sun and cloud and went about his work
for "the length of full seven years." But, when he died, he left the
sheepfold unfinished. The land was sold and went into a stranger's
hand. The cottage, named by men the EVENING STAR, is gone.
Only the great oak beside the door remained as a reminder of that
house of industry. And on the mountain side the pile of rocks lies
untouched, a poignant talisman of Michael's tragedy.

"Michael" is one of the best loved of all Wordsworth's writings.
The story draws close to a kind of loss and suffering that occurs in
some form to everyone. The tale is told as one coming from the
people, as one "believed by all." The poet is the communal spokesman. Yet the pathos which pervades the poem arises from the poet's
making a common story completely his own by speakng in his own
person and character with sheer, penetrating power. The diction is

pure and natural; colloquial phrases are touched with a dignity that gives them universal appeal. Simple statements of thought and feeling are given profound significance. They move to the ethical discovery, central in Wordsworth's moral teaching, "that suffering, when illuminated by love, creates its own nobility of heart."[5]

V *Preface to* Lyrical Ballads, *1800 and 1802*

The poems written in Germany and during the first year at Grasmere were gathered together for a second volume to *Lyrical Ballads* and were published with a Preface in 1800. The chief instigator of the Preface was Coleridge; however, the Preface was emphatically Wordsworth's composition and contained some opinions which Coleridge did not share. Years later Coleridge wrote a critique of it spelling out his points of disagreement with Wordsworth's style in poetry and with his ideas. Even at the time, Coleridge was conscious of certain conflicts which by 1802 made him "suspect that somewhere there is a *radical* difference in our theoretical opinions respecting poetry."[6]

The immediate purpose of the Preface was to disarm criticism and to straighten out readers. To accomplish this purpose, Wordsworth entered into a spirited defense of the poetic principles that had guided the experiment of the first *Lyrical Ballads*. Opposition and ridicule had stiffened his opinions; as a consequence, he moved unwarily to an extreme position on controversial topics, the most untenable having to do with his theory of language. He rashly asserted that there was no essential difference between the language of poetry and that of prose. Coleridge, who wholeheartedly supported Wordsworth in his attack upon the personificators and their stock-in-trade of poetic diction, could not accept his friend's declaration that the language of prose and metrical composition is the same. In *Biographia Literaria,* where he takes issue with Wordsworth, he had no difficulty in demonstrating that the *order* of words and the use and selection of those words would not be equally "fit and natural" in a prose composition and in metrical poetry.

Nor could Coleridge accept Wordsworth's contention that the language of low and rustic men is best adapted to poetic writing "because such men hourly communicate with the best objects from which the best part of language is originally derived"; nor his conjecture that these men because of their social condition "convey their feelings and notions in simple and unelaborated expressions."

Coleridge pointed out the ambiguity of "best objects," and he persuasively argued that good speech is the result of "good sense and natural feeling" rather than exposure to "best objects" (whatever they may be). He was unpersuaded that a poetic style based upon rustic speech was the formula for achieving "a more permanent and a far more philosophical language." The speech of rustics was little more than a negative ideal of a speech purified from all that was artificial and trivial.

It must be admitted that Wordsworth's concept of the use and function of language was narrow and limited. He mistakenly believed that the humble and rustic people among whom he had grown up had simple affections which they expressed in speech far removed from the insincerities of elegant society. He wrongly thought that men were nearer to Nature when they lived among mountains and that, when they were nearer to Nature, they spoke more purely and passionately. Wordsworth is not very persuasive nor consistent in his argument, for he admitted that even rustic speech needed to be "purified . . . from all lasting and rational causes of dislike and disgust." Wordsworth over-reached himself in his desire to convey the importance of the change he was trying to make in "poetic diction." If one strips away the extravagances into which he was betrayed, one sees that he was eminently right in his insistence that poetry must be a sincere expression of passion, not a decorative composition, and that its language must therefore be "a selection of language really used by men." Wordsworth saw more clearly, and showed perhaps more convincingly than any previous poet, that the language of passion may also be bare and austere and therefore in keeping with the syntax and structure of ordinary speech. Much of Wordsworth's noblest verse is of this kind.[7]

The enduring greatness of the Preface of 1800 (and 1802) lies not in the polemic against poetic diction and vitiated taste but in Wordsworth's speculations on the origin, nature, and purpose of poetry. He centers this discussion upon his now famous definition of poetry. "All good poetry," he said, "is the spontaneous overflow of powerful feelings: it takes its origin from emotion recollected in tranquility: the emotion is contemplated till, by a species of reaction, the tranquility gradually disappears, and an emotion, kindred to that which was before the subject of contemplation, is gradually produced, and does itself actually exist in the mind."

In poetic creation, Wordsworth is telling his reader, the recollected emotion is kindred but not identical to that of the actual situation which first aroused it. It is fed by continual influxes of emotion from collateral remembrances, so that the powerful feelings which overflow into poetry are both an increment and an idealization of the original emotion. Even if the original feeling were painful, or if painful associations were drawn to it, the overbalance of the mind during composition will be a state of enjoyment. A process of joy-inducing *katharsis* operates during poetic creation, a process which, according to Wordsworth, should also occur in the reader. Indeed, the poet has a duty to see that it does so: "[the Poet] ought especially to take care, that whatever passions he communicates to his reader, those passions, if the reader's mind be sound and vigorous, should always be accompanied with an overbalance of pleasure."

Wordsworth's meticulous description of the creative process is a truly great piece of psychological analysis. It is part of a passage of some three thousand words added to the Preface in 1802, which also includes his answer to the question "What is a Poet?" The poet, he says, is a man endowed with a "more than usual" capacity to perceive and feel and with a "greater promptness to think and feel without immediate external excitement." He must also have thought long and deeply.[8] The poet "thinks and feels in the spirit of human passion," and he does not write "for poets alone but for men." "The Poet, singing a song in which all human beings join with him, rejoices in the presence of truth as our visible friend and hourly companion."

Wordsworth believes with Aristotle that poetry is more philosophical than historical: "Its object is truth, not individual and local, but general, and operative." He also makes a claim that would raise it above science. The disciplines of analytical thought, he says, reflect only a part of human nature; but poetry is a reflection of the whole mind of man. "Poetry is the breath and finer spirit of all knowledge; it is the impassioned expression which is in the countenance of all Science . . . . Poetry is the first and last of all knowledge—it is as immortal as the heart of man." In the passages on poetry and the poet Wordsworth writes prose equal to any in our language.

Wordsworth was not only the daring experimenter in poetic language and techniques; he was also the social reformer and critic of the bad customs of his day. He saw the dangers that were threatening the spirit of man in his generation. War and industrialization were blunting the mind to an almost savage torpor causing men to seek "outrageous stimulation" in "frantic novels and sickly and stupid tragedies." Wordsworth believed that the human mind was capable of being excited without the use of gross and violent stimulants. He chose ordinary incidents and "great and simple affections" as the subject matter for his poetry. He wrote for all men, aimed to remove the film of familiarity, and break through the crust of custom. Each of the *Lyrical Ballads*, he said, has a worthy purpose: to extend the domain of sensibility for the delight, the honor, and the benefit of human nature; "to console the afflicted; to add sunshine to daylight, by making the happy, happier; to teach the young and gracious of every age to see, think, and feel, and, therefore, to become more actively and securely virtuous."[9]

The Preface to *Lyrical Ballads* was (and to some extent still is) a controversial document. It contains a number of ill-considered, poorly defended precepts which at the time were the cause of argument and tribulation. Coleridge wished that it had never been published. Readers today, of course, do not share that wish. For, however perverse Wordsworth may at times have been, something can be said for most of his original contentions. Moreover, along with the gross and misleading elements of his thought, there are the salutary and profound pronouncements that made the Preface the great and liberating treatise of its day. Along with the poems it helped to shape, it secured Wordsworth's fame—and altered the course of English poetry.

CHAPTER 4

The Prelude

T HE year 1798 was one of widespread pessimism in England: the conservatives were scornful of utopian dreams, and the reformers were disillusioned over any chance of improving society; the war with France had reached a state of crisis. In the midst of this national gloom, Wordsworth, who had recovered from his own disenchantment with political chimeras, was eager to share with others a way to regain hope and peace of soul. Early in March, spurred by Coleridge's enthusiasm, he undertook a long philosophical poem, which he hoped "to make of considerable utility," to be entitled *The Recluse; or Views on Man, on Nature, and on Human Life*.

Wordsworth launched into his new undertaking with high spirits; but, after turning out several hundred lines,[1] he was overwhelmed with doubts about his ability to carry through the tremendous task he had set for himself. He decided he should review his powers to determine "how far nature and education had qualified him to construct a literary work that might live." The result of this self-examination was *The Prelude*. It was Wordsworth's intention to make *The Prelude* introductory to *The Recluse*; but, because the new poem far outran the original scheme, ultimately reaching the great length of fourteen books and better than eight thousand lines, it was deemed not suitable for that purpose. However, *The Prelude* stands independently as a memorable account of the origin and development of the poetic mind and as the most vital work of Wordsworth's genius.

At Goslar in the winter of 1798-99 Wordsworth set to work in earnest on the poem of his early life by recalling all that Nature had done for him in childhood. The lines he then wrote make up the substantial part of Book I and include parts of Books V and XII. After his return to England in May, 1799, the inspiration came to him to dedicate the poem now shaping in his mind to Coleridge.

The dedication to his friend was a great incitement; without it, he probably would not have been able to carry the poem through to completion. For Coleridge was the friend of Wordsworth's genius as well as of his heart, a fact underscored throughout *The Prelude*. Probably sometime during the summer of 1799 Book II was composed.

However, after Wordsworth moved into Dove Cottage in December, 1799, he could not progress with his poem. Instead, much to Coleridge's disappointment, Wordsworth occupied himself composing sonnets and other short pieces. At last, in the fall of 1803, he roused again to the task and seems to have written in some coherent form the preamble and post-preamble (the first 271 lines of Book I). In the spring of 1804, under the stimulus of Coleridge's departure for Malta, Wordsworth turned again to the poem's composition and completed it through Book V. At this time he altered his plan for ending his self-examination with the dedication to poetry in his nineteenth year, to the fuller project of a poem including his experience in France, and bringing the story down to 1798, when he felt his powers were matured and ready for expression. This called for eight more books after the fifth, all of which were brought to completion in June, 1805.

The finished work fell far short of what Wordsworth had seemed capable of achieving. Partly for this reason and partly because it was a highly personal document, publication was withheld until after his death. But it was not laid aside and forgotten; often during the next thirty-five years he returned to *The Prelude* to revise it. The poem published in 1850 differs widely, therefore, from the one completed in 1805. Wordsworth had given it no title: it was known to his family and friends as "the poem to Coleridge" or as "the poem on his own early life." For its publication, Mary Wordsworth most appropriately chose *The Prelude* as its title.

I   *Synopsis*

The Prelude opens with the recording of a joyous hymn chanted by the poet to render thanks for his release from the bondage of the city. As the wind was blowing on his body, he felt within the breath of creative inspiration and was buoyed up with "A chearful confidence in things to come." After the spontaneous self-dedication, according to the next two hundred and fifty lines, he relaxed into passive contentment; contemplated various themes for a great work; was overcome wth indecision; and, finally baffled by his inability to compose, fell into a mood of morbid introspection and despair. Was it for a bafflement such as this, he asked himself, that the river Derwent had nourished him in childhood?

The poem properly begins with an account of the twofold discipline he had received from Nature: "Fair seed-time had my soul, and I grew up/Foster'd alike by beauty and by fear." Adventures from school days at Hawkshead through his twelfth year, which contributed ultimately to his poetic power, are recounted. These include such "incidents of fear" as his theft of a woodcock from another's trapline, the plundering of raven's eggs on the high crag, and the "severer intervention" of Nature's discipline when he stole a boat in the darkness. Then it was that a huge cliff "like a living thing" strode after him and for days "huge and mighty Forms" troubled his dreams. More quietly he tells of the ministry of Beauty: when he was skating, "the stars Eastward were sparkling clear"; at other times, how he would drink in "a pure organic pleasure" from the beauty "of curling mist" or from "the level plain/Of waters colour'd by the steady clouds."

Book II traces the poet's development from unconscious intercourse with Nature, as set forth in Book I, to an active awareness of "the sentiment of Being." The schoolboy episodes in the earlier part (to line 203) are intermediate, and the period covered in this section is from Wordsworth's thirteenth to his fifteenth year. During this time, while engaged in boyish sports among scenes of natural beauty, Nature was revealed collaterally. For example, the poet tells how, on an excursion to Furness Abbey, when with glee he and his companions were racing their horses through the chantry, he heard the singing of an invisible wren and was filled with a poignant desire to remain in that place forever "to hear such music."

With line 203 a new stage in Wordsworth's development commences. Beginning in his fifteenth and lasting until his seventeenth year, he relates how Nature was sought for her own sake. From boyish play, he turned to solitude, passionate friendship, vague yearnings and idealism, and the unutterable thoughts of youth. To "Nature's finer influxes" his mind then lay open, and he thrilled to discover in objects the manifold affinities not seen by others. On early morning walks alone among the hills he experienced moments of mystic calm, spiritual closeness to Nature, and a consciousness of "plastic power" within him. He had received so much from Nature that all his thoughts "were steep'd in feeling." In all things he "saw one life, and felt that it was joy." He laments the defection of those who have lost faith in mankind; and he concludes with an affectionate address to Coleridge, who, though reared in the city, has come to share his own deep devotion to Nature.

Book III tells of Wordsworth's first year at St. John's College, Cambridge. Upon his arrival, he was in high spirits and moved easily into the strange, motley world around him. Yet he had little regard for the program of college studies and had doubts about the reasons for his being there. When he was alone, he sensed a deep and quiet mental strength within himself. At times, he felt a spiritual contact with the illustrious poets who had preceded him at Cambridge—Chaucer, Spenser, and Milton. Mostly, he spent the year in a mixed round of social idleness and in halfhearted accession to academic duty. He did not find there the love of learning that should possess youth. How different, he thought, it must have been with the medieval lovers of truth who had resided at Cambridge. The year in retrospect seemed like a day at a museum: he suffered a barren sense of gay confusion, but something was left in the memory for future use.

Book IV begins in a joyous mood with the college youth on the heights overlooking Lake Windermere on his way back to Hawkshead for his first summer vacation. He had glad greetings from all the villagers and from old Dame Tyson, to whose memory Wordsworth pays a fine tribute. He experienced great happiness in seeing the throng of familiar things about the cottage that had been his home, and at night he especially enjoyed lying down again upon the bed where he had so often heard the roaring wind and clamorous rain and had watched "The moon is splendour couch'd among the leaves/Of a tall ash." Freed now from the confinement of college life, the poet tells with gratitude of how he returned to his solitary walks and how, on making again the familiar circuit of Esthwaite Lake, he was lifted into suprasensuous communion: "Gently did my soul/Put off her veil, and self-transmuted, stood/Naked as in the presence of her God." Trivial vanities often intervened to stop the course of lofty contemplation. But on one memorable occasion, when he was returning home alone after a night of revelry, the radiant beauty of the dawn so exalted him he was filled with a sense of solemn dedication. During this summer vacation, Wordsworth was also awakened to a new awareness of the worth and simple goodness of the plain-living country people: "With another eye," he says, "I saw the quiet Woodman in the Woods,/The Shepherd on the Hills." Book IV closes with an account of his surprise encounter in the darkness with an "uncouth shape," a vagrant soldier whom he befriended and aided.

Book V relates what Wordsworth owed to books in early life. It opens with the lament that consecrated books, worthy to endure forever, must perish. Related to this disconsolate thought is the nightmarish dream about an Arab intent upon carrying off all learning. The dreamer, who had been reading *Don Quixote* by the sea, fell into a sleep and dreamed. In his drean he was joined by an Arab mounted upon his dromedary bearing underneath one arm a stone (mathematics) and in the opposite hand a shining shell (poetry). From the shell there came a prophesy foretelling the destruction of the earth by deluge. On learning this forecast, the Arab moved foreward rapidly across the desert intent on burying his two books; and the dreamer followed him. When a glittering light revealed the waters of the deep advancing upon them, the Arab quickened his pace and was last seen "With the fleet waters of the drowning world/In chase of him." The dreamer woke in terror.

Wordsworth sympathizes with the Arab's anxiousness, for great books are Powers only less than Nature's self. He is grateful for the freedom allowed him as a schoolboy to roam widely in his reading rather than being confined by careful tutoring. In a satiric vein, he launches into an attack upon the child prodigy stuffed with false learning by the disciples of Jean Jacques Rousseau. To Wordsworth, it would be better to let the old fairy tales and romances, the rough and tumble of the schoolyard, and the secret ministries of Nature join in making their influence felt in shaping "A race of real children, not too wise,/Too learned, or too good." His own special treasure as a schoolboy was *Arabian Nights* which satisfied his "cravings for the marvelous." When he reached his early teens, the charm of romance yielded to the love of poetry, in which he found a sweet satisfaction, "a passion and a power." He concludes with an apology for omitting to say anything about the influence of books in his later years; but such acknowledgment he never made.

Book VI treats casually his second and third years at Cambridge without differentiating between them. Wordsworth lived more to himself and settled into more promising habits, but he continued to be indifferent to the prescribed course of study. Indeed, his summer vacations offered the most rewarding experiences during these years, the first of which was spent in the Lake Country in the company of his sister Dorothy and Mary Hutchinson. As he recalls that summer, the poet feels a strong inclination to add Coleridge to the group, though then unknown to them, and he pays a glowing tribute to his genius. The third summer vacation spent with his college mate, Robert Jones, in a walking tour of the Swiss and Italian Alps was truly a glorious, memorable adventure—one richly rewarding to him as a poet.

Book VII blends the experiences of two periods of residence in London: the first period subsequent to his graduation from college; the second, following his return from France. Before he ever went to the city, Wordsworth's youthful fancy had shaped marvellous visions of the wonders to be seen there. These gave way in due season; and, when he went to live intimately day by day in the motley, bustling metropolis, his keen and lively pleasures were intermixed with disappointments. He roamed the streets, watched intently the street entertainments, and beheld in the crowds "all specimens of Man." He enjoyed spectacles within doors: art galleries, pantomimic shows, melodrama at Sadler's Wells, and more solid entertainment at the theaters. He was distressed to see an innocent child surrounded by dissolute, debased humanity. A blind beggar became for him the symbol of "the utmost we know,/Both of ourselves and of the universe." With a touch of satire he portrays the young lawyer displaying his oratorical powers and the bachelor preacher winding "through many a maze,/A minuet course." In striking contrast with the daytime bustle is London at night in solemn calmness, beauty, and peace. Though blank confusion wearies the eye, there is in the city, to him who looks in steadiness, amidst "the press/Of self-destroying, transitory things/Composure and ennobling Harmony."

Book VIII reviews the steps that not only led Wordsworth to the love of Nature but ultimately to the love of Mankind. Man is brought into the ominous presense of Nature in a small gathering of country people holding a summer festival on the side of Mount Helvellyn. "How little They, they and their doings seem,/. . . and yet how great!" The nobility of man had early been impressed upon the boy Wordsworth through his admiration of the shepherds in the mountains. Their domain was more beautiful by far than any legendary paradise, and their life, fraught by challenges of danger and distress, was more noble than any other. With his concept of man thus exalted, Wordsworth, when confronted with wretchedness and vice in the city, remained steadfast in his trust of "Man ennobled."

But the love of Man was not predominant until the poet's twenty-second year. He reviews the growth of his love of Nature from the early years when she was secondary to his "own pursuits and animal activities," through the period of his youth when "wilful Fancy" fictionized natural objects, to "the time of greater dignity" when he felt "The pulse of Being everywhere, . . . One galaxy of life and joy." "Then rose Man, . . . as of all visible natures crown." In the city of London, that "Fountain of my Country's destiny," he felt most intensely the spiritual essence of human nature. The city was "thronged with impregnations" and "Affectingly set fourth, more than elsewhere/Is possible, the unity of man." Nature led him by slow gradations until the poet was independently established in his love of human kind.

In Book IX, Wordsworth says he went to France chiefly to learn the language, and for that purpose he chose to live at Orléans. On his way there he stopped for a few days at Paris and visited the sites made memorable by the revolution, but he did not feel emotionally involved. At Orléans, he was at first content to be a spectator; however, it was not long before he was won over to the revolutionary cause. The chief instrument in bringing about his conversion was, as has been noted, Michel Beaupuy, a royalist military officer who had turned patriot. Wordsworth had been bred up to democratic ways both at Hawkshead and afterward at Cambridge; therefore, the French Revolution "Seemed nothing out of nature's certain course." Hence, Beaupuy, who became Wordsworth's close companion, found him a ready convert. The patriot's arguments were given firm intellectual support from the French revolutionary philosophers and from that handbook of all good democrats, Plutarch's *Lives*. Wordsworth's conversion was emotionally confirmed when the two companions one day met a hunger-bitten victim of oppression and his friend excitedly said, " 'Tis against *that/* Which we are fighting." The remainder of Book IX is devoted to the tragic love story of Vaudracour and Julia, a fictionized account of Wordsworth's own affair with Annette Vallon. This recital was removed from *The Prelude* as hindering the forward motion of its central theme and published separately.

In Book X, the poet has arrived in Paris on his way back to England and shortly after the September Massacres. He ranged the city as he had before but more eagerly; and at night, as he lay on his bed, he felt "a substantial dread" and was filled with gloomy forebodings. During his presence there, the extremist Robespierre gained ascendancy; and Wordsworth inwardly prayed that a great leader with moderate temper might rise to lead the nation. Reluctantly, he returned home, but he was full of hope for France and for the cause of universal liberty among all peoples. When England's declaration of war on France suddenly came, Wordsworth was shocked to his deepest self; he felt that the war was both a tragedy and a blunder. Although the senseless slaughter of the Reign of Terror filled the poet with despair, he rationalized it as the necessary consequence of a reservoir of guilt "That could no longer hold its loathsome charge." A great lift was given to his spirit one summer evening at Leven's estuary following a visit to the grave of his schoolmaster, William Taylor, when, from a casual inquiry of a traveler, he received the stirring reply that *Robespierre was dead*. Filled with great joy, he pursued his way along the very sands upon which as a boy he had "in wantonness of heart" raced his horse with his schoolmates.

In Book X (Book XI of the final version), Wordsworth has kept faith with the ability of the people of France to settle their internal dissentions and to triumph over their enemies. He recalls with fervor how his own ideals for mankind were given strong support during the early years of the Republic: "Bliss was it in that dawn to be alive,/But to be young was very heaven." The whole earth then wore the promise of happiness such as one dreams of in a utopia, but this dream was now to be realized in the very world in which he lived. Even when Frenchmen engaged in excesses, the poet excused them on the grounds "That throwing off oppression must be the work/As well of license as of liberty."

When England challenged France with open war, his pride for his own country turned to shame. Subsequently, when France "changed a war of self-defence/For one of conquest," he still held stubbornly to his early belief in her cause. But strong emotional ties to his own country finally trapped Wordsworth in a conflict of allegiances from which he retreated to a delusion of security in the rational philosophy of Godwin. Following Godwin's lead, he dreamed that social freedom could be built upon that of independent intellect. It was not long before his speculations lured him into an intricate maze of contradictions, until, demanding *proof* and "wearied out with contrarieties," he "Yielded up moral questions in despair." At this juncture Coleridge, Dorothy, and "Nature's Self" helped to guide him back to his true self. Dorothy, in the midst of all, preserved him "still a Poet." Wordsworth closes the lengthy survey of his response to public events with an affectionate address to Coleridge, who is in Sicily; and he offers a devoted wish that his friend may there be restored to good health.

In Book XI (Book XII in 1850), Wordsworth reviews the period during which he became an idolater of analytical reason. At that time even Nature was not immune from contamination of his presumptuous habit of judging. He followed the "cult of the picturesque" in comparing scene with scene and in pampering himself "with meagre novelties/Of colour and proportion." Insatiably, he sought delights that pleased the sight, but not the mind. How different was his sister Dorothy's converse with Nature! Without intermeddling questioning, whatever scene she looked on yielded a sweetness that bespoke her own sweet presence. So it was with Dorothy's freedom of spirit that Wordsworth worshiped Nature in his early years among his native hills and so it was when he roamed through the Alps. But force of custom or aggravation of the times dulled his once vibrant communion with Nature. But at last he shook off the stultifying habit of analysis and again stood in Nature's presence "A sensitive and a creative soul." Our minds, he explains, are from early childhood nourished and invisibly repaired by "spots of time." He tells of two such "spots," one near Penrith Beacon when he had become half-faint with terror at the sight of initials carved in the turf marking the place where a murderer had been hanged; the other at his father's funeral (December, 1783) when he remembered his own trivial expectancy in anticipation of the Christmas holidays.

In Book XII (XIII in 1850), Wordsworth, restored to right reason and creative power, has found "once more in Man an object of delight." Sanguine schemes pleased him less, and he looked inquiringly at what makes the dignity of individual Man. Why is it, he asks, that "This glorious Creature" is to be found "One only in ten thousand?" To discover man as he really is, the poet turned to the public roads to watch and question those he met and to hold familiar talks with them. Because his faith in rural life to breed a good life was strengthened, he decided that simple, country folk would be the substance of his poetry.

Wordsworth was convinced that Nature had a passion and a power to shape the inner being of man and that poets especially have each his peculiar dower by which "he is enabled to perceive/Something unseen before" and from that influx create something that might become "a power like one of Nature's." To such a mood, he says, he was once lifted during a walk upon the Plain of Sarum when in vision he saw the primitive Britons offering living sacrifices on their altars. On his lonesome journey he composed a poem of familiar, everyday affairs ("The Female Vagrant") into which—so Coleridge said—he had infused touches of a higher power. Perhaps Coleridge's approval was a partial judgment of friendship. Nevertheless, Wordsworth remembers well that he seemed at that time to have sight of a new world, one fit to be recorded in verse for all to share.

Book XIII (Book XIV), the last book, features Wordsworth's excursion with his friend Jones and a guide up Mount Snowdon on a murky summer's night to see the sunrise from the top. During the ascent, the sky was low-hung with clouds that threatened rain; the climbers, hemmed in by fog and damp, could see nothing around them. Then, with the poet in the lead, the ground began to brighten as they neared the top; he instantly looked up to see the moon standing "naked in the Heavens." At his feet extended a huge sea of mist upon which the moon shone in single glory. Some distance away there was a break in the mist, "a deep and gloomy breathing-place," through which the roar of innumerable waters mounted as with one voice.

This majestic scene appeared to Wordsworth to be the perfect image of the poetic mind when actively possessed with creative power. This faculty, Imagination, gives to man liberty and intellectual love; it is the highest power that man may know. Wordsworth rounds out his recital with sincere and affectionate tributes to Dorothy and to Coleridge for the roles they played in shaping a poet's mind. He concludes with a prayerful wish that he may have "a few short years" in which to write poetry that will teach men to love what he and Coleridge have learned to love.

To a considerable extent *The Prelude* is autobiographical; but it obviously is not merely a narrative of the first twenty-seven years of its author's life. Wordsworth makes no attempt to give a faithful account of external happenings. Purely personal events are twisted out of normal order; some are omitted, and others are simplified so that the essential truth may be presented more clearly. Sometimes the facts of his life are completely ignored. Wordsworth is telling not so much the story of his life as recounting the rich imaginative experiences that were his; he is tracing the steps by which the mind absorbed and reshaped external circumstances until self-knowledge and imaginative power have been attained.

The Prelude's greatness does not consist, therefore, in its biographical accuracy. It is an idealization, not a factual rendering, of the poet's life. In it the author's penetration to the essential nature and power of the poetic mind transforms whatever is personal into the universal. As a balm for pessimism and a loadstone to direct his countrymen to new hope, *The Prelude* tells how a poet acquired true knowledge and, when he was led astray, how his flagging spirit was resuscitated. In the early books, Nature is shown as playing the leading role in awakening and instructing his faculties. In the middle books, he exposes himself as prodigal from Nature, betrayed by rationality. In the last books, he shows how imaginative power was restored and he became "a sensitive and creative soul" dedicated to the universal heart of man.

II   *Themes and Ideas*

The Prelude was not carefully thought out in advance. As it progressed, there were shifts in direction; and secondary materials were added that seem unrelated to the central theme. The initial purpose may be surmised from the famous section highly praised by Coleridge, "Wisdom and Spirit of the Universe" (Book I, 401-41),[2] first published in *The Friend* under the title "Growth of Genius from the influence of Natural Objects on the Imagination in Boyhood and Early Youth." Throughout Books I and II the emphasis is upon the power of Imagination to transform simple incidents. In the four years that passed after the completion of the second book, Wordsworth grew in the understanding of his objective. When he moved into the composition of the third book, he realized that the poem's real center, its unifying principle, was to be found in the Imagnation. Perhaps nowhere in the works of Wordsworth does the poetic passion burn with purer flame than

when he contemplates in this book the exalted role of Imagination
and the epical grandeur of the task he has set for himself:

> Of Genius, Power,
> Creation and Divinity itself
> I have been speaking, for my theme has been
> What pass'd within me. Not of outward things
> Done visibly for other minds, words, signs,
> Symbols or actions; but of my own heart
> Have I been speaking, and my youthful mind.
> O Heavens! how awful is the might of Souls,
> And what they do within themselves, while yet
> The yoke of earth is new to them, the world
> Nothing but a wild field where they were sown.
> This is, in truth, heroic argument
> And genuine prowess; which I wish'd to touch
> With hand however weak; but in the main
> It lies far hidden from the reach of words.
>   (vv. 171-85)

The faculty of Imagination, the poetic faculty par excellence,
becomes, then, the real hero, the presiding genius of *The Prelude*.
In the most awesome and haunting passages that tell of the Imagination (as in the sixth book following the narrative of the travelers'
crossing of the Alps), the poet reveals how this power has brought
him to "the highest bliss/That can be known." By means of it, the
invisible is revealed to him, and beauty is transmuted into truth.
Imagination finally leads to a moral victory for the poet in the attainment of intellectual love. In the process of acquiring Imagination, no one can help another; but Nature can and does assist—as
Wordsworth demonstrates throughout the poem. To follow his
demonstration, one needs to undersand what Wordsworth means
by Nature.

Partly as a result of happy childhood associations and partly as a
result of ideas inherited from eighteenth-century Deists, Wordsworth built a faith in the beneficent power of Nature. Like the
Deists, he held that God revealed himself in the beauties and
sublimities of untamed nature. Like them, he believed that the
natural world is the expression of divine wisdom with a view to the
well-being of the whole of creation and of mankind in particular.
But, unlike his eighteenth-century predecessors, Wordsworth

brought the Creator from His far-off heaven to inhabit this very present world. He was conscious of an animating spirit moving through all Nature with a shaping power, a drive and directive force. He felt a presence "far more deeply interfused"

> Whose dwelling is the light of setting suns
> And the round ocean and the living air,
> And the blue sky, and in the mind of man:
> A motion and a spirit, that impels
> All thinking things, all objects of all thought,
> And rolls through all things.
> ("Tintern Abbey," vv. 97-102)

The animating principle of universal Nature Wordsworth identifies with deity, but he is chary during the years 1797-1805 of using the word "God." There are a good many passages in *The Prelude* that suggest an approximation to pantheism (the belief that the universe is God and God is the universe, so that, if it were destroyed, He would no longer exist); for example, he writes in Book II (429-30), "in all things now/I saw one life, and felt that it was joy." But, for the most part, Wordsworth dismisses any literal pantheistic identification of the spirit life with the sum of physical things. Perhaps a better term to describe his idea of Nature is *panentheistic*, for he believed in a power that was both within and beyond earthly forms, a power within but also "far more deeply interfused." His representation of the spirituality of Nature is varied and free; for example, he repeatedly expresses an animistic belief that there are spirits or tutelary Powers who inhabit the solitudes. Quite literally he means that there is "a spirit in the woods" acting under the direction of the Deity.[3] Frequently, he thought of Nature as a spirit endowed with personality, a purposive intelligence who animates and guides the external world. So guided, Nature by extrinsic passion peopled his mind with grand and beauteous forms and made him love them.

The most important "fact" of Nature for Wordsworth is the "unity of all." Quite literally, God and Nature are one. There is no division between Man and Nature and none between Nature and God—all adhere in a mighty unity. "Each thing has a life of its own and we are all one life," wrote Coleridge, interpreting Spinoza. So, with Wordsworth, all forms of Nature are linked into "one galaxy of life and joy." Natural objects are interpenetrative in a fluid pattern with each other and with the mind of man. There is a constant interplay of external and internal. Wordsworth felt a mysterious presence flowing through surrounding things that ministered to him, quickened his sensibilities, and assisted his meditations. He shows us in *The Prelude* how this is so. He follows the steps by which as child, as youth, and as man he is led to the great end of creation, the reproduction of creative mind, the Imagination. And just as he received this triumphant ministration through Nature, so he believed, may other men receive it.

The spirit of Nature permeates *The Prelude*, and it serves directly in the complex development of the human mind. Wordsworth's explanation of this development is based upon theories stemming from David Hartley. According to Hartleian psychology, human knowledge originates in perceptions made by the five senses. These perceptions through association are transformed into the aggregates —the fears, hopes, beliefs—of mental life. All is built up from the outside; there is, however, from the first an activity or motion of the human spirit which transmutes the mental complexes into their appropriate personal values. Wordsworth's close adherence to Hartley's sensationalistic philosophy in "Tintern Abbey" shocked and alarmed even Coleridge, who initially had encouraged him in the use of it.

But it was not long before Wordsworth, following Coleridge's lead, modified and subordinated sensationalism. Wordsworth recognized from the first, even in "Tintern Abbey," that sensations were clothed with a strange radiance because they were informed by the creative mind. In Books I and II of *The Prelude*, where Hartleian psychology is prominent,[4] he portrays his childhood not as the period of sensations merely, but as the joyous time in which as "auxiliar light/Came from my mind," which bestowed new splendor on the external world. In these early books, Wordsworth tells of moments that transcended sense and were of a distinctly mystical quality:

> Oft in these moments such a holy calm
> Did overspread my soul, that I forgot
> That I had bodily eyes, and what I saw
> Appear'd like something in myself, a dream,
> A prospect in my mind.[5]
>
> (II, 367-71)

By the time he began the composition of Book III in 1803 a philosophy emerged which was distinctly unsensationistic. The mighty world of eye and ear was superseded by the mightier one of the mind. In the last books of *The Prelude* Wordsworth identifies as paramount in the moulding of personality a transcendental faculty which derives from a suprapersonal agency communicating its message to consciousness:

> This efficacious spirit chiefly lurks
> Among those passages of life in which
> We have had deepest feeling that the mind
> Is lord and master, and that outward sense
> Is but the obedient servant of her will.
>
>   (XI, 269-73)

The great paradox of Wordsworth is his simultaneous attachment to the senses and his need for a higher faculty which synthesizes, transfuses, and modifies experience. The poet gives great weight to the role of sensory factors in knowledge because he realizes "how exquisitely the external World is fitted to the Mind." But in *The Prelude* he far overreaches Hartleian mechanism by supplying a transcendental activity of the mind. This inward mental creativeness vitalizes the report of the senses and adds an imperishable increment of power to existence. This creative power Wordsworth identifies as Imagination.

Wordsworth has an exalted concept of Imaginaton. In Book XIII (168-70), he says Imagination "Is but another name for absolute strength/And clearest insight, amplitude of mind,/And reason in her most exalted mood." So Wordsworth defines Imagination, but the transcendent experience of it he was never able to describe; for it is not only ineffable but ultimately incomprehensible. No passage better illustrates the recondite mystery that confronted him than the one in Book VI where he recounts the adventure in crossing the Alps. At the climax of his recital Imagination lifted itself "like an unfather'd vapour" and halted his effort to continue. When he recovered and could go on, he recognized but could not describe the glory of that usurpation:

> To my Soul I say
> I recognize thy glory; in such strength
> Of unsurpation, in such visitings

> Of awful promise, when the light of sense
> Goes out in flashes that have shewn to us
> The invisible world, doth Greatness make abode,
> There harbours whether we be young or old.
> Our destiny, our nature, and our home
> Is with infinitude, and only there.
>
> (VI, 531-39)

Through Imagination the poet enters into communion with the invisible world; he apprehends the infinite and becomes aware of the eternal spirit that pervades and unifies all existence. Man himself becomes a Spirit living in Time and Space far diffused; man's spirit is merged with this spiritual Power, which is itself the great Imagination, World Soul, and "Reason in her most exalted mood." To participate in the creative act of perfect self-identification with the great Imagination is to know intellectual freedom; it is to experience the very love of God himself.

The creative Imagination works with the stuff of memory surcharged with emotion. Visitations of this active power Wordsworth identifies as "spots of time," and he sees them as occurring most frequently, but by no means exclusively, in childhood. Midway in Book XII, partly to explain his restoration as "a sensitive and creative soul," he tells of "spots of time" that in existence retain "a vivifying Virtue" by which "our minds/Are nourished and invisibly repaired." At its simplest level, the "spot" is a past event so charged and transformed that, when recalled to mind, the poet's imaginative power is revived and his moral being strengthened. This recall was not accomplished merely through mechanical recollection, but by means of the powerful emotion associated with and built upon the original experience.

In the first of the incidents recounted, the poet describes his already mentioned childhood adventure when he happened upon the site where a murderer had once been executed and he fled with terror from the place. Years later this fearful adventure is refracted through another memory, a benign one. As a college youth in the company of his sister and Mary Hutchinson, he roamed about during a summer holiday "in daily presence of this very scene." By a mysterious and complex transfer of power he felt a "radiance more sublime" from the remembrances of the first terror-haunted visitation. So, Wordsworth says, ". . . feeling comes in aid/Of feeling, and diversity of strength/Attends us, if but once we have been strong."

In another "spot of time" he tells of his turbulent impatience one Christmastime when he was waiting for the horses that were to bear his brothers and himself home. Not ten days later his father died, and the boy interpreted the event as a divine chastisement provoked by his impatience. In his maturity this crude belief had long been put aside, but the mysterious occurrence, charged with emotion and touched with infinity, made it one of those "spots of time" in his childhood to which he "often would repair and thence would drink,/As at a fountain."

In Book V, in the "spot of time" involving the boy who "blew mimic hootings to the owls," which was first published separately, Wordsworth explains how Nature assists in the development of Imagination. He has represented in this poem, he says in the 1815 Preface,

. . . a commutation and transfer of internal feelings, cooperating with external accidents to plant, for immortality, images of sight and sound, in the celestial soil of the Imagination. The Boy, there introduced, is listening, with something of a feverish and restless anxiety, for the recurrence of the riotous sounds which he had previously excited; and, at the moment when the intenseness of his mind is beginning to remit, he is surprized into a perception of the solemn and tranquillizing images which the Poem describes.

The boy's energies were braced in expectancy to hear the owls, then relaxed; and in that moment the beauty of the natural scene, falling upon his eye, carried far into his heart a sense of the enduring power of Nature.[6]

In much the same way in the "spot of time" memorializing the poet's experience in Simplon Pass, he shows how a consciousness of the terrible beauty of the mountain pass came upon him during the "dull and heavy slackening" of his feelings following the tidings of the peasant that he and his companion already *"had crossed the Alps."* During the travelers' climb, the physical senses were pitched to high expectancy; but they failed to report what should have been the climactic moment of their adventure. It was in the slackness that ensued that the Imagination fed upon the images of Nature—decaying lofty woods, waterfalls, shooting torrents, black drizzling crags, unfettered clouds—which became in recollection transformed into "symbols of Eternity,/Of first and last, and midst, and without end."

In the most exalted of all the "spots of time," the ascent of Mt. Snowdon, which concludes *The Prelude*, inner illumination comes from surprise and reversal rather than through the psychological sequence of tension and remission. Wordsworth and his companions, with the poet in the lead, were making their way up the mountain at the dead of night when the ground at his feet began to brighten. He looked up startled and saw the moon shining clear in the heavens far above his head and at his feet a huge sea of mist. From a "deep and gloomy" opening in the vapor some distance from him, there mounted the sound "of waters, torrents, streams/ Innumerable, roaring with one voice." In that deep thoroughfare, says Wordsworth, "Nature lodg'd/The Soul, the Imagination of the whole."

Nature often works, Wordsworth tells us, upon the outward face of things as with imaginative power. Nature thrusts itself forth upon the senses; then Imagination feeds upon the inner reality beyond it. Imagination moulds, abstracts, and combines—"By sensible impressions not enthrall'd/But quicken'd, rouz'd, and made thereby more apt/To hold communion with the invisible world." When the scene had passed away, it appeared to the poet "The perfect image of a mighty Mind,/Of one that feeds upon infinity." The single chasm through which the united sound of waters roared seemed analogous to the creative mind whence power arises from the dark abyss and takes shape in the world of light and form.

Wordsworth believed in an *anima mundi* operating in terms of benevolence and in some degree of purposiveness. But in *The Prelude* of 1805 he does not, as has been pointed out, portray external Nature as without flaw or as universally benign to man. There are dark places and terror in the world around him and dark places in the mind. In childhood, when he stole the woodcock from another boy's trap, Nature implanted in his mind "low breathings" coming after him. When he took the boat that belonged to another, "huge and mighty forms" moved slowly through his mind by day and were a trouble to his dreams. In young manhood, he woke in terror from the nightmare of the Arab carrying the stone and the shell to destruction. When he was in Paris soon after the September Massacres, the fear gone by pressed on him almost like the fear to come. As he contemplated the outrage and bloody violence done in the name of liberty, ghastly visions of despair filled his dreams.

Yet, for Wordsworth, the bleakness and terror never exist for

themselves alone; they potently serve that sense of religious sublimity with which Imagination invests them. "A dark inscrutable
workmanship" reconciles discordant elements and gives them direc-
tional force "to impregnate and to elevate the mind." Nature uses
ignoble means for noble ends:

> How strange that all
> The terrors, pains, and early miseries,
> Regrets, vexations, lassitudes interfused
> Within my mind, should e'er have borne a part,
> And that needful part, in making up
> The calm existence that is mine when I
> Am worthy of myself.
>
> (I, 344-50 [1850])

The Imagination mysteriously selects and transforms the elements
of fear, as well as those of beauty that will administer to the
strengthening of "the immortal spirit."

Wordsworth quite naturally assumed a dichotomy between conceptions of "beauty" and of "fear"—a dichotomy derived from a
whole century of speculation on the beautiful and the sublime.
These dual qualities were used not only to characterize the opposing
poles of the external world but also to indicate the range of human
emotion. Mr. Lindenberger calls attention to the rhetorical tradition, one with which Wordsworth was familiar, which distinguishes
between *pathos*, the sublime in Nature and the more violent emotions in man, and *ethos*, the beautiful in Nature and those emotions
in man which are calm and gentle. The progress from *pathos* to
ethos, according to this scholar, "is Wordsworth's image of the history of his own life and as such it provides a pattern for the organization for *The Prelude*." [7]

The first half of the poem moves from the awesome visionary
experiences of childhood to the "tamer argument" of the human
world of London; the second half advances from his experience of
the terrors of the revolution, with the corresponding turmoil in his
mind, to the attainment of inner peace. Until his residence in France
in his late youth, man had been subordinate to Nature, "His hour
being not yet come"; but Beaupuy converted him to the revolution
and his allegiance was given to the people. Still there is a stage beyond loyalty to the revolutionary cause. The revolution had been

born of violence and had been carried forward on a wave of terror.
Wordsworth, likewise, even to the very passing of his youth, had
"too exclusively esteem'd *that* love,/And sought *that* beauty,
which, as Milton sings,/Hath terror in it."

Hence, after his return to England, violent conflicting stresses
over the revolution and the war with France led the poet to rationalism; and rationalism led to the impairment of the Imagination and
moral bankruptcy. But, as he approached maturity, Nature bade
him "seek for other agitations, or be calm"; and Dorothy helped to
soften down his "over-sternness." Finally *pathos* (violence) was controlled and directed to *ethos* (calmness and love). The poet intends
the chastening process, described in Book XIII (211-68), to mark his
transition to manhood and his acceptance of a selfless or self-forget-
ting love. The attainment of "this love more intellectual" was a
moral victory for Wordsworth and is the climax of *The Prelude*.
Thus intellectual love is the second major theme of the poem,
and it is closely intertwined with the account of the growth of
Imagination:[8]

> Imagination having been our theme
> So also hath that intellectual love,
> For they are each in each, and cannot stand
> Dividually.
>
> (XIII, 185-88)

The person whose intellectual life has been grounded in Imagination is *capable* of love, and he can be taught to love. As Wordsworth
states it even more strongly: "This love more intellectual cannot be/
Without Imagination."

An important supporting theme of *The Prelude* is the love of
common man. This theme first makes its appearance in Book IV
when, during a summer vacation at Hawkshead, Wordsworth
viewed in a new perspective the goodness of the simple country
people living there. He saw with another eye the quiet woodman in
the woods, the shepherd on the hills, and even old Dame Tyson falling asleep over her Bible. His sympathies were also deeply stirred
at that time by his encounter with the vagrant soldier whom he
befriended and helped on his way. In Book VII, which tells of his
residence in London, he is witness to the pathos, the dignity, and

mystery of man in the great city, but somehow he seems isolated from the masses of mankind.

In Book VIII he reviews the steps by which the love of Nature led him to the love of mankind. The nobility of man, he reminds us, had early been impressed upon him as a boy through his admiration of the mountain shepherds. This idealization of individual shepherds and of the society of dalesmen in the Lake Country remained steadfast in his young manhood. These men of the pastoral community he consciously sets up in contrast to the brute masses of the city. In London he had felt intensely the "spiritual essence of Human nature" and the unity of man; but in the country his trust in "Man ennobled" was confirmed.

However, Wordsworth's trust had not been tested. For a long time following the "melancholy waste of hopes o'erthrown," when the French had turned a war of freedom into one of conquest, Wordsworth foundered desperately in search of steadfastness and knowledge. But at last the restoration of his creative Imagination lifted his "Being into magnanimity," and Nature deeply re-established intellectual love. Thus revived, with a clearer sense of what was excellent and right, he came to see that ambition and folly impel the rulers of the world and that the wealth of nations alone is lodged in individual man. Thereafter, he set his course to seek in Man as a person what there is of universal good.

As a result, he was especially anxious to learn the real worth and power of mind of those who lived by bodily labor. Eagerly he turned to the countryside and the public roads where he began to enquire and question those he met and to hold familiar talk with them. There he saw into the depth of human souls and found in lowly men dignity, steadfastness, and honor. Wordsworth recognizes that in rural communities excess of labor and poverty often thwart love; and love does not easily thrive in the cities. But in the country there are many living in the daily presence of Nature, who are rude in outward show, yet "men within themselves." He passionately declares that he will do justice in his verse to these simple men who too long have been neglected by snobbery:

> Of these, said I, shall be my Song; . . . my theme
> No other than the very heart of man
> As found among the best of those who live
> Not unexalted by religious hope,

> Nor uninformed by books, good books though few,
> In Nature's presence.
>
> (XII, 239-44)

The theme of common man is among the most exciting of the ideas that move through *The Prelude*. As the topic develops from book to book, the poet seems to glow with the sense of fresh discoveries. Best of all, he jubilantly realized that man as he idealized him in boyhood is still to be admired and is most worthy to be memorialized in his poetry.

Several topics which relate to the central themes of *The Prelude* are the ministry of books, the rejection of the "picturesque," and the poet's treatment of characters. In Book V, Wordsworth tells of what he "owed to books in early life." There is much uselessness, he says, in study and learning, especially of the sort pursued by a child prodigy in piling up rote knowledge under the strict guidance of a tutor. It would be better to have back again the old fairy tales and romances; better to let a boy roam wide in books of his own choosing than for him to be confined and protected. Tales of the marvelous, such as *Arabian Nights*, that charm away the hours and keep alive the sense of wonder are especially to be prized.

"Untaught things, creative, and enduring" seemed to Wordsworth much more important than what was learned in schools. He insists on letting the child be himself, on letting him gain emotional stability through the rough and tumble of the school grounds. Let mankind have, he says, a race of rugged, natural children doing wrong and suffering, yet "in happiness/Not yielding to the happiest upon earth."

> May books and nature be their early joy!
> And knowledge, rightly honor'd with that name,
> Knowledge not purchas'd with the loss of power!
>
> (V, 447-49)

The poet speaks with awe of the power in great books of science and poetry such as the Arab in the dream was bearing off to destruction. Wordsworth recounts the pleasures he received in reading words of poetry in tuneful order and of his discovery of "the great Nature that exists in works/Of mighty Poets." He finds visionary power embodied in the mystery of words. The right books rightly used, he concludes, are an aid to Imagination and a support to the lessons learned from Nature.

Soon after his return from France, Wordsworth tells us in Book XI, his faculties fell under the dominance of the analytic intellect and remained so enthralled until his deliverance by his sister Dorothy. His response to Nature was then contaminated; his mind was so far perverted that he began analyzing natural scenery in the fashion of the "picturesque" scenic hunters like Gilpin and Price. He became obsessed by the habit of comparing scene with scene and of observing the "meagre novelties of colour and proportion." Wordsworth also says that, at this time of intellectual thraldom, the tyranny of the bodily eye drove him insatiably to seek "new forms,/ New pleasure, wider empire for the sight."

His attitude toward Nature then was identical to that which Wordsworth experienced on his first visit to Tintern Abbey when his passion for colors and forms was rapacious and when the hold of physical Nature upon his eye was absolute. But the period of the eye's dominance (and the concomitant appeal of the pictorial and the picturesque in the landscape) did not last long. Through Dorothy's ministrations, Wordsworth escaped from the bondage under which he had fallen. He had felt too forcibly in early life the visitations of imaginative power for the imprisonment of his sight to last. In the course of time, the eye's eager delight was subdued by a mighty passion, and he stood again in Nature's presence "a sensitive and creative soul."

All the characters in *The Prelude* are solitaries: the blind beggar, the "girl who bore a Pitcher on her head," the lone Arab on his dromedary, the vagrant soldier, the boy who blew mimic hootings to the owls. Even Wordsworth's intimates are viewed in isolation: Michel Beaupuy, Dorothy, Coleridge in Sicily as "lonely wanderer," and the poet's beloved schoolmaster, William Taylor. At the center of this world of solitary figures stands, of course, the most important solitary of them all—the poet himself. In the various confrontations between Wordsworth and his solitaries, he usually establishes a dramatic interaction that results in a revelation of some sort. His encounter with the blind man illustrates how he does this.

When Wordsworth was moving through the crowds in London's overflowing streets, he tells us in Book VII, it seemed that every one that passed him by was a mystery. All shapes appeared as in a dream, neither knowing him, nor known. But once, lost amid the shifting pageant, he chanced upon the sight of a blind beggar propped against the wall and wearing upon his shirt a written paper to explain his story. Confronted with that spectacle his mind turned round "as with the might of waters": it seemed to him that in that label "was a type,/ Or emblem, of the utmost that we know,/ Both of ourselves and of the universe." In this dramatic meeting with the beggar, the poet kindled to an inward response. Out of what might have been a commonplace encounter came mystic communion and revelation.

Throughout *The Prelude*, Wordsworth casts himself in the reflector role. As he did in his chance meeting with the blind beggar, he surrounds his solitaries with a sense of mystery and then captures their mysteriousness as it rebounds to him. They are all, in one way or another, dramatic projections of the poet's self. Hence, each meeting with a solitary in its own special way advances the thematic development of *The Prelude*.[9]

III   *Language, Structure, and Style*

Wordsworth vowed, when nearing the completion of *The Prelude*, that, if he could henceforth "write a narrative Poem of the Epic kind," he should then "consider the *task* of my life over." One knows from his own testimony that he undertook *The Prelude* because he did not feel ready for the epic task: "I was unprepared to treat any more arduous subject, and diffident of my own powers."[10] But, when he was well launched into *The Prelude* and the way seemed clear before him, he acknowledged the epic impulse behind the poem on his own mind:

> O Heavens! how awful is the might of Souls,
> And what they do within themselves, while yet
> The yoke of earth is new to them, . . .
> This is, in truth, heroic argument.
>
> (III, 178-82)

In the preamble to *The Recluse*, Wordsworth had hailed Milton for justifying new areas worthier of epic treatment than wars of physical violence. Then, in his own poem of discovery, he went beyond Milton to find heroic argument in man's (indeed, in *one* man's) internal history. *The Prelude* developed into an epic of personal quest, a search for self-comprehension; but at the same time, it was to be universally representative. For, as Wordsworth says, "There's not a man/ That lives who hath not known his godlike hours." The hero in *The Prelude* became Everyman in an epic search for "majestic sway."

Besides blazing a trail for new thematic conquests, Milton also gave to Wordsworth the will to create a fully worked out poetic structure of epic scope. Ernest de Selincourt long ago took note of the epic structure in *The Prelude*.[11] The poem, de Selincourt observed, is not unlike an epic which, with its episodes, vicissitudes, and climax, goes a kind of circuit. The narrative begins at the end. The poet at the age of twenty-nine now "safe in haven relates the odyssey of his soul and imagination." The first eight books relate how Nature quickened his sensibilities and molded his mind in childhood and youth, how he was consecrated to his great task, and how his powers progressed and expanded through early manhood. The ninth book reveals the poet at the height of a "buoyant but untried faith." The tenth book recounts the unsettling of his hopes, the distress of mind, and the moral skepticism he suffered. The last books tell of recovery from despair, of reconciliation, and of the restoration of creative Imagination. The spiritual cycle at the close is completed; and the poet, like every epic hero, enters into his true heritage.

Through the years, Wordsworth made a number of changes in the structure of *The Prelude* that increased its over-all strength. He enhanced the dramatic appeal by adding, subtracting, or moving about various pieces. Several of the best parts were first written and published as separate poems and later skillfully woven into the whole: for example, "The Boy on Winander," "Simplon Pass," and "Influence of Natural Objects." The "spots of time" in Book XI, composed in 1798-99, were held back and used later as climactic examples of the power by which Imagination is restored.

Wordsworth, in revising the 1805 version, removed portions that impeded the forward movement or seemed irrelevant to his purpose. The story of Vaudracour and Julia, which is the concealed story of his passion for Annette Vallon, was seen in perspective to be transient rather than permanent in the growth of the poetic mind. The lengthy tale of the shepherd's son, who went to rescue sheep and had himself to be rescued, was eliminated from Book VIII. Its excision strengthened the continuity of the structural contrasts between the paradisical country of Wordsworth's boyhood and the various literary paradises of the past. These paradises, in turn, were set free to draw upon the appeal of fairy stories and romances in an earlier book. Throughout *The Prelude*, Wordsworth establishes links of contrast and parallelism that unify the structure. To those already mentioned may be added, for illustration, the summer festival of Helvellyn, Book VIII, placed in opposition to London's Bartholomew Fair, Book VII; and the return in Book X of the poet to the shores near Furness Abbey.

Repetition is a settled principle of organization in *The Prelude*. Again and again Wordsworth tries to find new ways to invoke the inexpressible, to reveal eternity in its innumerable guises. Often his attempts repeat themselves in his meetings with the various solitaries. Sometimes they take the form of a struggle for definition in "the spots of time." As the poem advances, progress toward revelation is by no means in a straight line nor on a steady course. Perhaps, as Mr. Lindenberger suggests, the repetitive pattern should be regarded as one of alternation—between fealty to the demands of "inner" reality and eternity and to those of the "external" world. During his soul's odyssey the poet not infrequently discovers new ways of looking at things through rebound from the negation of worldly experiences. The satiric episodes especially with their earthy bluntness serve to enhance the radiant, intuitive insights that precede or follow them.

Wordsworth was temperamentally adverse to satire, but he does use it effectively in *The Prelude* as a repetitive pattern of alternation. Satiric passages ("smudges of time") build up and set off passages of spiritual insight ("spots of time"). The satire comes chiefly in Books III, V, and VII, on Cambridge, false learning, and the emptiness of city life. Also briefly in Book XI the "cult of the picturesque" is ridiculed. In Book III Wordsworth protests compulsory chapel attendance and laments the shallowness of the college preachers:

> Our eyes are cross'd by Butterflies, our ears
> Hear shattering Popinjays; the inner heart
> Is trivial, and the impresses without
> Are of a gaudy region.

(vv. 456-59)

He is critical of academic authority and especially of the grave
Elders, "Men unscour'd, grotesque in character." Cambridge was a
kind of pageantry of the past world soon to be revealed to him in all
its folly in London. The satire of Book V is directed against the system of false learning propagated by the followers of Rousseau. They
create the child prodigy, perfect in learning and in books, treading a
path choked with grammars, but swollen with vanity and living "a
life of lies." In the city of London Wordsworth finds foolishness
scattered everywhere, but his scorn is most pointedly directed
against the empty eloquence of a young lawyer "winding away his
never-ending horn" and against the elegant, mincing ways of a
worldly London preacher:

> There have I seen a comely Bachelor,
> Fresh from a toilette of two hours, ascend
> The Pulpit, with seraphic glance look up,
> And, in a tone elaborately low
> Beginning, lead his voice through many a maze,
> A minuet course, and winding up his mouth,
> From time to time into an orifice
> Most delicate, a lurking eyelet, small
> And only not invisible, again
> Open it out, diffusing thence a smile
> Of rapt irradiation exquisite.
>
> (vv. 545-56)

The sardonic language of this Miltonic parody—indeed, the drab
descriptive language of most of Book VII—is a far remove from
the language of personal vision that precedes it in Book VI and that
follows it in Book VIII. So, too, the other satiric books fall roughly
into a pattern of repetitive alternation with what goes before and
what follows after. It is basic to the poem's design that Imagination
must first be impaired before its triumphant restoration at the end of
the poem. The repetitive alternations in Books III and IV, V and VI,
VII, and VIII support in lesser contrapuntal waves this cyclic pattern. *The Prelude* would have been much flatter and impoverished
if it had moved, as Wordsworth first planned it, directly from the
adolescent exultations of Book IV to the triumph he celebrates in the
final book. The point need not be labored about the repetitive
structure.

   The Prelude is not a miracle of architectonics, for Wordsworth did

not plan it carefully in advance nor follow any one purpose throughout. The poem is the more convincing because of its spontaneity.
Its truths are discovered by a great creative artist in the very process
of surveying his past and with no thesis to prove. At the same time,
the poet as craftsman has put together the pieces of his odyssey in
such a way that the result is a unified poem of masterful construction
and largeness of vision.

Wordsworth shaped the patterns of language in *The Prelude* to
reflect symbolically the experiences which his mind had with the
forms and images of Nature. At first he reacted in a sensuous way
to the physical world about him. As a child he

> . . . held unconscious intercourse
> With the eternal Beauty, drinking in
> A pure organic pleasure from the lines
> Of curling mist, or from the level plain
> Of waters colour'd by the steady clouds.
>   (I, 589-93)

From "pure organic pleasure"—"felt in the blood, and felt along
the heart"—the poet passed through sweet purgations until his
mind was shaped "to majesty" and consciously prepared for spiritual intercourse unprofaned by forms. This entrance into communion with "eternal Beauty" was the goal of his discursive mental
explorations in *The Prelude*. Yet, in the midst of his journeyings to
this visionary world, the poet had at all times a real solid world of
images about him.[12] This world of forms and images—water, islands,
mountains, breezes, and growing things—provides the basic setting
for the poem. When Wordsworth describes a stream he knew in
childhood, he can start out on the level of literal description; but
before the reader has read much further the stream has become a
metaphor for the workings of his imagination.

The dominating images of *The Prelude* are wind and water,
images which by their very nature serve as intermediaries between
the observable world and the higher, transcendental reality the
poet wishes to make visible. In the opening of the poem the breath
of the external wind and the inner breath of inspiration are brought
together and connected with the creative process. By such mergings
of the animate and inanimate worlds Wordsworth communicates in
poetic terms the sense of the spiritual unity of all existence which

he had felt so overwhelmingly on an intuitive level in early childhood. And, by moving freely from the real to the visionary world
and back again, he carries us with him in his adventure of discovery.

Some readers have felt that the language of *The Prelude* is overly
abstract. But Donald Davie in *Articulate Energy* (1955) has shown
that Wordsworth's vocabulary is neither abstract not concrete; it is
something between the two.[13] Its verbs are concrete and pinpoint
the main movements of Wordsworth's thought; the nouns and quali-
fying phrases re-create the full ebb and flow of the meditative process. Davie quotes and examines a key passage in Book II, the one in
which the infant at his mother's breast rouses to an awareness of his
existence; and Davie shows how, in the 1805 version especially,
Wordsworth conveys the power and the particularity of the situation
by the precisely discriminated energies of his verbs. Two or three
examples serve to illustrate the point: "the Babe,/ . . . Doth gather
passion from his Mother's eye!"; "his mind spreads,/ Tenacious of
the forms which it receives"; "Along his infant veins are interfus'd/
The gravitation and the filial bond/ Of nature." In such a passage as
the one analyzing the psychological stirrings of the babe, Wordsworth presents the meditating mind in all its fullness.

There is a great range and variety of style in *The Prelude*, as
would be expected in so long a poem. Fluctuations in subject matter
and mood call naturally for stylistic adaptations. For example, in
Book III, college life at Cambridge is viewed critically, even satiri-
cally; and it is accordingly presented in a matter-of-fact, sinewy
style. But, in Book IV, in sharp contrast to the style in Book III, there
is flowing, often eloquent poetry recounting the poet's suprapersonal communings with the living God. So, throughout the poem,
the style adjusts amply and sensitively to the changes called for by
the varied situations. There are few passages in *The Prelude* that
are rough or flatulent: "My drift hath scarcely,/ I fear, been obvious" (V, 290-91). When necessary, Wordsworth knew how to take
care of workaday details in a businesslike manner. The reader does
not object to following the poet through the plains and foothills, for
he knows that he will be led in time to the mountain tops.

Eminences in style emerge frequently; however, they do not usually continue for long stretches, but in passages of two to three dozen
lines where the thought and imagery unfold harmoniously together.
Readers of *The Prelude* soon learn to identify and cherish these
select passages, such as those recounting the theft of the boat (I,

401-27), the dedication to poetry (IV, 330-45), the boy on Winander
(V, 389-413), and Simplon Pass (VI, 556-72). Sometimes there are
gemlike passages that fuse in two or three lines, as for example:
"Bliss was it in that dawn to be alive,/ But to be young was very
heaven" (X, 693-94). Sometimes memorable phrases occur in isolation, such as, "The noble Living and the noble Dead" (X, 970).

Wordsworth was the master of all the rhetorical devices useful to
the poet, but he did not make a display of them. To make the skating scene more vivid, he used onomatopoeia: "All shod with steel,/
We hiss'd along the polish'd ice" (I, 460-61). To mimic the shouting
of the owls, he played upon enhancing vowel tones: "with quivering
peals,/ And long hallos, and screams, and echoes loud/ Redoubled
and redoubled; concourse wild/ Of mirth and jocund din!" (V,
401-4). He knew how to use rhetorical contrasts for emphasis: "I
grew up/ Foster'd alike by beauty and by fear" (I, 305-6). Certain
patterns of repetition he seems to have picked up from Milton. One
of the best examples of Miltonic repetition for stress of thought
and musical effect (which includes a triple repetition and a chias-
mus) is the passage where sound is translated into vision:

> . . . the soul
> Remembering how she felt, but what she felt
> Remembering not, retains an obscure sense
> Of possible sublimity, to which
> With growing faculties she doth aspire,
> With faculties still growing, feeling still
> That whatsoever point they gain, they still
> Have something to pursue.
>
> (II, 334-41)

Wordsworth also learned from Milton the sonorous use of proper
names, though he did not have the power to make names reverberate sublimely as did the author of *Paradise Lost*. Throughout
The Prelude, there are Miltonic verbal echoes, but especially in
those parts written in 1803 and after. Wordsworth borrows a phrase
from *Paradise Lost*, for example, for the opening of his preamble,
"The earth is all before me," (I, 15), which is an echo of the closing
lines of the expulsion of Adam and Eve, "The World was all before
them where to choose." Another notable borrowing from Milton occurs in the last line of the great passage on Simplon Pass. The awe-

some features of the pass are transformed in the poet's Imagination to types and symbols of Eternity, "Of first and last, and midst, and without end," which is an appeal to Revelation 1:8 ("I am Alpha and Omega, the beginning and the ending, said the Lord, which is, and which was, and which is to come, the almighty") that is also paraphrased by *Paradise Lost*, V, 165: "Him first, him last, him midst, and without end." Examples of Miltonic influence can easily be multiplied, but their use should not be exaggerated.[14] Whatever Wordsworth used from other authors or from the tradition of rhetoric, he made his own.

As has already been indicated in passing, *The Prelude* published posthumously in 1850 differs in many respects from the poem read to Coleridge in 1806. Wordsworth made important revisions in 1828, 1832, 1839, which altered the whole manner of the poem. The original was an intimate personal epistle addressed to Coleridge when the two were on the terms of closest intimacy. Wordsworth felt that, before the poem could be given to the public, he would have to make it less personal. He also wanted to amend faults of ambiguity and loose expression. In revising, he succeeded to a considerable extent in making the language more controlled and exact and the meaning clearer. Some of the finest passages are those written in the later years, such as the lines on Sir Isaac Newton (Book III). But the stylistic changes, by and large, are injurious to the freshness, naturalness, and frankness of the early version. Revision often obscured a simple, naïve experience: or it replaced the living fact with an intellectual statement about it.

Revision also resulted in vital changes in thought as well as in expression. The early text of *The Prelude* gives us a Wordsworth committed to a vibrant faith in "natural piety." But the pressure of years and crushing personal sorrows had Christianized his creed. As a consequence, the revised *Prelude* is overlaid with Christian thought. Accordingly, the original sections in which he exulted in the powers of his own mind, often in terms of sensationalistic-associationistic philosophy, are shorn of their daring and deliberately expressed in terms of dogmatic Christianity. In the revision, Wordsworth also tones down his attack on Cambridge; moreover, he presents France and the revolution with less glamor and with an increased conservatism. The later Wordsworth had forgotten much that the younger poet was trying to do in *The Prelude*. Consequently, his revisions were ruinous to both the honesty of the original and to its energy and freshness of style. Both versions of *The Prelude* are, of course, important; but the reader who wishes to capture the poet when he is most himself should concentrate on the 1805 version.

CHAPTER 5

Poems *in Two Volumes, 1807*

I N 1807 Wordsworth gathered together and published a number of poems, enough to make up two volumes, written since the publication of *Lyrical Ballads* (1800). The new poems differ substantially both in subject matter and in style from those in *Lyrical Ballads.* Many of them were composed in a great outburst of poetic inspiration in the spring of 1802. They include sonnets in the demanding Italian pattern, odes in both forms favored in the eighteenth century, and poems in a wide variety of meters. During his first year of residence in Grasmere in 1800 Wordsworth, who was inspired by imaginative sympathy for the shepherd folk in the Lake Country, immortalized the affections of pastoral life in "The Brothers" and "Michael." But by the end of 1800 the vein of pastoral poetry was spent, and Wordsworth needed time to work out new forms and to collect new experiences.

The year 1801 was one of comparative noncreativity; however, the poet was not idle. He undertook the modernization of three Chaucerian poems and thereby sharpened a facility in "rime royal" that was to benefit him in the composition of "Resolution and Independence." In 1802, he also found some promptings to his invention in the stanzaic patterns of Ben Jonson and Drayton. For his diction as well as his versification in the 1807 volumes he harked back to these and other favorite Elizabethan poets. From time to time he also adopted new stanzaic forms because of special associations. As a result, *Poems* of 1807 shows Wordsworth as experimenting in an extensive range of verse forms and often with spectacular success.

Of even greater significance than the advances of prosody in the new poetry is the shift in subject matter and mood. In *Lyrical Ballads* Wordsworth for the most part turned his back on his personal life, but in *Poems* of 1807 he found sources of inspiration in his own "heart-experience" and "soul-illumination." As in *Lyrical Ballads*, there are a number of narratives of human life in the 1807

125

volumes; but the stories are not bleak and naked; rather, they are rendered lyrically from the impulse of the poet's mood and reflect its atmosphere. In *Lyrical Ballads* there is no word of politics, but in *Poems* of 1807 one has a magnificent series of sonnets on public affairs.

Also, as Wordsworth faces the end of his youth in 1802, there is a movement toward greater concentration upon moral and spiritual problems. He becomes acutely aware of the fading of "the visionary gleam" and undertakes to answer the question "why" in the Immortality Ode. He begins to lose confidence in instinctive response to sustain his moral being and offers a mature adjustment in "Ode to Duty." Finally, when faced with the tragic loss of his dearly beloved brother John, he courageously submits, as he says in "Elegiac Stanzas," to a new control. In a number of significant ways, then, *Poems* of 1807, composed when Wordsworth was at the height of his powers, reveals an inward struggle from which emerged a man and a poet newly integrated around the imaginative idea of duty as the reality of love.

I *Sonnets*

Wordsworth told Landor that he once thought the sonnet an egregiously absurd form of composition. But one day in May, 1802, when his sister Dorothy read aloud to him the sonnets of Milton he was "singularly struck with the style of harmony, and the gravity, and republican austerity of those compositions." He took fire and produced three sonnets that same afternoon. The form proved to be congenial and in the years ahead he made extensive use of it. In all, he published over five hundred sonnets, covering a wide range of subjects in many of which can be found some of his best poetry.

One of the sonnets that he composed on that May afternoon was "I grieved for Buonaparte," the earliest of a flood tide of verse to be dedicated to national independence and liberty. Wordsworth was passionately alive at that time to the great drama of his country's struggle with France. During the brief interval of peace in 1802 he visited Annette and their child for a month at Calais. While there he wrote seven sonnets, only one of which was related to the reunion ("It is a beauteous evening calm and free"). This sonnet of spiritual amplitude and serenity he addresses to his daughter Caroline, "Dear child, dear girl," who bears within her the eternal presence of God.

The other sonnets all have to do with Wordsworth's zealous concern for European affairs and for England's part in them. Looking back from Calais at the "Fair Star of evening" stooping over England, he feels resurgent love for the country of his birth ("Composed by the Sea-side near Calais, August 1802"). All around him he discerns perpetual emptiness in the character and actions of the French people. But he is no less dismayed by the crowds of his own countrymen hastening to Paris to capture, if possible, a glimpse of Napoleon: "Ye men of prostrate mind, . . . /Shame on you, feeble Heads, to slavery prone!" ("Calais, August 1802"). Calais stirred vivid memories of his earlier visit to the city with Robert Jones in 1790 when French citizens were joyously celebrating the Fall of the Bastille and "faith was pledged to new-born Liberty" ("Composed near Calais, August 7, 1802"). But in August, 1802, when France proclaimed Napoleon first consul for life and decreed a state ceremonial in his honor, Wordsworth watched the people go indifferently about their tasks. To the poet, the contrast between then and now was agonizingly poignant ("Calais, August 15, 1802"). The promise of that "young dawn" had led to a dark noon presaging storm.

An ominous awareness of the great peril to liberty in England and Europe which Napoleon's rise to power forewarned was building up in Wordsworth. Liberty, which the young man had embraced, was now suddenly brought back into sharp focus. With militant energy Wordsworth released the fullness of his mind in stately and majestic regret over the loss of freedom for Venice, "eldest child of Liberty" ("On the Extinction of the Venetian Republic"). In the sonnet "To Toussaint L'Ouverture," he offered an emotional response to the heroic sacrifice of the Haitian leader who gave his life for freedom's sake. The poem closes with language that reverberates with the universal sharing of all creation in the cause of liberty.

Following the month's sojourn in Calais, Wordsworth returned to England; and there he continued his exhortations in liberty's defense. London looked quite different to him from what it had one month before as he had passed over Westminster Bridge on his way to France. In the famous sonnet "On Westminster Bridge" the city is a sight "touching in its majesty" in which all objects, conditions, and moods conspire to bring Nature and humanity into "an ennobling harmony." On his return to the city, he utters a cry of anguish over the worldliness of the present generation: "The homely beauty of the good old cause/Is gone." He calls upon Milton as the supreme example of moral virtue who in the stagnant present could lift men once again to "virtue, freedom, power":

> Milton! thou should be living at this hour:
> England hath need of thee: she is a fen
> Of stagnant waters: . . . We are selfish men;
> Oh! raise us up, return to us again;
> And give us manners, virtue, freedom, power.

"London, 1802"

In another sonnet, "Great Men Have Been Among Us," he celebrates other English leaders of the Civil War—Algernon Sidney, Andrew Marvel, James Harrington, and Young Henry Vane—but above them all towers the figure of Milton: "Thy soul was like a Star, and dwelt apart."

The notes sounded in the first London sonnets reverberate in those written when war with France was renewed in 1803 and through the entire series produced at intervals during the war. Prospects of invasion silenced Wordsworth's indignant rebukes and called forth what was heroic in his nature. "To the Men of Kent" is a spirited salute to the "Vanguards of Liberty" who did in times past win from the Normans "a gallant wreath." The crisis of Napoleon's victory at Jena in 1806, as empire after empire fell before the conqueror, roused an exultant battle cry of defiance: "And We are left, or shall be left, alone;/The last that dare to struggle with the Foe ..../O dastard whom such foretaste does not cheer!" ("November 1806"). During the war years Wordsworth's passion for liberty was tempered into a sinewy wisdom that also had something ennobling in it. Liberty, he declares, is not a free gift of Nature, but must be won and maintained at the cost "of ceaseless effort, vigilance, and virtue." It is not achieved by military victory nor shaped by governors trained in battle; nor will the protective barrier of the Channel waters save it: "By the soul/Only the nations shall be great and free."

The great sonnet "The World Is Too Much With Us" has the same mood—"Getting and spending, we lay waste our powers:/Little we see in Nature that is ours"—as those poems written in September, 1802, that lament the unworthiness of the times. The sonnet has a sea setting ("This sea that bares her bosom to the moon"), which may very well be a memory of Calais. In any event, it speaks with the same agitated passion that energizes the patriotic sonnets of 1802:

> For this, for everything, we are out of tune;
> It moves us not.—Great God! I'd rather be
> A Pagan suckled in a creed outworn;
> So might I, standing on this pleasant lea,
> Have glimpses that would make me less forlorn;
> Have sight of Proteus rising from the sea;
> Or hear old Triton blow his wreathèd horn.

Two splendid sea pictures are offered in sonnets about ships: "With Ships the Sea Was Sprinkled" and "Where Lies the Land to Which Yon Ship Must Go?" With the poet's help, one revives memories of days by the sea and pursues these ships "with a Lover's look." Three sonnets on sleep tell of agonized nights of sleeplessness, probably in the spring and summer of 1802, and of poignant supplications "To Sleep." One of these, which G. M. Harper calls "a perfect sonnet," opens with a series of beautiful images:

> A flock of sheep that leisurely pass by,
> One after one; the sound of rain, and bees
> Murmuring; the fall of rivers, winds and seas,
> Smooth fields, white sheets of water, and pure sky;
> I have thought of all by turns, and yet do lie
> Sleepless!

The diction is unpretending and the cumulative associations and rhythmic movement conducive to drowsiness. The rhyming, easy and natural, creates a relaxed response—"stealth," "wealth," "health." There is no need to know the reason for the poet's sleeplessness. The condition is common enough among all readers, as is the anguish in not being able, even with the most soothing incantations, to bring longed-for sleep.

Some critics of Wordsworth do not care for the patriotic sonnets. For example, John Jones finds "The famous sonnets read like exercises, repellent often in their provincial self-importance" (*The Egotistical Sublime*); or, F. R. Leavis sees the worst of the sonnets as "lamentable claptrap, and the best, even if they are distinguished declarations, are hardly distinguished poetry" (*Revaluation*). However, Middleton Murry thinks "the patriotic sonnets incomparably finer than any other poems in conscious praise of England"; and a goodly company of reputable judges share Murry's view.

The militant sonnets, whatever their worth as poems (and this writer places at least two of them very high—"To Toussaint L'Ouverture" and "London, 1802"), are important as a record of Wordsworth's advance from the poet of rapturous impulse to the poet of duty and fortitude. The emergence of Napoleon challenged Wordsworth's integrity and consummated the restoration of it. No poet of his temperament could pass through the tremendous experience of that struggle wholly unchanged. It quickened the stoic element in him and taught him to be less withdrawn in inspired contemplation and more concerned with the actual buffetings of life. It made him realize that "the dreary intercourse of daily life," which in Tintern Abbey days seemed so repellent to him, comes close to being the whole wisdom of life. In any case, it was in this mood of acceptance of the real world in terms of daily living that Wordsworth married Mary Hutchinson on October 4, 1802. This event foreshadows the poet's submission to the control of "Duty" two years hence and a still more sobering acceptance of life in 1805 that was demanded of him by the death of his brother John.

II *"Resolution and Independence"*

There are more of the essential features of Wordsworth's work in "Resolution and Independence" than in any other of the greater lyrics. Coleridge considered this fine poem especially characteristic of the author. It offers conflicting moods and responses: it ranges through joy and despondency, mystic insight and frugal moralizing, matter-of-factness in details of language, and glorification of the deepest passion. Dorothy records in her Journal (October 3, 1800) the incident upon which the poem was founded: "We met an old man almost double. He had had a wife, and 'she was a good woman, and it pleased God to bless us with ten children.' All of them were dead but one, of whom he had not heard for many years. He had been hurt in driving a cart, his leg broken, his body driven over, his skull fractured. His trade was to gather leeches, but now leeches were scarce, and he had not the strength for it." Two years later, Wordsworth created a new account of the meeting with the old leech-gatherer to which he united more recent experiences and moods.

The poem opens on a glorious morning after a night of storm in a mountain country. The world is joyous and alive: the songs of birds make a sweet orchestration against a background of "pleasant noise of waters." Visual images in the second stanza further testify to the morning's radiance and epitomize nature's vitality in a single brilliant image:

> —on the moors
> The hare is running races in her mirth;
> And with her feet she from the plashy earth
> Raises a mist, that, glittering in the sun,
> Runs with her all the way, wherever she doth run.

Into this idyllic scene Wordsworth introduces himself not merely as an observer but as a fellow sharer with his whole heart. "I describe myself," Wordsworth wrote in a letter to Sara and Mary Hutchinson, "as having been exalted to the highest pitch of delight by the joyousness and beauty of nature."[1]

> I saw the hare that raced about with joy;
> I heard the woods and distant waters roar;
> Or heard them not, as happy as a boy.

Then, in a sudden irrational change in mood from joy that could "no further go," he is plunged to one of lowest dejection:

> And fears and fancies thick upon me came;
> Dim sadness—and blind thoughts, I knew not, nor could name.

His anxieties range wide; then he begins to particularize them. He has lived his whole life "As if life's business were a summer mood"; now visions of hostile days overwhelm him of "Solitude, pain of heart, distress, and poverty." His mind is filled with thoughts of the miserable reverses that have befallen young poets:

> I thought of Chatterton, the marvellous Boy,
> The sleepless Soul that perished in his pride;
> Of Him who walked in glory and in joy
> Following his plough, along the mountain-side;
> By our own spirits are we deified:
> We Poets in our youth begin in gladness;
> But thereof come in the end despondency and madness.

His brother poets, Chatterton and Burns, had begun in gladness; but both had been cut down tragically in their youth. What happened to them (and what seems to be happening to Coleridge) could easily happen to him. Wordsworth's health at that time aroused in him great anxieties. He suffered from prostrating headaches and from sleeplessness, and he had fears that his often exhausting travails of sustained creativity might have to be paid for in the end.[2] He sums up the young poet's curse in the profoundly oracular line: "By our own spirits are we deified."

From his fit of depression, which has an element of the supernatural about it, he is rescued by what seems "almost an interposition of Providence." The lonely figure of the age-ravaged leech-gatherer appears as though miraculously summoned to confront the poet's ominous forebodings. Wordsworth drives home the helplessness of the old man: he is "the oldest man who ever wore gray hairs." Utterly alone, he is obviously unloved and uncared for; and his body is bent with infirmity. In a first draft the poet drew him with unsparing realism, likening him to the dead-alive figures in a cottage chimney corner: "He seem'd like one who little saw or heard/ For chimney-nook or bed or coffin meet." In response to shrewd criticism from his sister-in-law Sara Hutchinson, who failed to see the spirituality of the poem, Wordsworth cut out these lines and put in the famous similes of the stone and the sea-beast which serve as the imaginative core of the poem:

> As a huge stone is sometimes seen to lie
> Couched on the bald top of an eminence;
> Wonder to all who do the same espy,
> By what means it could thither come, and whence;
> So that it seems a thing endued with sense:
> Like a sea-beast crawled forth, that on a shelf
> Of rock or sand reposeth, there to sun itself;
>
> Such seemed this Man, not all alive nor dead,
> Nor all asleep—in his extreme old age.

In these and the following stanzas the old man is represented as at once real, almost grotesquely so; but, at the same time, he is an object of wonder and mystery. He has become merged with the landscape and associated with the primeval quality of life itself. He takes on a spiritual existence transcending the very processes of Nature, a source of permanence amidst the flux. By a skillful handling of imagery, Wordsworth suggests a connection between the leech-gatherer and something which is majestic and permanent in Nature: "Motionless as a cloud the old Man stood,/That heareth not the loud winds when they call;/And moveth all together, if it move at all."

The poet enters into conversation with him: "This morning gives us promise of a glorious day . . . . What occupation do you there pursue?" The old man answers, with feeble voice but with stately speech "such as grave livers do in Scotland use," that he came to the pond, old and poor as he was, to gather leeches—a hard and luckless trade by which, with God's help, he manages to make an honest living. Before the leech-gatherer finishes explaining his business to the poet, his words become muffled, and his figure fades into a dream landscape:

> The old Man still stood talking by my side;
> But now his voice to me was like a stream
> Scarce heard; nor word from word could I divide;
> And the whole body of the Man did seem
> Like one whom I had met with in a dream;
> Or like a man from some far region sent,
> To give me human strength, by apt admonishment.

Wordsworth has fallen into a mystic trance, just as he had before the blind beggar met on the streets of London on whom he gazed "As if admonished from another world." However, he was not yet ready to accept the solution to his foolish anxieties that the old man's words provided. His former thoughts return:

> the fear that kills;
> And hope that is unwilling to be fed;
> Cold, pain, and labour and all fleshly ills;
> And mighty Poets in their misery dead.

Lewis Carroll and Edward Lear in their parodies have made capital of the irrelevance of Wordsworth's response to the leech-gatherer. But Wordsworth is so enmeshed in the imaginatively fatal sin of willful despair that it takes a prolonged impact to arouse and free him. A second moment of vision echoes and elongates the first:

the lonely place,
The old Man's shape, and speech—all troubled me:
In my mind's eye I seemed to see him pace
About the weary moors continually,
Wandering about alone and silently.

Suddenly the poet is liberated into full awareness of the spirit life that animates, endures, and triumphs in the life of natural man. Wordsworth finally realizes that in the old man there has been no decay of the inner life to correspond to that of outer existence, and that despondency of spirit is not a necessary consequence of physical decline. When he understands the significance of the cheerful dignity of the decrepit old man, Wordsworth's tension is resolved, and he laughs himself to scorn. The last lines of the poem confirm in the simplest words—they are all that are needed—the truth of the experience for the poet: " 'God,' said I, 'be my help and stay secure;/I'll think of the Leech-gatherer on the lonely moor!' "

In few poems does Wordsworth achieve so great a perfection of form as he does in "Resolution and Independence." Though it contains striking contrasts in expression and style, they all move harmoniously toward the fulfillment of the poem's central purpose. The type of stanza used is ornate and very rare in Wordsworth's verse. Known as rhyme royal, it was picked up from his translations of Chaucer; it also derives from Chatterton's "Excelent Balade of Charitie." The elaborate double simile is another instance of complexity and refinement of style. Yet "Resolution and Independence" is basically a poem of profound simplicity. The one central incident is outwardly the most ordinary sort of occurrence.

The figure of the lonely leech-gatherer is drab; to some readers, even ludicrous. In an earlier version of the poem sent to Mary and Sara Hutchinson, Wordsworth included an account of the leech-gatherer's former life, his marriage, his ten children, and such matter-of-fact details as "He wore a cloak, the same as women wear . . ./And furthermore he had upon his back/Beneath his cloak, a round and bulky Pack." Wordsworth spiritedly defended these earthy details against the censures of Sara who criticized them as "tedious," though he amusingly enough omits some of them when the poem appeared in print. Even in its final form, however, there is an ample supply of prosaic features. These stand in startling contrast to the dignities and full musical resonance of the early stanzas with their Spenserian harmonies. Earthy detail and colloquial language were massively employed by Wordsworth not through any arbitrary whim, but because through them he could establish in universal terms the spiritual reality of the old man's existence. He could not have communicated in any other way a realization of "the native grandeur of the human soul" and its insuperable fortitude.

III   *Dove Cottage Lyrics and Memorials of a Tour in Scotland*

Poems of 1807 contains nearly all of Wordsworth's best-known lyrics and his most charming poems of flowers, birds, and butterflies. Markedly different from most of the poems in *Lyrical Ballads*, they represent Wordsworth predominantly as a nature poet. In practically all of them the influence of Dorothy is striking and noticeable. As a child and a young man Wordsworth preferred the austere beauty of the Lake Country and the Alps and had not paid much attention to the details of Nature. Dorothy, on the other hand, was most remarkable for her powers of observation and for her overriding enthusiasm for the smaller details and the gentler aspects of Nature. When the poet and his sister came to live together at Racedown, she transplanted her preferences and delights to her brother, a change he gratefully acknowledges in *The Prelude*. She softened down, he says, his oversternness and planted the crevices with flowers.

For seven long years the joyous companionship begun at Racedown was uninterrupted, but in the spring of 1802 life at Grasmere was approaching an end. William and Dorothy were soon to leave Dove Cottage for some months to go to France and later to Yorkshire for William's marriage. The lyric entitled "A Farewell" (composed May 29, 1802, which apprehends the moment of their departure, is addressed in affectionate terms to the "sweet garden-cottage" where the brother and sister had known near-perfect "soul companionship." The poem offers a loving tribute to William's bride as the new mistress of Dove Cottage, but it makes no attempt to hide the emotional crisis involving the end of years of private intimacy between the brother and sister.

Other lyrics anticipating the coming change dwell with bittersweet poignancy on the poet's recollections of his childhood with Dorothy. An early member of the group is "The Sparrow's Nest." The chance discovery of a sparrow's nest in the shrubbery at Dove

Cottage garden brought back "a vision of delight" of a similar nest in the hedge at his father's home which, as children, he and his sister had intently watched. Even then, "a little Prattler among men," Dorothy in visiting the sparrow's nest had those "humble cares and delicate fears" which in maturity continued to be a blessing to the poet. In another poem, "To a Butterfly," he recalls again how, even as a child, Dorothy set an example of tenderness.

There are also poems in which Wordsworth recounts their shared adult experiences; of these, the most famous is the poem on daffodils. This kind of poem he would not have written had he not learned to see through Dorothy's eyes. One windy day in April, 1802, as the poet and his sister were passing through Gowbarrow Park along the shore of Lake Ullswater, they saw "a crowd,/A host of golden daffodils,/Fluttering and dancing in the breeze." In her journal passage on the daffodils Dorothy has made full use of her imagination in describing them. She endowed the daffodils with human attributes—"some rested their heads upon these stones as on a pillow for weariness; and the rest tossed and reeled and danced, and seemed as if they verily laughed with the wind." She likens the long belt of them along the shore to a busy highway of jostling people with "here and there a little knot, and a few stragglers" that in no way disturb the simplicity and unity of the show. In all of Dorothy's many recordings of the sights and sounds of Nature, none surpasses the touch of creative magic she displays here.

When her brother set out to make a poem about their adventure, which wasn't until several years later (c. 1804), he had his work cut out for him. What he does is to intensify the immediacy of the experience by confining it to his own person and to dramatize it by heightening the sense of sudden discovery. At the moment of revelation the wind was blowing over the lake directly on all that was before it, awakening both the waves and the crowd of daffodils into agitated motion. When Wordsworth recalled the original experience, perhaps through reading Dorothy's account of it, his tranquility was stirred by the awakening of the creative spirit which, even as the wind gave life to external Nature, gave to the "forms and images" living in his memory "a breath and everlasting motion." In the poem the wind's action draws all parts of the composition together and relates them to the whole. It is the breath which, in the climax of recollection, fills his heart with pleasure and sets it to dancing with the daffodils. Though the subject of the daffodil stanzas is, as Wordsworth reminds the reader, rather an elementary and primarily an ocular impression, it is worth noting that this lyric reports what must be a nearly universal response to natural beauty. For "I Wandered Lonely as a Cloud" is not only the most popular of all Wordsworth's lyrics; it is also the most frequently anthologized poem in the English language.

The Dove Cottage poems, coming as they do midway between youth and middle age, alternate between the happy and the darker moods of the poet. Among the more joyous lyrics must be numbered "The Green Linnet," in which Wordsworth, from his sequestered orchard seat, greets "the happiest guest/In all this covert of the blest":

> Amid yon tuft of hazel trees,
> That twinkle in the gusty breeze,
> Behold him perched in ecstasies,
>   Yet seeming still to hover;
> There! where the flutter of his wings
> Upon his back and body flings
> Shadows and sunny glimmerings,
>   That cover him all over.

In this song of welcome to the linnet, the poet magically joins the art of great word painting to felicitous music that seemingly takes its very life and motion from the bird itself.

Free and cheerful, also, are the flower poems in which Wordsworth hails the small celandine, ill-requited "Herald of the Spring," and the daisy, "unassuming Common-place/Of Nature." In these poems Wordsworth elaborates upon the idea that delight in the beauties of flowers is self-created—"my own delights I make"—and fancifully pursues with an easy, joyous inventiveness his responses to their habits and even moralizes upon them. Not all the flower poems, however, are lighthearted; one, at least, "The Small Celandine" (composed in 1804), is as bleak as the early ballads. On a rough spring day the poet discovered an old Celandine, "an altered form,/Now standing forth an offering to the blast,/And buffeted at will by rain and storm." Wordsworth's brooding mind wonders at the helplessness of the flower that in its youth had always been protectively responsive to sun and cold, "a flower of wiser wits." Now it "cannot help itself in its decay." In splenetic mood, the poet observes a close parallel between the flower's state and that

of man. In the last stanza he draws the moral in what could be a
trite maneuver. But the encounter with the real flower is so genuinely an encounter of a middle-aged man threatened by his own
helplessness that meaning and symbol are joined with absolute
naturalness.

Paralleling to some extent the austere thought evoked by the
lesser Celandine are the famous lines on "Yew-Trees." All his life
Wordsworth was enthralled by the beauty, majesty, and antiquity
of living trees, but nowhere is his response to trees more magnifi-
cently expressed than in this poem. He begins by describing the
solitary yew of Lorton Vale "of vast circumference and gloom profound" of form and aspect too magnificent ever to be destroyed.
But of still worthier note are the fraternal Four of Borrowdale. With
figured verse and with a more artful diction than he customarily
uses, the poet majestically summons up the awesome spirit of primeval mysteries in the umbrageous presence of these huge trees.
In *Modern Painters* Ruskin calls "Yew-Trees" "the most vigorous
and solemn bit of forest landscape ever painted." Wordsworth himself placed it among the poems of imagination.

The more sonorous temper of "Yew-Trees" is also found in "The
Affliction of Margaret," written in 1804 perhaps originally for inclusion in a new edition of *Lyrical Ballads*. It is a heart-rending
poem on the maternal grief of "a poor widow of Penrith." "She kept
a shop," says Wordsworth, "and when she saw a stranger passing by,
she was in the habit of going out into the street to enquire of him
after her son." Her pathetic plea is cast in majestic phrase and
rhythm that go beyond any of Wordsworth's earlier ballads:

> Perhaps some dungeon hears thee groan,
> Maimed, mangled by inhuman men;
> Or thou upon a desert thrown
> Inheritest the lion's den;
> Or hast been summoned to the deep,
> Thou, thou and all thy mates, to keep
> An incommunicable sleep.

But this brief survey of the Dove Cottage poems may be concluded on a happier note with a few comments about one of Wordsworth's most delightful pieces: "Stanzas written in my Pocket-copy
of Thomson's *Castle of Indolence*." In Spenserian stanzas, a form he
rarely used, Wordsworth describes himself and Coleridge during

their joyous companionship in the early Grasmere days. The first four stanzas describe Wordsworth and the next three Coleridge, each a happy spirit indulging himself in his own eccentric behavior. With fine imaginative insight Wordsworth has shared with the reader the intriguing vagaries of the genius of himself and his friend and the intense reality of their happiness.

In August, 1803, William and Dorothy set off with Coleridge on a tour of Scotland; but, because of ill-health, Coleridge separated from his companions at Loch Lomond. The Wordsworths continued on by themselves, visiting the Highlands and stopping over for a week with Sir Walter Scott at Lasswade. Their six weeks' journeying brought them into contact with a mass of new impressions which Dorothy records in *Recollections of a Tour Made in Scotland.* What the two travelers sought most of all was an emotional involvement in landscape to which a human figure was linked. Just such a scene unfolded before them when they came suddenly at dusk upon a lonely Highland boy calling the cattle home for the night:

His appearance was in the highest degree moving to the imagination: mists were on the hillsides, darkness shutting in upon the huge avenue of mountains, torrents roaring, no house in sight to which the child might belong; his dress, cry, and appearance all different from what we had been accustomed to. It was a text, as Wm. has since observed to me, containing the whole history of the Highlander's life—his melancholy, his simplicity, his poverty, his superstition and above all, that visionariness which results from a communion with the unworldliness of nature.[3]

For Wordsworth the supreme gift of the tour was precisely such moments of visionariness that fed his imagination and became transformed in the due course of time into poetry. He made no poem upon the Highland lad in his isolation; he chose instead the lonely Highland girl working and singing by herself as she harvested the grain.

During their tour Wordsworth and his sister would have seen women reaping the grain and timing the strokes of the sickle to the harvest song. Upon his return home he composed "The Solitary Reaper" after reading the following sentence in Thomas Wilkinson's *Tour in Scotland*: "Passed a female who was reaping alone: she sung in Erse, as she bended over her sickle; the sweetest voice I ever heard: her strains were tenderly melancholy, and felt delicious long after they were heard no more." Wilkinson's words tersely and

admirably establish the facts of the poem, but Wordsworth's tren-
chant imaginative recollection vitalizes the loneliness, melancholy,
simplicity, and, most of all, the mysteriousness associated in his
mind with the people of the Highlands. He underscores the reaper's
isolation by repeating four times over in the first stanza that she is a
single human figure in the landscape.

The aloneness of the singer is intensified in the second stanza
when she is compared to the lone nightingale singing in far-off
Arabia and to the solitary cuckoo "Breaking the silence of the seas/
Among the farthest Hebrides." The melancholy tone and rhythm
established in the first stanza are developed in the third stanza.
Mysteriousness is achieved by means of the reaper's song. The
spectator cannot understand her foreign tongue; hence, the theme
of her "melancholy strain" is shrouded in mystery. The poet, in
contemplating the possible theme of the song, pushes back the
boundaries of time and space. The theme, whatever it is, could be
past, present, or future; it could be some personal domestic sorrow
or some universal loss; it could be near at hand, at home, or distant.
The mystery of her plaintive song in that remote place becomes
interpenetrated in the reader's consciousness with the mystery of all
human experience outside the limit of time and space. Wordsworth
not only captures the whole history of the Highlander's life; he
isolates for one brief moment the mystery of sorrowing humanity in
the melancholy song of the reaper. He reaches the furthest limits
of imaginative awareness; yet he avoids all commonplace conven-
tionalities and falsifications of reality. The girl remains steadfastly
the simple Highland lass cutting and binding the grain and singing
at her work.

Another fine poem that closely and imaginatively involves a
human figure with the landscape is "To a Highland Girl." Wordsworth says that his sister described "this delightful creature and her
demeanor particularly" in her Journal. In the poem she becomes the
unifying center of a conflux of romantic recollections, enlivened by
merriment, mellowed by kindness, but made unforgettable and
radiant through beauty. The poet has no more claim upon the Highland girl as a person than as "a wave of the wild sea." Imaginative
re-creation transforms the memory of her to visionary loveliness,
"heavenly bright," such as one might envisage in a dream. Yet she
also belongs, "in the light of common day," to the scene of gray
rocks, household lawn, half-veiling trees, waterfall, silent bay, and

the quiet road by the cabin. Like the skylark, she is "true to the kindred points of heaven and of home."[4]

The poem that probably best expresses the spirit of the Scottish tour is "Stepping Westward." The courteous greeting of "two well-dressed women" along the shore of Loch Katrine—"What, you are stepping westward?"—wrought an enchantment upon the poet that opened up the spiritual meaning of his wanderings. The greeting was made "in one of the loneliest parts of that region" and seemed a sound "without place or bound," a token opening into infinity. It told the travelers, though they were traveling as "guests of chance," that their stepping westward was "A kind of *heavenly* destiny"; that, in the journey ahead, they had "spiritual right/To travel through that region bright." With this transcendental vision evoked by the friendly greeting of the Highlanders there mingled also "a human sweetness" that would accompany the travelers on their endless way.

One of the finest lyrics of the tour, "Yarrow Unvisited," resulted from Wordsworth's contact with Scott and the balladry of Scott's countryside. It is a kind of "recollection" in reverse; for, though William and Dorothy have not been to Yarrow and William jauntily refuses to indulge his sister's wish to go there, he touches the thought of it with his own imagination: "We have a vision of our own;/Ah! why should we undo it?" The meter is the same as the "Leader Haughs," a poem by the "Minstrel" Burn, one of the last true wandering minstrels of the border. Other ballads, also, contributed to "Yarrow Unvisited," particularly the exquisite ballad of Hamilton beginning "Busk ye, busk ye, my bonny bonny Bride/ Busk ye, busk ye, my winsome Marrow!" By drawing upon real balladry and adding playful touches of dialect, Wordsworth created in "Yarrow Unvisited" a truly delightful piece of Border minstrelsy.

IV   *"Ode: Intimations of Immortality from
Recollections of Early Childhood"*

Wordsworth's great "Ode on Immortality" is not easy nor wholly clear. A basic difficulty of interpretation centers around what the poet means by "immortality." T. M. Raysor offers an impressive array of evidence for believing that Wordsworth "was thinking of an individual immortality which even took the form of resurrection of the body."[5] But Alan Grob, who finds that Mr. Raysor draws his evidence substantially from the years after the ode was written, sees nothing in works prior to 1804 implying any conviction of hopes beyond the grave.[6] The majority of scholars believe, along with Mr. Grob, that the term "immortality" in this poem does not mean the endlessness of life; instead, it means the infiniteness of human consciousness.[7] The poet's primary task is the search for identity whereby the natural man can apprehend a continuous unity of consciousness, resting upon the abiding presence of a "spirit-life" which is immortal through all phases of his life.

The Ode was built upon a grave crisis. In mid-March, 1802, Wordsworth was visited by Coleridge, who complained despairingly of a loss of his creative powers. Induced by his mood, Wordsworth also became fearful that his own imaginative vision might be failing him. One week after Coleridge's departure and in answer to his challenge to the doctrine of hope, Wordsworth composed within five days "To the Cuckoo," "My Heart Leaps Up," and the opening stanzas to the Immortality Ode. On March 23 Dorothy entered in her Journal: "a mild morning, Wm. worked at *The Cuckoo* poem." The recollection of the cuckoo's voice on that day —it was not physically heard, for the first cuckoo did not arrive until the first of May that year—called into consciousness those "visionary hours" when the earth was apprehended with "bliss ineffable" and the poet saw in all things "one life and felt that it was joy."

It was a short leap to the Rainbow poem, composed on March 26, in which Wordsworth reasserts his faith in the on-going beauty and joyousness of existence. Wordsworth did not see the rainbow at the time of the poem's composition, any more than he had heard the bird's voice when he wrote the poem on the cuckoo; he is probably recalling a rainbow he had seen in boyhood on a day of wild storm in the vale of Coniston.[8] But, through imaginative re-collection, Wordsworth found himself transported, as he had during the composition of the cuckoo poem, to another sphere of being—to one more real than that of the senses. When he had such ecstatic experiences, he felt that he had passed outside time into eternity. In the Rainbow poem he poignantly expresses the hope that the rapturously beautiful sights of Nature that in childhood opened to him another world through vision would continue to do so as long as he lived.

The next day, March 27, "a divine morning, at breakfast, Wm. wrote part of an Ode." Now he confronts directly the fact that, with the passing of the years, the glory which had transfigured all things for him in boyhood had faded; and he no longer sees things "apparelled in celestial light" except when meditation on the cuckoo's cry or recollection of the rainbow's splendor brought him once again to that world of vision:

> There was a time when meadow, grove, and stream,
> The earth, and every common sight,
>   To me did seem
>   Apparelled in celestial light,
> The glory and the freshness of a dream.
> It is not now as it hath been of yore;—
>   Turn wheresoe'er I may
>   By night or day,
> The things which I have seen I now can see no more.

So he states the irrevocable separation from past splendors and wrestles with the problem of his loss through the next three stanzas. In the second stanza the poet declares that all the lovely objects of Nature are lovely still, but in their presence he has changed: for him the glory is gone. In the third stanza, he forces a vigorous response to the joyousness of all creatures around him on that glad May morning:

> Now, while the birds thus sing a joyous song,
>   And while the young lambs bound
>   As to the tabor's sound,
> To me alone there came a thought of grief:
> A timely utterance gave that thought relief,
>   And I again am strong.

The "timely utterance" must have been the Rainbow poem written just the day before the Immortality Ode was begun and expressing the conviction that the paradisaical vision of his childhood has been recovered and will survive in the future. So the response becomes affirmative: "The cataracts blow their trumpets from the steep;/ No more shall grief of mine the season wrong." The cataracts, echoes, winds, and the shouts of the shepherd boy have a mnemonic effect which causes the poet to participate in the holiday spirit of renewal. But the affirmative movement is of short duration. For, although Wordsworth enters sympathetically into the joyousness of Nature, still for him a particular kind of vision was withheld:

> —But there's a Tree, of many, one,
> A single Field which I have looked upon,
> Both of them speak of something that is gone:
>> The Pansy at my feet
>> Doth the same tale repeat:
> Whither is fled the visionary gleam?
> Where is it now, the glory and the dream?

So the fourth stanza ends on a discordant note expressing a heavy sense of loss and an implicit demand for an explanation of the cause of it.

In stanzas V-VIII Wordsworth projects an explanation for his loss of vision that is based on the doctrine of pre-existence[9]—one probably suggested to him by Coleridge. Both poets had realized the profound significance of childhood in the growth to mature manhood. In considering the recovery of his imagination as recounted in *The Prelude*, Wordsworth places great emphasis upon the part played by the restorative power of imaginative moments recollected from his own childhood:

> O! mystery of man, from what a depth
> Proceed thy honors. I am lost, but see
> In simple childhood something of the base
> On which thy greatness stands.
>> (*Prelude* XII, 272-75)

Now a reading of Plato and the neo-Platonists suggested that the dreamlike moments experienced in childhood were simply carry-overs from the spirit realm from which the soul descended. Gradually, as the natural child grew up and forgetfulness set in, the celestial brightness dimmed and finally completely faded away. The universal myth of pre-existence, though alien to Wordsworth's mind and connected to no other of his writings, provided him with an account of his experience based upon authority. When Wordsworth was criticized for teaching the strange doctrines of pre-existence, he defended himself in a fine metaphor: "Archimedes said that he could move the world if he had a point whereon to rest his machine. . . . I took hold of the notion of pre-existence as having sufficient foundation in humanity for authorizing me to make for my purpose the best use of it I could as a poet." So Wordsworth put into the single, consistent myth of pre-existence experiences which were universal and that had happened to him but which remained untranslatable except in mythical terms.

To give his myth validity, Wordsworth sets up Coleridge's small son Hartley, the "six years' Darling of a pigmy size," as a living example of the child possessed of power and domination. What is imperial about the child of the Ode is his visionary power that makes it possible for him to move into another world. He becomes "a mind/ That feeds upon infinity"; though "deaf and silent," he reads "the eternal deep." The child is transfigured into the symbol of life triumphant, sovereign and immortal; over him, "Immortality Broods like the Day." The child, of course, in time will grow up and lose his regal powers. Indeed, he bends all his efforts to grow up, "at strife" with his own blessedness. Hence, the poet asks him wonderingly, "Why with such earnest pains doth thou provoke/ The years to bring the inevitable yoke?" And he forlornly concludes: "Full soon thy Soul shall have her earthly freight,/ And custom lie upon thee with a weight,/ Heavy as frost and deep almost as life!"

In contemplating the fate of the child, the poet finds himself confronted with an impass. The problem of the loss of ecstatic vision, he discovers, cannot be resolved upon the presumptive evidence of pre-existence. For the logic of pre-existence led Wordsworth to the inescapable conclusion that maturity is a time of inevitable darkness and grief—a conclusion that ran counter to his own experience and to human experience in its totality. When he resumed the composition of the poem two years later, Wordsworth was on firmer ground.[10]

In the concluding stanzas of the Ode, the poet is now convinced that the visionary splendor glimpsed in childhood is gone past recall; but he is equally certain that the indestructible elements that generate youth's vision persist in all stages of man's development. These "first affections," whatever they may be, are yet the "fountain light of all our day." Having once been, they still must be; and man can in thought revive them and be grateful for them. The ecstatic contemplation of Nature is past, but now in its place the philosophic mind reads the "music of humanity" interfused everywhere in the visible scene. Thus the child is indeed father of the man. Childhood has the vision and manhood the wisdom, and their days are bound to one another by a continuous, indestructible spiritual energy. So the poet finds strength not only in the "primary sympathies" that by "invisible links" ally Nature to the affections, but also in "soothing thoughts that spring/ Out of human suffering." The child knows the natural world, but man has come to know the human world as well.

The controlling theme of the Ode is, therefore, identical with that of *The Prelude*: both poems trace the growth of the human heart. In childhood, imagination opens up the glory and the infinitude of Nature; in manhood, Nature inspires human affections that will bring strength and comfort. Hence, the poet still responds joyously to "Fountains, Meadows, Hills, and Groves." He has but relinquished "one delight" (the old visionary power) to live beneath Nature's more habitual sway (the companionship that keeps "watch o'er man's mortality"). As he wished it in the Rainbow poem, the poet's days are joined "each to each by natural piety." At the poem's close, the world of Nature becomes wedded to the world of man. All existence becomes significant and precious for its human-heartedness:

> Thanks to the human heart by which we live,
> Thanks to its tenderness, its joys, and fears,
> To me the meanest flower that blows can give
> Thoughts that do often lie too deep for tears.

Some critics have found weaknesses in the Ode. Coleridge heads the list with his complaint that the lines addressing the child as "Thou best Philosopher" is an instance of mental bombast—"thoughts and images too great for the subject." Mr. Pottle finds the poem marred by disparate ideas; other readers are troubled by what seem to be inflated thoughts and forced piety.[11] However, the majority of competent judges acclaim the "Ode on Immortality" to be Wordsworth's most splendid poem. In no other poem are poetic conditions so perfectly fulfilled. There is the right subject, the right imagery to express it, and the right meter and language for both. Wordsworth happily chose the form of ode as best suited to the majestic subject with which he deals. The form was suggested by a disputation he and Coleridge had over the odes of Ben Jonson and by Coleridge's own use of the form. Wordsworth had never previously used such a meter, but in his poem it moves along with freedom and majestic dignity as though it came "as naturally as leaves to a tree."

The stately metrical form is matched by a simple but majestic structure: the three parts turn upon a crisis, an explanation, and a consolation. Some critics of the Ode complain of the abrupt transitions in the poem, particularly of the prolonged break occasioned by the pre-existence theme. But one must not be disturbed nor misled by the inclusion of this section. Besides the superb poetry of the fifth stanza, for which every lover of poetry is grateful, the Platonic middle section gives a shuttle-like movement and largeness to the Ode. Wordsworth uses this section to set off the lamentations of the first part against the exultations of the third and, as a great lever, to lift his theme. The concluding section rises to a moral grandeur beyond what would have been possible without the stanzas on pre-existence.

The language of the Ode is stately, varied, and beautiful; the imagery is fresh and radiant. Images of light recur throughout the poem to give coherence and splendor to the theme. Also a humbler imagery emerges from time to time: that of the flower, the natural symbol of the beauties of Nature which are the "breath of God," which threads its way through the poem until it reaches the climax of meaning in "the meanest flower that blows." The primary symbol in the poem is, of course, the child whose presence is continuous. Enough has been said already about the child's symbolic significance—enough, indeed, about the range of meaning and value given by a variety of readers to this amazing lyric.

V   *"Ode to Duty," "Elegiac Stanzas," and* *"The Happy Warrior"*

"Ode to Duty," composed early in 1804, had its origins in conversations with Coleridge, who was conducting an investigation with himself on the nature and dislike of doing one's duty.[12] The poem ties in with the heroical last stanzas of the "Ode on Immortality." In the "Ode to Duty," as with the more famous ode, the poet accepts the law of life fulfilled in terms of human love and self-sacrifice as a welcome replacement for the rapturous visions and unchartered freedom of his youth. Two types of characters are described in the poem as fulfilling duty's ordinance. First there are those (stanzas two and three) who instinctively with glad innocence do duty's work and know it not:

> [Those] who, in love and truth,
> Where no misgiving is, rely
> Upon the genial sense of youth:
> Glad Hearts! without reproach or blot;
> Who do thy work, and know it not.[13]

Second (stanzas four and five), there are those who, by transcending self, knowingly and willingly, submit to duty as objective law. In this class Wordworth places himself, not through any catastrophe nor "strong compunction," but because, as he confesses, he has too long relied on his own freedom of choice and seeks the "repose" to be found in external control:

> Me this unchartered freedom tires;
> I feel the weight of chance desires:
> My hopes no more must change their name,
> I long for a repose that ever is the same.

Duty is invoked as the law of the universe. Nature takes a prominent place in the scheme of existence; but now the supreme power that moves the sun and the other stars is identified with the moral law: "Thou dost preserve the stars from wrong;/ And the most ancient heavens, through/ Thee, are fresh and strong." The bond to Nature acquires a new name, and Wordsworth sets himself in a new relationship to it.

In a stanza included in the 1807 edition, but subsequently omitted, Wordsworth described a third situation, an ideal as yet unattained in this world, in which human desire and self-interest spontaneously coincide with duty so that moral victory is always enhanced by enjoyment:

> Yet not the less would I throughout
> Still act according to the voice
> Of my own wish; and feel past doubt
> That my submissiveness was choice:
> Not seeking in the school of pride
> For "precepts over dignified,"
> Denial and restraint I prize
> No farther than they breed a second Will more wise.

In this statement of the ideal of duty, according to Mr. Stallknecht, Wordsworth is following Schiller's doctrine of the *schöne Seele*, a subtle restatement of Kant. In Schiller's eyes, there is something beautiful about a character whose desires and interests have grown to coincide with duty itself. Hence Wordsworth, following Schiller, is advocating not blind submission to duty but free, eager acceptance of a moral law which cannot be interpreted as satisfying one's immediate desires. Although Wordsworth never reprinted the stanza quoted, Mr. Stallknecht sees the spirit of Schiller's "beautiful soul" reflected in the entire ode. Thus in man's imperfect world, persons of the second class, which includes the poet, win peace of mind by a self-imposed inner control and by happy acceptance of the guidance of a higher power. In the "Ode to Duty" Wordsworth has given a dignified self-renunciation and a movingly honest confrontation to the law of life.

On February 6, 1805, Captain John Wordsworth of the merchant service went down with his ship off Portsmouth. He was the best-loved of William's brothers, "a Poet in everything but words," and his loss was an intense shock. For two months after John's death, William wrote nothing at all; but by May he was able to finish *The Prelude*. However, it was the next year before he felt equal to the task of memorializing his brother in verse. He did so in "Elegiac Stanzas suggested by a Picture of Peele Castle in a Storm." The picture was by Sir George Beaumont, and Wordsworth saw it in his patron's home during a visit to London in 1806. The poem was written soon afterward.

The tragic drowning of his brother confirmed the predominant soberness of life expressed in the closing stanzas of the "Ode on Immortality" and the "Ode to Duty." This devastating experience brought the poet's earlier and later moods into actual and acute antagonism. In "Elegiac Stanzas" the contrast between his present and former self are set forth in the pictorial symbol of Peele Castle. The poem opens with the recollection of pleasant memories of a summer month spent on the coast overlooking the castle eleven years before. At that time the sea remained serenely calm day after day and the air still:

> How perfect was the calm! it seemed no sleep;
> No mood, which reason takes away, or brings:
> I could have fancied that the mighty Deep
> Was even the gentlest of all gentle Things.

If then, Wordsworth says, his had been the painter's hand to express what he saw, he would have added "the gleam,/ The light that never was, on sea or land,/ The consecration, and the Poet's dream." But this remoteness in his soul the poet rejects as illusory; in its place he accepts the consequences of human tragedy:

> So once it would have been,—'tis so no more;
> I have submitted to a new control:
> A power is gone, which nothing can restore;
> A deep distress hath humanised my Soul.

Beaumont's picture of the castle in the raging storm now seems a truer representation of life than the placid scene Wordsworth viewed as a young man. The storm with "the lightning, the fierce wind, and trampling waves" all remind him of the dreadful night John lost his life. No longer can he "behold a smiling sea" and be what he has been:

> Farewell, farewell the heart that lives alone,
> Housed in a dream, at distance from the Kind!
> Such happiness, wherever it be known,
> Is to be pitied; for 'tis surely blind.

> But welcome fortitude, and patient cheer,
> And frequent sights of what is to be borne!
> Such sights, or worse, as are before me here.—
> Not without hope we suffer and we mourn.

Two years before in the Immortality Ode Wordsworth took comfort in the enduring love of Nature which survived the loss of vision. But now life is no longer a chronicle of heaven; like the castle, life braves the ravaging storm. One does not have "soothing thoughts that spring/Out of human suffering"; instead, one has "fortitude, and patient cheer." With John's death, Wordsworth is forever separated from the unique spiritual joy he knew in youth. He accepts his loss and welcomes fortitude, which makes that and all other loss to come endurable. The last line of the poem suggests to some readers the Christian consolation of life after death. However one may choose to read that line, it is a fact that Wordsworth hereafter, who earlier said "we find our happiness [here] or not at all" (*Prelude* X, 728), turned toward the solace of traditional Christianity.

A second poem honoring his brother, "The Happy Warrior," also confirms the poet's new stoic attitude. The tragic death of Lord Nelson in the autumn of 1805, whose heroic person the nation idolized, was the occasion for the lines. But Wordsworth himself said it was John's character that largely inspired them. The poem is by no means simply a eulogy of military life; the Happy Warrior is an heroic person in any walk of life who lives in obedience to an "inner light" or indwelling law. What guides him is the same power that "preserves the stars from wrong." He is a kind of personified ideal of the "Ode to Duty."

With the momentous group of poems written in 1804—"Ode on Immortality," "Ode to Duty," "Elegiac Stanzas," and "The Happy Warrior"—a great turning point in Wordsworth's thought is marked as he passed from a period of sheer self-dependence to one of vigorous stoicism and traditional Christian faith in his later life. The new-found austerity appears also in "The Song at the Feast of Brougham Castle" and in "The White Doe of Rylstone," stories of heroic martyrdom composed in 1807. In these poems, as in the great odes and the elegiac verses to his brother, fortitude and love, when put to proof in adversity, are transmuted to wisdom— even to beatification.

CHAPTER 6

The Excursion *and After*

S OMEWHERE between 1805 and 1807 Wordsworth's poetic vitality began slowly to decline. With the fading of inspiration he thirsted for peace of mind—a desire that drove him gradually to adopt the sentiments, attitudes, and forms of convention. After years of self-questing and challenge, he no longer sought primarily to reform the reading public but more often to remind his readers of what they already knew and accepted. His poetical method, tone, and style also changed considerably. These alterations in thought and expression are reflected in *The Excursion* (1814), the major work of the poet's middle years.

The evolution of Wordsworth's opinions in this work and later ones was both honest and intelligible. He was not, as some have charged, "a renegade" to his faith nor were his human sympathies contracted. Moreover, even as inspiration declined, Wordsworth's prosodic skills and technique continued to develop; much of the later poetry is, therefore, of high artistic merit. Foremost among the achievements of the later time is the revision of *The Prelude*, undertaken in 1839, in which the poet created new beauties and at the same time clarified and strengthened his poetry.[1] Other outstanding pieces of the later years include "Laodamia," "After-Thought," "Mutability," and "Surprised by Joy." The last-named has been called "the most poignant sonnet in the English language."

I The Excursion

Wordsworth thought that *The Excursion* was the crowning expression of his genius, but not many critics have been very happy about it. Jeffrey's "This will never do!" sounded the battle cry of contemporary opposition that was echoed by Hazlitt and others and later confirmed by Matthew Arnold. In his essay on Wordsworth (1888), Arnold agreed that *The Excursion* could "never be to the disinterested lover of poetry a satisfactory work." Yet many of

Wordsworth's contemporaries rated the poem highly. To Charles Lamb, it was "the noblest conversational poem I have ever read"; and Keats acclaimed it as "one of the three things to rejoice at in this age." It went through seven editions in the poet's lifetime and helped immeasurably to build up his reputation. However, soon after Wordsworth's death, *The Excursion* fell into almost total neglect from which it has not yet recovered. *The Prelude* has rightfully replaced *The Excursion* in critical esteem. Nevertheless, in spite of its failure to measure up to the lofty aspirations of the Prospectus, *The Excursion* remains an important, memorable work.

The "argument" of *The Excursion* is the vindication of man's right to hope by overcoming despondency and re-establishing genuine knowledge. In Book I, the theme of optimism is introduced by "The Ruined Cottage," a tragic story but one that suggests consoling thoughts. It is told to the Poet by the Wanderer, the prime sponsor for Hope, whose own life history, to give authenticity to his views, is graphically set before us. The theme is expanded in Books II, III, and IV by the introduction of the rebellious, disillusioned Solitary, who impinges the cause of Hope. Book IV, the heart of the poem, contains the bulk of the Wanderer's exhortations to the Solitary to correct his despondency. In Book V, the Pastor, who is introduced, supports the cause of Hope with a series of stories (Books V-VII) about those who lie buried in the churchyard. Finally, in Books VIII and IX the Wanderer applies the theme to a criticism of the social conditions of England.

As first conceived by Wordsworth and Coleridge while in the Quantock Hills, *The Excursion* was to be completely original.[2] Coleridge had predicted that his friend would achieve immortality with his "Recluse" as the first and finest philosophical poem, and Wordsworth himself in the highly original Prospectus seemed on the way to fulfillment of his friend's prediction. But when he came to write *The Excursion* (identified by Wordsworth as "the second part of a long and laborious work to consist of three parts and to be called *The Recluse*") his inspiration flagged. Instead of initiating a new genre, he fell back upon a kind of didactic poetry of retirement that was common in the eighteenth century, and was represented by such works as Edward Young's *Night Thoughts*, Mark Akenside's *The Pleasures of Imagination*, and William Cowper's *The Task*. To this dominant type in blank verse, Wordsworth merged the poetry of philosophical dialogue, of which the most notable example is John Thelwall's *The Peripatetic*; illustrative tales of humble life found in such poems as Shenstone's "School-mistress" and especially Crabbe's "Parish Register"; and meditations on life and death derived from the then popular funeral elegies.

There was some originality in Wordsworth's synthesis of tradi-tional materials; but, on the whole, it must be admitted, *The Excursion* has a disappointing air of archaism. The poem's greatest novelty and to many its most attractive feature is its setting in the Lake Country. The scenery described, though not recorded in detail, resembles the region of Furness Fells, except the scene of Margaret's story in Book I, which is a common in Somersetshire or Dorsetshire. Book II takes the reader to the cottage of the Solitary, situated on the high ridge between the Great and Little Langdales, and there the crucial debate of Book IV is held. With the introduction in Book V of the Pastor, the scene shifts to the village of Grasmere. All in all, the natural surroundings make a great contribution to the poem, especially to the opening and close.

Each of the major characters in *The Excursion*, as all critics since Hazlitt have realized, is a personified aspect of Wordsworth himself. The Solitary is professedly drawn from a certain Joseph Fawcett, "a preacher at a dissenting meeting-house at the Old Jewry in London." But his characterization is, in fact, largely taken from Wordsworth as he later interpreted himself during his contact with the French Revolution and his subsequent disillusionment over its failure. The story of the Solitary's suffering resulting from the deaths of a daughter and a son followed by the death of his wife closely parallels Wordsworth's loss of two of his own children within a single year a short time before *The Excursion* was completed. Something of the authentic Wordsworth also comes through in the Solitary's response to mountain glory. When the storms ride high, he has heard the mysterious music which the mountains give forth to Wordsworth's ear. The Solitary, too, like the poet on Snowdon, has had his rapturous vision on the mountain. But, unlike Words-worth, the Solitary has not mastered his bitterness: he remains cynical, apathetic, and arrogant. He is what Wordsworth might have become if Dorothy and Coleridge had not rescued him.

The Wanderer, the leading character of *The Excursion*, is a de-tached spectator of rural life. He was brought up under the three-fold influence of Nature, strict family tradition, and the reverential worship of God. His boyhood and youth and that of Wordsworth, as set forth in the early books of *The Prelude*, are nearly identical. The original of the Wanderer was a "packman" Wordsworth had known during schooldays in Hawkshead. He admired the occupation and defended the suitablility of such a character to take a prominent role in *The Excursion*. Wordsworth said the Wanderer "represented an idea of what I fancied my own character might have become under the circumstances."

In the first book the Wanderer's character opens up a new perspective for the poet; unfortunately, as the poem progresses, he becomes at times unattractive because of his self-righteousness. The Pastor is hardly more than a narrator of other poeple's lives, though it is obvious that Wordsworth admires him and partly shares his views. The Poet brings Wordsworth in as the spokesman for the whole. Thus the reader sees that each of the main characters bears resemblances to the poet himself. The whole poem is, indeed, but a thinly veiled account of how Wordsworth achieved a victorious adjustment over the years to a series of crippling blows to his own hopes.

The action of *The Excursion* is spread over five summer days and includes only four main characters. As a story involving these characters it has little to recommend it, though some of the stories they tell have high merit. The vital center of interest is the doctrinal plot. This center is firmly established in Book I with the biographical account of the Wanderer and with the story of "The Ruined Cottage." Through the ministry of Nature and ardent thought the Wanderer had attained to Hope and Wisdom: "Unoccupied by sorrow of its own,/His heart lay open; . . . he could *afford* to suffer/ With those whom he saw suffer." His heart grieved for Margaret whose tragic story he tells to show that it is possible, by means of active faith in divine wisdom, to convert earthly sorrows into positive good.[3]

In Book II the reader becomes acquainted with the Solitary, whom be learns about first through the Wanderer so the reader can get a proper perspective on the Solitary's errors and frailties. A sick man and not a philosopher, his illness consists of uncontrolled vacillations between excesses of self-complacency and personal grief, apathy and zealous revolutionary ardor, voluptuous immorality and cynical misanthropy. The discovery of his copy of

Candide—"this dull product of a scoffer's pen"—reveals to the Wanderer how impoverished and prideful the Solitary had become. When the Solitary makes an appearance, one discovers that he still possesses true sensibilities: he greets the Wanderer with "an amicable smile" and comforts a weeping child; he responds to the wild beauty of the mountains. But his utter lack of faith is confirmed by the story he tells of the poor old pensioner driven to his death by the heartless indifference of a housewife. Even when the Solitary descends the mountain after finding the old man, the vision of a "mighty city" wrought by the great clouds piling up after the storm can have no meaning for him. He wants to believe, but he can not.

At the opening of Book III, the mountain setting is read symbolically. The Wanderer sees in nature's forms "a semblance strange of power intelligent." But the Solitary can see the varied shapes before them only as "the sport of Nature." He regards the botanist or geologist who never bothers about the riddle of existence as happier than the Wanderer; and happiest of all is the thoughtless cottage boy. For the Solitary, death is "a better state than waking." As support for his despondency, the Solitary relates the story of his shattered life. His vain, self-indulgent youth was altered with marriage to a lovely bride. Two children were born to their union, and they lived in undisturbed wedded happiness for seven years. Then abruptly both children died; soon after, his grief-stricken wife followed them, leaving him "on this earth disconsolate." Life became for him empty and meaningless.

From his dejection he was roused by the shock of the storming of the Bastille, and he becomes a convert to the French Revolution. But, when the French nation turned aggressor and when the zealots in England abandoned liberty's cause, the Solitary decided to leave his own country and to seek in America the "archetype of human greatness." But he soon became disillusioned with democracy in America and with "Primeval Nature's child," the Indian, who proved to be "A creature, squalid, vengeful, and impure." From his futile quest he returned to a sequestered existence in the Lake Country whence he looks apathetically upon the stream of life encompassed by evil; he cherishes no hope but that his "particular current soon will reach/ The unfathomable gulf, where all is still!"

In Book IV, the Wanderer, who steadfastly confronts the difficulties raised by the story of the Solitary, offers a way for him to overcome his despondency. The Sage opens his discourse by accepting the basic assumption of the Solitary that there is unavoidable suffering and evil in the world. But "the calamities of mortal life" may be offset by faith in a benevolent, superintending providence "Whose everlasting purposes embrace/ All accidents, converting them to good." A trust in this infinite benevolent power is inspired by the beauty of the natural world and is supported by the enduring strength of moral law. Duty, aspiration, and hope exist outside the exigencies of change and are eternal. Thus, the Solitary has no right to despair because the glowing visions of his youth have faded.

The Wanderer, too, once experienced "fervent raptures" that are now gone forever; but he does not merely because of his loss sink into apathy. Moreover, the Wanderer has also shared the Solitary's faith in "social man." If he shares it no longer, it is not because his hope for humanity has flagged but because he realizes that it takes time for mankind to be redeemed. The revolutionists have forgotten that man's nature cannot be changed in a day; man must learn "that unless above himself he can/ Erect himself, how poor a thing is Man!" The Sage urges the Solitary to live a normal country life, to revisit the scenes of his youth, and (in a very Wordsworthian formula) to revive early memories, "the hiding places of man's power." For "Strength attends us if but once we have been strong." One should rejoice in Nature and, if tired with systematic thinking, let the fancy lead to superstition's airy dreams. Even superstition opens up a sort of truth that is better than doubt and despair.

In a famous passage, which enchanted the author of *Endymion*, the Wanderer tells how the enlightened Greek shepherd or hunter created divine forms from the living presence of Nature. He counsels the Solitary to throw aside cynical Voltaire and to drink deep at the fountain of living experience and reality as did the Greeks. The Wanderer's argument culminates with a passage of remarkable beauty (vv. 1058-76). The soul, he says, has power to transmute all obstructive elements of its experience into new sources of strength. Despondency is corrected by calling into play "the mind's *excursive* power." And he concludes: "So, build we up the Being that we are;/ Thus deeply drinking-in the soul of things,/ We shall be wise perforce."

With the opening of Book V, the group leaves the mountain

solitude, descends into the valley, and arrives at the village church. The Solitary reopens the problem of the predominance of evil by attacking baptism as an empty pretense and by reiterating his charge that the value of life declines from youth to age. The Pastor, who joins the disputants, gives his support to the Wanderer's optimistic faith in a benevolent providence. He asserts that solace for the calamities of life may be in part achieved by him "who can best subject/ The will to reason's law," but that human reason alone has limitations. An inward faith is also required, one supported by active energy, tenderness of heart, and dignity of soul. In answer to the Solitary's request to supply specific examples from life in place of abstract assertions, the Pastor offers the story of the sequestered quarryman and his wife as proof that happiness and virtue can exist in spite of arduous poverty. The Solitary objects that theirs is the exception rather than the rule and cites as more typical the case of the old Pensioner.

In Books VI and VII, the Pastor tells a series of tales about the tenants of the churchyard to show, in a variety of ways, how some persons overcome their sorrow or suffering and some do not. The stories, offered as "solid facts" from real life, support the wisdom of reasonable optimism. Wordsworth lets the stories speak for themselves, though the intended moral is not far to seek. The Pastor, encouraged by the Poet, agrees to limit his narratives chiefly to those that excite feelings of the higher ethical sort: love, esteem, and admiration. However, he does feel that tales of evil sometimes should be told as a challenge to virtue.

Book VI opens with the story of the rejected lover who achieved a victory by giving himself to science and "Nature's care" (an illustration of the means of restoration recommended to the Solitary in Book IV). This story is followed by the account of the persevering miner who is redeemed, like one of Browning's characters, by his strength of purpose. Exactly opposite is the tale of the prodigal son, who in weakness followed dissolute ways in the city but returned repentent to his parents' door. The harmonizing influence of solitude is illustrated by the story of the Jacobite and the Hanoverian, who though dire enemies in the world, found peace and affection in constant fellowship during their retirement. Much can be learned, the Pastor reminds his listeners, "in the preverseness of a selfish course" as exemplified in the story of the proud and despotic mother. After a prolonged resistance to benign influences, the mother achieves peace when she realizes the transience of her devotion to worldly passions.

In contrast to the tale of the avaricious matron, there follows the tragic and deeply moving story of Ellen. She is deserted by her lover and suffers other humiliations after the birth of her child, but in the end she is purified and ennobled by an edifying submission to divine will. At the insistence of the Wanderer, the Parson relates the story of Wilfrid Armathwaite, a shepherd who seduced his own maidservant. Unable to find forgiveness in himself or bear the weight of his shame, he took his own life. The gloom of this tale is relieved by the charming picture which closes Book VI of the widower who finds consolation for his bereavement in the affection and joy which survive in his six daughters.

In one of the best-told stories of the series, a tale which opens Book VII, a pampered worldly clergyman is forced to take a modest curacy among the mountains. By accepting his lot and by faithfully performing his narrow duties, he finds spiritual equanimity. There follows a pair of stories about men with bodily afflictions who create full lives for themselves. The deaf man cultivates the grace of "pure contentedness" and becomes a source of hope to others. The blind man triumphs over his defect by actively engaging his remaining senses to enrich his mind until it is truly enlightened.

The series of stories closes with two tales that link Grasmere with the wider world. The first of these is about a heroic youth who leads forth a troop of volunteers from the peaceful valley during the alarm of Napoleon's threat to invade. Death came to the youth from a moment's rashness, and he was buried with "a soldier's honours." The second of the tales is a kind of epitaph on a knight of Elizabeth's time, Sir Alfred Irthing, who fulfilled his vow "to redress wrong." The stories of the mountain youth and the knight emphasize the transience of human glory; the restless generations go to their decay while "the vast Frame/ Of social nature changes evermore." At the end of Book VII, the Wanderer courteously thanks the Pastor for all the stories he has told and asserts that they may be accepted as "words of heartfelt truth" tending to teach patience under affliction, faith, hope, love, and reverence. By their example, the Solitary is offered the means of restoring his sense of "belonging" to life and his ultimate regeneration.

In the final section, Books VIII and IX, the Wanderer appraises the contemporary state of English society as it has been affected by the Industrial Revolution. He sees towns burgeoning, "barren wilderness erased," Britain's ships peopling the high seas, and a mighty navy defending the blessed isle "of Liberty and Peace." He exults in the mastery "of the forces of Nature" to serve his will. But he is alarmed at the heavy price paid for material progress by injury to the health of workers and corruption of the "old domestic morals of the land." He sees families broken up by factory labor and children enslaved to weakness and stupidity. The Solitary pointedly asks if there haven't always been and if there aren't now tens of thousands of children living in the country who are denied "liberty of mind" by abject poverty and unremitting toil. This challenging question leads the Wanderer to the climactic response that opens Book IX: " 'To every Form of being is assigned'/ Thus calmly spoke the venerable Sage,/ 'An *active* Principle.' "

The "active Principle" pervades the universe; its noblest seat is the human Mind. In response to this power, man is free "to obey the law of life, and hope, and action." Even old age is not separated from "the stir of hopeful nature." But human injustice has brought about inequalities that obstruct the operation of the active principle. To achieve "liberty of mind" for all classes, the Wanderer calls upon England to "complete her glorious destiny" by providing universal education. The famous passage beginning "O for the coming of that glorious time/ When . . . this imperial Realm,/ While she exacts allegiance, shall admit/ An obligation, on her part, to *teach*/ Them who are born to serve her and obey; . . ." (293 ff.) is hardly great poetry, but it is an intellectually courageous utterance and the climax on the constructive side of the argument of *The Excursion*. It is a link to the earlier poetry mainly addressed to the correction of despondency, and it reaffirms the liberty of mind founded on virtue. At the close of the poem, the Solitary has not been restored to hope; but Wordsworth seems to have planned his rehabilitation for some future work. In any case, the Solitary's recovery is not vital to the thematic structure.

Wordsworth's primary purpose in *The Excursion* is to expound a philosophy, though not in any sense formally to announce a system. Basic to his teaching is the constantly recurring theme that Nature is permeated with an active intelligence that is universal and the source of all men's highest thoughts and feelings. This active soul of Nature spreads beyond itself communicating good; it is the freedom of the universe. Any man who has lost hope may be restored to virtue by opening his mind to universal truths which are innate, immutable, and transcendental. In the process of recovering, however, human reason alone is not enough since it is liable to error. The entire story of the Solitary is, in fact, an example of the abuse of rationalistic thinking.

The Wanderer says that the wildest superstitions are preferable to pure reason. Reasoning is an invaluable secondary power, but self-knowledge must be guided and enlightened by Imagination. Since the source of enlightenment is Nature, the Wanderer calls upon the Solitary to correct his irregular habits of living by communicating with Nature with the full power of the *excursive* mind. By following this course, he will apprehend eternal moral truths, gain self-control and self-respect, and be reawakened to love for his fellow men. The path of Duty that the Wanderer exhorts the Solitary to follow is not, in any strict sense, Christian Duty. The concept of Duty, like Hope, is basically utilitarian. Virtue is the simple produce of the common day; joy is found "in widest commonalty spread." In establishing his philosophic position, Wordsworth makes slight use of the language of Christian doctrine. He skillfully and unobtrusively fuses naturalistic belief with tradition. Even the Pastor generalizes about his faith and shows at times a bias for neo-Platonic natural piety. Nevertheless, *The Excursion* does teach Christian faith and virtue and, in many respects, is more specifically religious than any of Wordsworth's previous works.

The Excursion cannot be considered an altogether satisfactory poem. As a whole, it lacks dramatic and narrative vigor. The reader is confronted by that "species of ventriloquism," of which Coleridge complains, "where two are represented as talking, while in truth one man only speaks." A common criticism is that Wordsworth has dealt unfairly with the Solitary by making him a man of straw. In answering the Solitary's arguments, the Wanderer admittedly is at times dogmatic and pietistic. However, Wordsworth does not intend for the two adversaries to meet on equal terms. The Solitary is a "sick" man and needs help. This help the Wanderer magnanimously offers even though it may at times seem to be given in a patronizing manner.

In the matter of style, it must be admitted that there is a decline from what is Wordsworth's best. There is an abundance of conscious artifice, inflated rhetoric, and prolixity. The use of personification has increased, imagery is frequently decorative and ornamental,

and there is an inflated use of prosaic words ("disencumbering")
and of negative adjectives ("unambitious," "unsubstantialized").
Words of Latin derivation predominate over those of Anglo-Saxon
origin; the double negative (always a favorite device of Wordsworth)
is much too common; and there is too frequent use of parenthesis.
In the narratives employed to correct despondency, Wordsworth
inclines to force his points at the expense of the stories.

But *The Excursion* cannot be dismissed as the tiresome, inflated
preaching of an aging poet. The central character, the Wanderer,
has many qualities to recommend him. Though his role as peddler
was ridiculed by Jeffrey, the choice was a characteristic and right
decision for Wordsworth. The Wanderer represents the successful
embodiment of the poet's unifying impulse of philosophy. He is
the chosen vehicle to transmit the spiritual and infinite as an
active force for truth, goodness, and love. The stories told by the
Pastor offer a remarkable range of character types handled by
Wordsworth with knowledge and power. Many of them were the
life stories and love stories of Grasmere people personally known
to the poet. These characters of the real world were individualized
by the author with numerous vivid details and unique characteristics.

Though the style of *The Excursion* has its shortcomings, as has
been indicated, it still contains "much wisdom, much beauty, and
very little that does not in some way bear the stamp of a great
mind."[4] There are many lovely images and individual passages and
lines noteworthy for particular reasons, such as that on the shell
held to the ear of the child (Book IV), the passage praising natural
but mute poets (Book I), the picture of the moon (Book IV), the
Wanderer's youthful transports (Book I), the Solitary's speech on
the twin peaks of Langdale and his account of the ending of the
storm and his mystical vision (Book III), the child's imaginative
flight initiated by listening to the minstrels (Book VII), the
Solitary's account of love (Book III), and the famous chronicle of
the origin of the Greek shepherd's religion (Book IV). Wordsworth's
power to describe landscape remained "unimpaired and often
strangely moving." This talent he reveals in countless small, deft
strokes and in elaborate sketches like that of the white ram who
is reflected in the still lake in Book IX.

In summary, in spite of shortcomings, *The Excursion* is a great
and significant document of Wordsworth's mind in a transitional
phase before it has settled into the dogmas of orthodoxy and con-

servatism. The poem has splendid bursts of eloquence, bold arguments lighted with felicities of phrase, fresh depictions of natural
scenery, and courageous expositions of social philosophy.

II   The White Doe of Rylstone

The White Doe of Rylstone, begun in October, 1807, and finished
in February, 1808, was not published until 1815, one year after
The Excursion. Although *The White Doe* came earlier and is
touched with the ethereal magic of Wordsworth's earlier poetry,
it shares with *The Excursion* the problem of human suffering.
Moreover, in both poems the problem originates from the poet's
confrontation of "keen heart-anguish" in his own life. In *The
Excursion*, as has already been pointed out, the response of the
Solitary to the deaths of his two children and of his wife closely
parallels Wordsworth's heartbreak over the loss of his own two
children. Similarly, Emily's lonely conquest of sorrow in *The White
Doe* matches the poet's victory over numbing grief after the death
of his brother John. Because of Wordsworth's intimate, personal involvement with suffering, the poem is in many ways his profoundest
exercise of the spirit; he himself believed it to be "in conception
the highest work he had ever produced."

For his story Wordsworth combined history with legend: the
rising of the northern earls during the reign of Queen Elizabeth I
(as told in Thomas Percy's *Reliques*) with the weekly visit of a white
doe at Bolton Priory (as set forth in T. D. Whitaker's *History and
Antiquities of the Deanery of Craven*). To these two elements, fused
by poetic imagination, he added a third agent, missing from the
original action: Emily, daughter of the Nortons. Richard Norton,
father of nine sons and a daughter, joined the rebellious earls in
support of the Catholic religion; but Wordsworth skillfully hints
that some of the rebels were motivated by conditions other than
religious ones. Norton's motives, however, are sincere; and the
poet treats him sympathetically. No attempt is made in the poem
to give a true or rounded account of the rebellion. There is no
mention, for example, of Mary Queen of Scots though in history
she was a prime mover in the quarrel.

Wordsworth also leaves out the maneuvers and retreat of the
earls and concentrates on the Nortons alone in their glory and
misery. The intricacies of history have given way to the simplicity
of poetry. There is no avoidance of moving action, only a rigorous

selection of it focusing upon the martyrdom of Emily. For the spiritualized conception of Emily's character, as Wordsworth acknowledges in the Dedication to Mary, the "celestial" Una of Spenser's *Faerie Queene* served him as a glorious example. "The gentle Una . . . pierced by sorrow's thrilling dart,/ Did meekly bear the pang unmerited." So Emily was singled out in *The White Doe* to endure the cruel hammer blows of Fate and to achieve over "pain and grief" a spiritual triumph.

The first canto is set in a period after the death of Emily, in order to create in the mind of the reader an aura of expectation and to establish what Wordsworth calls "the shadowy influence of the Doe." "Soft and silent as a dream" she comes each Sunday morning to the churchyard of "Bolton's moulding priory" where, during divine service, she quietly lies beside a grassy grave. She emerges as a creature with supernatural overtones and implicitly as a creature which, in Wordsworth's language, "by connection with Emily is raised as it were from its mere animal nature into something mysterious and saint-like." The Doe's kinship with Emily is anticipated by the creature's reclining beside a grave which was "the favoured haunt of Emily in her last years." The Doe's spiritual affinity is "Presumptive evidence" of involvement with a higher being; for, by the formula explained in a passage from Bacon's *Of Atheism* that is prefixed to the poem, beasts are ennobled by dependence on Man, just as Man is made noble by the protection and favor of God. The Doe, then, is established in the first canto as the emblem of Emily's spiritualization. The remainder of the poem is an "explanation" of the transfiguration of Emily and the Doe.

The second canto opens bleakly with the introduction of the "solitary Maid" whose only companion is "her sylvan Friend" and who exists in "a dearth/Of love upon a hopeless earth." The cause of her woes is a banner of war which, at her father's command, she embroidered with the sacred cross and wounds of Christ. The banner symbolizes the tragic action with which Emily and others had become involved. For Emily, it is a sign of impending disaster; for her father, a symbol of martial courage in a righteous cause; for the poet and reader, an emblem of Emily's patience.[6]

When the call came for Norton to join the rebels, he was confronted with a divided family. His eldest son, Francis, pleads with him not to go to war. But Norton, with "a look of holy pride,"

seizes the banner, thrusts it into another's hands, and leads forth
eight sons to battle. Left behind in scorn, Francis grapples with
his heart agony, is cleansed from despair, and envisages massive
suffering but one not futilely negative. He decides to join his
brothers unarmed, though he utterly forswears his father's course.
When he sees Emily left alone, innocent of any offense to God or
man, he speaks words to her counseling patience, which at first she
does not understand. She realizes well enough that the action of her
father will bring suffering; but she must learn, as Francis explains,
that suffering requires action to master it:

> depend
> Upon no help of outward friend;
> Espouse thy doom at once, and cleave
> To fortitude without reprieve.

Emily cannot see what she is to become. Her temptation, as Francis
foresaw, is still to hope for the safety of her family or for some
change in the fortune of war.

But, in the next three cantos, Emily's patience emerges. She sup-
presses her desire to intercede in her father's doings. She knows
that her duty is not to interfere in the course of events, but "in
resignation to abide / The shock and finally secure / O'er pain and
grief a triumph pure." Emily carries Wordsworth's meaning for
what suffering holds of "permanent, obscure, and dark," but
which also partakes of infinity. The *conquest* of her sorrows is the
crucial *action* of the poem.

After the father and brothers are led off to execution, the survival
of Francis provides a ray of hope. Emily is encouraged by the
report that her brother has recovered the banner. Just as she had
earlier resisted the attention of the Doe, so she now withdraws
from the total acceptance of her doom. She still cannot realize the
magnitude of her afflictions, but not for long. The sixth canto
recounts the capture and death of Francis. On another level, it
describes "the hammering of the final nail in the crucifixion of
Emily" when she throws herself upon her brother's grave and is
overwhelmed with "the whole ruth / And sorrow of the final truth!"

As the burial of Francis is the consummation of Emily's earthly
sorrow, so the final canto is the consummation of her "anticipated
beatification" through the "apotheosis" of the Doe. At the end of
long wanderings in grief and trouble, Emily returns to Rylstone.

She is forlorn, but her soul stands fast, sustained by memory and reason, and "held above/ The infirmities of mortal love;/ Undaunted, lofty, calm, and stable,/ And awfully impenetrable." With the return of the Doe, Emily is cheered and fortified; she is able to revive the memories of the past, "undisturbed and undistrest." Natural haunts calm and cheer her; when the church bells sound their Sabbath music—"God us ayde"—her heart joins them in prayer. On favored nights she often goes to Bolton to look upon St. Mary's shrine and the grave of Francis; there she sits "forlorn, but not disconsolate." When she returns from the abyss of thought, she does not mourn but rejoices in life. However, her sanction is *inward* and stands apart from human cares; hence she can proffer affection only to a creature of celestial significance—to the radiant Doe whose presence pervades the poem like a spirit, suggesting the mystic beauty of another world. She shadows forth the joyful serenity that Emily's tortured spirit finally achieves. Wordsworth makes clear Emily's accomplishment and her relationship to the Doe in a letter to Coleridge in 1808:

[Emily] is intended to be honoured and loved for what she *endures*, and the manner in which she endures it; accomplishing a conquest over her own sorrows (which is the true subject of the Poem) by means, partly, of the native strength of her character, and partly by the persons and things with whom and which she is connected; and finally after having exhibited the "fortitude of patience and heroic martyrdom," ascending to pure, ethereal spirituality, and forwarded in that ascent of love by communion with a creature not of her own species, but spotless, beautiful, innocent, and loving in that temper of earthly love to which she alone can conform.[7]

In the closing lines the poet announces the culmination of Emily's triumph:

> From fair to fairer; day by day
> A more divine and loftier way!
> Even such this blessèd Pilgrim trod,
> By sorrow lifted towards her God.

Since the suffering of Emily "is permanent . . ./ And has the nature of infinity," after her death her beatified spirit survives in the Doe—

> Who, having filled a holy place,
> Partakes, in her degree, Heaven's grace;
> And bears a memory and a mind
> Raised far above the law of kind.

The Doe remains the living emblem of that "fortitude of patience" which looks through finite suffering to infinite salvation.

The question may well be asked as to why Wordsworth did not have Emily return to society where her faith might be fulfilled by works. One of Wordsworth's basic purposes in writing his poetry, as attested by his letter to Lady Beaumont at the very period when he was about to write *The White Doe,* was to console the afflicted. Emily's victory is obviously directed to this purpose; for, by picturing her as having no outward stimulus or reward, except the unquenchable triumph of her own soul, her victory is most completely demonstrated. As Wordsworth says: "Everything that is attempted by the principal personages in *The White Doe* fails, so far as its object is external and substantial. So far as it is moral and spiritual it succeeds."

Emily's valor is set in sharp contrast to that of her father whose heroism is external. But hers is no less militant: she made "a *conquest* over her own sorrows." Wordsworth similarly triumphed in his battle with despair following the death of his brother John. When he came to write *The White Doe,* he dared address himself calmly "to scale the dizzy cliffs of anguish where mortal senses reel" because his own feelings about his brother's death gave him guidance in his ascent. In that soul-searching Wordsworth found the ministry of Nature by itself insufficent; hence, he sought support and guidance in religious faith. Having won his own struggle with despondency, Wordsworth, unlike the heroine of Rylstone, directed his hope and ministry to the outer world. But, in the years following *The White Doe,* he did so with the increasing help of the teachings of orthodox religion.

III   *The Later Poetry*

After *The Excursion,* though there appeared not much more that was great and distinctive in his poetry, Wordsworth was always ready to employ new approaches to make his offerings attractive. He sought fresh materials for his poems not only from "natural objects" but from the literature and history of Classical times. He also adopted a new metaphorical attitude and tended to use his subjects more directly as symbols of meaning. At the time he was helping his son John prepare for college, his interest was revived in Greek and Roman mythology. The immediate result of this renewed interest was the composition of "Laodamia" and "Dion."

"Laodamia," founded on the description of the underworld in Virgil's *Aeneid*, Book VI, was composed while *The Excursion* was being prepared for the press and was first published in *Poems* (1815). This poem, Wordsworth said, "cost me more trouble than almost anything of equal length I have ever written." It tells how Laodamia is allowed by the Gods, in answer to her fervent prayer, to converse for a brief space with her husband Protesilaus, the first warrior to die at Troy. When Laodamia sees her husband, she passionately longs to embrace him and revive "the joys of sense." But she is sternly told by Protesilaus to control her rebellious passion: "for the Gods approve/The depth, and not the tumult, of the soul;/A fervent, not an ungovernable, love." He adjures her to "mourn meekly" and await with patience "Our blest reunion in the shades below."

But Laodamia's passion is too strong. When the wraith is summoned away, in a transport of grief she falls dead on the floor of the palace. Wordsworth, who was deeply involved in the human implications of this tragedy, had great difficulty in settling on a satisfactory ending. In the first printed version he deviated from the myth in letting the overpassionate Laodamia go altogether free from punishment. In 1827, however, he was persuaded to change her doom, in agreement with Virgil, to one more severe: she must wander for eternity "in a grosser clime" in Hades "apart from happy Ghosts." Five years later Wordsworth relented his severity toward Laodamia and at the last doomed her only "to wear out her appointed time." Thus, he finally settled, much to his credit, upon a compromise between myth and his own heart. Like "Laodamia," the story of "Dion" is based upon the Classics (the source is Plutarch) and, also like it, has an exalted moral strain. When Dion is tempted unjustly to shed human blood, though ostensibly for the public good, the judgment upon him is absolute: "Him, only him, the shield of Jove defends, / Whose means are fair and spotless as his ends."

In 1818, long after Wordsworth had taken his conscious farewell to visionary life, a radiant sunset seen from the mound in front of his home at Rydal revived in him a momentary glimpse of glory. He tells with an intermingling of joy and pain of the sudden illumination from another world in the well-known lines "Composed upon an Evening of Extraordinary Splendour and Beauty." The experience has close associations with the Immortality Ode. The splendor of the sunset recalls

                                the light
            Full early lost, and fruitlessly deplored.
            Which, at this moment, on my waking sight
            Appears to shine, by miracle restored.

However, the "visionary gleam" has an ephemeral luster that quickly fades, and the poem resulting from it really has little of the old magic. Wordsworth first included it with *Poems of Imagination,* but he later transferred it to the group of *Evening Voluntaries.*

As the years advanced, Nature came to provide delightful interludes for the poet rather than transforming experience. A composite of such interludes resulted in a sonnet series describing the Duddon River. The poet had from his youth onward "many affecting remembrances" associated with the stream which he weaves together in an imaginary day's ramble from its rise at the top of Wrynose Pass as it ripples, winds, and widens on its way to the sea. In the sonnets recording this ramble Wordsworth is much less concerned with giving pleasure through pictorial images (though these are not lacking) than with providing stirring thoughts to elevate the mind. He intertwines his own private affections, memories, and hopes with the ever-changing landscape; and he joins to them the legendary and historical associations with this lovely stream.

When published in 1820, *The River Duddon* was "more warmly received" than any other of Wordsworth's writings. Most readers found the symbolism easy to understand, and they could enjoy the pleasant human links skillfully made by the poet with the onflowing stream and the pastoral and mountain landscape. Actually, there is nothing noteworthy about the thirty-three miscellaneous sonnets marking the river's course to the sea. However, in "After-Thought," in which the poet sums up the symbolic meaning of the poetical journey from mountain to ocean, he has written one of the greatest of all his sonnets. Here time and space are transcended. The river which flows out and loses itself in the sea is the eternal life-force of man's spirit as it emerges from the unknown, runs its earthly course, and merges again with the eternal. It represents the spiritual oneness of Man and Nature deeply interfused, "what was, and is, and will abide."

Wordsworth was able over the years intuitively to reconcile his religion of Nature with the doctrine of the Anglican Church without any compromise to either. In 1822 he published *Ecclesiastical*

Sonnets in which he traces the history of the English church from its beginnings. At no time in this series does he exploit or defend religious dogma; of open didacticism there is hardly a trace. As the poetical chronicle unfolds, Wordsworth stands as "spectator ab extra" watching over the new forces and ways of the church developing through the centuries. Throughout the sequence, the theme is handled with tolerance and wisdom. In occasional detached or isolated moments there is an inrush of magnificent poetry, like that in which the poet in "King's College Chapel" opens the way to infinity, or in "Mutability" finds that "Truth fails not" but the forms that enshrine her gradually melt "like frosty rime."

During his middle and later years, Wordsworth's love of traveling did not abate; and he often used the objects and experiences of his tours as the subjects for new poems. During the summer of 1814, the poet made a second visit to Scotland with Mary and Sara Hutchinson. In the company of James Hogg he visited Yarrow River and wrote the central piece "Yarrow Visited" in a trilogy which began with "Yarrow Unvisited" in 1803 and ended with "Yarrow Revisited" in 1831.[8] When he first visited the stream, he realized that what he saw in the light of day rivaled the delicate creation of "fond imagination." And, as the sunshine played upon its surface, he was led to anticipate a future joy in the recollection of "Thy genuine image, Yarrow!" The beauty of Nature never lost its power to delight the poet in moments recollected in tranquility. Even after seventeen years had passed and Wordsworth had again beheld the "unaltered face" of the river in the company of Walter Scott and contrasted the change the years had brought to himself and the "Great Minstrel of the Border," he concluded by observing that Yarrow's image was "dearer still to memory's shadowy moonshine."

But "Yarrow Revisited," Wordsworth himself said, was too heavily laden with the pressure of fact for the verses to harmonize satisfactorily with the two preceding poems. Scott was about to set out for Italy in a vain search for health and came back only to die. When the group returned from Yarrow and forded the Tweed to Abbotsford, the sun cast upon the Eildon Hills "a rich but sad light." Wordsworth sensed that it would be the last time Scott would cross that beloved river. A few days later he composed a farewell sonnet to Scott, "A trouble, not of clouds, or weeping rain." An equally noble tribute to his friend written at that time also vibrates in the splendid Trosachs sonnet. In 1835, when Wordsworth received news of the death of Hogg, he vividly recalled his visits to Yarrow with the Ettrick Shepherd and Scott, and he composed on the spot a magnificent personal elegy to their memory. Also included in this "extempore effusion" were Coleridge, Lamb, Crabbe, and Felicia Hemans who, within the short span of three years, had joined them in "the sunless land."

Wordsworth's fame grew slowly over the years, but in the last decade it almost overwhelmed him. When in 1839 Oxford honored him with a doctor's degree, the ovation which greeted him was one of the most tremendous the university had ever witnessed. On Southey's death, Wordsworth was made poet laureate. At last he came to realize that the prophetic words he had written long years before in simple confidence to comfort Lady Beaumont were being fulfilled. In that earlier time when his poems were scorned, he bade her to trust that their destiny would be "to console the afflicted; to add sunshine to daylight, by making the happy happier; to teach the young and the gracious of every age to see, to think, and feel, and therefore, to become more actively and securely virtuous." As he hoped, the poems have faithfully performed that service.

In April, 1850, full of years and honors, William Wordsworth, one of England's greatest poets, died. He lies buried in the churchyard of Grasmere beneath the shade of yew trees planted by his own hand and in the sound of the incessant murmuring of the mountain stream. So the "ceaseless music" of running water, which at the beginning of life, as he tells the reader, quickened his gift of poetry, accompanies his spirit still. And the music he made flows without ceasing to all who give ears to hear it.

CHAPTER 7

Conclusion

WILLIAM Wordsworth was the most truly original genius of his age and exerted a power over the poetic destinies of his century unequaled by any of his contemporaries. Wordsworth's originality was recognized early by Coleridge, who, during his last year of residence at Cambridge, became acquainted with *Descriptive Sketches*. "Seldom, if ever," wrote Coleridge in *Biographia Literaria* in remembrance of that occasion, "was the emergence of an original poetic genius above the literary horizon more evidently announced." With the publication of *Lyrical Ballads*, the challenge of the new kind of poetry was quickly acknowledged and accepted by the public at large.

But, if Wordsworth set new directions and new values as to what was possible in poetry, he also called forth ridicule and opposition. Lord Jeffrey, who thought that the poet was "too ambitious of originality," held that what he was attempting would never do. Wordsworth himself foresaw that there would be resistance, but he did not foresee the extent of it, and cautioned readers that they would "perhaps frequently have to struggle with feelings of strangeness and awkwardness." For two decades Jeffrey did not relent in his abusive attack on Wordsworth, but the poet remained to the end unshaken in the rightness of his poetic innovations.

In his considered statement on the subject of the poet's creative freedom ("Essay Supplementary to the Preface," 1815), Wordsworth observes in a passage often quoted, that, in so far as a poet is great and "at the same time original," he has the task of creating the taste by which he will be enjoyed; the great poet will, therefore, "clear and often shape his own road." Francis Jeffrey succeeded measurably in slowing down the public acceptance of Wordsworth; but, by the early 1820's, by virtue of his own great strength the poet had gained such headway with the public that Jeffrey found it prudent to retire from the field. Thereafter the opposition among critics and readers alike quickly faded, and Wordsworth's fame steadily rose until it reached a high point in the 1830's. In his declining years Wordsworth was acknowledged as the pre-eminent living British poet; and, when he died, he was honored and revered by a wide public. Shortly after his death, his popularity receded somewhat and reached an ebb around 1865.

In the late 1870's a highly significant essay by Leslie Stephen provoked a famous reply by Matthew Arnold, which stimulated new interest in Wordsworth among scholars and general readers. Since Arnold's time, critical studies and biographies have multiplied; and readers have grown in numbers with the years. Today, there are few responsible critics who would question Wordsworth's right to a place among the foremost English poets. Wordsworth does not, to be sure, meet with the ready acceptance accorded Chaucer, Shakespeare, and Milton. There is a certain pedestrian tone, an unfortunate element of prosiness that is easy to laugh at and easy to find dull. Often matter-of-fact, even banal, details are inextricably intertwined in his works with the most inspired and sublime passages. Coleridge and others since have complained of the inconstancy and disharmony of Wordsworth's style.

Some readers have also been unhappy about his compulsion to moralize. But Wordsworth wished to be thought of as a teacher or as nothing. In this role he might have found more ready acceptance if he had been mindful of Dryden's golden maxim (a maxim which he accepts in theory) that Poesy only instructs as it delights. He might have employed more often than he did the light touch of humor, but he generally eschews that saving grace. Some readers have felt that Wordsworth lacked the gift of dramatic imagination and, in some respects, the storyteller's art. But, granting a good deal, even granting that in some of Wordsworth's best work there are occasional flaws that are difficult to excuse, there yet remains a massive body of poetry written at the height of his powers which has an immense variety of excellences and a wide and unfading appeal.

The greatness of Wordsworth's best work proceeds from a calm, almost elemental, strength. He possessed a weight of character, an extraordinary emotional force and reach of intellect, and a tremendous imaginative power. The source of his strength lay within his own extraordinary powers of awareness. He saw things that other people do not see, or see but dimly; and he saw them with singular frequency and vividness. His poetic impulse came to him through some perfectly familiar experience, such as beholding the rainbow or hearing the shout of the cuckoo. From an impression simply and purely sensuous, he would establish a mood of mind or feeling in which "the object contemplated was suddenly released from the tie of custom and became a source of mysterious exaltation" (Havens). In such brief, intensely charged moments Wordsworth experienced a feeling of release; sensation blanked out, consciousness was almost completely lost, and he became "living soul." Through frequent repetitions of these periods of transcendent ecstasy, Wordsworth became overpoweringly aware of the reality and importance of the spiritual world. This spiritual world, however, is not an isolated state but the sensible world more fully apprehended. Everything is apocalyptic, but everything, too, is natural. An auxiliary light from the mind bestowed new splendor on the forms and colors of earth. A "wonderful interchange" went on between the poet and everything about him, "they flowing into him, he going out to them. His soul attracted them to itself, as a mountain-top draws the clouds, and at their touch woke up to feel its kinship with the mysterious life that is in all nature and in each separate object of nature."[1]

Wordsworth is the poet of many things besides, but it is in his relation to Nature that his poetic inspiration originates. It was among the "grand and permanent forms" of Nature that he most unmistakably *felt* the wisdom and spirit of the universe. There was confirmed his faith in the dignity and independence of Man. Through both Man and Nature alike there rolls the divine something "more deeply interfused." The mergence of the human figure with Nature gave it that degree of dignity and virtue which alone would allow it to become, for Wordsworth, a worthy symbol of human life. Wordsworth's typical human figures—the Solitary Reaper, the Wanderer, Lucy, the Old Cumberland Beggar—are those which are most intimately "engaged" with their natural background. His most authentic voice sounds in those passages where Man and Nature are "bound each to each in natural piety."

The Mind of Man "wedded to this goodly universe/In love and holy passion" is the haunt, and the main region, of Wordsworth's song. He probes the deepest secrets of the human mind and the inner heart of man whether in rapturous communion or in heroic conflict. In his most significant work he is a psychologist who deals with "the primary laws of our nature" and the fundamental passions. But he is psychological not pathological. When he treats of sex, it is in a normal and healthful fashion. His lines to Annette, for example, are elemental and moving:

> The house she dwelt in was a sainted shrine
> Her chamber-window did surpass in glory
> The portals of the East, all paradise
> Could by the simple opening of a door,
> Let itself in upon him.

There is nothing distortingly pathological about these verses. They are primary, nobly plain, wholesomely sincere. As Arnold said, they have the permanence of "what is really life." Wordsworth's preoccupation is with a distinctively human naturalness; a sanity and spiritual health lay at the core of his poetry and lasted a lifetime.

His interest in psychology caused him often to choose peasants, children, defectives, and old people to search the human spirit for those universal laws that govern every man's being. With true sympathy and profound imaginative insight he has reached into the humblest hearts and discovered in the primary affections a true source of joy and strength for living. Out of a boy's random feelings, a mother's sorrow, or a leech-gatherer's gossip about his trade he framed his songs, which rise from lowliest origins to the universality and nobility of Greek tragedy. Wordsworth's deepest concern was for the betterment of mankind through a fuller, happier realization of hidden resources within each individual.

Wordsworth is still in the great Renaissance tradition which saw the poet as a responsible human spokesman. He was the guardian of the social health. "There is scarcely one of my poems which does not aim to direct attention to some moral sentiment," he writes to Lady Beaumont. He purposes "to console the afflicted . . . to teach the young," to make man "wiser, better, and happier." Doomed, as all men are, "to go in company with Pain, and Fear," he learned to bear the shocks of life with honor and turned grief to account. He felt that poems could alter persons and bring health to society. Where health was departing from society, it was the poet's duty to call society back. Wordsworth's unique experiences, particularly his residence in France during the revolution, as well as his genius, gave him an unequaled perspective for interpreting the essential thoughts and passions of his age. In the political realm,

he was led to hope—not mistakenly, as it proved—that his countrymen might be roused by an appeal to the ideals of freedom to a
renewed sense of their strength and their responsibility.

Wordsworth's insight led him to perfect a new kind of poetry
which not only stemmed the classical decay but gave a forward
impetus to English and American thought and expression that has
hardly yet subsided. His diction and style, as Coleridge long ago
pointed out, is peculiarly his own and "cannot be imitated, without
its being at once recognized as originating in Mr. Wordsworth."
At its best, his style is unsurpassed in its naked idiomatic force and
its quiet unadorned beauty of word and phrase. It excels in epigram-
matic power, dignity, ampleness, poignant intensity, and vigorous
masculinity. Wordsworth is not at all a monotonous poet but
exhibits a great variety in style, mood, and subject matter. Among
the short lyrics alone there is a long roll call of perennial favorites
displaying his extraordinary variety in form and range in material.
Nor does Wordsworth lack a sense of humor as it was for a long time
fashionable to believe. Much of his humor is something which might
be called "a joyous parody of life" and is characteristically droll;
much of it "comes from a twisting of simplicity, seeing the humble
in a warm or wry light."[2] As for variety and vitality of pure poetic
expression, "Where," asks Mr. Herbert Read, "can you match the
wealth of Shakespeare except in Wordsworth?"

Wordsworth is pre-eminent for the truth of his report about
Nature and he is one of the great poets of the human heart. His
poetry has penetrated beyond the show of things to the realm of the
universal. As a poet gifted with "the Vision and the Faculty divine,"
he has seized upon those profound spiritual relationships that exist
among Man, Nature, and the Eternal World. Some of the truths
advanced by Wordsworth which were startlingly new to his
generation and were revered by the Victorians may no longer seem
exciting. Some portions of his report on Nature may need quali-
fying. But one should not willingly yield the gains he has won for
man. He has handed on an impressive body of philosophical
speculation which stimulates thought and challenges meditation.

Indeed, his observations have a strikingly modern bearing: "For
a multitude of causes, unknown to former times, are now acting
with a combined force to blunt the discriminating powers of the
mind, and, . . . to reduce it to a state of almost savage torpor. The
most effective of these causes are the great national events which

are daily taking place, and the increasing accumulation of men in cities, where the uniformity of their occupations produces a craving for extraordinary incident, which the rapid communication of intelligence hourly gratifies."[3] For many a sufferer looking up from the dark Satanic mills of the twentieth century, Wordsworth has the "healing power" to fortify the spirit. He endures because of the great power with which he transmits the joy offered in Nature; and the joy offered all men in the simple affections and duties of their daily lives.

Notes and References

Chapter One

1. Fenwick note, *Poems*, I, 319.

2. Z. S. Fink in *The Early Wordsworthian Milieu* (Oxford, 1958), pp. 23-42, has shown how Wordsworth refashioned incidents and images of his personal experience in the Lake Country to the traditional purposes of the topographical poem without ever sacrificing the truth of fact to the picturesque.

3. In the "sunset storm" passage (*Descriptive Sketches*, vv. 332-47), there is an isolated instance where Wordsworth reaches inner vision—not through a blending of images of sight but through a supercharged excess of them. For an excellent discussion of this passage and the problems relating to Wordsworth's imaginative vision see G. H. Hartman, "Wordsworth's *Descriptive Sketches* and the Growth of the Poet's Mind," *Publications of the Modern Language Association*, LXXVI (1961), 519-27.

4. S. T. Coleridge, *Biographia Literaria*, ed. J. Shawcross (Oxford, 1907), Chapter IV.

5. Wordsworth's contact with the radical circle of his publisher, Joseph Johnson, would have made him intimately acquainted with Godwin's writings.

6. *The Prelude*, Book X (1805), 806-30.

7. *The Early Letters of William and Dorothy Wordsworth*, ed. Ernest de Selincourt (Oxford, 1935), p. 120.

8. Wordsworth and Godwin saw much of each other in 1795 when Godwin was at the height of his fame. The two men met and corresponded with something like regularity until Godwin's death in 1836.

9. See *Poems*, I, 345-49.

10. *Ibid.*, p. 342.

11. John F. Danby, *The Simple Wordsworth* (London, 1960), p. 77.

12. "The Ruined Cottage," completed at Racedown in the spring of 1797, was revised and expanded in February, 1798, and eventually became the first book of *The Excursion*.

13. F. W. Meyer, *Wordsworth's Formative Years* (Ann Arbor, 1943), p. 246.

Chapter Two

1. Coleridge to Lady Beaumont, April 3, 1815. *Collected Letters of Samuel Taylor Coleridge*, ed. E. L. Griggs (Oxford, 1956-59), IV, 564. Hereafter, *Collected Letters*.

2. Coleridge to Joseph Cottle, June 8, 1797; *Collected Letters*, I, 325.

3. Christopher Wordsworth, *Memoirs of William Wordsworth* (London, 1851), II, 288-89.

4. William Wordsworth to Francis Wrangham, June 5, 1808, *The Letters of William and Dorothy Wordsworth: The Middle Years*, p. 224.

5. Robert Mayo, "The Contemporaneity of the *Lyrical Ballads,*" *Publications of the Modern Language Association*, LXIX (1954), 495.

6. Helen Darbishire, *The Poet Wordsworth* (Oxford, 1950), p. 61.

7. S. M. Parrish, "Dramatic Technique in the *Lyrical Ballads,*" *Publications of the Modern Language Association*, LXXIV (1959), 85-97.

8. John F. Danby, *The Simple Wordsworth* (London, 1960), p. 50.

9. Coleridge, *Biographia Literaria*, ed. Shawcross, II, 35.

10. "My First Acquaintance with Poets," 1823, in *Complete Works of Hazlitt*, ed. P. P. Howe (London, 1930), XVII, 118.

11. The following passage in Gilpin should be compared with "Tintern Abbey": "Many of the furnaces, on the banks of the river, consume charcoal, which is manufactured on the spot; and the smoke, which is frequently seen issuing from the sides of the hills; and spreading its thin veil over a part of them, beautifully breaks their lines, and unites them with the sky."

Chapter Three

1. "I Travelled among Unknown Men" was composed in April, 1801, after Wordsworth's return to England, but it re-creates perfectly the nostalgic love of his own country during the wintertime at Goslar.

2. Cf. the lines from "Tintern Abbey": "that serene and blessed mood/ In which . . . we are laid asleep in body, and become a living soul . . . [and] see into the life of things."

3. *Poetical Works*,V, pp. 406-7.

4. April 9, 1801, *Early Letters*, p. 266.

5. Mary Moorman, *William Wordsworth: The Early Years* (Oxford, 1957), p. 500.

6. Samuel Taylor Coleridge to William Sotheby, *Collected Letters of Coleridge*, II, 444.

7. The language of rustic life progressively disappeared from Wordsworth's work and was formally retained only in theory. In the second *Lyrical Ballads* and thereafter, Wordsworth replaced the repetition, the uneducated syntax, the extremely bald vocabulary of the Alfoxden poems with the tone of cultivated conversation, flexible and straightforward, controlling the passion and detail, and not controlled by them. The

extremes of the two styles may be seen by comparing the opening of "The Thorn," with its repetition and helplessness in syntax, to that of "Michael" where all is firm and well ordered.

8. Pablo Picasso has explosive words for those who would place the artist on the level of mediocrity: "What do you think an artist is—an imbecile with a brush or pen? An artist is a man who must see more widely, think more deeply, feel more strongly than others of his time."

9. William Wordsworth to Lady Beaumont, May 21, 1807, *Letters of William and Dorothy Wordsworth: The Middle Years*, p. 126.

Chapter Four

1. Helen Darbishire thinks that Wordsworth probably wrote at this time the memorable lines "On Man, on Nature, and on human life" which he appended to the Preface of *The Excursion* as "a kind of Prospectus" to *The Recluse*.

2. All references to *The Prelude* are to the corrected and revised edition by Helen Darbishire, 1959, and the references are to the 1805 text unless otherwise stated.

3. See, for example, Book I, 400-405:

> Ye Presences of Nature, in the sky
> And on the earth! Ye visions of the hills!
> And Souls of lonely places! can I think
> A vulgar hope was yours when Ye employ'd
> Such ministry.

4. See, for example, Book I, 351-55, 431-41, 571-85, 609-40; Book II, 51-55, 237-75.

5. Cf. "Tintern Abbey," vv. 45-49:

> . . . we are laid asleep
> In body, and become a living soul:
> While with an eye made quiet by the power
> Of harmony, and the deep power of joy,
> We see into the life of things.

6. See Wordsworth's elaboration of the point to De Quincey. Thomas De Quincey, *Literary Reminiscences* (Boston, 1851), I, 308-9.

7. Herbert Lindenberger, *On Wordsworth's "Prelude,"* 1963, pp. 28-38.

8. See the excellent article on this topic by Francis Christensen, "Intellectual Love: The Second Theme of *The Prelude*," *Publications of the Modern Language Association*, LXXX (1965), 69-75.

9. Cf. Lindenberger, *op. cit.*, pp. 209-19.

10. To Sir George Beaumont, May 1, 1805. *Letters: Early Years*, p. 489.

11. Introduction to the first edition, 1926, p. xxvii.

12. See Book VIII, 593-604.

13. See Davie's chapter on the syntax of Wordsworth's *Prelude*, pp. 106-16.

14. See, for example, Book VIII, 119-45, which is strongly reminiscent in style, construction, and phrasing of *Paradise Lost*, IV, 208-47. For additional illustrations of Milton's influence, consult R. D. Havens, *The Mind of a Poet* (Baltimore, 1941), Index "Milton," p. 652.

Chapter Five

1. *Early Letters*, p. 305.

2. In a letter to Miss Taylor he said: "I intend to devote my life to literature, if my health will permit me."—*Early Letters*, p. 269. Wordsworth aged early; his spirit and energy burned him out. He seems to be anticipating the loss of his powers in Stanza VII.

3. Dorothy Wordsworth, *Recollections of a Tour Made in Scotland*, ed. Ernest de Selincourt (Oxford, 1952), I, 286.

4. Some of the lines addressed to the Highland girl overflowed and became the germ of "She was a Phantom of delight," the poet's lovely tribute to his wife, Mary Hutchinson.

5. "The Themes of Immortality and Natural Piety in Wordsworth's Immortailty Ode," *Publications of the Modern Language Association*, LXIX (1954), 861-75.

6. "Wordsworth's Immortality Ode and the Search for Identity," *Journal of English Literary History*, XXXII (1965), 32-61.

7. Cf., for example, A. C. Bradley, *Oxford Lectures on Poetry* (London, 1909), pp. 129-41; Arthur Beatty, *William Wordsworth* (Madison, Wis., 1922), pp. 84-86; and Lionel Trilling, *The Liberal Imagination* (New York, 1942), pp. 129-53.

8. See Mary Moorman, *William Wordsworth*, I, 526.

9. Coleridge was attracted early to neo-Platonic speculations on pre-existence and degraded Intelligences and had written a sonnet on the birth of his son Hartley expressing a feeling, which he often had, that "the present has appeared like a vivid dream or exact similitude of some past circumstance."

10. Wordsworth says that "two years at least passed between the writing of the four first stanzas and the remaining parts." But he was often mistaken about the dating of his poems. An impressive body of evidence has been brought together that has convinced this writer, at least, that Wordsworth composed most, if not all, of the stanzas on pre-existence in early summer of 1802. For a full reporting of the evidence see John D. Rea, "Coleridge's

Intimations of Immortality from Proclus," *Modern Philology*, XXVI (1928), 201-13, and Herbert Hartman, "The 'Intimations' in Wordsworth's 'Ode'," *Review of English Studies*, VI (1930), 129-48.

11. See D. A. Stauffer, "Cooperative Criticism," *Kenyon Review*, IV (1942), 133-44.

12. See Mary Moorman, *William Wordsworth*, II, 1-7.

13. The poet has in mind his sister Dorothy as he described her in *The Prelude*, XII, 155-58.

Chapter Six

1. See p. 123 in this book for an account of these revisions.

2. Coleridge wished his friend to address a poem "to those, who, in consequence of the complete failure of the French Revolution have thrown up all hopes of the amelioration of mankind, and are sinking into an almost epicurean selfishness, disguising the same under the soft titles of domestic attachment and contempt for visionary *philosophes*." *Memoirs of William Wordsworth*, by Christopher Wordsworth, I, 159.

3. For a full account and appraisal of the story of Margaret see pp. 39-42 in this book.

4. J. S. Lyon, *The Excursion: A Study* (New Haven, 1950), p. 140. For a detailed anaylysis of this poem's structure and style see Lyon, pp. 122-38.

5. *Memoirs*, II, 313.

6. See James A. W. Heffernan, "Wordsworth on Imagination: The Emblemizing Power," *Publications of the Modern Language Association*, LXXXI (1966), 394. Mr. Heffernan offers an excellent interpretation of *The White Doe*.

7. *Letters: Middle Years*, I, 197-98.

8. See p. 141 for a discussion of "Yarrow Unvisited."

Chapter Seven

1. J. C. Shairp, *Studies in Poetry and Philosophy* (Edinburgh, 1868).

2. See J. E. Jordan's excellent article "Wordsworth's Humor," *Publications of the Modern Language Association*, LXIII (1958), 81-93.

3. Preface to *Lyrical Ballads*, 1800.

Selected Bibliography

PRIMARY SOURCES

A. *Poems:*

The Poetical Works of William Wordsworth. Ed. Ernest de Selincourt and Helen Darbishire. Oxford: Clarendon, 1940-49. 5 vols. A second edition of volumes I-III was issued by Miss Darbishire in 1952-54.

The Poetical Works of William Wordsworth. Ed. Thomas Hutchinson. New York: Oxford University Press, 1911. The standard one-volume edition with Wordsworth's arrangement of the poems.

The Complete Poetical Works of William Wordsworth. Ed. A. J. George. Cambridge: Houghton Mifflin, 1904. Poems are arranged in chronological order.

Lyrical Ballads. Ed. R. L. Brett and A. R. Jones. London: Methuen, 1963. The text of the 1798 edition with the additional 1800 poems and preface. Provided with an introduction and notes.

The Prelude, or Growth of a Poet's Mind. Ed. Ernest de Selincourt. Oxford: Clarendon, 1926. Second edition, revised by Helen Darbishire, 1959. The text of 1805 is printed opposite the text of 1850, with variant readings, notes, and commentary.

The White Doe of Rylstone. Ed. Alice P. Comparetti. Ithaca: Cornell, 1940. Introduction gives a full account of composition, sources, and critical estimates.

The Ecclesiastical Sonnets of William Wordsworth. Ed. Abbie Findlay Potts, New Haven: Yale, 1922. Discusses manuscripts, composition, and structure of the series. Copious notes.

B. *Prose and Letters:*

The Prose Works of William Wordsworth. Ed. Alexander B. Grosart. London: Moxon, 1876. 3 vols. Better than the two-volume edition by William Knight. London: Macmillan, 1896.

Wordsworth's Preface to Lyrical Ballads. Ed. W. J. B. Owen, with an Introduction and Commentary. Copenhagen: Rosenkilde and Bagger, 1957.

The Critical Opinions of William Wordsworth. Compiled by Markham L. Peacock. Baltimore: Johns Hopkins Press, 1950.

The Early Letters of William and Dorothy Wordsworth: (1787-1805). Ed. Ernest de Selincourt. Oxford: Clarendon, 1935. 2nd ed., revised by Chester L. Shaver, 1967.

The Letters of William and Dorothy Wordsworth: The Middle Years. Ed. E. de Selincourt. Oxford: Clarendon, 1937. 2 vols.

The Letters of William and Dorothy Wordsworth: The Later Years. Ed. E. de Selincourt. Oxford: Clarendon, 1939 3 vols.

The Correspondence of Henry Crabb Robinson with the Wordsworth Circle (1808-1866). Ed. Edith J. Morley. Oxford: Clarendon, 1927. 2 vols.

Some Letters of the Wordsworth Family . . . . Ed. Leslie N. Broughton. Ithaca: Cornell, 1942.

Wordsworth and Reed: The Poet's Correspondence with his American Editor, 1836-1850. Ed. Leslie N. Broughton. Ithaca: Cornell, 1933.

SECONDARY SOURCES

A. *Bibliographies:*

HEALEY, GEORGE H., ed. *The Cornell Wordsworth Collection: A Catalogue.* Ithaca: Cornell, 1957. Useful for information about early editions and primary documents.

HENLEY, ELTON F., and STAM, DAVID H., eds. *Wordsworthian Criticism, 1945-1964: An Annotated Bibliography.* New York: New York Public Library, 1965. Continues the work begun by Logan.

LOGAN, JAMES V. *Wordsworthian Criticism: A Guide and Bibliography.* Columbus: Ohio State, 1947. Reprinted 1961. Annotated bibliography with an introductory chapter on Wordsworth's critical reputation.

The student should consult also: (1) the annual bibliography of the Romantic movement in *English Language Notes,* formerly in *Philological Quarterly* (1950-65) and before that in *English Literary History* (1937-49); (2) the annual bibliographies in *Publications of the Modern Language Association* and in the Modern Humanities Research Association's *Annual Bibliography of English Language and Literature;* (3) volume III of *The Cambridge Bibliography of English Literature,* 1940, with its *Supplement* of 1957; (4) *The English Romantic Poets: A Review of Research,* ed. Thomas M. Raysor (New York: Modern Language Association, 1950, revised 1956).

B. *Biography:*

DE SELINCOURT, ERNEST. *Dorothy Wordsworth: A Biography.* Oxford: Clarendon, 1933. Fullest, best account of Wordsworth's sister. To be used along with *Journals of Dorothy Wordsworth,* ed. E. de Selincourt (London: Macmillan, 1941), in 2 vols.

HARPER, GEORGE M. *William Wordsworth: His Life, Works, and Influence.* New York: Scribner's, 1916. 2 vols. Revised, abridged edition appeared in 1929. Once the standard biography; now superseded by Mary Moorman's.

HERFORD, CHARLES H. *Wordsworth.* New York: Dutton, 1930. Most dependable brief life; includes critical appraisals of the poetry.

MEYER, GEORGE W. *Wordsworth's Formative Years.* Ann Arbor: Michigan, 1943. Study of the poet's early life and works from sources other than *The Prelude.*

MARGOLIOUTH, H. M. *Wordsworth and Coleridge, 1795-1834.* London: Oxford University Press, 1953. Compact, well-balanced account of the celebrated friendship between the two poets.

MOORMAN, MARY. *William Wordsworth: A Biography. The Early Years, 1770-1803.* Oxford: Clarendon, 1957. A second volume covering *The Later Years, 1803-1850*, was published in 1965. The standard biography.

C. *Criticism: General:*

BANNERJEE, SRIKUMAR. *Critical Theories and Poetic Practice in the "Lyrical Ballads."* London: Williams and Norgate, 1931. Admirably compact, but should be supplemented and modified by later studies by Josephine Miles, M. H. Abrams, and others.

BATESON, F. W. *Wordsworth: A Re-interpretation.* London: Longmans, 1954. 2nd ed., 1956. Stimulating criticism; marred by unsupportable theorizing of an "incestuous" relationship between the poet and his sister.

BATHO, EDITH C. *The Later Wordsworth.* Cambridge University Press, 1933. Reprinted, New York: Russell and Russell, 1963.

BEACH, J. W. *The Concept of Nature in Nineteenth-Century English Poetry.* New York: Macmillan, 1936. Excellent orientation to Wordsworth's naturalism (chapters II-VI), but Beach's judgment on the value of the poet's mystic faith should be checked by the evaluations of Rader, Stallknecht, Weaver, and others.

BEATTY, ARTHUR. *William Wordsworth: His Doctrine and Art in Their Historical Relations.* Madison: Wisconsin, 1927. Emphasizes Wordsworth's indebtedness to the associational psychology of David Hartley.

BLOOM, HAROLD. "William Wordsworth," *The Visionary Company: A Reading of English Romantic Poetry.* Garden City, N. Y.: Doubleday, 1961. Stimulating readings of selected poems; excellent on "spots of time" in *The Prelude.*

BRADLEY, A. C. *Oxford Lectures on Poetry.* London: Macmillan and Co., 1909. Wordsworth the most sublime of poets since Milton.

CHRISTENSEN, FRANCIS. "Creative Sensibility in Wordsworth," *Journal of English and Germanic Philology*, XLV (1946), 361-68.

CLARKE, COLIN C. *Romantic Paradox: An Essay on the Poetry of Wordsworth*. New York: Barnes and Noble, 1963. Wordsworth's poetry has a far richer texture and is more loaded with ambivalent meanings than has hitherto been recognized.

COLERIDGE, SAMUEL T. *Biographia Literaria*. London: Fenner, 1817. Chapters IV, XIV, XVII-XX are important on Wordsworth's poetical theory and practice.

DANBY, JOHN F. *The Simple Wordsworth: Studies in the Poems 1797-1807*. London: Routledge, 1960; New York: Barnes and Noble, 1961. Useful for the sensitive reading of some of the "simple" poems: "The Fountain," "The Solitary Reaper," and "The White Doe."

DARBISHIRE, HELEN. *The Poet Wordsworth*. The Clark Lectures, Trinity College, Cambridge, 1949. Oxford: Clarendon, 1950. Excellent appraisal of Wordsworth's poetic achievement.

DAVIS, JACK, ED. *Discussions of William Wordsworth*. Boston: D. C. Heath, 1963. Representative selection of the best criticism of Wordsworth by Coleridge, Arnold, Bradley, Willey, Abrams, Leavis, and others.

DUNKLIN, GILBERT T., ED. *Wordsworth: Centenary Studies Presented at Cornell and Princeton Universities*. Princeton University Press, 1951. Poet reappraised in studies by Douglas Bush, Frederick A. Pottle, Earl Leslie Griggs, John Crowe Ransom, B. Ifor Evans, Lionel Trilling, Willard L. Sperry.

FERRY, DAVID. *The Limits of Mortality: An Essay on Wordsworth's Major Poems*. Middletown: Wesleyan University Press, 1959. Challenging study; will doubtless provoke disagreement at times. See as a corrective Alan Grob, "Wordsworth's Nutting," *Journal of English and Germanic Philology*, LXI (1962), 826-32.

GARROD, H. W. *Wordsworth: Lectures and Essays*. Oxford: Clarendon, 1923; second edition, 1927. Emphasis is on Wordsworth's poetry up to 1805.

HARTMAN, GEOFFREY H. *Wordsworth's Poetry 1787-1814*. New Haven and London: Yale, 1964. Illuminating study containing useful bibliographies of criticism.

HEFFERNAN, JAMES A. W. *Wordsworth's Theory of Poetry*. Ithaca: Cornell University Press, 1969. Expertly unravels the tangled threads of Wordsworth's poetic theory and elucidates his concept of imagination.

JONES, [HENRY] JOHN. *The Egotistical Sublime: A History of Wordsworth's Imagination*. London: Chatto and Windus, 1954. Examines with brilliance the development of Wordsworth's creative mind.

KNIGHT, G. WILSON. *The Starlit Dome: Studies in the Poetry of Vision*. London: Oxford, 1941. Reissued London: Methuen, 1959. Contains an important essay on Wordsworth.

KROEBER, KARL. *The Artifice of Reality: Poetic Style in Wordsworth, Foscolo, Keats, and Leopardi.* Madison and Milwaukee: Wisconsin, 1964. Perceptive commentary on Wordsworth's style.

MARSH, FLORENCE. *Wordsworth's Imagery: A Study in Poetic Vision.* New Haven: Yale University Press, 1952. A valuable examination of Wordsworth's imagery and style.

MILES, JOSEPHINE. *Wordsworth and the Vocabulary of Emotion.* Berkeley and Los Angeles: California, 1942. *University of California Publications in English,* Vol. XII, No. 1. See also No. 2 in this series by the same author, *Pathetic Fallacy in the Nineteenth Century.* Draws important inferences about Wordsworth's changes in style, mood, and intent.

MURRY, ROGER N. *Wordsworth's Style: Figures and Themes in Lyrical Ballads of 1800.* Lincoln: University of Nebraska Press, 1967. Penetrating analyses of Wordsworth's language and handling of poetic figures.

NOYES, RUSSELL. *Wordsworth and Jeffrey in Controversy.* Bloomington: Indiana University Press, 1941. Historical account of Jeffrey's attack on the poet and its consequences.

————. *Wordsworth and the Art of Landscape.* Bloomington: Indiana University Press, 1968.

PERKINS, DAVID. *Wordsworth and the Poetry of Sincerity.* Cambridge, Mass.: Harvard, 1964. Perceptive, sensitive criticism of a considerable body of Wordsworth's poetry. See also this author's chapter on Wordsworth in *The Quest for Permanence.* Cambridge, Mass.: Harvard, 1959.

RADER, MELVIN. *Presiding Ideas in Wordsworth's Poetry. University of Washington Publications in Language and Literature,* 1931, Vol. VIII, No. 2. One of the most valuable studies of Wordsworth's idealism. Revised and enlarged as *Wordsworth; A Philosophical Approach.* Oxford: Clarendon Press, 1967.

STALLKNECHT, NEWTON P. *Strange Seas of Thought: Studies in William Wordsworth's Philosophy of Man and Nature.* Durham: Duke, 1945. Reprinted, Bloomington: Indiana University Press, 1958.

TODD, F. M. *Politics and the Poet: A Study of Wordsworth.* London: Methuen, 1957. Sound study of Wordsworth as a thinking, feeling man of his time.

WEAVER, BENNETT. *Wordsworth: Poet of the Unconquerable Mind.* Ann Arbor, Michigan: The George Wahr Publishing Co., 1965. Psychological approach used to interpret the interrelations of sense experience and imagination in Wordsworth's poetry.

WHITEHEAD, ALFRED NORTH. *Science and the Modern World.* New York: New American Library, 1925. Republished in Mentor Books (paperback), 1948. Notable defense of Wordsworth's philosophy.

WILLEY, BASIL. "On Wordsworth and the Locke Tradition." *The Seventeenth Century Background.* London: Chatto and Windus, 1934.

English "scientific" tradition conditioned much of Wordsworth's thought.

—————— *The Eighteenth Century Background.* London: Chatto and Windus, 1940. Continues elucidation of Wordsworth's natural philosophy in its historical context.

WOODRING, CARL. *Wordsworth.* Boston: Houghton Mifflin, 1965. Compact, scholarly introduction to the poetry and prose.

WORDSWORTH, JONATHAN. *The Music of Humanity: A Critical Study* of *Wordsworth's "Ruined Cottage."* New York: Harper and Row, 1969. Reconstructs "The Ruined Cottage" from early manuscript into virtually a new poem. Full commentary on its composition, literary background, symbolism, and its relationship to "The Pedlar."

D. *Criticism: The Prelude:*

BURTON, MARY E. *The One Wordsworth.* Chapel Hill : North Carolina, 1942. Argues that the revisions in later drafts of *The Prelude* represent stylistic improvements rather than changes in outlook.

CHRISTENSEN, FRANCIS. "Intellectual Love: The Second Theme of *The Prelude*," *Publications of the Modern Language Association*, LXXX (March, 1965), 69-75.

HAVENS, RAYMOND D. *The Mind of a Poet: A Study of Wordsworth's Thought with Particular Reference to* The Prelude. Baltimore: Johns Hopkins, 1941. Detailed commentary supplements the notes to the de Selincourt edition of *The Prelude.*

LEGOUIS, ÉMILE. *The Early Life of William Wordsworth, 1770-1798: A Study of "The Prelude."* Paris, 1896. Trans. J. W. Matthews, 1897. Reprinted with new material, 1921 and 1932. New York: Dutton. The first scholar to place *The Prelude* at the center of Wordsworth's corpus. Much of historical criticism still unsuperseded.

LINDENBERGER, HERBERT. *On Wordsworth's* Prelude. Princeton University Press, 1963. Series of related essays on the poem's language, style, theme, and structure.

POTTS, ABBIE FINDLAY. *Wordsworth's* Prelude: *A Study of Its Literary Form.* Ithaca: Cornell, 1953.

E. *Criticism: The Excursion:*

LYON, J. S. The Excursion: *A Study.* New Haven: Yale, 1950. Full historical and critical commentary.

PIPER, H. W. *The Active Universe: Pantheism and the Concept of the Imagination in the English Romantic Poets.* London: Athlone (University of London), 1962. Has several good chapters on *The Excursion.*

Index